Web Development with JavaServer Pages

Web Development with
JavaServer Pages

DUANE K. FIELDS
MARK A. KOLB

MANNING

Greenwich
(74° w. long.)

For online information and ordering of this and other Manning books, go to www.manning.com. The publisher offers discounts on this book when ordered in quantity. For more information, please contact:

Special Sales Department
Manning Publications Co.
32 Lafayette Place   Fax: (203) 661-9018
Greenwich, CT 06830   email: orders@manning.com

 Manning Publications Co.   Copyeditor: Elizabeth Martin
32 Lafayette Place   Typesetter: Tony Roberts
Greenwich, CT 06830   Cover designer: Leslie Haimes

Printed in the United States of America
2 3 4 5 6 7 8 9 10 – CM – 03 02 01 00

brief contents

contents

Working with databases   **178**

Architecting JSP applications   **209**

preface

In late 1998 we were asked to develop the architecture for a new website. Our employer, a vendor of enterprise software for system and network management, had an unconventional set of requirements: that the site be able to provide product support data customized for each customer; and that the support data be tailored to the software the customer had already purchased, as well as the configurations already selected.

Of course, the website needed to look sharp and be easy to navigate. Management software, which of necessity must be flexible and support a wide range of operating conditions, tends to be very complex. This particular software was targeted at Internet and electronic commerce applications, so using the web as a major component of product support was a natural fit. By personalizing web-based support for each customer, this inherent complexity would be reduced, and the customer experience improved. But how to accomplish that ... and how to do it within the time constraints the project required?

What we needed was an architecture that would give everyone on the team, both the designers and the programmers, as much freedom as possible to work unhindered in the limited time available. The ability of these two groups to progress independently, without costly rework, was crucial. A solution that could provide dynamic content as an add-on to otherwise conventional HTML files clearly was the best approach. We briefly considered, then just as quickly dismissed, the notion of building our own dynamic context system. There just wasn't enough time to deliver both a publishing system and a website.

At the time we were already familiar with Java servlets. Indeed, servlets were a key element of the architecture of the product to which this site would be devoted. We mulled over using servlets for the site itself but were concerned with how this would affect those responsible for the content, graphics, and layout of the site.

As we researched the problem further we were reminded of an ongoing initiative at Sun Microsystems called JavaServer Pages (JSP). JSP was still being refined, and Version 1.0 was months away. However, it was intended to become a standard Java technology, and it used Java servlets as its foundation. It also allowed us to implement dynamic content on top of standard HTML files. Best of all, it worked! As we became more familiar with JSP, we found that it worked very well indeed.

As is often the case, there were some rough spots as the JSP specification went through major changes along the way. Hair was pulled, teeth were gnashed, lessons were learned. Fortunately, we obtained a great deal of help from the JSP community—the developers at Sun and the other JSP vendors, as well as our fellow early adopters.

This book thus serves a twofold purpose. First, we hope to help future users of JSP by sharing the hard-earned lessons of our experience. We offer them what we hope is a helpful guide to the current JSP feature set: JavaServer Pages is now at version 1.1 and the need for published reference material has long been recognized.

Second, we offer this book as an expression of gratitude to the current community of JSP developers in return for the assistance they provided when we needed it. Thanks to all.

acknowledgments

We recognize the support and understanding of the many people who helped make this book possible. We acknowledge:

T. Preston Gregg, our development manager, for allowing us to make the early leap to a JSP architecture, before the technology was considered ready for prime time. This head start was painful at times, but ultimately proved a boon to our web development projects. It also gave us the experience necessary to develop this text, for which we are equally grateful. Other colleagues who advised us during the writing of the this book include Kirk Drummond and Ward Harold.

The JSP design team at Sun Microsystems, especially Eduardo Pelegrí-Llopart. His assistance and attentiveness to our queries was critical to the success of this effort.

The teeming millions of Java and JSP developers who continue to offer their insights and expertise to the development community through their unselfish participation in mailing lists, newsgroups, and the web. Double thanks to everyone participating in the Jakarta and Apache projects for their outstanding work in the Open Source arena. You are all instrumental to the continuing success of Java and establishing it as a lingua franca for Internet development.

Our publisher, Marjan Bace, for giving us this opportunity, and our editor, Elizabeth Martin, for her yeoman's effort in polishing this manuscript. Their insights and guidance were invaluable to the completion of this book.

Our reviewers, whose comments, criticisms, and commendations throughout the development of this book advised, corrected, and encouraged us. Our deep appreciation is extended to Michael Andreano, Ruslan Belkin, Drew Cox, Jose Luis Diaz, Sergio Queijo Diaz, Richard Friedman, Dennis Hoer, Paul Holser, Vimal Kansal,

Sachin Khanna, Daniel Kirkdorffer, JJ Kuslich, Eric Lunt, Dave Miller, Vincent Partington, Harold Sasaki, Edward Toupin, Wong Kok Wai, and Paul Williamson. We are also indebted to Ted Kennedy, our review editor, for coordinating this imposing task.

Our friends, families, and coworkers for their unfailing support, assistance, and tolerance throughout the writing process. Without them this book could not have been possible.

about this book

JavaServer Pages is a technology that serves two different communities of developers. Page designers use JSP technology to add powerful dynamic content capabilities to web sites and online applications. Java programmers write the code that implements those capabilities behind the scenes.

Web Development with JavaServer Pages is intended to present this technology to both groups. It is impossible in a book of this length to provide all the background information required by this subject, and, for this reason, we do not attempt to describe the HTML markup language. It is assumed that the reader is sufficiently familiar with HTML to follow the examples presented. It is likewise assumed that the reader is familiar with URLs, document hierarchies, and other concepts related to the design, operation, and management of web servers.

We also do not include a primer on the Java programming language. As with HTML, there is a wealth of reference information available on the language itself. Our focus here is strictly on JavaServer Pages. Obviously, JSP interacts strongly with Java and HTML, as well as other technologies such as HTTP servers and databases. The interactions between JSP and these technologies will be covered in depth, but the details of these related technologies are beyond the scope of this book.

What, then, can the reader expect to be covered in this book?

Chapter 1 answers the question, what is JSP and how did the technology evolve? This chapter is an overview of how this new technology can be used to add dynamic content to web pages, and the benefits it provides compared to other dynamic content systems.

Chapter 2 presents introductory examples, as well as an overview of the basic conventions for JSP tags. This is followed by a discussion of how JSP interacts with the web server and the end user's browser, and how JSP pages actually work to produce dynamic content. As it covers all of the major aspects of JSP technology at a high level, this chapter is geared toward both Java programmers and page designers.

Chapters 3 and 4 introduce the four basic categories of JSP tags: directives, scripting elements, comments, and actions. The use and syntax of all standard JSP tags is presented, with the exception of those specific to JavaBeans. The first three categories are covered in chapter 3.

Chapter 4 introduces action tags, and describes the implicit Java objects accessible from all JSP pages. In both of these chapters, particular emphasis is placed on the application of these tags and objects to dynamic content generation via scripting. The scripting examples use the Java programming language, and may be of secondary interest to page designers. Because this chapter introduces most of the major functionality provided by JavaServer Pages, it is intended for a general audience.

Chapters 5 and 6 cover JSP's component-centric approach to dynamic page design through the use of JavaBeans and JSP Bean tags. The JSP tags covered in chapter 5 allow page designers to interact with Java components through HTML-like tags, rather than through Java code. This chapter will introduce the JavaBeans component model, and demonstrate JSP's interaction with JavaBeans through the use of the JSP Bean tags.

Chapter 6 builds on this foundation, teaching Java programmers how to develop their own JavaBeans for use with JSP.

Chapter 7, geared primarily toward Java developers, covers techniques for working with databases through JSP. Nowadays, most large-scale web sites employ databases for at least some portion of their content. Ad management, user registration information, inventory records, and community services are all quite commonly handled through a database. JSP and relational databases make a good combination. The relational database gives us the organizational capabilities and the performance necessary to manage dynamic data. By combining the power of a relational database with the flexibility of JSP for content presentation and front-end design, it is practical to build rich, interactive interfaces to your data.

In chapter 8, we discuss several architectural models useful for developing JSP applications. We examine the various architectural options available when we combine JSP pages with servlets, Enterprise JavaBeans, HTML, and other software elements to create web-based applications. The introductory material in this chapter, as well as the final section on selecting an architecture, are geared toward a general audience. The bulk of this chapter, which focuses on how these architectural models are implemented, is geared toward Java programmers.

In chapter 9, we apply the JSP programming techniques we covered in previous chapters to the development of a real world, enterprise web application. In a chapter-length example, we will be developing a system for managing and presenting lists of frequently asked questions (FAQs). This chapter is based on a project the authors recently completed for a major software company's customer support site. The presentation aspect of this chapter should be of interest to page designers, while the implementation aspects should be of interest to programmers.

Whatever architecture you have selected for your JSP development, an application isn't useful until it is successfully deployed. The JSP and servlet specifications have introduced several new facilities for easing and improving the deployment of Java-based web applications. Chapter 10 explains Sun's new Web Archive format and how it can be used to create packaged JSP applications. Since both code and pages are stored together in a packaged application, this chapter should be of interest to all JSP developers.

In chapters 11 and 12 we present a number of examples of JSP programming, which should be of interest to both page designers and programmers. The examples of form management, interface design, and error handling in chapter 11 have been designed to be representative of common tasks for which you might employ JSP. Chapter 12 focuses on full-fledged applications that illustrate the various techniques and practices presented in the other chapters of this book.

Chapter 13 covers the development, deployment, and use of custom tag libraries. This material focuses primarily on the implementation of custom tags by Java programmers. From the perspective of jointly designing a set of application-specific tags, page designers may find some benefit in reviewing the introductory sections of this chapter, which discuss the types of functionality that can be provided by custom JSP tags. In chapter 14, we expand upon the topic of custom tags with additional examples that take advantage of more advanced features of Java and JSP.

There are five appendices in this book. Appendix A provides instructions for installing and running Tomcat, the free reference implementation for both servlets and JavaServer Pages jointly developed by Sun Microsystems and the Apache Software Foundation. Tomcat provides an Open Source, zero-cost platform for JSP development that is fully compliant with the published specifications. This chapter assumes no programming knowledge, but does require familiarity with the operating system on which the software is to be installed.

Java applets are small applications that run within the context of a web browser. Appendix B describes the `<jsp:plugin>` action, a cross-platform tag for specifying applets which use Sun Microsystem's Java Plug-in technology in order to take advantage of the Java 2 platform within the browser. This appendix is directed at Java programmers.

As is the case with any major software technology in use today, there is a wealth of information on JSP and related topics available online. Appendix C provides a listing of mailing lists, newsgroups, and web sites of relevance to both categories of JSP developers, accompanied by brief descriptions of the content available from each.

Appendix D, serving as a quick reference, summarizes the use and syntax of the standard (i.e., built-in) JSP tags available to page designers.

Appendix E, geared toward Java programmers, lists all of the Java classes introduced by the JSP and servlet specifications to supplement the standard Java class library for web-based application development. Summary descriptions of these classes and their methods are provided, as is a table of the JSP implicit objects.

Source code

The source code for all of the examples called out as listings in the book is freely available from our publisher's web site, www.manning.com/fields, and from the book's companion web site, www.taglib.com. The listings are organized by chapter and topic and include the source for both Java classes and JSP pages used in the examples. If any errors are discovered updates will be made available on the web.

Code conventions

Courier typeface is used to denote code (JSP, Java, and HTML) as well as filenames, variables, Java class names, and other identifiers. When JSP is interspersed with HTML, we have used a bold Courier font for JSP elements in order to improve the readability of the code. Italics are used to indicate definitions and user specified values in syntax listings.

about the authors

DUANE K. FIELDS, web applications developer and Internet technologist, has an extensive background in the design and development of leading edge Internet applications for companies such as IBM and Netscape Communications. Duane lives in Austin, Texas, where he consults, does Java applications development, and tries to find more time to fish. He frequently speaks at industry conferences and other events and has published numerous articles on all aspects of web application development from Java to relational databases. He is a Sun Certified Java Programmer, an IBM Master Inventor, and holds an engineering degree from Texas A&M University. He can be reached at his website at www.deepmagic.com.

MARK A. KOLB, Ph.D., is a reformed rocket scientist with graduate and undergraduate degrees from MIT. A pioneer in the application of object-oriented modeling to aerospace preliminary design, his contributions in that field were recently recognized with a NASA Space Act Award. With over 15 years' experience in software design, Mark's current focus is on Internet applications, ranging from applet-based HTML editors to server-side systems for online product support and fulfillment. Mark resides in Round Rock, Texas, with his family and a large stack of unread books he's hoping to get to now that this one is done. His home on the web is at www.taglib.com.

author online

Purchase of *Web Development with Java Server Pages* includes free access to a private Internet forum where you can make comments about the book, ask technical questions, and receive help from the authors and other JSP users. To access the forum, point your web browser to www.manning.com/fields. There you will be able to subscribe to the forum as well as receive information on how to access the forum once you are registered.

about the cover illustration

The cover illustration of this book is from the 1805 edition of Sylvain Maréchal's four-volume compendium of regional dress customs. This book was first published in Paris in 1788, one year before the French Revolution. Its title alone required no fewer than 30 words.

> *"Costumes Civils actuels de tous les peuples connus dessinés d'après nature gravés et coloriés, accompagnés d'une notice historique sur leurs coutumes, moeurs, religions, etc., etc., redigés par M. Sylvain Maréchal"*

The four volumes include an annotation on the illustrations: "gravé à la manière noire par Mixelle d'après Desrais et colorié." Clearly, the engraver and illustrator deserved no more than to be listed by their last names—after all they were mere technicians. The workers who colored each illustration by hand remain nameless.

The remarkable diversity of this collection reminds us vividly of how distant and isolated the world's towns and regions were just 200 years ago. Dress codes have changed everywhere and the diversity by region, so rich at the time, has melted away. It is now hard to tell the inhabitant of one continent from another. Perhaps we have traded cultural diversity for a more varied personal life—certainly a more varied and interesting technological environment.

At a time when it is hard to tell one computer book from another, Manning celebrates the inventiveness and initiative of the computer business with book covers based on the rich diversity of regional life of two centuries ago, brought back to life by Maréchal's pictures. Just think, Maréchal's was a world so different from ours people would take the time to read a book title 30 words long.

Introduction

1

Welcome to *Web Development with JavaServer Pages*. This book has been written to address the needs of a wide audience of web developers. You may have only recently heard about this exciting new technology for developing dynamic web content, or perhaps you have already begun to use JavaServer Pages in your own projects. You may be a HyperText Markup Language (HTML) designer with little or no background in programming, or a seasoned Java architect. In any case, this book will show you how to use JavaServer Pages to improve the look and maintainability of dynamic web sites and web-based applications, and ease the design and development process. So, without further ado, let's begin our look at JavaServer Pages.

1.1 What is JSP?

JavaServer Pages—JSP, for short—is a Java-based technology that simplifies the process of developing dynamic web sites. With JSP, web designers and developers can quickly incorporate dynamic elements into web pages using embedded Java and a few simple markup tags. These tags provide the HTML designer with a way to access data and business logic stored inside Java objects without having to master the complexities of Java application development.

Think of JSP as a type of server-side scripting language, although, as we'll see later, it operates quite differently behind the scenes. JavaServer Pages are text files, usually with the extension .jsp, that take the place of traditional HTML pages. JSP files contain traditional HTML along with embedded code that allows the page designer to access data from Java code running on the server. When the page is requested by a user and processed by the HyperText Transport Protocol (HTTP) server, the HTML portion of the page is passed straight through. The code portions of the page, however, are executed at the time the request is received, and the dynamic content generated by this code is spliced into the page before it is sent to the user. This provides for a separation of the HTML presentation aspects of the page from the programming logic contained in the code, a unique benefit we'll consider in detail below.

1.2 Evolution of dynamic content technologies

For the simplest web requests, a browser requests an HTML document, and the web server finds the corresponding file and returns it. If the HTML document includes any images, the browser will in turn submit requests for the image documents, as well. As described here, all of these requests are for static files. That is, the documents that are requested never change depending upon who requested them, when they were requested, or which (if any) additional parameters were included with the request. New versions of the documents might be placed on the server, but at any given time, every request for those documents returns exactly the same results. In such cases, the web server needs only to locate the file corresponding to the requested document, and respond to the web browser with the contents of that file.

Much of the data delivered over the web today, however, is dynamic in nature. Up-to-the-minute stock prices and the latest weather reports can be viewed. A user's personal email messages and appointment calendar can be managed. Consumers can add contents to that e-commerce staple, the online shopping cart, by clicking on a picture of the item they wish to buy. All of this data is transient in nature, because the information it is based on is constantly changing, or because it must be personalized for each individual viewer, or both.

Dynamic web content, then, requires that the web server do some additional processing of the corresponding request in order to generate a customized response. In addition to the URL of the request, the form of this customized response might be dependent upon additional parameter values included with the request. Alternatively, it might be based on the date and time, the location on the network from which the request was made, or on some representation of the identity of the user making the request. Indeed, the exact details of the response might depend upon a combination of some or all of these factors.

1.2.1 Common Gateway Interface

The earliest HTTP servers did not include any built-in mechanisms for generating responses dynamically. Instead, interfaces were provided for calling other programs to translate requests into run-time content. The first standard for dynamic web content was based on the Common Gateway Interface, or CGI, which specified a mechanism for web servers to pass request information to external programs, which were then run by the web server to generate responses at runtime. The Perl language is a popular choice for writing CGI programs, but CGI codes can be written in any language that can be called as a stand-alone program by the HTTP server. For example, a CGI program could be written in any scripting language supported by the local operating system. Alternatively, it could be written in C and compiled into native object code. CGI programs could even be written as Java applications.

When Sun Microsystems first introduced Java technology to the computing community, it was in the context of small programs, referred to as *applets*, which could be delivered over the Internet and run within web browsers. From the beginning, Java could also be used to write stand-alone applications, but interactive programs running inside the browser certainly received most of the early attention.

Nevertheless, Java-based CGI programs first appeared shortly after Java was made available to the public in 1995. It was eventually recognized that the benefits of the Java platform applied equally as well to the server as to the client, and today server-side Java plays a prominent role in the continuing evolution of the Java platform.

The traditional CGI approach to generating dynamic content has some inherent inefficiencies, which ultimately limit its applicability to large-scale deployment of web-based applications. As indicated in figure 1.1, CGI programs run outside the web server. This means that a new process must be started to execute a CGI program. There is some overhead associated with creating and communicating with this separate process, and each process requires its own share of the local machine's memory resources. Furthermore, CGI programs are designed to handle only a sin-

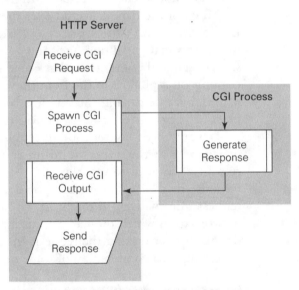

Figure 1.1   Server process for running CGI programs

gle request, after which they return their results to the web server and exit. This means that each time a request for dynamic content is received by the web browser, it must start a new process for running the corresponding CGI program for that specific request, send it the request information, wait for results, then pass those results back in its response to the browser. These days, it is not uncommon for popular web sites to be handling thousands of simultaneous requests, so even if the inefficiencies of individual CGI program execution are fairly small, they quickly add up to significant performance penalties.

As a result, a number of vendors have introduced new systems for dynamic generation of web content. In some cases, new HTTP servers that provide built-in dynamic content capabilities have been introduced. Today, however, the HTTP server market has come to be dominated by a small number of suppliers, making such all-in-one approaches less commercially viable. Current dynamic content systems more typically take the form of add-on code modules that leverage server-specific application programming interfaces (APIs) in order to interact directly with the web server process. By plugging in as a subprocess of the web server, these systems avoid much of the overhead associated with conventional CGI programs, and offer dynamic content capabilities with much better scalability than the traditional approach.

As indicated earlier, dynamic content generation requires the server to process requests at run time in order to construct an appropriate request-specific response. Instructions are required in order to perform this processing, so at one level or another it is clear that some programming is required. As a result, many of the most popular dynamic content systems, such as Allaire's ColdFusion, Microsoft's Active Server Pages, Netscape's Server-Side JavaScript, and PHP (an Open Source hypertext preprocessor) enable dynamic content to be specified using scripting languages. The use of scripting languages is a particularly appropriate choice here because web developers are used to rapid turnaround when testing their web pages: as soon as the HTML in a static web page is modified, the results of that change can be viewed in a web browser. By relying on scripting languages that do not require a lengthy edit-compile-link cycle before any code can be run, these dynamic content tools provide the same immediate feedback web developers have grown accustomed to with HTML.

Similarly, in recognition of the page-centric nature of web development, these tools enable scripts for dynamic content generation to be embedded directly in the web pages in which the dynamic content is to appear. The static elements of the page, governing page layout and base content, can be coded in HTML in the usual manner. Appearing alongside this static HTML in the source document are the scripts for generating the dynamic content. When the document is requested by an end user, the web server will pass along the static HTML elements, which often comprise the bulk of the page, unchanged. The scripts, however, will be turned over to the dynamic content system for execution, with the results of running these scripts embedded into the document in place of the script's original source code. Because the static HTML elements provide a framework into which the dynamic content generated by the scripts will be inserted, such tools are commonly referred to as *template systems*.

1.2.2 ColdFusion

The primary differences among template systems, then, lie in their scripting languages, and the capabilities provided therein. ColdFusion, from Allaire, provides a set of HTML-like tags which were initially targeted at embedding database queries into web pages, but it has since been extended to support a wide variety of data sources for dynamic content generation. The adoption of HTML-like tags has the advantage that there is a single, consistent style of syntax throughout the page; the ColdFusion tags are comfortable to web designers because they look just like the other tags present in the document. ColdFusion supports both UNIX and Microsoft Windows platforms.

1.2.3 Active Server Pages

Microsoft's Active Server Pages, often abbreviated ASP, support multiple scripting languages, including PerlScript, Jscript, and VBScript. PerlScript is based on Perl, and Jscript is based on JavaScript but the default scripting language for ASP is VBScript, a subset of Microsoft's popular Visual Basic programming language. VBScript includes support for accessing ActiveX components, which are compiled code objects that can encapsulate virtually any functionality, including database access and file manipulation. A large body of commercial off-the-shelf ActiveX components is available, and Microsoft provides tools and documentation for writing your own, as well. The major limitation of ASP, however, is that it is available only with Microsoft's Internet Information Server (IIS), running under the Windows NT operating system.

NOTE   As a result of its popularity, a number of vendors have developed tools for deploying ASP on other platforms. Chili!Soft, for example, has an ASP product for the Apache HTTP server running on the UNIX platform, which even supports interoperability between Active Server Pages and server-side Java (i.e., servlets and JSPs). Unfortunately, ASP derives much of its power from its support for ActiveX components, which, at least at the time of this writing, are not widely available on non-Microsoft platforms.

1.2.4 Server-Side JavaScript

As you might expect, Server-Side JavaScript (SSJS) uses JavaScript as its scripting language. JavaScript is an object-oriented language (based on prototypes rather than classes) with a C-like syntax, but, although it has a similar name, it is not Java. SSJS is an extension of the core JavaScript language, which is also the basis for the popular client-side JavaScript language used for scripting web browsers. SSJS adds built-in features for database and email support, session management, and interoperability with server-side Java classes using Netscape's LiveWire technology. In a departure from the other dynamic content systems described here, SSJS is a compiled language. A collection of web pages containing SSJS is compiled into a web application that is executed whenever the corresponding URLs are requested. Like compiled Java code, compiled SSJS is not platform-specific with respect to hardware or operating system. SSJS is, however, specific to Netscape's HTTP servers (i.e., Netscape Enterprise Server and Netscape Application Server).

1.2.5 *PHP*

A fourth dynamic content system that is growing in popularity is PHP. PHP was originally an acronym for Personal Home Page tools. As its scope and functionality have grown over the years, that moniker is no longer adequate and the software is now referred to only as PHP. Like JavaScript, PHP employs a C-like syntax, and provides strong support for pattern matching and database access. Extensions for communicating with other network resources, such as mail and directory servers, are also available. Unlike most of the other dynamic content systems now available, however, PHP is an Open Source product. As with other Open Source products, such as the Linux operating system and the Apache HTTP server, PHP is not a commercial product. It is instead the result of contributions from a community of interested developers, freely contributing to and supporting its code base. One important result of its Open Source nature is that PHP is now available on a large number of platforms. PHP is compatible with Windows NT and several UNIX operating systems, and with a number of HTTP servers, such as Apache, Microsoft's IIS, and Netscape Enterprise Server.

1.2.6 *Java servlets*

In light of the importance of dynamic content generation to web development then, it was natural for Sun to propose extensions to Java in this domain. In much the same way that Sun introduced applets as small Java-based applications for adding interactive functionality to web browsers, in 1996 Sun introduced servlets as small Java-based applications for adding dynamic functionality to web servers. Java servlets have a programming model similar to CGI scripts, insofar as they are given an HTTP request from a web browser as input, and are expected to locate and/or construct the appropriate content for the server's response.

Unlike traditional CGI programs that require spawning a new process to handle each new request, all of the servlets associated with a web server run inside a single process. This process runs a Java Virtual Machine (JVM), which is the platform-specific program for running (cross-platform) compiled Java programs. As illustrated in figure 1.2, instead of creating a process for each request, the JVM creates a Java thread to handle each servlet request. Java threads have much less overhead than full-blown processes, and execute within the processor memory already allocated by the JVM, making servlet execution considerably more efficient than CGI processing. Since the JVM persists beyond the life of a single request, servlets can also avoid many time-consuming operations, such as connecting to a database, by sharing them among all requests. At the same time, because servlets are written in Java, they enjoy all the benefits of the core Java platform: an object-oriented programming model, automatic memory management, cross-platform portability, and access to the rich collection of Java APIs now available for accessing databases, directory servers, network resources, and so forth.

When reduced to their essence, servlets provide a Java-based methodology for mapping HTTP requests into HTTP responses. Generating dynamic web content using servlets then, is accomplished by means of Java code that outputs the HTML (or other data) representing that content. In the case of HTML data, one approach is for the Java code to construct strings containing the appropriate markup text and then print those strings on the output stream associated with the HTTP response. This is often referred to as the out.println approach, because a significant portion of the resulting code consists of lines that start with this (or a very similar) sequence of characters.

Another option is to take a more object-oriented approach to modeling the response data, by first constructing

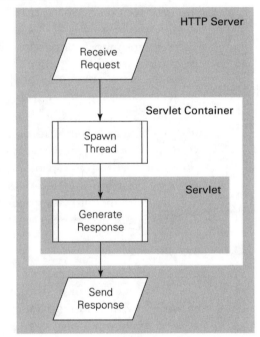

Figure 1.2   Server process for running servlets

a model of the page being constructed as a collection of Java objects. Many web pages, for example, can be modeled as a hierarchy of textual elements, including a title, various levels of headings, and paragraphs of text providing the content for each section, subsection, and so on. Java classes could be defined which represent each of these textual elements, as well as the page itself. The classes for the textual elements would provide methods for accessing and modifying their content. The page class would provide methods for adding and removing textual elements. When generating dynamic content, then, an instance of the page class is created, to which instances of the appropriate title, heading, and paragraph classes are then added. Once the complete model of the page was constructed, other methods could be called to render these objects as strings of HTML to be sent back as the servlet's response.

One popular library of Java classes that enables this style of dynamic content generation is the Element Construction Set (ECS), which, like PHP, Apache, and Linux, is an Open Source software effort. One of the key advantages of this object-oriented approach to dynamic content generation is that it lends itself to supporting multiple forms of document output. ECS, for example, supports output in both HTML and XML, and can be extended to support additional formats, as needed.

In a similar manner, the Swinglets toolkit from Javelin Software allows developers to construct servlet output using a set of components modeled after those of Java's Swing library of user interface components. The Swinglets library provides several classes for data presentation, including tables, links, buttons, and radio buttons. Data is added to these interface components, which may then be rendered in various formats, including HTML, Dynamic HTML, and WML (Wireless Markup Language, an HTML-like language geared toward wireless devices such as mobile phones).

A potential disadvantage of this approach, however, is that all document contents, both static and dynamic, reside in program source code. As a result, any change to such a document requires intervention by a programmer. An HTML page designer cannot change the layout of the page unless the associated source code is changed. Indeed, any change to the static elements of the document, such as changing the URL of a link or image, requires corresponding changes to the source code. This dilemma also applies to the `out.println` approach.

1.2.7 JavaServer Pages

As discussed earlier, incorporating dynamic content must ultimately involve some form of programming to describe how that content is generated. Program code, however, tends to be expensive to create and to maintain, so minimizing the need for programming is often a desirable goal. Combining this goal with Sun's objective for robust, full-featured support for Java on the server, a Java-based template system, JSP, was the natural result.

JSP is something of a hybrid among template systems, because it supports two different styles for adding dynamic content to web pages. Like ASP, SSJS, and PHP, scripts can be embedded in JSP pages containing actual programming code. In the case of JSP, this programming code is typically Java. (Actually, the JSP specification allows for the possibility of alternative scripting languages. See chapter 3, "Programming JSP scripts," for details.) Like ColdFusion, JSP supports a set of HTML-like tags that interact with Java objects on the server, without the need for raw Java code to appear in the page. In fact, the JSP 1.1 specification takes this capability a step further, by providing a tag extension mechanism that allows developers to create libraries of custom tags that can be loaded into a JSP page. These custom tags can then be used on the page just like the standard JSP tags.

NOTE   As a demonstration of the power of this approach, it is interesting to note that Live Software, makers of the JRun servlet software, have developed a set of custom JSP tags which reproduce the tags used in Allaire's ColdFusion product. This product, effectively a cross-platform, Java-based clone of Cold-Fusion, was released in May 1999 as <CF_Anywhere>. Allaire was sufficiently impressed by this feat that in June 1999, it bought the company.

Servlets and JavaServer Pages first appeared as part of Sun's Java Web Server product, an HTTP server written in Java. Sun eventually released the servlet technology as a standard Java extension. JSP soon followed, with the first draft API specifications appearing in 1998. The JavaServer Pages 1.0 Specification was released in June 1999, thus ensuring a stable, well-defined platform for vendors to build against.

Soon after Sun published the Java servlet specification, other companies began to add support for the base servlet architecture to their products. Since JSP functionality itself is typically implemented using the servlet technology, other servlet products could readily take advantage of it, and web developers quickly discovered its advantages.

As such, a number of third-party products are now available for adding servlet and JSP functionality to existing web servers. Two of the more popular products in this category are JRun from Live Software and New Atlanta's ServletExec. In addition, in June 1999 Sun Microsystems and the Apache Software Foundation announced the Jakarta Project, the goal of which is an Open Source implementation of servlets and JSP that will also serve as one of the reference platforms for these technologies.

As an essential element of feature-rich web sites and web-based applications, dynamic content generation continues to be the focus of much attention in the web development community. JSP is now positioned to play a major role in the ongoing evolution of web technology, and we look forward to seeing the next generation of online tools, services, and diversions that will be enabled by JavaServer Pages.

1.3   *JSP and Java 2 Enterprise Edition*

JSP is now an integral part of developing web-based applications using Java. Because of its ability to separate presentation from implementation logic by combining standard markup text with scripting elements and object-oriented components, JSP provides an excellent front-end technology for applications that are deployed over the web.

1.3.1 Java platform editions

In June 1999, Sun Microsystems announced that the Java 2 software platform would be split into three editions, aimed at different categories of hardware deployment platforms. The traditional Java Runtime Environment, or JRE, which contains all of the core classes in the formal language specification (including, for example, the standard networking, utility, and graphical user interface classes), has been renamed the *Java 2 Standard Edition*, or J2SE. The J2SE is targeted toward traditional desktop computing platforms, such as Microsoft Windows and Apple Macintosh personal computers.

A subset of the core classes, targeted toward handheld devices (for example, PDAs—personal digital assistants—such as the 3Com PalmPilot), embedded processors (such as Internet-enabled toasters), and so-called "information appliances" (e.g., digital TV set-top boxes), comprises the *Java 2 Micro Edition*, or J2ME. The goal of J2ME is to provide a Java environment with minimal footprint, that nevertheless supports the Java vision of Write Once, Run Anywhere™ program code.

At the opposite extreme from J2ME is the *Java 2 Enterprise Edition*, or J2EE. Rather than subtract from the Java 2 core, as the micro edition does, J2EE bundles the core Java classes with extensions targeted toward enterprise application development. For example, J2EE includes support for Enterprise JavaBeans, which provides a set of standard abstractions for accessing corporate data stores, such as databases and directory servers, with automatic support for transaction management and resource pooling.

Given the inherent complexity involved in designing, constructing, and maintaining large-scale enterprise applications, however, Sun's specification of J2EE includes a set of guidelines for developing software using the J2EE platform. These guidelines take the form of a recommended base software architecture referred to as the *J2EE Application Model*.

1.3.2 Web-based applications

A key element of the J2EE Application Model is the use of the web as a preferred mechanism for data delivery between the application and the end user, relying on the web browser as a primary user interface for enterprise software. The advantage of this approach is that the web browser, in just the few short years since the birth of the World Wide Web, has been established as a ubiquitous, cross-platform, *de facto* standard for accessing data over the network. When an application relies on the web browser for its user interface, there is no need for end users to install any additional software to run the application. And as new versions of the application are developed and deployed on the server, end users automatically start using the new version: end users need not take any local action to upgrade to the latest version.

To facilitate web-based applications, then, both servlets and JSP are required elements of the J2EE specification. And while both technologies can be used to dynamically generate HTML to be sent to an end user's web browser, only JSP enforces a strong separation between the presentation logic involved in displaying data and the business or programming logic used to generate that data in the first place. This separation means that the design of the user interface, embodied in a set of JSP pages, can be carried out independently from the design of the other code that runs on the server (e.g., interpreting requests, formulating database queries, and manipulating results). This independence leads to much more robust applications, since changes to one part of the application generally do not require corresponding changes to other parts. Specifically, when using JSP, changes to the presentation of the data (e.g., formatting of the data, design of the associated graphics, overall page layout) do not require any changes to the underlying server code that supplied that data in the first place.

Given Sun's selection of servlets and JSPs as major components of J2EE, it is clear that support for these technologies will continue to grow. Even now, it is more the rule than the exception that enterprise web application servers, such as Netscape Application Server, IBM WebSphere, and BEA WebLogic, include support for both servlets and JSPs.

In addition to growth in the market for software to deploy JSP, it is anticipated that improved development tools will soon be available. Currently, JSP development is essentially a manual process, but several of the web authoring tool vendors have announced support for JavaServer Pages in upcoming releases of their products, including Drumbeat 2000 from Macromedia, IBM's Visual Age for Java, and HomeSite from Allaire. JSP's built-in support for component-based design using JavaBeans, discussed in a later section, promises to enable a new set of tools for creating dynamic web pages graphically, using a visual programming approach to drag and drop server-side Java components into WYSIWYG editing tools. The ability to create sophisticated JSP pages without ever seeing HTML tags, let alone Java code, may soon be a reality.

1.4   *JSP benefits*

JSP offers several benefits as a system for dynamic content generation. First of all, as a Java-based technology, it enjoys all of the advantages that the Java language provides with respect to development and deployment. As an object-oriented language with strong typing, encapsulation, exception handling, and automatic memory management, use of Java leads to increased programmer productivity and more robust code. Because there is a standard, published API for JSP, and because compiled Java bytecode is portable across all platforms that support a JVM, use of JSP does not lock you into using a specific hardware platform, operating system, or server software. If a switch in any one of these components becomes necessary, all JSP pages and associated Java classes can be migrated over as is. Because JSP is vendor-neutral, developers and system architects can select best-of-breed solutions at all stages of JSP deployment.

In addition, because it enables full access to the underlying Java platform, JSP can readily take advantage of all of the other standard Java APIs, including those for cross-platform database access, directory services, distributed computing, and cryptography. This ability to leverage a wide range of data sources, system resources, and network services means that JSP is a highly flexible solution for creating feature-rich web-based applications.

JSP itself offers several advantages as a system for dynamic content generation. Among these are improved performance over CGI and a programming model that emphasizes component-centric application design. This programming model enables developers using JSP to maintain a strict separation between the presentation elements of a web application and its underlying implementation. This separation, in turn, facilitates a division of labor within the web development team by establishing a well-defined interface between application development and page design.

1.4.1   *Performance*

Conventional CGI codes exist as external programs from the HTTP server. When the server receives a request to be handled via CGI, it spawns one new process for each request to execute the CGI code. This makes it easy for the web server to handle multiple simultaneous requests requiring the same CGI program, but in most operating systems, process creation is rather expensive: memory and other system resources must be allocated and data and program code loaded before the code is run. Since CGI programs are designed to generate a single response for a single request, they execute quickly. After a CGI program has finished running, however, additional operating system resources are consumed when its process is destroyed.

As we will see in chapter 2, JSP is typically implemented via servlets. When a web server receives a request for a JSP page, it forwards it to a special process dedicated to handling servlet execution. This process is referred to as the *servlet container*. In the context of JSP, it is referred to as the *JSP container*.

JARGON   In older literature on server-side Java technologies, these containers are also referred as "engines"—that is, the *servlet engine* and the *JSP engine*.

The servlet container is normally a separate process from the HTTP server, due primarily to the fact that the servlet container is a Java process, running a JVM, while most HTTP servers are written in other languages. The key factor here is that, for servlet containers associated with conventional HTTP servers, there is only one additional process for the servlet container, which handles all servlet-related requests, including JSP. This process is initiated when the HTTP server starts up, and continues to run until the HTTP server is shut down. Rather than create a completely new process for each request requiring dynamic content generation, all such requests are forwarded by the HTTP server to a single servlet container process.

TIP   For those HTTP servers that are written in Java, there is no reason the servlet container cannot be run as part of the same process. In fact, for many of the HTTP servers which are written in Java, all of the functionality of the HTTP server is implemented via servlets, including the handling of requests for both JSP and HTML files, so there is no distinction whatsoever between the HTTP server and the servlet container.

It is still a requirement that the servlet container handle multiple requests for a given servlet or JSP at the same time, but this is accomplished via Java threads, rather than full-fledged processes. Threads are similar to processes, in that many threads can be running simultaneously within a JVM. Threads require considerably less overhead to create and destroy than processes, however; for this reason they are sometimes referred to as *lightweight processes*. Because they use less resources, they are much more efficient than processes. For example, spawned processes often copy the memory of the parent process, whereas threads share memory with the parent thread. As a result, servlets and JSPs are much more efficient than traditional CGI programs for generating dynamic web content.

> **NOTE** As a matter of fact, all of the code running within a Java Virtual Machine is part of one thread or another. When a JVM first starts up, it creates an initial set of threads for managing itself (e.g., running the garbage collector, listening for user interface events), as well as a thread for running user code. This code can in turn create and run its own threads, as is the case for a servlet container using threads to handle HTTP requests.

For even greater performance, some servlet containers are capable of running "in process," as part of the HTTP server process itself, even for those HTTP servers which are not written in Java. This makes communication of requests and responses between the servlet container and the HTTP server much more efficient, and is accomplished by running the servlet container itself as a thread within the HTTP server. IBM's WebSphere, for example, supports in-process operation as an option, and the servlet container built into Version 4 of Netscape's iPlanet server products only runs in process.

Furthermore, because all servlet and JSP requests are handled by the same process (i.e., the JVM), it is very easy for them to share resources, and thereby improve performance. For example, database access is much quicker when employing a pool of reusable database connections that always remain open. Since CGI programs start a separate process for each request, it is much more difficult for them to share resources. In the case of database access, for example, each CGI request must typically open its own connection to the database, and close that connection when the request is done. This adds additional overhead, which the servlet container can avoid by creating a connection pool during startup, and then sharing these connections among individual request threads.

As you are probably aware, Java class files are compiled to platform-independent bytecode rather than native assembly code. The job of the JVM is to interpret this bytecode and turn it into platform-native instructions at run-time. Because of this extra layer of interpretation required to run Java code, it is necessarily the case that Java code will run slower than an equivalent program written in another programming language (for example, C or C++) and compiled to native code. Given this fact, it might seem like Java would be a poor choice for dynamic content generation, since the speed with which requests can be turned into responses has a direct impact on the amount of traffic that can be handled by a web server.

Recall, however, that most dynamic content generation systems in wide use today rely on interpreted scripting languages. The most popular language for CGI programming is Perl, an interpreted scripting language. Active Server Pages and

PHP are based on interpreted scripting languages. Server-Side JavaScript, like Java, is compiled into a platform-independent format, so it also requires a run-time interpreter. ColdFusion tags are likewise interpreted at run-time on a per-request basis.

Compared to the most popular alternatives, then, JavaServer Pages does not suffer a relative performance hit because of its reliance on an underlying interpreter. Furthermore, because of the popularity of Java as a programming language, many techniques have been introduced in recent years for improving Java run-time performance, such as Just-In-Time (JIT) compilation and generational garbage collection. In practice, then, Java performance is more than adequate for dynamic content generation, given adequate server hardware. At the same time, hardware and operating systems vendors continue to actively research new methods for improving JVM performance, as they compete for top honors in various Java benchmarks. And as Java performance continues to improve, the performance of JavaServer Pages also improves. So, while Sun Microsystems and all of the other vendors of servlet and JSP products continue to work on the performance of the basic JavaServer Pages API, JSP also benefits indirectly from all of the resources being devoted to Java performance in general.

1.4.2 *Reusable components*

Although JavaServer Pages enables programmers to implement dynamic content generation by including Java source code directly in web pages, it also includes a set of HTML-like tags for interacting with Java objects residing on the server. In particular, these tags are designed for creating, querying, and modifying server-side *JavaBeans*.

JavaBeans are objects, written in Java, whose implementations conform to a set of conventions designed to promote modularity and reusability. JavaBeans uses a programming style that leads to self-contained chunks of program code that encapsulate related data, functionality, or behavior, which may be used and reused in multiple contexts without having to know the details of their inner operation. As a result, JavaBeans can readily be connected together and combined in order to provide more sophisticated or application-specific capabilities. The generic computer term for an object that exhibits this sort of plug-and-play interoperability is a *component*. JavaBeans, then, is one example of a component programming model. Others include Microsoft's ActiveX (which plays a similar role in Active Server Pages to the role of JavaBeans in JavaServer Pages) and CORBA, a component interoperability standard developed by the Object Management Group (OMG), an industry consortium for distributed, cross-platform, object-oriented middleware.

A component, then, is a stand-alone object representing a collection of properties and behavior. Because these properties and behavior can be accessed without regard for the underlying implementation, it is possible to describe a component's capabilities independent of the programming language in which it was originally written. A component could be used in a second programming language (for example, a scripting language), or even be applied using visual tools, with no program code at all. In the case of JavaServer Pages, components written as JavaBeans are accessed not by means of a programming language, but via an alternate syntax. Specifically, JSP provides HTML-like tags for accessing JavaBeans on a page, and for displaying and modifying their properties. For complete details, see chapter 5.

The primary virtue of component-centric design is reusability. Because components are required to be self-contained, programmers do not have to understand any complicated relationships between objects in order to be able to use them. A component may call on other objects behind the scenes, but the abstract interface through which the component is accessed and manipulated, if designed properly, will mask the underlying complexity. Because components tend to be targeted towards specific tasks—representing a particular set of data, performing a specific behavior—it is easy to determine what functionality the component provides, and therefore under what circumstances it should be used. To some extent, components are reused by virtue of the fact that they are easy to use in the first place.

The benefit of this reusability is productivity. If a component is already available to perform some task, that is one less piece of code that needs to be written, debugged, and maintained. Furthermore, components are generally not context-sensitive. For example, the same JavaBean can be deployed in a servlet, an applet, or a JSP page, creating additional opportunities for reuse.

1.4.3 *Separating presentation and implementation*

By taking advantage of JSP's built-in support for JavaBeans, it becomes possible to maintain a strict separation between data presentation—the display of information to the end user—and program implementation—the code used to generate that information in the first place. The benefit of decoupling these two aspects is that changes to one can be made without requiring any changes to the other. The way data is displayed (e.g., font selection, color scheme, page layout) can be revised without ever having to modify any Java code. Similarly, as long as the component interfaces remain unchanged, the underlying implementation can be rewritten (e.g., to improve performance or maintainability) with no effect on any JSP pages that use those components.

Given this goal, then, JSPs provide a very simple and elegant means of maintaining the separation of these two elements of a web-based application: syntax. By leveraging JSP's HTML-like tags for accessing JavaBeans and their properties, JSP pages can be written that contain no Java source code. If none of the available tags provides the functionality needed, you can, if so inclined, write your own application-specific tag library using the JSP tag extension mechanism. If the JSP page contains only tags and no Java code, the first requirement for enforcing separation of presentation and implementation has been met, since there is no implementation code mixed in with the presentation code.

The second requirement is equally easy to describe: there should be no HTML code in your JavaBeans. At first blush, this might sound like an absurd notion. (JavaBeans are written in Java, not HTML!) However, there's nothing stopping a programmer from creating a JavaBean whose properties include strings of HTML code. A JSP page could then access these properties, inserting that HTML code into the page through the corresponding property tags. It may be tempting to give your JavaBean the ability to, say, generate a large HTML table from the results of a database query, but any time it is necessary to change the appearance of the table, that Bean must be edited, compiled, and tested before that change can be put into effect. For this reason, in order to achieve separation of presentation and implementation, it's also necessary to keep presentation code out of the implementation code.

There will be times, though, when generating HTML code programmatically is the best solution. Consider an on-line banking application implemented via Java-Server Pages. There would likely be JavaBeans representing a customer's accounts, as well as each of the transactions involving those accounts. For maximum reusability, good component-centric design would dictate that these application-oriented JavaBeans would model only the banking aspects of accounts and transactions, and would not include properties that return, say, account balances in HTML format. These Beans could then be readily deployed in other application contexts (e.g., a Java applet), which have no use for such web-oriented baggage. It would likely prove fairly cumbersome, however, to write a JSP page that uses these Beans to display, say, the last 10 transactions for an account. This is primarily because JSP does not include any built-in tags for iterating through Bean properties. To solve this dilemma, it appears that you have no choice but to either include Java scripting code in the JSP, or provide for HTML output by the Bean.

Fortunately, JavaServer Pages provides a third alternative, specifically geared toward programmatic generation of HTML using Java code. As suggested in figure 1.3, this is the role of JSP's tag extension mechanism, which allows Java programmers to implement new JSP tags and package them in application-specific libraries that may then be imported into individual JSP pages. For this hypothetical banking application, then, the best way to maintain separation between presentation and implementation is to develop a set of custom tags for representing complex account information, such as transaction lists, via HTML.

Custom tags still have the problem that, in order to change the display of data controlled via custom tags, programming is required. This is unavoidable, however, if programmatic generation of HTML is required. The advantage of implementing HTML generation via custom tags is two-fold. First, custom tags provide a means for avoiding Java code in the JSP files themselves. JSP files can continue to rely on a single, consistent, HTML-like syntax. Second, on the programming side, the HTML generation is isolated within the tag library code. The tag library will likely have dependencies upon your JavaBeans code, but not *vice versa*. Custom tags provide a well-defined interface

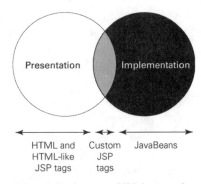

Figure 1.3   Support of JSP features for the separation of presentation and implementation.

between the presentation and implementation, without contaminating the JSP files with implementation code, or the Bean properties with presentation code.

1.4.4   *Achieving division of labor*

An important side effect of this decoupling of presentation and implementation through JSP is that it promotes a clear division of labor in the development and maintenance of web applications for dynamic content generation. It is the rare individual indeed who possesses outstanding skills in both programming and artistic design. Although many companies try, rarely are they fortunate enough to find a first class web designer who also possesses strong Java development skills or the corollary, a true Java guru with strong graphics and layout skills.

As a result, most web application development teams are cross-functional in nature, representing multiple specialties. Designers, graphic artists, and HTML coders are responsible for the presentation. Java programmers and system architects are responsible for the implementation. Large corporate teams may also include editors, marketing consultants, database administrators, network engineers, and system administrators. All of the team members have important contributions to make to the focus, design, and content of the web application, but when it comes time for actual implementation, efficiency will be a direct result of the extent to which the participants are able to work independently. When a clear division of labor can be put in place, such that the need to coordinate work between team members is minimized, work on multiple parts of the implementation can be carried out simultaneously. Studies have repeatedly shown that communication is the major bottleneck in team productivity; if communication needs can be reduced during the critical implementation phase, the productivity rewards can be great.

Similarly, when changes to the application are required after initial development, the fewer team members that need to be involved in order to effect that change, the more quickly the modification can be put in place. For example, an important concern for an on-line service provider is the usability of their web site: Is content easy to find? Are services easy to use? Usability, then, is critical to customer satisfaction and retention. In the interest of usability, the presentation aspects of a web application may undergo almost constant review and revision. The implementation of the business and programming logic behind the application, however, tends to evolve much more slowly.

If the team members responsible for these two elements of the application can work independently, then, both the initial development and later refinements can be carried out more efficiently. As described above, JSP's support for component-centric design promotes the establishment of clear interfaces for accessing the functionality of server-side objects implemented as JavaBeans. The HTML-like tags provided by JavaServer Pages for accessing JavaBeans can then take advantage of these interfaces to achieve (and enforce) separation of presentation and implementation.

In practical terms, this means that page designers can focus on HTML and application engineers can focus on Java. The team as a whole develops the requirements that drive the web application's design. The programmers then translate these requirements into a set of properties and behaviors to be implemented as Java-Beans. These properties and behaviors then provide the foundation for dynamic content generation to be leveraged by the presentation team via JavaServer Pages. And, once this foundation is established, both teams can work independently to refine their contributions to the application—e.g., enhancing the look and feel of the application, or increasing its run-time efficiency—without negatively impacting the performance of the other team.

Fundamentals

2

Now that you've seen an overview of JSP, where it has come from, and what it offers, it's time to dive into the technology itself. Subscribing to the theory that it's better to jump in headfirst than to wade in one step at a time, we'll immediately look at a few examples, followed by a discussion of the basic syntax of JSP tags. Next, we'll consider the requirements for setting up a web server for use with Java-Server Pages. Finally, we'll examine how the technology actually works, and discuss how the implementation of JSP affects its operation.

2.1 Writing your first JSP

Our first objective in this chapter is to set the stage with examples that illustrate the flexibility and power of JSP as a solution for dynamic content generation. We won't focus too much on the details—there will be plenty of that later. The intent here is simply to give you an idea of the ground to be covered in the coming chapters.

2.1.1 About the examples

As indicated in chapter 1, a strength of JSP is its ability to provide dynamic content generation via a familiar, HTML-like syntax. At the same time, however, this familiar syntax can make it difficult for those new to JSP to immediately recognize where its elements are being used within a page. Therefore, in the examples in this book that combine JSP elements with other static content (typically HTML), we have adopted the convention of marking JSP tags in such pages and page fragments in **boldface**. The intent of this convention is to enable readers to easily distinguish JSP content from the surrounding static document content.

2.1.2 Hello, World!

No software book would be complete without an example that prints out "Hello, World!" so here is a JSP that does just that:

```
<HTML>
<BODY>
Hello, World!
</BODY>
</HTML>
```

At this point, you're probably thinking, "Hey! That's nothing but HTML!" And you're exactly right. It is nevertheless, a valid JSP file. This file could be added to the document hierarchy of a web server configured to run JSP and, if it were assigned the proper extension (typically .jsp), then any request for this document would be interpreted as a JSP request. The web server would forward the request to the local

JSP container for processing. Naturally, the JSP container wouldn't find any actual JSP elements, and so would simply output the HTML as written. This is a fairly roundabout way of delivering a static HTML document, but it would certainly work.

2.1.3 *Hello, World! revisited*

Having established the fairly uninteresting fact that all valid HTML documents are also valid JSP documents, let's consider a more motivating example. Here's a file that generates content dynamically through the use of a pair of JSP tags that support scripting:

```
<HTML>
<BODY>
<% String visitor = request.getParameter("name");
if (visitor == null) visitor = "World"; %>
Hello, <%= visitor %>!
</BODY>
</HTML>
```

Without getting into the details, this JSP first declares a Java `String` variable named `visitor`, and then attempts to initialize it from the current HTTP request. If no value for this variable is present in the request, a default value is assigned. A JSP expression is then used to insert the value of this variable into the HTML output of the page.

Request parameters are passed into JSP pages using the normal HTTP parameter mechanisms. For HTTP GET requests, encoded parameter values are simply appended to the URL. For HTTP POST requests, a more complicated protocol is used to send parameter data behind the scenes. In practice, URLs longer than 255 characters can be problematic, so POST requests are the standard when a large amount of parameter data is required.

WARNING   This length restriction on URLs is driven by backward-compatibility with older software. The HTTP/1.1 specification actually imposes no *a priori* limits on URL length, but there are older servers, proxies, and browsers that cannot handle URLs which exceed this 255-character limit.

For the purposes of this example, let's assume the URL for this JSP page is http://server/webdev/fundamentals/helloScript.jsp. If a web browser were used to request this URL via an HTTP GET request, the JSP container would process this page and respond with the following:

```
Hello, World!
```

If the appropriate parameter value were added to this URL, however, a different result would be obtained. If the requested URL was http://server/webdev/fundamentals/helloScript.jsp?name=Flynn, for example, the response from the JSP container would instead be:

```
Hello, Flynn!
```

In the first case, without the parameter value, the script used the default value for the page's `visitor` variable. In the second case, the script retrieved the value of the `name` parameter from the request, and so was able to generate more personalized dynamic content.

If you were to use a web browser to try out these examples, you might be tempted at this point to use the browser's **View Source** command to look at the HTML in this response. If you were to do so, you might expect to see the contents of the original JSP file. Instead you would see something like the following:

```
<HTML>
<BODY>
Hello, Flynn!
</BODY>
</HTML>
```

If you are new to dynamic content generation, you may be wondering what happened to all of the JSP tags (e.g., `<%= visitor %>`). This result looks like someone slipped in the file from the previous section, inserting the name "Flynn" in place of some of the original text.

In fact, that's very close to what's actually happening. Keep in mind that the web browser sees only the response from the web server to its request, which may or may not correspond to some original source document. The browser has no way of knowing that, when the web server receives a request corresponding to a JSP page, that request is forwarded to the JSP container for processing. It is the JSP container that reads and interprets the code in the corresponding file to generate the dynamic content, inserting the results into the static content already on the page, and returning the completed page to the HTTP server. This is the page that is then sent back to the browser, with no evidence whatsoever of the activity that took place behind the scenes to construct it. As far as the browser knows, it's just reading a straight HTML file. It is this HTML from the response that is displayed by the browser when you apply the **View Source** command.

2.1.4 *Hello, World! the Bean edition*

In addition to support for scripting, JSP includes tags for interacting with Java-Beans. To give this subject of "Hello, World!" implementations the full attention it deserves, it is necessary to provide a third example JSP that demonstrates this approach, as well.

Before a JSP using the JavaBeans tags can be presented, however, we first need a Bean for it to use. Here is the source code for a Bean called `HelloBean`, which has one property, called `name`:

```
package com.taglib.wdjsp.fundamentals;
public class HelloBean implements java.io.Serializable {
  String name;

  public HelloBean () {
    this.name = "World";
  }
  public String getName () {
    return name;
  }
  public void setName (String name) {
    this.name = name;
  }
}
```

If you are a Java programmer, you can see from this code that JavaBeans are implemented via ordinary Java classes, which adhere to a set of conventions for instantiating themselves, and for accessing and setting their properties. For all the details on these conventions, see chapter 6. For now, note that the `HelloBean` class has a constructor that takes no arguments, but which assigns a default value to the `name` property. This property, whose value is an instance of Java's `String` class, is accessed via a method called `getName()`. It is modified via a method called `setName()`, which takes a single argument of the same type as the property itself (i.e., class `String`).

Given this definition of the `HelloBean` class, it may be used in a JSP file as follows:

```
<HTML>
<BODY>
<jsp:useBean id="hello" class="com.taglib.wdjsp.fundamentals.HelloBean"/>
<jsp:setProperty name="hello" property="name" param="name"/>
Hello, <jsp:getProperty name="hello" property="name"/>!
</BODY>
</HTML>
```

The first JSP tag to appear in this page is the `<jsp:useBean>` tag. As its name suggests, it is used to indicate that a Bean of a particular class will be used on this page. Here, the `HelloBean` class is specified. In addition, an identifier, `hello`, is specified for the Bean instance. This identifier may be used to refer to the Bean later on in the JSP file.

The `<jsp:setProperty>` tag appears next. In the form shown here, this tag is used to modify the `name` property of the `hello` Bean based on the value of the `name` parameter in the request. In effect, then, this tag says that the request should be searched for a parameter named `name`, and, if one is found, its value should be copied from the request to the Bean's `name` property.

The final JSP tag in this file, `<jsp:getProperty>`, is used to access the value of a Bean property and insert it into the page in place of the original tag. In this case, the tag retrieves the `name` property of the Bean associated with the `hello` identifier.

Assume, then, that the URL for this JSP page is http://server/webdev/fundamentals/helloBean.jsp. If this page is accessed via an HTTP GET request with that URL the output will be, as before,

```
Hello, World!
```

This is because the default value of the `name` property is the string `"World"`. No parameter was provided from which the `<jsp:setProperty>` tag could set the property's value, so the default value—set by the constructor that was called as a result of the `<jsp:useBean>` tag—was used.

Suppose, though, that the URL http://server/webdev/fundamentals/helloBean.jsp?name=Alan was used to access this page. In this case, the `<jsp:setProperty>` tag would find a parameter with the same name as one of the Bean's properties (i.e., `name`). The parameter value would be used to set the corresponding property value, such that the response to this request would be:

```
Hello, Alan!
```

In this case, it took two files to create this dynamic content, the Java source code file which defined the Bean class and the JSP file that created, modified, and accessed the Bean in order to produce that content. In the previous script-based example, all of the code was included in the single JSP file.

As discussed in the previous chapter, and is evident from these two examples, the Bean-based approach promotes reusability of code (multiple JSPs could take advantage of the `HelloBean` class without needing to write any additional Java code) and the separation of presentation from implementation (one file contains only HTML and HTML-like tags, the other contains only Java). As is also evident, the Bean-based approach requires more work up front, in order to achieve the same results.

2.1.5 Hello Real World

While the "Hello, World!" examples demonstrate the capabilities JSP provides for dynamic content generation, the actual functionality of these examples is not particularly inspiring. In an effort to remedy this, we provide here a peek at a real-world application of JSP. Listing 2.1 presents the source code for a JSP page that implements a web-based client for looking up domain registration information via the Internet-standard Whois protocol.

At this point, it certainly isn't expected that readers new to JSP will be able to follow the code in this listing. In fact, the details of this particular example won't be presented until the end of chapter 12. There's clearly a lot of ground to cover between here and there, so don't be alarmed if this listing makes no sense to you. As stated earlier, the primary reason for including this example here is to demonstrate that JSP can be used for more than just toy problems that insert people's names into a web page.

At the same time, there are a few preliminary observations that can be made about this JSP page, even at this early stage. First of all, we can see that it employs a combination of scripting tags and JavaBeans tags. No actual network programming code is apparent, however; presumably the protocol implementation details are taken care of by the Bean. Where the scripting tags are used, they appear to be focused primarily on presentation details, such as setting up form tags.

In addition, the HTML in this file is fairly complex. The form has several input fields, and uses a table to manage the overall layout. (A screen shot of this page can be seen in figure 12.4.) The bottom line is that JSP allows the developer to combine the full power of the Java programming language with rich web-based user interfaces, while maintaining a clear line of separation between the presentation of that interface and the underlying implementation of the application.

Listing 2.1   Source code for a real-world JSP example

```
<jsp:useBean id="whois" scope="session"
            class="com.taglib.wdjsp.byexample.WhoisBean">
  <jsp:setProperty name="whois" property="serverList"
                   value="whois.internic.net,whois.register.com"/>
</jsp:useBean>
<jsp:setProperty name="whois" property="*"/>
<HTML>
<HEAD><TITLE>Whois Client</TITLE></HEAD>
<BODY BGCOLOR="white">
<TABLE bgcolor="tan" align="center" border="1" cellpadding="10">
<FORM action="<%= HttpUtils.getRequestURL(request) %>" method="GET">
<TR><TD>
```

```
<INPUT type="submit" value="Whois">
<INPUT type="text" name="query" SIZE="20"
       value="<jsp:getProperty name="whois" property="query"/>">
 
<B>Record Types:</B>
<SELECT name="options" SIZE="1">
<OPTION <%= whois.getOptions().equals("")?"selected":"" %>
VALUE="">All
<OPTION <%= whois.getOptions().equals("Do")?"selected":"" %>
VALUE="Do">Domain Only
<OPTION <%= whois.getOptions().equals("Person")?"selected":"" %>
VALUE="Person">People Only
<OPTION <%= whois.getOptions().equals("Organization")?"selected":"" %>
VALUE="Organization">Organizations Only
</SELECT>
<P></P>
<B>Whois Server:</B>
<INPUT TYPE="RADIO" NAME="serverList"
<%= whois.getServerList().equals("whois.internic.net,whois.register.com")
    ?"checked":"" %> VALUE="whois.internic.net,whois.register.com">
Both  
<INPUT TYPE="RADIO" NAME="serverList"
<%= whois.getServerList().equals("whois.register.com")?"checked":"" %>
VALUE="whois.register.com">
Register.com  
<INPUT TYPE="RADIO" NAME="serverList"
<%= whois.getServerList().equals("whois.internic.net")?"checked":"" %>
VALUE="whois.internic.net">
Network Solutions
<P></P>
<TEXTAREA rows="24" cols="80">
<jsp:getProperty name="whois" property="results"/>
</TEXTAREA>
</TD></TR>
</TABLE>
</FORM>
</BODY>
</HTML>
```

2.2   *Tag conventions*

Having seen some examples, now, let's take a closer look at the types of tags JSP provides. In chapter 1, the JSP tags were referred to as HTML-like. This is true to the extent that JSP tags—like HTML tags—all begin and end with angle brackets, that is., the < and > characters. In point of fact, however, the JSP tags fall into two basic categories: scripting-oriented tags inspired by ASP, and a full set of tags based on the Extensible Markup Language, (XML).

2.2.1 Scripting-oriented tags

The ASP-derived tags are easily recognized by their delimiters. They all start with the characters `<%` and end with the characters `%>`. An additional character may appear after the initial `<%`, such as `!`, `=`, or `@`, to further proscribe the meaning of the tag. Examples include:

```
<%! double radius = 7.5; %>
<%= 2 * Math.PI * radius %>
<% if (radius > 10.0) {
    out.println("Exceeds recommended maximum. Stress analysis advised.");
    } %>
<%@ include file="copyright.html" %>
```

Note that all these tags are self-contained. All of the information relevant to the tag, and all of the data it will act on, is contained within the individual tags themselves. In contrast, many HTML tags appear in pairs. For example, the `<I>` and `</I>` tags have the effect of italicizing any text they contain. The contained text is referred to as the *body* of its containing tags. None of these scripting-oriented JSP tags have bodies.

NOTE   The use and functionality of the scripting-oriented tags will be described in detail in chapter 3.

2.2.2 XML-based tags

The second type of JSP tag follows XML syntax and conventions. XML syntax is very similar to HTML, but adds a few rules which remove some of the vagueness of its sister language. For example, XML tags are case sensitive. In HTML, `<title>` is merely an alternate spelling of the `<TITLE>` tag. In XML, these are treated as two different tags, which may each have their own meaning. XML requires that all attribute values appearing within a tag must be quoted, using either single or double quotes. (In HTML, quotes around attribute values are optional, unless the attribute value contains white-space characters.) XML also makes a distinction between tags within the document that contain a body, and those that do not. Specifically, a tag which does not contain a body uses `<` as its opening delimiter, and `/>` as its closing delimiter. For example,

```
<jsp:forward page="admin.jsp"/>
```

Tags that do have body content use the same conventions as HTML. The opening tag uses `<` as its opening delimiter, and `>` as its closing delimiter. The closing tag uses `</` as its opening delimiter, and `>` as its closing delimiter. Here is a sample JSP tag with body content:

```
<jsp:useBean id="login"
             class="com.taglib.wdjsp.fundamentals.UserBean">
  <jsp:setProperty name="login" property="group" value="admin"/>
</jsp:useBean>
```

In this case, the body content is another JSP tag. The tag in the body does not itself have a body, so it follows the previous convention.

XML provides capabilities for developers to extend it on an application-specific basis. In order to allow tags from multiple XML applications to appear in the same document, XML has introduced the notion of namespaces for identifying which tags are associated with which application. This is accomplished by prepending a namespace identifier, followed by a colon, to the beginning of each tag's name. As seen in the previous example, the JSP tags are in the "jsp" namespace, so each tag begins with `jsp:`. XML namespaces also come into play when using JSP tag libraries. When incorporating an extended tag library into a JSP page, you are required to specify the namespace to use with that library's tags.

There are two motives for JSP to adopt XML syntax rather than HTML. The first is machine readability. The additional rules imposed by XML are intended to avoid some of the ambiguities of HTML, and thereby make it easier for programs to parse it. Since JSP is implemented by software that reads JSP pages and translates them into the appropriate Java program calls behind the scenes, streamlining this process—as long as it does not impede the process of developing those pages in the first place—is to everyone's advantage.

The second motive is a bit more far-reaching. Because of its greater flexibility, there is an expectation within the industry that XML will, with HTML, become one of the primary document types on the World Wide Web. Those involved in the ongoing development of the JSP specification through Sun's Java Community Process share this expectation, and want to ensure that JSP is equally relevant for dynamic generation of both HTML and XML content. By using XML syntax for most of the JSP tags (and providing XML alternatives for all the others), JSP is poised to be an excellent solution for dynamic generation of web content now, and for years to come.

TIP   Although the examples in this book focus primarily on using JavaServer Pages for generating HTML, there is no reason JSP cannot be used to generate content for other types of text-based documents. Just as JSP tags can be embedded within what is otherwise a valid HTML document to supply dynamic content, they may also be embedded in, for example, an otherwise valid XML document to be delivered over the web. For an example of XML generation using JSP, see chapter 11.

One aspect in which JSP departs from both HTML and XML conventions is in its support for embedding tags within one another. First, any JSP tag can be embedded within the document's HTML tags, in order to supply tag content dynamically. In addition, JSP allows for the embedding of JSP tags within other JSP tags, under certain circumstances. Specifically, a few of the XML-based JSP tags allow the values for a limited subset of their attributes to be specified using JSP expressions. Here is an example:

```
<jsp:setProperty name="login" property="visits"
                 value="<%= previousVisits + 1 %>"/>
```

Such embedded tags—referred to as *request-time attribute values*—may look strange, but they turn out to be very useful in practice. More on request-time attribute values, including the restrictions placed on their use, will be presented in the next three chapters.

NOTE   Details on the majority of JSP's XML-based tags will be presented in chapters 3 and 4. A few of these tags, however, are specific to JSP's built-in support for the JavaBeans component programming model. Descriptions of these tags will be covered in chapter 5.

2.3   *Running JSP*

Having seen some examples and reviewed the basic syntax, you should now have a basic understanding of *what* JSP can do. We next turn our attention to *how* it does these things. First, we'll look at the basic requirements for adding JSP capability to a web server. From that foundation, we'll discuss how JSP pages actually work to generate dynamic content in response to an HTTP request, and then consider how the underlying implementation interacts with the server in areas such as output buffering, session management, and application scalability. The chapter concludes with a discussion of how the JSP container handles errors that occur when processing JSP pages.

2.3.1 *Adding JSP support*

The most basic requirement for using JSP is a web server. Here, *server* implies both hardware, in the form of a computer accessible over the Internet or a corporate intranet, and software, in the form of an HTTP server, running on that hardware. Some of the most popular HTTP servers are Apache (an Open Source HTTP server), Netscape Enterprise Server, Netscape Application Server, and Microsoft Internet Information Server.

In addition to the HTTP server, software implementing a JSP container is required. Certain HTTP servers, such as the 4.0 versions of Netscape Enterprise and Application Servers, include built-in support for servlets and JSP. Also in this category are those HTTP servers that are themselves written in Java. Java Web Server from Sun and Jigsaw, an Open Source server from the World Wide Web Consortium (W3C), are two such examples.

Most large web sites, however, run HTTP servers written in more traditional programming languages, which are compiled into native code. This is done for performance reasons, so that all network operations and access to static file data (images, normal HTML files, etc.) is as efficient as possible. In order to use JavaServer Pages with one of these HTTP servers, it is necessary to add a third-party JSP container.

Fortunately, a number of vendors are now offering JSP containers that offer compatibility with all of the common native-code HTTP servers. Open Source implementations are also available. A comprehensive list, with pointers to their respective web sites, is available in appendix C. As mentioned in chapter 1, many web application servers include a JSP container. Furthermore, given the inclusion of JSP as a required element of Java 2 Enterprise Edition, support for this technology by server vendors should continue to grow. Again, see appendix C for further details.

It is fortunate that all of the major HTTP server vendors have provided Application Programming Interfaces (APIs) for integrating dynamic content generation with the core HTTP functionality. For example, Netscape provides an API common to all of its HTTP servers called NSAPI (Netscape Server Application Programming Interface). The analogous API for Microsoft Internet Information Server is ISAPI (Internet Server Application Programming Interface). These APIs provide function libraries that third-party developers can use to implement the efficient transfer of requests and response data between the HTTP server and their own add-on tools.

In the Apache HTTP server, third-party add-on tools are referred to as modules. In older versions of Apache, it was necessary to recompile the source code for the HTTP server in order to add support for a new module. Newer versions of Apache support dynamic loading of modules at run time based on the contents of a configuration file.

Most providers of JSP containers include an installation program that will take care of the details of configuring your web server to support JavaServer Pages. If not, consult the software documentation accompanying the JSP container for configuration details. Many of these products include online support forums where you can get assistance from vendor representatives, and from other members of their respective user communities.

The details of configuring these servers and add-on JSP containers are beyond the scope of this book. In the interest of ensuring that all readers have access to an environment for creating, running, and testing JavaServer Pages, however, we have included instructions for obtaining and operating Tomcat, the JSP reference implementation, in appendix A, "Running the reference implementation." Tomcat, developed jointly by Sun Microsystems and the Apache Software Foundation through the Jakarta project, is a software package which serves as the reference implementation for both servlets and JSP. Freely available for download from the Apache web site, it includes a rudimentary HTTP server, as well as support for interoperation with the Apache web server. As a free tool that defines the behavior that all other implementations are intended to follow, Tomcat is an excellent platform for experimenting with the technology, and developing and validating your applications.

Once a JSP container has been installed and configured, using it is relatively straightforward. JSP files are added to the normal document hierarchy of the HTTP server, and are distinguished from other web documents using a special file extension. This extension is typically .jsp, although most JSP containers will allow you to change this, or supplement it with alternative JSP file extensions.

Any Java classes referred to by your JSP files need to be installed somewhere on the Java class path used by the JSP container. It is usually possible to add your own, user-specified directories to this class path; you may find it convenient to add a directory specifically for storing the Java classes used in your JSP files. Once all of these elements are in place, you're ready to start serving dynamic web content from JSP pages.

2.3.2 *How JSPs work*

Now that we've reviewed a few examples and looked at how JSP support can be added to a web server, all the pieces are in place for considering the details of JSP operation. As indicated, JSP processing starts with a request for a JSP document. Such requests are indicated by URLs that employ a special file extension. Typically, the file extension .jsp is used, but it is usually possible to configure the JSP container to recognize alternate or additional file extensions.

Servlets

Although the JSP specification does not mandate any one specific approach for implementing JavaServer Pages, it is currently the case that all major JSP implementations are based on servlets. As a first step in understanding how JSPs work, then, it is helpful to understand how servlets work.

As already mentioned, servlets are a Java-based analog to CGI programs, implemented by means of a servlet container associated with an HTTP server. A set of URLs and/or URL patterns is specified as being handled by the servlet container, so that whenever a request for a URL matching this set is received by the HTTP server, that request is forwarded to the servlet container for processing. For example, the URL http://server/account/login might be mapped to the servlet class `com.taglib.wdjsp.fundamentals.LoginServlet`. When the HTTP server receives a request for this URL, the server forwards this request to the servlet container, which in turn forwards it to an instance of the `LoginServlet` class.

The forwarding of requests is accomplished by packaging all of the request data—URL, origin of the request, parameters and parameter values, and so forth—into a Java object. A similar Java object is constructed representing the response. This response object has methods for setting the status code of the response, and for accessing the output stream which will hold the results of processing the request. The servlet classes are responsible for defining service methods to handle the various types of HTTP requests, including a `doGet()` method for handling HTTP GET requests and a `doPost()` method for handling HTTP POST requests. The objects constructed by the servlet container to represent a single request and its corresponding response are passed as arguments to these methods, which are then called by the servlet container on a per-request basis.

Given a request object and a response object, the service method accesses the properties of the request and performs the appropriate computations on this data in order to construct its reply. The HTML that comprises that reply is written to the output stream associated with the response object. After the service method has finished running, the servlet container sends the contents of the response object back to the HTTP server, which in turn sends the response back to the web browser which submitted the request in the first place. Multiple simultaneous requests for a servlet are handled by running each call to the servlet's service methods in a separate thread.

JavaServer Pages

From this description, you can begin to imagine how this approach might be extended to support JavaServer Pages. After all, JSP execution starts with a request for a JSP page, processing is done on the JSP tags present on the page in order to generate content dynamically, and the output of that processing, combined with the page's static HTML, must be returned to the web browser. By adding a few extra steps to the basic servlet process, however, performance can be improved considerably.

The primary component of a servlet-based implementation of JavaServer Pages is a special servlet often referred to as the page compiler. The container is configured to call this servlet for all requests with URLs that match the JSP file extension, and it is the presence of this servlet and its associated Java classes that turns a servlet container into a JSP container. As its name suggests, the task of this servlet is not just finding JSP pages in response to such requests, but actually compiling them: each JSP page is compiled into a page-specific servlet whose purpose is to generate the dynamic content specified by the original JSP document.

Thus, whenever the HTTP server receives a request for a URL corresponding to a JSP, that request is sent to the JSP container, which invokes the page compiler servlet to handle the request. If this is the first time a request has been received for a particular JSP file, this servlet compiles the JSP file into a servlet.

To compile a page, the JSP page compiler parses through its contents, looking for JSP tags. As it parses the file, it translates its contents into the equivalent Java source code which, when executed, will generate the output indicated by the contents of the original file. Static HTML is translated into Java strings, which will be written unmodified and in their original sequence into an output stream. JSP tags are translated into Java code for generating dynamic content: Bean tags are translated into the corresponding object and property calls, while scripting elements are transferred as is. This code will be mixed in with the output of the original static HTML, so that the dynamic content is inserted into the output in the correct location. This source code is then used to write the service methods for a servlet, such that running it for a request has the effect of producing the content specified by the original JSP file. Once all the servlet code has been constructed, the page compiler servlet calls the Java compiler to compile this source code and add the resulting Java class file to the appropriate directory in the JSP container's class path.

Once the compiled JSP page servlet is in place, the page compiler servlet then invokes this new servlet to generate the response for the original request. Of course, this parsing, code generation, and compiling incurs quite a bit of overhead. Fortunately, these steps are required only the first time a request for a given JSP page is received. All subsequent requests can be passed directly to the already-compiled page servlet for immediate processing.

As long as the contents of the original JSP page remain unchanged, there is no need to generate a new servlet, since the Java code corresponding to those contents remains the same. For this reason, the very first step taken by the JSP page compiler when it receives a request for a JSP is to check the time stamp for the JSP file corresponding to the requested URL, to determine when that file was modified or created. The page compiler will also check the time stamp on the compiled servlet for this JSP page. If no compiled servlet is found, or if the time stamp on the JSP file is more recent than the one on the compiled page servlet, then a new servlet must be generated. This means that the (new or modified) JSP file must be parsed and translated into source code, and this new source code must be compiled. If the compiled servlet is newer than the JSP file, however, no new compilation is required and control can be transferred directly to the servlet to finish processing the request, saving considerable time. So while the first request for a new or recently modified JSP page will be slow, all later requests go straight to the compiled servlet for response generation.

This process is summarized in flowchart form in figure 2.1, where web browser requests are received by the HTTP server, and JavaServer Pages requests are routed to the page compiler servlet running in the JSP container. The JSP container then checks whether or not the servlet for the requested JSP page is up-to-date: Does a compiled servlet exist for this page, and, if so, is it newer than the current contents of the JSP page? If not, the JSP container must go through the process of parsing the page, generating the source code, and compiling it. The newly compiled servlet is then loaded into the servlet container. If the JSP page servlet is current, then the JSP container needs to make sure that the servlet is currently loaded, since it may have been unloaded after its original creation due to lack of use. In either case, control may then be transferred from the page compiler servlet to the JSP page servlet, which then handles the request. The response is generated by the JSP page servlet and routed back to the HTTP server, for return to the web browser.

This unique page compilation feature lends additional performance benefits to JavaServer Pages, in comparison to other dynamic content systems. As discussed, most dynamic content systems rely on special tags, interpreted scripting languages, or a combination. For most of these systems, the file containing these tags and/or scripts must be parsed each time the document is requested. This parsing incurs overhead that is avoided with JavaServer Pages, since JSP files are parsed only the first time they are requested. JSP will be slower than other approaches for this first request, because of the compilation step, but will be faster than the other approaches for all subsequent requests.

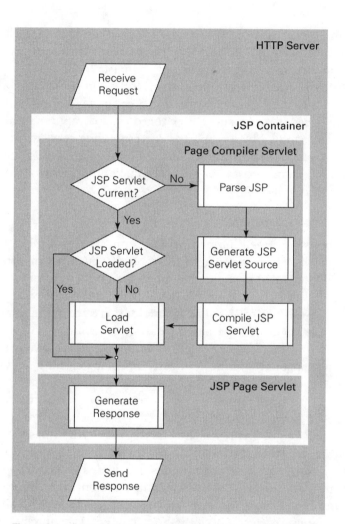

Figure 2.1 Server process for creating and running JSP servlets

TIP   There are also mechanisms in JSP for avoiding the performance hit associated
with compiling a page the first time it is requested. For example, a JSP page
can be pre-compiled by the JSP container before any user requests for it are
received. Alternatively, a JSP page can be deployed via a Web Archive file in
the form of a compiled servlet. For details, see chapter 10.

In addition, because of the way the JVM that is running inside the JSP container operates, the code associated with a JSP servlet class tends to remain resident in the system memory of the web server. As long as new requests for that JSP are being received on a regular basis, the servlet code remains loaded into the memory allocated to the JVM. Access to data and code stored in a computer's physical memory is much quicker than access to data and code stored on a computer's hard disk. Because JSP requests are handled by loading the corresponding servlets into memory and running them, rather than reading the JSP file from the local file system, JSP again enjoys a performance boost over content generation systems that rely on repeatedly reading files from disk.

2.3.3 *Buffered output*

At a high level, the basis of the HTTP protocol is requests and responses. Web browsers submit requests to web servers, which return documents or other web content in response. While HTTP is one of the more straightforward network protocols, there is some behind-the-scenes activity in the sending of requests and responses that complicates the process. For example, there are actually multiple types of requests, which affect how parameter data is transmitted to the server. Requests can also be accompanied by *header* information, which is typically used for identifying the type and capabilities of the browser, controlling caching, and returning cookie data.

Similarly, the HTTP protocol allows the server to send additional information back to the client in the form of response headers. These headers are sent back along with the requested web content, which is therefore referred to as the *body* of the response. Response headers are primarily used for sending status information about the request back to the browser. Like request headers, they may also be used for controlling caching, and for setting cookie data. An important limitation of response headers, however, is that the web browser expects to receive all of the header information before it receives any of the body content. One might therefore expect that if a JSP page needs to send header data back to the browser, then the response headers would have to be specified before any JSP output is generated to be sent back as the body of the response. If, for example, a JSP page wanted to set a cookie, it might be assumed that setting it would have to occur at the very beginning of the page. After all, since JSPs are processed sequentially from top to bottom, any attempt to set a cookie after outputting body content, either dynamic or static, would be too late.

One behavior that the HTTP protocol does not support is retracting responses after the server has started sending them. The web server cannot start sending a document to a browser, change its mind, and then ask the browser not to display it. The web server could abort the document transmission, but the browser will simply display whatever content it received up until the response was aborted. There is nothing in the protocol that enables the server to stop the browser from displaying content once it has been sent. This constraint also might be expected to carry over to JSPs. It would suggest that, once processing has begun on a JSP, it cannot forward processing to a different JSP, without also displaying whatever contents had been generated before the forwarding took place. For example, if an error occurred midway through the processing of a page, all the content generated before that time would show up in the browser, followed by the error message. There would be no way to discard the earlier output and display only the error message, or to forward control to a special error-handling page.

Fortunately, these potential limitations have been recognized—and overcome—by the software engineers who are responsible for the JSP architecture. In order to address these restrictions in the underlying HTTP protocol, the JavaServer Pages specification requires that all JSP implementations support the buffering of output from JSP pages. This means that, as a JSP is being processed, the page's content is not automatically sent to the browser as it is being generated. Instead, all page content is temporarily stored in an output buffer. Only after the entire page has been processed, will the output stored in the buffer be sent to the browser as the body of an HTTP response from the server.

Since the output is being buffered, it becomes possible to specify header information at any point in the processing of a JSP page. For example, a JSP could include code (or a custom tag) that conditionally sets a cookie, and that code (or tag) could appear on the JSP page wherever the page author wishes. Because the output is buffered, the author is assured that the body of the response won't be sent until the whole page has been processed, so it will necessarily be the case that the response header for setting this cookie will be sent before the response body is sent.

Buffering the output from a JSP page also opens up the possibility of discarding it. Although HTTP responses cannot be retracted, the use of buffered output in JavaServer Pages means that sending the response (both headers and body) can be postponed until all of the content needed for the response has been generated. Thus, during construction of the content it becomes possible to decide not to send that content, but to start over with a new response. This decision could be based on program logic associated with the JSP page (in the form of an embedded script or tag), or it could result from the detection of an error while processing the page.

With respect to implementation, buffered output is a feature built into every JSP servlet generated by the JSP page compiler. The output of a JSP servlet, which is a combination of the static content present in the original JSP page and the dynamically-generated content corresponding to the page's JSP tags, is sent to an output stream which automatically directs it to an output buffer.

There is one important caveat associated with this buffering of JSP output: the output buffer is finite in size. When the output buffer is full and can hold no more text, its contents are automatically flushed. Before the buffer is emptied, however, its current contents are sent on to the browser, so that they will not otherwise be lost. As a result, the server will begin sending its response, including any headers that the JSP servlet has thus far determined are necessary. The current contents of the output buffer are also sent, as part of the response body. After the output buffer has been emptied, processing of the JSP servlet resumes, with any new output being sent as a continuation of the response body whenever either (a) the output buffer becomes full and must be flushed again, or (b) the end of the JSP servlet is reached. Of course, once the first part of the response body has been sent, it is no longer possible to send additional headers, or to recall any of the body content already sent to the browser.

TIP   Alternatively, the JSP container can be configured to raise an exception if and when the output buffer becomes full. See chapter 3 for details.

In practice, however, it is rare for a JSP output buffer to become full and require flushing before the entire page has been processed. The default buffer size is 8K, which is more than sufficient for most web pages with dynamic content. If a JSP page does generate more than 8K of output, however, it is also possible to increase the size of the output buffer on a per-page basis. The directives for setting the output buffer size or, if desired, disabling output buffering, are described in chapter 3.

2.3.4   *Session management*

Another idiosyncrasy of the HTTP protocol is that it is stateless. What this means is that HTTP servers do not keep any information about the browsers that are connecting to them from one request to another. After a request is received and a response returned, the server forgets all about the computer that browser is running on. The next time it receives a request from that network host, that request is treated just the same as if it were the first from that machine.

While this makes for a very simple and therefore reliable protocol, it also makes more advanced web applications, such as personalized content generation, more difficult. In order to customize content for an individual user, that user must first be identified. Currently, most web sites use some form of username/password login to accomplish this. If multiple customized pages will be viewed, a mechanism for keeping track of users is required, given that they would probably find it unacceptable to be presented with a new login challenge for each separate page request.

Similarly, if data input is spread across multiple forms prior to final processing, the results of each individual form submission must be stored and cross-referenced against the submitters' identities. A classic example of multiform input is the ubiquitous shopping cart application common to e-commerce web sites. The user browses a catalog of items, using forms to select items (and corresponding quantities) from multiple catalog pages for addition to a single shopping cart. Once the user is finished shopping, a checkout page is provided for confirming the order and supplying payment and shipping information. Throughout this process, the contents of the shopping cart—and its association with a specific visitor to the site—must be maintained.

This process of trying to maintain state across multiple HTTP requests is referred to as *session management*, the idea being that all of a user's requests for pages from a web server during a given period of time are actually part of the same interactive session. JavaServer Pages includes built-in support for session management, by taking advantage of the capabilities provided by the Java servlet API. Servlets can use either cookies or URL rewriting to implement session management, but the details of session management are hidden at the JSP level.

NOTE The primary motivation behind the introduction of HTTP cookies was session management. Cookies enable a web server to store short strings of data in the web browser, such that this data will be sent back to the server with each subsequent request for a web page hosted on that server. (Cookies are sent back only to the originating server, or other servers in the same network domain.) Session management is readily implemented via cookies by generating a unique session identification number for each user and storing that session ID in a cookie.

The disadvantage of the cookie-based approach is that a user may choose to disable support for cookies in his or her web browser. An alternative approach is to use URL rewriting. This technique appends the session ID as a request parameter to all URLs that link to pages local to the web server. URL rewriting tends to require more work on the part of the site developers, since all references to URLs must be generated dynamically, in order to include the appropriate user-specific session ID.

From the perspective of JSP development, the availability of session management can simply be assumed. JSP provides an implicit object (see chapter 3) named `ses-sion`, which represents an individual user's interactive session with the web server. Any JSP page that participates in session management can store items in this `ses-sion` object, and subsequently retrieve or remove them later, based on the user's interaction with the site. For example, the `session` object could be used to store login information or the contents of a shopping cart, and this stored data can then be accessed by any JSP page on the server.

Storing large amounts of data in the `session` object can be problematic, however, for sites with a large userbase. If you store 5 kilobytes (K) of data in each user's session, this translates to 5 megabytes (MB) of memory—in some combination of physical memory and virtual memory—if there are 1000 users with active sessions. If you must manage data for a million active sessions, then 5 gigabytes (GB) of memory would be required. Based on the available hardware, then, the amount of data stored in the session has a direct impact on the number of simultaneous users that can practically be supported.

TIP   As a Java developer, you can estimate the size of an object you are considering for storage in a user's session via Java's serialization facility. Write the object class to implement the `java.io.Serializable` interface, create a prototypical instance of the object, and then save the object to disk via the `writeObject()` method of `java.io.ObjectOutput`. The size of the resulting file will provide an indication of the object's memory footprint. In fact, this will typically be a conservative estimate, since the serialization format adds extra overhead, such as class and version information, which is not needed by objects that reside in a running JVM.

Note that implementing the `java.io.Serializable` interface is desirable for all objects that are to be stored in sessions, independent of concerns about memory footprint. This is because some JSP containers are able to store session information to disk during shutdown, so that it may be restored upon restart. There are also JSP containers which utilize serialization to transfer session information between JVMs running on separate machines, in order to perform on-the-fly load balancing.

A common approach for reducing memory utilization of session data is to store only references to data (a username or an ID number, for example) in the session. Actual session-specific data is then stored in some other repository, such as a database, to be accessed as needed using the reference information residing in the session as the key for restoring it from the repository.

In any event, all objects stored as session data for a user will eventually be reclaimed by the JSP container whenever the user's session times out. Given that HTTP is a stateless protocol, there is no way for the JSP container to know that a user has left the web site and is no longer using the session. Indeed, the user may have even quit using the web browser altogether, but HTTP has no provision for relaying this information to the web server. Instead, each `session` object keeps track of the last time it was requested by a servlet or JSP page. After a predetermined period of time has elapsed in which no requests were made, the user's session is considered to have expired, and is no longer valid. At this point, all system memory associated with the `session` object, including that of any application-specific objects stored in it, becomes available for removal from the JVM. The next time the user returns to the site, an empty `session` object will be created; no information is carried over from sessions that have expired.

TIP The time-out period for JSP sessions is a configuration variable of the JSP container. Most JSP containers provide a control panel application or a configuration file for setting its value. In addition, programmatic access to this value is provided by the `getMaxInactiveInterval()` and `setMaxInactiveInterval()` methods of the `javax.servlet.http.HttpSession` interface, of which the `session` object discussed in this section is an instance.

2.3.5 *Scalability*

A critical concern for those responsible for creating, running, and maintaining large, high-volume web sites is scalability. The most impressive feature list in the world means nothing if your web server cannot provide those services to all of the users who wish to use them, or if those users are frustrated by a server that is not sufficiently responsive.

Given the approach to implementing JavaServer Pages described earlier, it is clear that the scalability of JSP is a direct result of the scalability of Java servlets. Fortunately, the scalability of servlets is quite good. Because it uses a multithreaded approach to handling simultaneous requests, rather than the multiprocess approach required by conventional CGI programs, many more simultaneous requests can be handled via servlets than by CGI for a given hardware configuration.

As the discussion in the previous sections might suggest, the primary limitation on servlet—and hence JSP—performance is system memory. Servlet requests are handled by loading the compiled servlet class (if it has not already been loaded) into the portion of the system's memory that has been allocated for use by the JVM. The more memory that is available for use by the JVM, the more servlets and JSPs can be loaded. The servlet container is able to unload servlets that are not in use, and reload them when they are needed again, but if a significant portion of the site relies on servlets and JSPs, providing ample memory for Java is highly recommended. Output buffering and session management only add to the burden placed on system memory, and these effects are multiplied by the number of simultaneous users.

Unfortunately, there are no hard and fast rules for sizing the memory requirements of a web server intended for the deployment of JSP. The servlets generated by JSP pages vary in size, and the overall memory requirements for the JVM and the web server itself are strongly influenced by the kinds of computations that will be performed by those servlets, and the other types of applications that they will be accessing. Database and cryptography applications, for example, tend to be rather memory-intensive. If a multitier architecture is being used to connect to the database remotely, however, the impact on the local server's memory is driven more by the amount and structure of the data being accessed, than by the fact that a database is being used to access it.

A second consideration for scalability is load distribution. Providing multiple machines over which the server load can be spread is a common strategy for the deployment of web-based applications. As such, it is best to structure your application architecture from the very beginning to allow for the possibility of distributed processing. One way to accomplish this is by allocating the functionality across multiple hosts. For example, one machine acts as the database server, another handles e-commerce transactions such as credit card processing, and yet another serves up web content such as JSP pages. Another approach is to replicate the complete functionality across a set of similarly configured machines, and use a load-balancing scheme to parcel out requests to those machines which are the most lightly loaded. A third and fairly popular approach among heavily trafficked sites is to combine these techniques: distributing functionality across multiple arrays of similarly configured machines.

JavaServer Pages is fairly amenable to all three of these load distribution schemes. The one aspect of JSP that tends to complicate distributed processing is session management, because an end user's session is represented by a Java object that resides in the memory of an individual JVM. If session management is not required by your application, then of course this is not an issue. Similarly, if your load distribution is based solely on distributing functionality, this is usually not a problem, since only one machine is responsible for serving JSP pages, and all sessions will reside on that machine. If, however, multiple servers are providing JSP content and you need to use JSP session management, some mechanism is required for managing sessions across multiple servers.

One way to solve this problem is to use a customized load-balancing scheme that keeps track of which server a session is stored on. The first time a user connects to the site (i.e., before a session object has been created), that user's request is forwarded to the machine that currently has the lightest load. This server assignment is recorded, however, and all subsequent requests from that user will be directed to the same server, regardless of its current load. This ensures that the user's requests will all be handled by the same JVM, the one in which their session object resides. A number of products that provide this capability are currently available. The Apache web server, for example, can be configured to distribute requests across multiple secondary servers, and use session information to direct all of an individual user's requests to the same secondary server.

A second solution that extends this approach is to use a JSP container that supports *session migration*. In this approach, a group of servers running the same JSP container software is able to copy session objects from one server to another on an as-needed basis. Thus, if the load balancing software decides that a particular user's requests now need to be handled by a different server, that second server is able to copy the user's session data from the machine that was previously handling their requests. Again, a number of JSP containers implement this behavior. Optional support for session migration is now part of version 2.2 of the Servlet API specification, so it is likely that vendor support for these features will continue to improve.

Ultimately, the most accurate way to determine if a given solution is scalable is to try it. In practice, this uncomfortable observation applies to just about all web application technologies, not just JavaServer Pages. This doesn't mean, however, that you have to build a complete system before you know whether or not it will scale. Instead, you can develop a simple prototype that exercises the most processor- and memory-intensive tasks you expect to be performing in your final application, and test that prototype. If the prototype exhibits acceptable scaling behavior, then the production system should likewise perform to your satisfaction.

To aid in this endeavor, a number of software packages for stress-testing web applications are freely available. These tools let you specify the URL to be requested, and the rate at which requests should be sent to the server. The software then repeatedly sends new requests for the indicated URL, which may correspond to a servlet or JSP, and collects statistics on response times. With such tools, it is very simple to assess the scalability of the server software under expected customer use, by monitoring its responsiveness to this simulated load. A comprehensive listing of such tools is included in appendix C, but examples are JMeter, an Open Source tool from the Apache Software Foundation, and ServletKiller from Live Software. It might surprise you to discover that among the primary sources for these tools are the vendors of servlet and JSP containers themselves. On the other hand, there is perhaps no better testament to the general scalability of servlet and JSP solutions than that the vendors themselves encourage you to test their limits.

2.3.6   *Error handling*

As indicated earlier, the automatic compilation feature of JavaServer Pages has significant impact on JSP performance. At the same time, because compilation takes place behind the scenes, without any intervention from the web developer, the technology remains accessible to nonprogrammers, supporting a separation of presentation and implementation tasks that leads to productive division of labor in web application development.

Compilation errors

Because JSP compilation does not take place under the control of a Java programmer, however, and because the occasional typographical error is unavoidable, anyone developing with JavaServer Pages will eventually encounter a compilation error while testing their pages. Recall that JSP compilation is initiated by a web browser submitting a request for a new JSP page or one that has recently changed. As a result, if compilation errors are encountered they will be reported through the browser when the server reports that it is unable to complete a request for a particular page. Compilation errors can be due to simple typos, such as a misspelled class or property name in a JavaBeans tag, or they may be the result of more complicated problems, such as a flaw in the logic or syntax of an embedded script.

Although the exact form of an error report varies from one implementation to another, most JSP containers currently available display an error message that is based on the code in the JSP servlet, rather than in the original JSP page. As such, it may require the intervention of a Java programmer to decipher the error message. If the compilation error is merely the result of a misspelling, however, the misspelling is usually carried straight through to the JSP servlet source code, so a quick perusal of the code listing included in the error report may be enough to find the source of the problem. If this approach proves unsuccessful, then by all means recruit the help of an experienced Java programmer. Java compilation problems due to logic or syntax errors are usually quite easy to resolve, if you are familiar with the language. The assistance of an expert can often get you back up and running in short order.

TIP   If you're using version 5 of Microsoft Internet Explorer as your web browser on the Windows platform, you may find while debugging that the browser is intercepting the error messages from your JSP pages. To turn off this feature, select the **Internet Options...** item from the **Tools** menu, and then click on the **Advanced** tab. Under the section heading **Browsing**, turn off the checkbox labeled **Show friendly HTTP error messages**.

Run-time errors

Whereas compilation errors associated with JSPs might be frustrating for web designers but only slightly annoying for Java developers, unexpected JSP run-time errors are welcomed by no one. Compilation errors will occur only after a new JSP page is added, or an existing page is modified, and will prevent that page from being viewed until the cause of the error has been found and repaired. With run-time errors, a JSP could have been running successfully for days, and then suddenly stop working, even though the text of the corresponding JSP page has not been modified.

Like compilation errors, a run-time error will manifest itself as an error message displayed in the web browser. Depending upon the configuration of your JSP container, a run-time error message may be accompanied by a *stack trace* report, which lists the Java method calls that were pending when the error occurred. The stack trace report, so called because it traces the execution sequence (i.e., the stack of instructions) all the way back to the method call which initiated the current thread, allows you to identify what the JSP container was doing when the error condition arose. As such, it provides a good starting point for tracking down the problem.

If this is a newly deployed page, then the presence of a run-time error likely indicates only that additional debugging is required. If this is a page that has been in place and working for some time, then uncovering the cause of the problem may be more difficult. One potential source of run-time errors is changes in server and/or network configuration. Web-based applications often rely on multiple, distributed data sources. This allows for a modular architecture, with optimal utilization of computational resources, but introduces multiple points of failure. If there is a problem with network access, a machine is temporarily offline, or changes have been made to a data source (e.g., the database server was moved to a new machine, a password has expired), the potential for a JSP run-time error is quite high. If the stack trace for a run-time error indicates that it occurred while trying to access a network server or other external data repository, checking the status of the resource in question and verifying configuration information should be among your first steps in trying to resolve the problem.

If no configuration issues are found, then another possibility is that the error is due to some infrequent combination of circumstances that your original program logic does not take into consideration. A good strategy for resolving such bugs is to check all of the log files associated with the web server, the JSP container, and any other resources used by the JSP page which is generating the run-time error. If logging has been turned off or minimized, you may need to set logging levels higher in order to more precisely identify the circumstances which lead to the run-time error. Finally, you may also need to instrument the JSP page and/or any associated Java-Beans with additional logging code as a debugging aide.

TIP   For a mission-critical web site or application, a proactive approach to code instrumentation and logging is highly recommended. When server downtime is unacceptable, there is no substitute for having complete and accurate logs the *first* time a problem occurs.

Programming JSP scripts

This chapter covers

- Using JSP directives
- JSP scripting elements
- Flow of control via scriptlets
- Comments in JSP pages

In the previous chapter, much emphasis was placed on leveraging component-centric design to promote the separation of presentation and implementation. By taking advantage of JSP's built-in support for server-side JavaBeans, it is possible to write JSP pages that contain only HTML and HTML-like tags. Doing so yields considerable benefits with respect to code reuse, application maintainability, and division of labor. This "purist" approach to JSP development is not always the most practical solution, however. Circumstances may dictate the use of an alternative approach: JSP pages with embedded scripts, typically referred to as *scripting elements.*

For example, when developing an application prototype, the schedule may not provide developers with sufficient time for a full-scale component design effort. Of course, if the design is not based on JavaBeans, then the JSP Bean tags (see chapter 5) will be of little use. The scripting tags, however, can apply the full expressive power of the underlying Java language, and are, therefore, fully compatible with whatever data model you select, JavaBeans or otherwise.

Furthermore, even if you are using JavaBeans, the capabilities of the built-in JSP Bean tags are somewhat limited. If your needs go beyond the creation of server-side JavaBeans and the access and modification of their properties, you will either need to use (and perhaps even write) a custom tag library, or take advantage of the existing scripting tags. Like JavaBeans component design, creating a custom tag library requires a considered approach that your development schedule may not permit. Designing a custom tag library is only justified when you know you will be using its custom tags over and over again. Reusability is a key element of tag library design, and a key reason that good library design tends to be difficult and time-consuming. If such an effort is infeasible, the scripting tags are available to supply any required functionality not provided by the standard Bean tags.

What scripts lack in abstraction, then, they more than make up for in power. This power results, of course, from the ability of scripts to express arbitrary computations in the associated scripting language. With the full strength of a programming language at their disposal, scripts are the ultimate tool of last resort when developing JSP: if you can't find another way to do something, you can always write a script. And, as suggested earlier, there are also times when scripts are the first tool of choice.

3.1   Scripting languages

The default scripting language for JSP is, naturally enough, Java. Unless otherwise specified, the JSP parser assumes that all scripting elements on a page are written in

Java. Given that JSP pages are compiled into Java servlets, this assumption makes the translation of scripts into servlet code very straightforward.

The JSP specification, however, allows JSP implementers to support alternative scripting languages as well. To be acceptable for use with JSP, a scripting language must meet three requirements:

- It must support the manipulation Java objects. This includes creating objects and, in the case of JavaBeans, accessing and modifying their properties.
- It must be able to invoke methods on Java objects.
- It must include the ability to catch Java exceptions, and specify exception handlers.

More succinctly, for a scripting language to be compatible with JSP, it needs to have sufficient expressive power to take advantage of the capabilities provided by the JSP platform. For example, if a scripting language cannot access Java objects and call their methods, it cannot read request parameters, participate in session management, or set cookies. The core functionality of JSP is made accessible to web developers via Java objects, so a scripting language that cannot use these objects is of limited utility.

If a scripting language is able to interact with Java objects, or can be extended to interact with Java objects, then it is a good candidate for integration with a JSP container. Caucho Technology, for example, has developed a JSP container called Resin, which is integrated with the company's Java-based implementation of the JavaScript scripting language. As a result, Resin supports both Java and JavaScript as its scripting languages. Support for alternative scripting languages makes JSP accessible to a larger development community by giving developers who are uncomfortable with Java syntax the option to use a different programming language in their JSP pages.

Unfortunately, while alternative languages for JSP scripting are supported by the JSP specification, portable mechanisms for integrating scripting languages with JSP containers are not. Such a mechanism is under consideration for a future version of JSP, but the only JSP scripting language that is universally available at the time of this writing is Java. For this reason, we will use Java as the scripting language for all of the examples in this book. If you are using a JSP container that supports any scripting languages other than Java, please consult your software documentation for further details on the use of those alternatives.

3.2 JSP tags

JSP provides four major categories of markup tags. The first, *directives*, is a set of tags for providing the JSP container with page-specific instructions for how the document containing the directives is to be processed. Directives do not affect the handling of individual requests, but instead affect global properties of the JSP page that influence its translation into a servlet.

Scripting elements are used to embed programming instructions, written in the designated scripting language for the page, which are to be executed each time the page is processed for a request. Some scripting elements are evaluated purely for their side effects, but they may also be used to generate dynamic content that appears in the output of the page.

Comments are used for adding documentation strings to a JSP page. JSP supports multiple comment styles, including one which enables documentation to appear in the output from the page. Other JSP comments can only be viewed in the original JSP file, or in the source code for the servlet into which the page is translated.

Actions support several different behaviors. Like scripting elements, actions are processed for each request received by a page. Actions can transfer control between pages, specify applets, and interact with server-side JavaBeans components. Like scripting elements, actions may or may not generate dynamic content. All custom tags incorporated via extended tag libraries take the form of actions.

The remaining sections of this chapter cover the first three categories of JSP tags, while the fourth will be presented in chapters 4 and 5. The individual tags included in these categories are introduced, and their use is described.

3.3 JSP directives

Directives are used to convey special processing information about the page to the JSP container. For example, directives may be used to specify the scripting language for the page, to include the contents of another page, or to indicate that the page uses a custom tag library. Directives do not directly produce any output that is visible to end users when the page is requested; instead, they generate side effects that change the way the JSP container processes the page.

3.3.1 Page directive

The page directive is the most complicated JSP directive, primarily because it supports such a wide range of attributes and associated functionality. The basic syntax of the page directive is as follows:

```
<%@ page attribute1="value1" attribute2="value2" attribute3=… %>
```

White space after the opening `<%@` and before the closing `%>` is optional, but recommended to improve readability. Like all JSP tag elements, the `page` directive supports an XML-based syntax, as follows:

```
<jsp:directive.page attribute1="value1"
                    attribute2="value2" attribute3=... />
```

Attribute specifications are identical for the two tag styles, and there are eleven different attributes recognized for the page directive. In the examples to follow, we will use the first style, only because it is slightly less verbose and therefore appears more frequently in JSP pages that are created manually. Keep in mind that these two tag styles are interchangeable.

Table 3.1   Attributes supported by the `page` directive

Attribute	Value	Default	Examples
info	Text string	None	info="Registration form."
language	Scripting language name	"java"	language="java"
contentType	MIME type, character set	See first example	contentType="text/html; charset=ISO-8859-1" contentType="text/xml"
extends	Class name	None	extends="com.taglib.wdjsp.MyJspPage"
import	Class and/or package names	None	import="java.net.URL" import="java.util.*, java.text.*"
session	Boolean flag	"true"	session="true"
buffer	Buffer size, or false	"8kb"	buffer="12kb" buffer="false"
autoFlush	Boolean flag	"true"	autoFlush="false"
isThreadSafe	Boolean flag	"true"	isThreadSafe="true"
errorPage	Local URL	None	errorPage="results/failed.jsp"
isErrorPage	Boolean flag	"false"	isErrorPage="false"

A summary of the eleven attributes supported by the `page` directive is presented in table 3.1, and individual discussions of each attribute follow. In view of this large number of attributes, you will likely find it very convenient that JSP allows you to specify multiple `page` directives on a single page. With the exception of the `import` attribute, however, no individual `page` directive attribute may be specified multiple times on the same page. This means an attribute cannot appear multiple times within the same directive, nor can it appear in multiple directives on the same page.

For example, the following sequence of page directives is valid, since the only attribute that is repeated is the import attribute:

```
<%@ page info="This is a valid set of page directives." %>
<%@ page language="java" import="java.net.*" %>
<%@ page import="java.util.List, java.util.ArrayList" %>
```

The following page directive, however, is not valid, because the session attribute occurs twice:

```
<%@ page info="This is an invalid page directive" session="false"
        buffer="16k" autoFlush="false" session="false" %>
```

Similarly, this sequence of page directives is invalid because the info attribute is repeated:

```
<%@ page info="This is not a valid set of page directives." %>
<%@ page extends="com.taglib.wdjsp.MyJspPage"
        info="Use my superclass." %>
```

Unrecognized attributes are also invalid. If a JSP page contains any invalid page directives, a translation-time error will result when the JSP container attempts to generate the source code for the corresponding servlet.

Info attribute

The info attribute allows the page author to add a documentation string to the page that summarizes its functionality. This string will then be available for use by the JSP container or other tools in a programmatic manner for displaying the summary information. There are no restrictions on the length or contents of the documentation string, but author, version, and copyright information are commonly included, as in the following example:

```
<%@ page info="The CLU homepage, Copyright 1982 by Kevin Flynn." %>
```

The default value for the info attribute is the empty string.

Language attribute

The language attribute specifies the scripting language to be used in all scripting elements on the page. All JSP containers are required to support Java as a scripting language, and this is the default if the language attribute is not explicitly specified. As indicated earlier in the chapter, support for other scripting languages is optional, and varies among JSP implementations. Here is how the language attribute is used to specify Java as the scripting language:

```
<%@ page language="java" %>
```

Note that if the `include` directive is employed, scripting elements in the included page must use the same scripting language as the current page.

ContentType attribute

This attribute is used to indicate the MIME type of the response being generated by the JSP page. Although MIME stands for Multipurpose Internet Mail Extensions, MIME types are also used to indicate the type of information contained in an HTTP response, and this is the context in which they are used in JSP. The most common MIME types for JSP are `"text/html"`, `"text/xml"`, and `"text/plain"`, indicating responses in HTML, XML, and plain text formats, respectively. To specify that a JSP document is generating XML content, for example, this attribute is specified as follows:

```
<%@ page contentType="text/xml" %>
```

The default MIME type for JSP pages is `"text/html"`.

The `contentType` attribute can also be used to specify an alternate character set for the JSP page. This enables page authors to deliver localized content using the language encoding most appropriate for that content. The character set is specified via the `contentType` attribute by appending a semicolon, the string `charset=`, and the name of the desired character set to the end of the attribute value. (An optional space is permitted between the semicolon and `charset=`.) For example, to specify an HTML response using the (default) ISO-8859-1 character set, the following directive would be used:

```
<%@ page contentType="text/html; charset=ISO-8859-1" %>
```

Note that if the response to be generated by a JSP uses an alternate character set, the JSP page must itself be written in that character set. Of course, the JSP container can't know a page is using an alternate character set until it reads the `page` directive that specifies the character set, so only character sets that allow specification of this directive are valid for use in a JSP page. Once the directive has been read by the JSP container (i.e., using the default character set), it can switch to the indicated character set for the remainder of the page. All the characters read before switching character sets, however, must be compatible with the final character set.

The official registrar for both MIME types and character sets is the Internet Assigned Numbers Authority (IANA). This standards body maintains lists of all of the valid MIME types and character set names.

Extends attribute

The `extends` attribute identifies the superclass to be used by the JSP container when it is translating the JSP page into a Java servlet, and is specified as follows:

```
<%@ page extends="com.taglib.wdjsp.myJspPage" %>
```

There is no default value for this attribute. If this attribute is not specified, the JSP container is free to make its own choice of JSP servlet class to use as the superclass for the page. Note that if you do specify this attribute, JSP imposes certain restrictions on the specified superclass. If, as is typically the case, the JSP page is being delivered via the HTTP protocol, then the specified superclass must implement the `javax.servlet.jsp.HttpJspPage` interface. If an alternate protocol is being used, then the specified superclass must implement the `javax.servlet.jsp.JspPage` interface. (The API documentation for these classes is available from Sun Microsystems, and is included with the JSP reference implementation described in appendix A.)

In practice, this attribute is very rarely used. This is because the default behavior, letting the JSP container select the superclass for the page, typically yields the best performance. The vendors of JSP containers devote considerable resources to tuning their implementations, including optimization of their default page superclasses. Except when you have very specific needs not anticipated by your JSP vendor, it is unlikely that writing and optimizing your own page superclass will be worth the effort.

Import attribute

Unlike the `extends` attribute, use of the `import` attribute is quite common, because it extends the set of Java classes which may be referenced in a JSP page without having to explicitly specify class package names. (In other words, because it saves typing.) All Java classes and interfaces are associated with a package name; to completely specify a class, the package name must be prepended to the class name. For example, the above discussion of the `extends` attribute makes mention of an interface named `javax.servlet.jsp.HttpJspPage`. This is actually a reference to an interface named `HttpJspPage`, which resides in the `javax.servlet.jsp` package.

NOTE   Java programmers will notice from the discussion that follows that the `import` attribute of the `page` directive has an analogous role to Java's `import` statement, used when writing Java class files. This is, of course, no coincidence. When a JSP page is compiled into a servlet, any `import` attributes are translated directly into the corresponding `import` statements.

The advantages of packages are twofold. First, packages make it easy to keep track of classes that are related in functionality and origin, since these are typically used as the criterion for grouping a set of classes together into a package. Second, they make it possible to avoid class naming collisions between different developers (or groups of developers). As long as the developers put their classes into separate packages, there will not be any conflicts if some of the classes share the same name.

For example, the Java 2 Standard Edition includes two classes (actually, one class and one interface) named `List`. One resides in the `java.awt` package, and represents a user interface component for selecting one or more items from a scrolling list. The second resides in the `java.util` package, and represents an ordered collection of objects. Users of these classes distinguish between the two via their package names.

It can become very tedious, however, to always have to refer to classes using their package names. The `import` attribute can be used to identify classes and/or packages that will be frequently used on a given page, so that it is no longer necessary to use package names when referring to them. This is referred to as *importing* a class or package into the JSP page. To import a specific class, simply specify its name (including the package) as the value of the `import` attribute, as in the following:

```
<%@ page import="java.util.List" %>
```

If this directive is present in a JSP page, the `java.util.List` class can be referred to on that page by simply using the unqualified class name, `List`, also called its *base name*. This will hold true anywhere on the page a class name might appear in a JSP element—including both scripting elements and Bean tags—except in the `<jsp:plugin>` tag (see appendix B).

It is also possible to import an entire package into a JSP page, in cases where multiple classes from the same package are being used. This is accomplished by specifying the name of the package, followed by a period and an asterisk, as the value of the `import` attribute:

```
<%@ page import="java.util.*" %>
```

This example directive has the effect of importing all of the classes in the `java.util` package into the current JSP page, such that any class in the `java.util` package may now be referred to using only its base name.

As mentioned previously in this chapter, `import` is the only attribute of the `page` directive that may occur multiple times within a single JSP page. This allows JSP developers to import multiple classes and/or packages into the same page, via multiple `page` directives with `import` attributes, or multiple `import` attributes within the same `page` directive, or a combination of both. In addition, the `import` attribute itself supports importing multiple classes and/or packages via a single attribute value, by separating the items to be imported using commas. For example, the following directive imports an interface, a class, and a package using a single `import` attribute:

```
<%@ page import="java.util.List, java.util.ArrayList, java.text.*" %>
```

The space character following the comma is optional, but recommended for improved readability.

Based on the discussion above, you may be wondering what would happen if you tried to import two classes that have the same base name, as in the following:

```
<%@ page import="java.util.List, java.awt.List" %>
```

The JSP container considers this to be an illegal statement, and will refuse to process a JSP page that includes such an ambiguity. You might instead try to import these two classes using their packages, as follows:

```
<%@ page import="java.util.*, java.awt.*" %>
```

In this case, however, the conflict is resolved by allowing neither of the two List classes to be referred to by its base name. Instead, both must use their fully qualified class names, which include their package names. In order to be able to refer to one of the two classes by its base name, you will have to explicitly import that class, as in the following:

```
<%@ page import="java.util.*, java.awt.List" %>
```

Using this last directive, the List class from the java.awt package can be referred to via its base name, but the List class from the java.util package must be referred to using its full name, java.util.List.

Finally, note that, as a convenience for JSP developers, every page for which Java is selected as the scripting language automatically imports all of the classes from the following four packages: java.lang, javax.servlet, javax.servlet.http, and javax.servlet.jsp.

Session attribute

The session attribute is used to indicate whether or not a JSP page participates in session management (as described in chapter 2). The value for this attribute is a simple boolean indicator, either true or false. For example, to specify that a page is not part of a session, the following form is used:

```
<%@ page session="false" %>
```

The default value for this attribute is true; by default then, all pages participate in session management. If a JSP does not interact with the session, then a slight performance gain can be obtained by setting this attribute to false. Note, however, that the session implicit object, described in chapter 4, is available only on pages for which the session attribute is set to true.

Buffer attribute

The `buffer` attribute controls the use of buffered output for a JSP page. To turn off buffered output, so that all JSP content is passed immediately to the HTTP response, this attribute should be set to `none`, as follows:

```
<%@ page buffer="none" %>
```

Alternatively, this attribute can be used to set the size of the output buffer in kilobytes, by specifying the attribute value as an integer, followed by the character string "`kb`". For example:

```
<%@ page buffer="12kb" %>
```

The default value for this attribute is `"8kb"`. Note that the JSP container is allowed to use an output buffer larger than the requested size, if it so chooses; the specified value can therefore be thought of as the minimum buffer size for the page. This allows the JSP container to optimize performance by creating a pool of output buffers and using them as needed, instead of creating an output buffer for every JSP page request.

Buffering the output of JSP pages is generally a good practice to follow, primarily because it enables transferring control from one page to another (e.g., via the `<jsp:forward>` action, described in chapter 4). This enables you to retract all of the output generated so far by a page, including headers and cookies, for replacement with the contents of another page.

In particular, output buffering allows you to make full use of the `errorPage` attribute of the `page` directive, discussed later, to forward control to a user-friendly error page when exceptions arise in the course of JSP processing. Such custom error pages are greatly preferred over the output of JVM error messages in the middle of what otherwise appears to be normal output. In addition, error pages can be scripted to notify the webmaster or the development team when a run-time error occurs, yielding a dual benefit: the end user sees an unintimidating and perhaps apologetic message that there was a problem in responding to their request, while the implementers receive a full report detailing the context and circumstances of the error. (For further details, see the error-handling example in chapter 11.)

If, as recommended, you elect to use buffered output, it is key that you select an appropriate buffer size. This is because, as indicated in chapter 2, if the output from the page is able to fill the buffer, most of the benefits of buffering—including the ability to forward to an alternate page—will be lost. Fortunately, estimating the size of your output is a rather straightforward, if tedious, exercise. If your output is primarily English text, then one character of output will consume one byte of data in your output buffer. Other encodings use multiple bytes of data for representing individual characters. Once you know the size of the characters you will be using, the next step is to estimate the number of characters that will be generated by the page.

Each character of static text in the original JSP page will of course translate into one character's worth of data in the final output. For dynamically generated content, a conservative approach is to estimate the maximum number of characters corresponding to each JSP element which generates output. After summing all of these character counts, multiply by the number of bytes per character to compute the required buffer size, dividing by 1,024 to convert bytes into kilobytes. You will likely find that the default value of 8K is sufficient for most JSP pages, but pages which generate significant amounts of dynamic content may need correspondingly larger output buffers.

AutoFlush attribute

This attribute is also used for controlling buffered output. In particular, this attribute controls the behavior of the JSP container when the page's output buffer becomes full. If this attribute is set to `true` (the default), the output buffer will automatically be flushed, and its current contents sent to the HTTP server for transmission to the requesting web browser. Page processing then resumes, with any and all new content being buffered until the buffer once again becomes full, or the end of the page is reached. This attribute is set as follows:

```
<%@ page autoFlush="true" %>
```

As mentioned in chapter 2, note that once the buffer has been flushed and its initial contents sent to the browser, it is no longer possible for the JSP page to set response headers or forward processing to a different JSP page.

If the `autoFlush` attribute is instead set to `false`, the JSP container will not automatically flush the buffer when it becomes full. Instead, it will raise an exception, which will have the effect of halting processing of the JSP page and displaying an error page in the browser that originally requested the page. The class of the exception raised under these circumstances is implementation-specific. Also, keep in mind that it is illegal to set the `autoflush` attribute to `false` when the `buffer` attribute is set to `none`. In other words, the JSP container cannot be set to signal an exception when the output buffer becomes full if there is no output buffer in the first place.

The best setting for this attribute will vary from page to page. If the amount of output that might be generated by a page is unpredictable, the `autoFlush` attribute should be set to `true`. Under such circumstances, overflowing the output buffer is a very real possibility, so you need to ensure that the page's contents will be delivered to the browser, rather than an error message. If you also might need to set response headers on this page, or conditionally forward to another page, the decision to do so should be made near the beginning of the page, in order to guarantee that these actions will take place before the buffer might be flushed and the opportunity for taking these actions is lost.

If, however, you need to keep your options open as long as possible with respect to setting response headers or forwarding to another page, then setting `autoFlush` to `false` is the appropriate choice. In this case, it is critical that the page's output buffer be large enough for any conceivable output that might be generated by the page. If not, you again risk the possibility that, if it turns out the output buffer must be flushed, the end user will see an error message rather than your page contents.

IsThreadSafe attribute

The `isThreadSafe` attribute is used to indicate whether your JSP page, once it is compiled into a servlet, is capable of responding to multiple simultaneous requests. If not, this attribute should be set to `false`, as in the following:

```
<%@ page isThreadSafe="false" %>
```

When this attribute is set to `false`, the JSP container will dispatch outstanding requests for the page sequentially, in the order they were received, waiting for the current request to finish processing before starting the next. When this attribute is set to `true` (the default), a new thread is created to handle each request for the page, such that multiple requests for the page are handled simultaneously.

If at all possible, this attribute should be set to its default value of `true`. If not, performance will suffer dramatically whenever multiple users try to access the JSP page at the same time, since each subsequent user will have to wait until all previously submitted requests have been handled before processing of their request can begin. If the page is heavily trafficked, or its content generation is at all computationally intensive, this delay will likely not be acceptable to users.

Whether or not this attribute can be set to `true`, however, is usually dependent upon its use of resources. For example, if your JSP page creates and stores a database connection that can only be used by one end user at a time, then, unless special measures are taken to control the use of that connection, the page cannot safely be accessed by multiple threads simultaneously. In this case, the `isThreadSafe` attribute should be set to `false`, or else your users are likely to encounter run-time errors when accessing the page. If, however, your JSP page accesses a pool of database connections and waits for a free connection before it begins processing, then the `isThreadSafe` attribute can probably be set to `true`.

Setting `isThreadSafe` to `false` is certainly the more conservative approach. As indicated above, however, this yields a significant performance penalty. Fortunately, the thread safety of a JSP page is typically dependent more upon *how* resources are used, rather than *what* resources are used. If you are not a Java developer and are concerned about whether or not your page is safe for multithreading, the best approach is to consult an experienced programmer; if the page is not thread-safe as is, it can usually be made thread-safe.

TIP   Judicious use of Java's `synchronized` keyword is the best approach to ensuring thread safety. All access to objects that are shared across multiple JSP pages, or across multiple invocations of the same JSP page, should be synchronized if there is the potential for inconsistency or deadlocks should those objects be simultaneously accessed and/or modified by multiple threads. In this vein, you should carefully examine all static variables, and all objects used by JSP pages whose scope is either `session` or `application` (as discussed in chapter 4), for potential thread safety issues.

Finally, you also need to be aware that, even if a JSP page sets the `isThreadSafe` attribute to `false`, JSP implementations are still permitted to create multiple instances of the corresponding servlet in order to provide improved performance. In this way, the individual instances handle only one request at a time, but by creating a pool of servlet instances, the JSP container can still handle some limited number of simultaneous requests. For this reason, you still must consider the resource usage even of pages that are not marked thread-safe, to make sure there are no potential conflicts between these multiple instances. Given this harsh reality, you are usually better off biting the bullet and making sure that your page is fully thread-safe. This discussion of the `isThreadSafe` attribute is presented here in the interest of completeness, but the bottom line is that if you're tempted to set this attribute's value to `false`, you will be doing both yourself and your users a favor if you reconsider.

ErrorPage attribute

This attribute is used to specify an alternate page to display if an (uncaught) error occurs while the JSP container is processing the page. This alternate page is indicated by specifying a local URL as the value for this attribute, as in the following:

```
<%@ page errorPage="/webdev/misc/error.jsp" %>
```

The error page URL must specify a JSP page on the same server as the original page. As in this example, it may be an absolute URL, which includes a complete directory specification. Alternatively, a relative URL may be specified, in which case any directory information included in the URL is appended to the directory information associated with the current page, in order to form a new URL. In the context of the `errorPage` attribute, absolute URLs start with a forward slash, while relative URLs do not.

The default value for this attribute is implementation-dependent. Also, note that if the output of the JSP page is not buffered and any output has been generated before the error occurs, it will not be possible to forward to the error page. If the output is buffered and the `autoFlush` attribute is set to `true`, once the buffer becomes full and is flushed for the first time, it will likewise become impossible to forward to the error page. As you might expect, if `autoFlush` is `false`, then the exception raised when the buffer is filled will cause the JSP container to forward control to the page specified using the `errorPage` attribute.

IsErrorPage attribute

The `isErrorPage` attribute is used to mark a JSP page that serves as the error page for one or more other JSP pages. This is done by specifying a simple boolean attribute value, as follows:

```
<%@ page isErrorPage="true" %>
```

When this attribute is set to `true`, it indicates that the current page is intended for use as a JSP error page. As a result, this page will be able to access the `exception` implicit object, described in chapter 4, which will be bound to the Java exception object (i.e., an instance of the `java.lang.Throwable` class) which caused control to be forwarded to the current page.

Since most JSP pages do not serve as error pages, the default value for this attribute is `false`.

3.3.2 Include directive

The second JSP directive enables page authors to include the contents of one file in another. The file to be included is identified via a local URL, and the directive has the effect of replacing itself with the contents of the indicated file. The syntax of the `include` directive is as follows:

```
<%@ include file="localURL" %>
```

Like all JSP tags, an XML variant of this directive is also available. Its syntax is as follows:

```
<jsp:directive.include file="localURL" />
```

There are no restrictions on the number of `nclude` directives that may appear in a single JSP page. There are also no restrictions on nesting; it is completely valid for a

JSP page to include another JSP page, which itself includes one or more other JSP pages. As mentioned earlier, however, all included pages must use the same scripting language as the original page.

As in the URL specification for the `errorPage` attribute of the `page` directive, the value of the `include` directive's `file` attribute can be specified as an absolute path on the local server, or relative to the current page, depending upon whether or not it starts with a forward slash character. For example, to include a file in a subdirectory of the directory that the current JSP page is in, a directive of the following form would be used:

```
<%@ include file="includes/navigation.jsp" %>
```

To include a file using an absolute path on the local server, the following form would be used:

```
<%@ include file="/shared/epilogue/copyright.html" %>
```

The decision whether to use a common top-level directory for shared content, versus directory-specific files, depends upon the overall design of your web site or application hierarchy. A combination of both approaches may also be appropriate.

As indicated in figure 3.1, the `include` directive has the effect of substituting in the contents of the included file before the page is translated into source code and compiled into a servlet. The contents of the included file may be either static text (e.g., HTML) or additional JSP elements that will be processed as if they were part of the original JSP page. This means that it is possible to make reference in the included page to variables that are local to the original page, and vice versa, since the included page effectively becomes part of that original page. In practice, this approach can lead to software maintenance problems, since it breaks the modularity of the individual files. If used in a disciplined manner, though, it can be helpful to isolate code that appears repeatedly across a set of JSP pages into a single file, and use the `include` directive to share this common code.

NOTE   For C and C++ developers, the JSP `include` directive is a direct analog of the `#include` directive provided by the preprocessor for those two languages.

As described in chapter 2, the JSP container will automatically rebuild and recompile the servlet associated with a JSP page whenever it detects that the file defining the page's contents has been modified. This only applies to the file for the JSP page itself, however, not to any files which have been incorporated via the `include` directive. The JSP container does not keep track of file dependencies

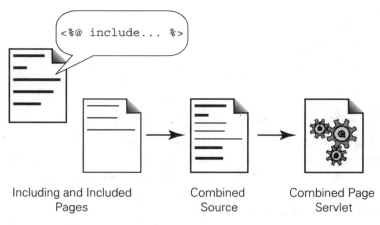

Figure 3.1   Effect of the `include` **directive on page compilation**

resulting from the use of this directive, so modifications to included files will not automatically trigger the generation of a new JSP servlet. The easiest way to force the construction of a new servlet is to manually update the modification date on the file for the including page.

TIP   On the UNIX platform, the easiest way to update a file's modification date is via the `touch` command. Unfortunately, there is no direct equivalent on the Windows platform. Alternate Windows command shells are available which provide this functionality, or you can simply open the file in an editor and save its contents, unchanged.

JSP also provides an alternative means for including the contents of one JSP file within another, via the `<jsp:include>` action, described in chapter 4. Unlike the `include` directive, which treats the contents of the file to be included as if it were part of the original page, the `<jsp:include>` action obtains the contents of the file to be included at the time the request for the original page is being handled, by forwarding the request to the included page and then inserting the results of processing this secondary request into the results of the original page.

3.3.3   *Tag library directive*

This directive is used to notify the JSP container that a page relies on one or more custom tag libraries. A tag library is a collection of custom tags that can be used to extend the functionality of JSP on a page-by-page basis. Once this directive has been used to indicate the reliance of a page on a specific tag library, all of the custom tags defined in that library become available for use on that page. The syntax of this directive is as follows:

```
<%@ taglib uri="tagLibraryURI" prefix="tagPrefix" %>
```

An XML variant is also available:

```
<jsp:directive.taglib uri="tagLibraryURI" prefix="tagPrefix" />
```

In both cases, the value of the `uri` attribute indicates the location of the Tag Library Descriptor (TLD) file for the library, and the `prefix` attribute specifies the XML namespace identifier that will be prepended to all occurrences of the library's tags on the page. For example, the following directive loads in a tag library whose TLD is accessible via the local URL /EncomTags:

```
<%@ taglib uri="/EncomTags" prefix="mcp" %>
```

Within the page in which this directive appears, the tags defined by this library are accessed using the prefix `mcp`. A tag from this library named `endProgram`, then, would be referenced within the page as `<mcp:endProgram/>`. Note that all custom tags follow XML syntax conventions.

Because the tag prefix is specified external to the library itself, and on a page-specific basis, multiple libraries can be loaded by a single page without the risk of conflicts between tag names. If two libraries both define tags with the same name, a JSP page would still be able to load and use both libraries since it can distinguish those tags via their prefixes. As such, there are no restrictions on how many tag library directives may appear on a page, as long as each is assigned a unique prefix. If, however, the JSP container cannot find the TLD at the indicated location, or the page references a tag that is not actually defined in the library (based on the contents of the TLD), an error will result when the JSP container tries to compile the page.

The construction of custom tag libraries and their associated TLDs is described in chapter 13. The deployment of custom tag libraries is presented in chapter 10.

WARNING   For security reasons, the JSP specification mandates that JSP containers are allowed only to read TLDs that are stored on the local server. Similarly, the Java classes implementing a library's custom tags must also be stored locally. Some JSP containers, however, currently allow page authors to specify URLs referencing complete tag library JAR files in the `uri` attribute of the `taglib` directive. Support for this behavior is intended to ease development, but keep in mind that downloading arbitrary Java code from a remote URL and running that code on your web server is a rather risky proposition.

3.4 Scripting elements

Whereas the JSP directives influence how the page is processed by the JSP container, scripting elements enable developers to directly embed code in a JSP page, including code that generates output to appear in the results sent back to the user. JSP provides three types of scripting elements: declarations, scriptlets, and expressions. Declarations allow the developer to define variables and methods for a page, which may be accessed by other scripting elements. Scriptlets are blocks of code to be executed each time the JSP page is processed for a request. Expressions are individual lines of code. Like scriptlets, they are executed for every request. The results of evaluating an expression, however, are automatically inserted into the page output in place of the original expression tag.

All scripting elements in a page are written in the scripting language designated for the page via the `language` attribute of the `page` directive, as described above. In the absence of an explicit specification of the scripting language, it is assumed by the JSP container that the scripting language is Java. Recall, as well, that if the `include` directive is used to incorporate the contents of one JSP page into another, both pages must use the same scripting language. Finally, none of the tags for the JSP scripting elements support attributes.

3.4.1 Declarations

Declarations are used to define variables and methods specific to a JSP page. Declared variables and methods can then be referenced by other scripting elements on the same page. The syntax for declarations is:

```
<%! declaration(s) %>
```

Note that multiple declarations may appear within a single tag, but each declaration must be a complete declarative statement in the designated scripting language. Also note that white space after the opening delimiter and before the closing delimiter is optional, but recommended to improve readability. The XML version of this syntax is:

```
<jsp:declaration> declaration(s) </jsp:declaration>
```

The two forms are identical in effect.

Variable declarations

Variables defined as declarations become instance variables of the servlet class into which the JSP page is translated and compiled. Consider the following declaration of three variables:

```
<%! private int x = 0, y = 0; private String units = "ft"; %>
```

This declaration will have the effect of creating three instance variables in the servlet created for the JSP page, named x, y, and units. These variables can be referenced by any and all other scripting elements on the page, including those scripting elements that appear earlier in the page than the declaration itself.

When declaring JSP instance variables, it is important to keep in mind the potential that multiple threads will be accessing a JSP simultaneously, representing multiple simultaneous page requests. If a scripting element on the page modifies the value of an instance variable, all subsequent references to that instance variable will use the new value, including references in other threads. If you wish to create a variable whose value is local to the processing of a single request, this may be done in a scriptlet. Declared variables are associated with the page itself (through the servlet class), not with individual requests.

Since variables specified via JSP declarations are directly translated into variables of the corresponding servlet class, they may also be used to declare class variables. Class variables, also referred to as static variables, are variables whose values are shared among all instances of a class, rather than being specific to an individual instance. When the scripting language is Java, class variables are defined using the static keyword, as in the following example:

```
<%! static public int counter = 0; %>
```

The effect of this declaration is to create an integer variable named counter that is shared by all instances of the page's servlet class. If any one instance changes the value of this variable, all instances see the new value.

In practice, because the JSP container typically creates only one instance of the servlet class representing a particular JSP page, there is little difference between declaring instance variables and declaring class variables. As explained earlier, the major exception to this rule is when a JSP page sets the isThreadSafe attribute of the page directive to false, indicating that the page is not thread-safe. In this case, the JSP container may create multiple instances of the page's servlet class, in order to handle multiple simultaneous requests, one request per instance. To share a variable's value across multiple requests under these circumstances, the variable must be declared as a class variable, rather than an instance variable.

When the isThreadSafe attribute is true, however, it makes little practical difference whether a variable is declared as an instance variable or a class variable. Declaring instance variables saves a little bit of typing, since you don't have to include the static keyword. Class variables, though, do a somewhat better job of conveying the typical usage of declared JSP variables, and are appropriate regardless of the setting of the isThreadSafe attribute.

Method declarations

Methods defined via declarations become methods of the servlet class into which the JSP page is compiled. For example, the following declaration defines a method for computing factorials:

```
<%! public long fact (long x) {
      if (x == 0) return 1;
      else return x * fact(x-1);
    } %>
```

As with variable declarations, declared methods can be accessed by any and all scripting elements on the page, regardless of the order in which the method declaration occurs relative to other scripting elements.

DEFINITION The factorial of a number is the product of all of the integers between that number and 1. The factorial function is only valid for non-negative integers, and the factorial of zero is defined to be one. The standard mathematical notation for the factorial of a variable x is $x!$ Thus, $x! = x *$ $(x-1) * (x-2) * \dots * 1$. For example, $5! = 5 * 4 * 3 * 2 * 1 = 120$. The method definition provided here implements this definition in a recursive manner, by taking advantage of the fact that $0! = 1$, and the observation that, for $x > 0$, it is true that $x! = x * (x-1)!$

In addition, multiple method definitions can appear within a single declaration tag, as can combinations of both variable and method declarations, as in the following:

```
<%! static private char[] vowels =
      { 'a', 'e', 'i', 'o', 'u', 'A', 'E', 'I', 'O', 'U' };
    public boolean startsWithVowel (String word) {
      char first = word.charAt(0);
      for (int i = 0; i < vowels.length; ++i) {
        if (first == vowels[i]) return true;
      }
      return false;
    }
    static private String[] articles = { "a ", "an " };
    public String withArticle (String noun) {
      if (startsWithVowel(noun)) return articles[1] + noun;
      else return articles[0] + noun;
    }
%>
```

This declaration introduces two methods and two class variables. The `withArticle()` method, which relies upon the other variables and methods included in the declaration, can be used to prepend the appropriate indefinite article to whatever character string is provided as its argument.

As with class variables, class methods may be specified using JSP declarations. Class methods, also known as static methods, are methods associated with the class itself, rather than individual instances, and may be called without requiring access to an instance of the class. In fact, class methods are typically called simply by prepending the name of the class to the name of the method. Class methods may reference only class variables, not instance variables. In practice, because it is generally not possible to obtain (or predict) the name of the servlet class corresponding to a particular JSP page, class methods have little utility in the context of JSP.

Handling life-cycle events

One particularly important use for method declarations is the handling of events related to the initialization and destruction of JSP pages. The initialization event occurs the first time the JSP container receives a request for a JSP page. The destruction event occurs when the JSP container unloads the servlet class, either because the JSP container is being shut down, or because the page has not been requested recently and the JSP container needs to reclaim the resources (e.g., system memory) associated with its servlet class.

These events are handled by declaring special life-cycle methods that will automatically be called by the JSP container when the corresponding event occurs. The initialization event is handled by a method named `jspInit()`, and the destruction event is handled by a method named `jspDestroy()`. Neither method returns a value or takes any arguments, so the general format for declaring them is as follows:

```
<%! public void jspInit () {
      // Initialization code goes here...
    }
    public void jspDestroy () {
      // Destruction code goes here...
    }
%>
```

Both methods are optional. If a JSP life-cycle method is not declared for a JSP page, the corresponding event is simply ignored.

If the `jspInit()` method is defined, the JSP container is guaranteed to call it after the servlet class has been instantiated, but before the first request is processed. For example, consider a JSP page that relies upon a pool of database connections in order to collect the data used to generate its contents. Before the page can handle any requests, it needs to ensure that the connection pool has been created, and is available for use. The initialization event is the standard JSP mechanism for enforcing such requirements, as in the following:

```
<%! static private DbConnectionPool pool = null;
    public void jspInit () {
      if (pool == null) {
        String username = "sark", password = "mcpr00lz";
        pool = DbConnectionPool.getPool(this, username, password);
      }
    } %>
```

Here, a class variable is declared for storing a reference to the connection pool, an instance of some hypothetical `DbConnectionPool` class. The `jspInit()` method calls a static method of this class named `getPool()`, which takes the page instance as well as a username and password for the database as its arguments, and returns an appropriate connection pool, presumably either reusing an existing connection pool or, if necessary, creating one.

In a similar manner, if the `jspDestroy()` method is defined, it will be called after all pending requests have been processed, but just before the JSP container removes the corresponding servlet class from service. To continue the example introduced above, imagine the following method declaration for the page destruction event:

```
<%! public void jspDestroy () {
      pool.maybeReclaim(this);
    } %>
```

Here, the connection pool is given a chance to reclaim its resources by calling its `maybeReclaim()` method with the page instance as its sole argument. The implication here is that if this page is the only consumer of connection pools that is still using this particular pool, the pool can reclaim its resources because this page no longer needs them.

3.4.2 *Expressions*

Declarations are used to add variables and methods to a JSP page, but are not able to directly contribute to the page's output, which is, after all, the objective of dynamic content generation. The JSP expression element, however, is explicitly intended for output generation. The syntax for this scripting element is as follows:

```
<%= expression %>
```

An XML variant is also provided:

```
<jsp:expression> expression </jsp:expression>
```

In both cases, the *expression* should be a valid and complete scripting language expression, in whatever scripting language has been specified for the page. The effect of this element is to evaluate the specified expression and substitute the resulting value into the output of the page, in place of the element itself.

JSP expressions can be used to print out individual variables, or the result of some calculation. For example, the following expression, which uses Java as the scripting language, will insert the value of π into the page's output, courtesy of a static variable provided by the `java.lang.Math` class:

```
<%= Math.PI %>
```

Assuming a variable named `radius` has been introduced elsewhere on the page, the following expression can be used to print out the area of the corresponding circle:

```
<%= Math.PI * Math.pow(radius, 2) %>
```

Again, any valid scripting language expression is allowed, so calls to methods are likewise permitted. For example, a page including the declaration of the `fact()` method presented above could then insert factorial values into its output using expressions of the following form:

```
<%= fact(12) %>
```

This particular expression would have the effect of substituting the value 479001600 into the contents of the page.

These three expressions all return numeric values, but there are no restrictions on the types of values that may be returned by JSP expressions. Expressions can return Java primitive values, such as numbers, characters, and booleans, or full-fledged Java objects, such as strings and JavaBeans. All expression results are converted to character strings before they are added to the page's output. As indicated in table 3.2, various static `toString()` methods are used to convert primitive values into strings, while objects are expected to provide their own `toString()` methods (or rely on the default implementation provided by the `java.lang.Object` class).

Table 3.2   Methods used to convert expression values into strings

Value Type	Conversion to String
boolean	`java.lang.Boolean.toString(boolean)`
byte	`java.lang.Byte.toString(byte)`
char	`new java.lang.Character(char).toString()`
double	`java.lang.Double.toString(double)`
int	`java.lang.Integer.toString(int)`

Table 3.2 Methods used to convert expression values into strings (continued)

Value Type	Conversion to String
float	`java.lang.Float.toString(float)`
long	`java.lang.Long.toString(long)`
object	`toString()` method of object's class

You may have noticed that no semicolon was provided at the end of the Java code used in the example JSP expressions. This is because Java's semicolon is a statement delimiter. A semicolon has the effect of transforming a Java language expression into a program statement. In Java, statements are evaluated purely for their side effects; they do not return values. Thus, leaving out the semicolon in JSP expressions is the right thing to do, because the JSP container is interested in the value of the enclosed code, not its side effects.

Given that this scripting element produces output only from expressions, not statements, you may be wondering if there is a convenient way to do conditional output in a JSP page. Java's standard `if/then` construct, after all, is a statement, not an expression: its clauses are evaluated purely for side effects, not value. Fortunately, Java supports the oft-forgotten tertiary conditional operator, which does return a value based on the result of a conditional test. The syntax of Java's tertiary operator is as follows:

```
test_expr ? true_expr : false_expr
```

Each operand of the tertiary operator is itself an expression. The `test_expr` expression should evaluate to a boolean value. If the value of `test_expr` expression is `true`, then the `true_expr` expression will be evaluated and its result returned as the result of the tertiary operator. Alternatively, if the value of `test_expr` expression is `false`, then the `false_expr` expression is evaluated and its result will be returned.

The tertiary operator can thus be used in a JSP expression as in the following:

```
<%= (hours < 12) ? "AM" : "PM" %>
```

In this particular example, the value of the `hours` variable is checked to determine whether it is less than twelve. If so, the tertiary operator returns the string `"AM"`, which the JSP expression then inserts into the page. If not, the operator returns `"PM"` and, again, the JSP expression adds this result to the page output.

TIP The tertiary operator is particularly convenient for use in JSP expressions not just for its functionality, but also for its brevity.

3.4.3 *Scriptlets*

Declarations and expressions are intentionally limited in the types of scripting code they support. For general purpose scripting, the appropriate JSP construct is the *scriptlet*. Scriptlets can contain arbitrary scripting language statements which, like declarations, are evaluated for side effects only. Scriptlets do not, however, automatically add content to a JSP page's output. The general syntax for scriptlets is as follows:

```
<% scriptlet %>
```

Scriptlets can also be specified using XML notation, as follows:

```
<jsp:scriptlet> scriptlet </jsp:scriptlet>
```

For either tag style, the `scriptlet` should be one or more valid and complete statements in the JSP page's scripting language. Alternatively, a scriptlet can leave open one or more statement blocks, which must be closed by subsequent scriptlets in the same page. In the case where the JSP scripting language is Java, statement blocks are opened using the right brace character (i.e., {) and closed using the left brace character (i.e., }).

Here is an example of a scriptlet which contains only complete statements:

```
<% GameGrid grid = GameGrid.getGameGrid();
   Recognizer r1 = new Recognizer(new Coordinates(grid, 0, 0));
   Recognizer r2 = new Recognizer(new Coordinates(grid, 100, 100));
   r1.findProgram("Flynn");
   r2.findProgram("Flynn"); %>
```

This scriptlet fetches one object via a class method, which it then uses to instantiate two new objects. Methods are then called on these objects to initiate some computation.

Note that a page's scriptlets will be run for each request received by the page. For the above example, this means that two new instances of the `Recognizer` class are created every time the JSP page containing this scriptlet is requested. Furthermore, any variables introduced in a scriptlet are available for use in subsequent scriptlets and expressions on the same page (subject to variable scoping rules). The foregoing scriptlet, for example, could be followed by an expression such as the following:

```
<%= r1.statusReport() %>
```

This expression would then insert the results of the `statusReport()` method call for instance `r1` into the page's output. Later scriptlets or expressions could make additional references (such as method calls, or inclusion in argument lists) to this instance and the `r2` instance, as well the `grid` object.

If you wish to control the scoping of a variable introduced by a scriptlet, you can take advantage of JSP's support for leaving code blocks open across multiple script-lets. Consider, for example, the following JSP page which reproduces the above scriptlet, with one small but important modification:

```
<html>
<body>
<h1>Intruder Alert</h1>
<p>Unauthorized entry, dispatching recognizers...</p>
<% GameGrid grid = GameGrid.getGameGrid();
   { Recognizer r1 = new Recognizer(new Coordinates(grid, 0, 0));
     Recognizer r2 = new Recognizer(new Coordinates(grid, 100, 100));
     r1.findProgram("Flynn");
     r2.findProgram("Flynn"); %>
<h2>Status</h2>
<ul>
<li>First Recognizer: <%= r1.statusReport() %>
<li>Second Recognizer: <%= r2.statusReport() %>
</ul>
<% } %>
Alert Level:<%= grid.alertLevel() %>
</body>
</html>
```

In this case, the first scriptlet introduces a new program block before creating the two `Recognizer` instances. The second scriptlet, towards the end of the page, closes this block. Within that block, the `r1` and `r2` instances are said to be *in scope*, and may be referenced freely. After that block is closed, these objects are *out of scope*, and any references to them will cause a compile-time error when the page is compiled into a servlet by the JSP container. Note that because the `grid` variable is introduced before the block is opened, it is in the page's top-level scope, and can continue to be referenced after the second scriptlet closes the block opened by the first, as in the call to its `alertLevel()` method near the end of the page.

The reason this works has to do with the translation of the contents of a JSP page into source code for a servlet. Static content, such as HTML code, is translated into Java statements which print that text as output from the servlet. Similarly, expressions are translated into Java statements which evaluate the expression, convert the result to a string, and print that string value as output from the servlet. Scriptlets, however, undergo no translation at all, and are simply inserted into the source code of the servlet as is. If a scriptlet opens a new block without also closing it, then the Java statements corresponding to any subsequent static content or JSP elements simply become part of this new block. The block must ultimately be closed by another scriptlet, or else compilation will fail due to a Java syntax error.

NOTE Java statements corresponding to a JSP page's static content, expressions, and scriptlets are used to create the _jspService() method of the corresponding servlet. This method is responsible for generating the output of the JSP page. Directives and declarations are also translated into servlet code, but do not contribute to the _jspService() method and so are not affected by scoping due to scriptlets. On the other hand, the JSP Bean tags, discussed in chapter 5, are translated into Java statements for the _jspService() method and therefore are subject to scoping restrictions introduced via scriptlets.

3.5 *Flow of control*

This ability of scriptlets to introduce statement blocks without closing them can be put to good use in JSP pages to affect the flow of control through the various elements, static or dynamic, that govern page output. In particular, such scriptlets can be used to implement conditional or iterative content, or to add error handling to a sequence of operations.

3.5.1 *Conditionalization*

Java's if statement, with optional else if and else clauses, is used to control the execution of code based on logical true/false tests. Scriptlets can use the if statement (or the appropriate analog if the scripting language is not Java) to implement conditional content within a JSP page. The following page fragment, for example, uses the fact() method introduced earlier in this chapter to compute the factorial of a page variable named x, as long it is within the appropriate range:

```
<% if (x < 0) { %>
   <p>Sorry, can't compute the factorial of a negative number.</p>
<% } else if (x > 20) { %>
   <p>Sorry, arguments greater than 20 cause an overflow error.</p>
<% } else { %>
   <p align=center><%= x %>! = <%= fact(x) %></p>
<% } %>
```

Three different blocks of statements are created by these scriptlets, only one of which will actually be executed. If the value of x is negative, then the first block will be executed, causing the indicated static HTML code to be displayed. If x is greater than 20, the second block is executed, causing its static HTML to be displayed. Otherwise, the output from the page will contain the static and dynamic content specified by the third block, including the result of the desired call to the fact() method.

3.5.2 *Iteration*

Java has three different iteration constructs: the `for` loop, the `while` loop, and the `do/while` statement. They may all be used via scriptlets to add iterative content to a JSP page, and are particularly useful in the display of tabular data. Here, for example, is a page fragment which uses the `fact()` method defined earlier in this chapter to construct a table of factorial values:

```
<table>
<tr><th><i>x</i></th><th><I>x</I>! </th></tr>
<% for (long x = 0l; x <= 20l; ++x) { %>
   <tr><td><%= x %></td><td><%= fact(x) %></td></tr>
<% } %>
</table>
```

Static HTML is used to create the table and its headers, while a `for` loop is used to generate the contents of the table. Twenty-one rows of data are created in this manner, as indicated in the screen shot in figure 3.2. The other iteration constructs may be used in a similar manner. In addition to generating row data for HTML tables, another common use for iteration scriptlets is looping through a set of results from a database query.

3.5.3 *Exception handling*

As described in chapter 2, the default behavior when an exception is thrown while processing a JSP page is to display an implementation-specific error message in the browser window. In this chapter, we have also seen how the `errorPage` attribute of the `page` directive can be used to specify an alternative page for handling any uncaught errors thrown by a JSP page. A third option allows even finer control over errors by incorporating the standard Java exception-handling mechanisms into a JSP page using scriptlets.

If a block of code on a JSP page has the potential of signaling an error, Java's exception handling construct, the `try` block, may be used in a set of scriptlets to catch the error locally and respond to it gracefully within the current page. By way of example, consider the following alternative declaration for the factorial method presented earlier:

```
<%! public long fact (long x) throws IllegalArgumentException {
      if ((x < 0) || (x > 20))
        throw new IllegalArgumentException("Out of range.");
      else if (x == 0) return 1;
      else return x * fact(x-1);
    } %>
```

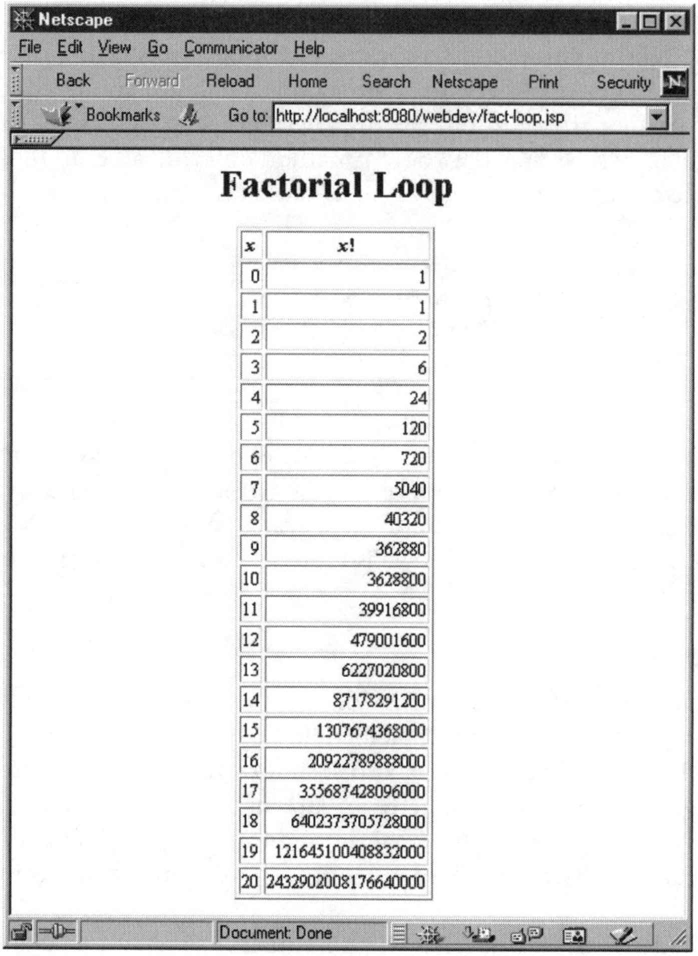

Figure 3.2 Tabular results generated by the iteration example

This version of the method verifies that the method's argument is within the valid range for this calculation, signaling an `IllegalArgumentException` if it is not.

Using this version of the method, we could consider an alternative implementation of the example presented in the foregoing section on conditionals, as follows:

```
<% try { %>
  <p align=center> <%= x %>! = <%= fact(x) %></p>
<% } catch (IllegalArgumentException e) { %>
  <p>Sorry, factorial argument is out of range.</p>
<% } %>
```

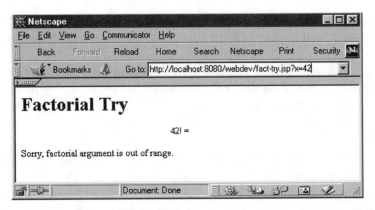

Figure 3.3   Failure results generated by the first exception handler example

Like the earlier example, the intent here is to print out the result of a factorial calculation, or display an error message if the calculation cannot be made. In this case, a `try` block is established around the expression which calls the `fact()` method. If this call raises an `IllegalArgumentException` the `catch` block will handle it by printing an error message. If no exception is raised, the content enclosed by the `catch` block will be ignored, and only the successful results are displayed.

The former behavior is demonstrated in the screen shot presented in figure 3.3. Here, an attempt to calculate the factorial of 42 has been made, but this is out of the range of permitted values for the `fact()` method. (This is because Java integer values of type `long` are limited to 64 bits. Twenty is the largest integer whose factorial can be expressed using 64 bits.) As a result, the `IllegalArgumentException` is thrown, and then caught. Notice that all of the output generated up until the call to the `fact()` method appears on the page. This is because the corresponding servlet code for this output does not raise any exceptions, and therefore is executed when the page is processed. As soon as the call to `fact()` occurs, however, the exception is raised and control is transferred to the `catch` block, which then prints out the error message.

In order to suppress the equation output altogether, the code on the JSP page must be rearranged to call the `fact()` method before any of that output is generated. One possible approach is to rewrite the first scriptlet as follows:

```
<% try {
    long result = fact(x); %>
  <p align=center> <%= x %>! = <%= result %></p>
<% } catch (IllegalArgumentException e) { %>
  <p>Sorry, factorial argument is out of range.</p>
<% } %>
```

In this case, the factorial value is computed in the scriptlet itself, at the beginning of the `try` block, and stored in a new local variable named `result`. This variable is then used in the expression which displays the factorial value, rather than directly calling the method, as before. And because the method call now precedes any output, if an exception is thrown, control will be transferred to the `catch` block before the output in the `try` block begins.

3.5.4 *A word of caution*

As you can see from these examples, scriptlets that introduce enclosing blocks are very powerful. Short of using custom tag libraries, they are the only means available in JSP to implement conditional or iterative content, or to add custom exception handlers to a page. At the same time, excessive use of these scriptlets can lead to maintainability problems.

The primary reason for this is readability. The fact that Java delimiters (i.e., { and }) appear adjacent to the HTML-like scriptlet delimiters (i.e., `<%` and `%>`) introduces a syntax clash, which can make these tags difficult to follow. Adhering to an indentation convention, as the examples here do, can help address this issue, particularly when there are several lines of content interleaved between the scriptlet that opens a block and the scriptlet that closes it.

As discussed in chapter 1, maintenance of JSP pages is often shared by individuals skilled in Java programming and others who are skilled in page design and HTML. While it is certainly true that HTML has tags that must appear in pairs in order to have meaning, the notion that some scriptlets are stand-alone while others are mutually dependent is somewhat foreign to those familiar with HTML syntax but not Java syntax. As the preceding examples demonstrate, there are cases where three or more scriptlets are required to implement conditional logic or exception handling, a scenario that has no parallels in HTML.

As a result, modifying and debugging pages that make heavy use of scriptlets such as these can be complicated. If the web designers on a team are uncomfortable with the syntax issues, it is not unlikely that they will involve the programming staff when making even minor changes to a page. Likewise, if there is a problem with the display of a page, a joint effort may be required to resolve it.

3.6   *Comments*

If the number of ways comments can be expressed in a language is an indication of its power, then JSP must be the most powerful dynamic content system around: there are three different ways to insert comments into a JSP page. These three styles of comments themselves divide into two major types, comments that are transmitted back to the browser as part of the JSP response, and those that are only visible in the original JSP source file.

3.6.1   *Content comments*

Only one of the three comments styles falls into the first group. These are referred to as content comments, because they use the comment syntax associated with the type of content being generated by the JSP page. To write a comment that will be included in the output of a JSP page that is generating web content, the following syntax is used:

```
<!-- comment -->
```

Those familiar with HTML and XML will recognize that this is the standard comment syntax for those two markup languages. Thus, a JSP page that is generating either HTML or XML simply uses the native comment syntax for whichever form of content it is constructing. Such comments will then be sent back to the browser as part of the response. Since they are comments, they do not produce any visible output, but they may be viewed by the end user via the browser's View Source menu item.

   Since these comments are part of the output from the page, you can, if you wish, include dynamic content in them. HTML and XML comments can, for example, include JSP expressions, and the output generated by these expressions will appear as part of the comment in the page's response. For example:

```
<!-- Java longs are 64 bits, so 20! = <%= fact(20) %> is
    the upper limit. -->
```

In this case, the computed value of the factorial expression will appear in the comment that is actually sent to the browser.

3.6.2   *JSP comments*

JSP comments are independent of the type of content being produced by the page. They are also independent of the scripting language used by the page. These comments can only be viewed by examining the original JSP file, and take the following form:

```
<%-- comment --%>
```

The body of this comment is ignored by the JSP container. When the page is compiled into a servlet, anything appearing between these two delimiters is skipped while translating the page into servlet source code.

For this reason, JSP comments such as this are very useful for commenting out portions of a JSP page, as when debugging. In the following page fragment, for example, only the first and last expressions, displaying the factorials of 5 and 9, will appear in the page output:

```
5! = <%= fact(5) %><br>
<%--
6! = <%= fact(6) %><br>
7! = <%= fact(7) %><br>
8! = <%= fact(8) %><br>
--%>
9! = <%= fact(9) %><br>
```

All of the other expressions have been commented out, and will not appear in the page's output. Keep in mind that these comments do not nest. Only the content between the opening comment delimiter, `<%--`, and the *first* occurrence of the closing delimiter, `--%>`, is ignored.

3.6.3 *Scripting language comments*

Finally, comments may also be introduced into a JSP page within scriptlets, using the native comment syntax of the scripting language. Java, for example, uses `/*` and `*/` as comment delimiters. With Java as the JSP scripting language, then, scripting language comments take the following form:

```
<% /* comment */%>
```

Like JSP comments, scripting language comments will not appear in the page's output. Unlike JSP comments, though, which are completely ignored by the JSP container, scripting language comments will appear in the source code generated for the servlet.

Scripting language comments can appear by themselves in scriptlets, as the form above implies, or may accompany actual scripting code, as in the following example:

```
<% long valid = fact(20);
   long overflow = fact(21); /* Exceeds 64-bit long! */
%>
```

In this case, the comment will again appear in the source code of the corresponding servlet.

Scripting language comments can also appear in JSP expressions, as long as they are also accompanied by, or part of, an expression. For example, all of the following JSP expressions are valid:

```
<%= /* Comment before expression */ fact(5) %>
<%= fact(7) /* Comment after expression */ %>
<%= fact(9 /* Comment inside expression */) %>
```

A JSP expression that contains only a comment, but not a scripting language expression, is not valid, and will result in a compilation error.

Java also supports a second comment syntax, in which the characters // are the opening delimiter, and the closing delimiter is the end of the line. This comment syntax can also be used in JSP pages, as long as the scriptlet or expression in which it is used is careful to include the end-of-line delimiter, as in the following examples:

```
<% long valid = fact(20);// This one fits in a 64-bit long.
   long overflow = fact(21);// This one doesn't.
%>

5! = <%= fact(5) // Getting tired of factorial examples yet?
%>
```

If the scriptlet or expression does not include the end-of-line delimiter, there is a danger that the content immediately following it may be commented out when the JSP page is translated into a servlet. Consider, for example, the following JSP page fragment:

```
Lora's brother is over <%= fact(3) // Strange ruler... %> feet tall!
```

Depending upon the implement of the JSP container, it is possible that the code generated to print out the character string " feet tall!" may appear in the servlet source code on the same line as the code corresponding to the JSP expression. If so, this code will be commented out in the servlet source code and never appear in the output from the page. In fact, it is also possible that part of the code generated for the expression itself will be commented out, in which case a syntax error will result the first time the page is compiled. For this reason, the fully delimited Java comment syntax (i.e., /* ... */) is the preferred style for JSP usage, particularly in JSP expressions.

Actions and implicit objects

This chapter covers

- Types of JSP implicit objects
- Accessing and applying implicit objects
- Attributes and scopes
- Action tags for transfer of control

Three types of JSP tags were introduced in chapter 3: directives, scripting elements, and comments. The remaining type, actions, will be introduced here. Actions encapsulate common behavior into simple tags for use from any JSP page. Actions are the basis of the custom tag facility described in chapters 11 and 12, but a number of standard actions are also provided by the base JSP specification. These standard actions, presented later in this chapter, are supported by all JSP containers.

Before we look at the standard actions, however, we will first consider the set of Java objects that the JSP container makes available to developers from each page. Through their class APIs, these objects enable developers to tap into the inner workings of the JSP container and leverage its functionality. These objects can be accessed as built-in variables via scripting elements. They may also be accessed programmatically by JavaBeans (chapter 5), servlets (chapter 8) and JSP custom tags (chapters 13 and 14).

4.1 *Implicit objects*

As the examples presented in chapter 3 suggest, the JSP scripting elements provide a great deal of power for creating, modifying, and interacting with Java objects in order to generate dynamic content. Application-specific classes can be instantiated and values from method calls can be inserted into JSP output. Network resources and repositories, such as databases, can be accessed to store and retrieve data for use by JSP pages.

In addition to objects such as these, which are completely under the control of the developer, the JSP container also exposes a number of its internal objects to the page author. These are referred to as *implicit objects*, because their availability in a JSP page is automatic. The developer can assume that these objects are present and accessible via JSP scripting elements. More specifically, these objects will be automatically assigned to specific variable names in the page's scripting language. Furthermore, as summarized in table 4.1, each implicit object must adhere to a corresponding API, in the form of a specific Java class or interface definition. Thus, it will either be an instance of that class or interface, or of an implementation-specific subclass.

Table 4.1   JSP implicit objects and their API's for HTTP applications

Object	Class or *Interface*	Description
page	*javax.servlet.jsp.HttpJspPage*	Page's servlet instance.
config	*javax.servlet.ServletConfig*	Servlet configuration data.
request	*javax.servlet.http.HttpServletRequest*	Request data, including parameters.
response	*javax.servlet.http.HttpServletResponse*	Response data.
out	*javax.servlet.jsp.JspWriter*	Output stream for page content.
session	*javax.servlet.http.HttpSession*	User-specific session data.
application	*javax.servlet.ServletContext*	Data shared by all application pages.
pageContext	*javax.servlet.jsp.PageContext*	Context data for page execution.
exception	*java.lang.Throwable*	Uncaught error or exception.

The nine implicit objects provided by JSP fall naturally into four major categories: objects related to a JSP page's servlet, objects concerned with page input and output, objects providing information about the context within which a JSP page is being processed, and objects resulting from errors.

Beyond this functional categorization, four of the JSP implicit objects—request, session, application, and pageContext—have something else in common: the ability to store and retrieve arbitrary attribute values. By setting and getting attribute values, these objects are able to transfer information between and among JSP pages and servlets as a simple data-sharing mechanism.

The standard methods for attribute management provided by the classes and interfaces of these four objects are summarized in table 4.2. Note that attribute keys take the form of Java string objects, while their values are referenced as instances of java.lang.Object.

Table 4.2   Common methods for storing and retrieving attribute values

Method	Description
setAttribute(key, value)	Associates an attribute value with a key (i.e., a name).
getAttributeNames()	Retrieves the names of all attributes associated with the session.
getAttribute(key)	Retrieves the attribute value associated with the key.
removeAttribute(key)	Removes the attribute value associated with the key.

4.1.1 *Servlet-related objects*

The two JSP implicit objects in this category are based on the JSP page's implementation as a servlet. The `page` implicit object represents the servlet itself, while the `config` object stores the servlet's initialization parameters, if any.

Page object

The `page` object represents the JSP page itself or, more specifically, an instance of the servlet class into which the page has been translated. As such, it may be used to call any of the methods defined by that servlet class. As indicated earlier in this chapter, the `extends` attribute of the `page` directive may be used to specify the servlet class explicitly, otherwise an implementation-specific class will be used by the JSP container when constructing the servlet. In either case, the servlet class is always required to implement the `javax.servlet.jsp.JspPage` interface. In the specific case of web-based JSP applications built on HTTP, the servlet class must implement the `javax.servlet.jsp.HttpJspPage` interface. The methods of this class are presented in appendix E.

In practice, the `page` object is rarely used when the JSP scripting language is Java, because the scripting elements will ultimately be incorporated as method code of the constructed servlet class, and will automatically have access to the class's other methods. (More specifically, when the scripting language is Java, the `page` object is the same as the `this` variable.) For other scripting languages, however, the scripting variable for this implicit object grants access to all of the methods provided by the `javax.servlet.jsp.JspPage` interface, as well as any methods that have been defined for the page via method declarations.

Here is an example page fragment that utilizes this implicit object:

```
<%@ page info="Page implicit object demonstration." %>
Page info:
<%= ((javax.servlet.jsp.HttpJspPage)page).getServletInfo() %>
```

This expression will insert the value of the page's documentation string into the output from the page. In this example, note that because the servlet class varies from one page to another, the standard type for the `page` implicit object is the default Java type for nonprimitive values, `java.lang.Object`. In order to access methods defined by the `javax.servlet.jsp.HttpJspPage` interface, the `page` object must first be cast to that interface.

Config object

The `config` object stores servlet configuration data—in the form of initialization parameters—for the servlet into which a JSP page is compiled. Because JSP pages are seldom written to interact with initialization parameters, this implicit object is rarely used in practice. This object is an instance of the `javax.servlet.Servlet-Config` interface. The methods provided by that interface for retrieving servlet initialization parameters are listed in table 4.3.

Table 4.3 Methods of `javax.servlet.ServletConfig` interface for accessing initialization parameters

Method	Description
getInitParameterNames()	Retrieves the names of all initialization parameters.
getInitParameter(name)	Retrieves the value of the named initialization parameter.

Due to its role in servlet initialization, the `config` object tends to be most relevant in a page's initialization routine. Consider, for example, the following variation on the sample `jspInit()` method presented earlier in this chapter:

```
<%! static private DbConnectionPool pool = null;
    public void jspInit () {
      if (pool == null) {
        String username = config.getInitParameter("username");
        String password = config.getInitParameter("password");
        pool = DbConnectionPool.getPool(this, username, password);
      }
    } %>
```

In this case, rather than storing the username and password values directly in the JSP page, they have been provided as initialization parameters and are accessed via the `config` object.

Values for initialization parameters are specified via the deployment descriptor file of a web application. Deployment descriptor files are described in chapter 10.

4.1.2 Input/Output

These implicit objects are focused on the input and output of a JSP page. More specifically, the `request` object represents the data coming into the page, while the `response` object represents its result. The `out` implicit object represents the actual output stream associated with the `response`, to which the page's content is written.

Request object

The `request` object represents the request that triggered the processing of the current page. For HTTP requests, this object provides access to all of the information associated with a request, including its source, the requested URL, and any headers, cookies, or parameters associated with the request. The `request` object is required to implement the `javax.servlet.ServletRequest` interface. When the protocol is HTTP, as is typically the case, it must implement a subclass of this interface, `javax.servlet.http.HttpServletRequest`.

The methods of this interface fall into four general categories. First, the `request` object is one of the four JSP implicit objects that support attributes, by means of the methods presented in table 4.2. The `HttpServletRequest` interface also includes methods for retrieving request parameters and HTTP headers, which are summarized in tables 4.4 and 4.5, respectively. The other frequently used methods of this interface are listed in table 4.6, and provide miscellaneous functionality such as access to the request URL and the session.

Among the most common uses for the `request` object are looking up parameter values and cookies. Here is a page fragment illustrating the use of the `request` object to access a parameter value:

```
<% String xStr = request.getParameter("num");
   try { long x = Long.parseLong(xStr); %>
     Factorial result: <%= x %>! = <%= fact(x) %>
<% } catch (NumberFormatException e) { %>
     Sorry, the <b>num</b> parameter does not specify an
     integer value.
<% } %>
```

In this example, the value of the `num` parameter is fetched from the request. Note that all parameter values are stored as strings, so conversion is required before it may be used as a number. If the conversion succeeds, this value is used to demonstrate the factorial function. If not, an error message is displayed.

When utilizing the `<jsp:forward>` and `<jsp:include>` actions described at the end of this chapter, the `request` object is also often used for storing and retrieving attributes in order to transfer data between pages.

Table 4.4   Methods of the `javax.servlet.http.HttpServletRequest` interface for accessing request parameters

Method	Description
`getParameterNames()`	Returns the names of all request parameters
`getParameter(name)`	Returns the first (or primary) value of a single request parameter
`getParameterValues(name)`	Retrieves all of the values for a single request parameter.

Table 4.5 **Methods of the** `javax.servlet.http.HttpServletRequest`
interface for retrieving request headers

Method	Description
`getHeaderNames()`	Retrieves the names of all of headers associated with the request.
`getHeader(name)`	Returns the value of a single request header, as a string.
`getHeaders(name)`	Returns all of the values for a single request header.
`getIntHeader(name)`	Returns the value of a single request header, as an integer.
`getDateHeader(name)`	Returns the value of a single request header, as a date.
`getCookies()`	Retrieves all of the cookies associated with the request.

Table 4.6 **Miscellaneous methods of the** `javax.servlet.http.HttpServletRequest` **interface**

Method	Description
`getMethod()`	Returns the HTTP (e.g., `GET`, `POST`) method for the request.
`getRequestURI()`	Returns the request URL, up to but not including any query string.
`getQueryString()`	Returns the query string that follows the request URL, if any.
`getSession(flag)`	Retrieves the session data for the request (i.e., the `session` implicit object), optionally creating it if it doesn't already exist.
`getRequestDispatcher(path)`	Creates a request dispatcher for the indicated local URL.
`getRemoteHost()`	Returns the fully qualified name of the host that sent the request.
`getRemoteAddr()`	Returns the network address of the host that sent the request.
`getRemoteUser()`	Returns the name of user that sent the request, if known.
`getSession(flag)`	Retrieves the session data for the request (i.e., the `session` implicit object), optionally creating it if it doesn't already exist.

Response object

The `response` object represents the response that will be sent back to the user as a result of processing the JSP page. This object implements the `javax.servlet.Servlet-Response` interface. If it represents an HTTP response, it will furthermore implement a subclass of this interface, the `javax.servlet.http.HttpServletResponse` interface.

The key methods of this latter interface are summarized in tables 4.7–4.10. Table 4.7 lists a pair of methods for specifying the content type and encoding of a response. Table 4.8 presents methods for setting response headers, while those in table 4.9 are for setting response codes. The two methods in table 4.10 provide support for URL rewriting, which is one of the techniques supported by JSP for session managment. For a full listing of all the methods associated with the `javax.servlet.http.HttpServletResponse` interface, consult appendix E.

Table 4.7 **Methods of the** `javax.servlet.http.HttpServletResponse`
interface for specifying content

Method	Description
`setContentType()`	Set the MIME type and, optionally, the character encoding of the response's contents.
`getCharacterEncoding()`	Returns the character encoding style set for the response's contents.

Table 4.8 **Methods of the** `javax.servlet.http.HttpServletResponse`
interface for setting response headers

Method	Description
`addCookie(cookie)`	Adds the specified cookie to the response.
`containsHeader(name)`	Checks whether the response includes the named header.
`setHeader(name, value)`	Assigns the specified string value to the named header.
`setIntHeader(name, value)`	Assigns the specified integer value to the named header.
`setDateHeader(name, date)`	Assigns the specified date value to the named header.
`addHeader(name, value)`	Adds the specified string value as a value for the named header.
`addIntHeader(name, value)`	Adds the specified integer value as a value for the named header.
`addDateHeader(name, date)`	Adds the specified date value as a value for the named header.

Table 4.9 **Response code methods of the** `javax.servlet.http.HttpServletResponse` **interface**

Method	Description
`setStatus(code)`	Sets the status code for the response (for non-error circumstances).
`sendError(status, msg)`	Sets the status code and error message for the response.
`sendRedirect(url)`	Sends a response to the browser indicating it should request an alternate (absolute) URL.

Table 4.10 **Methods of the** `javax.servlet.http.HttpServletResponse`
interface for performing URL rewriting

Method	Description
`encodeRedirectURL(url)`	Encodes a URL for use with the `sendRedirect()` method to include session information.
`encodeURL(name)`	Encodes a URL used in a link to include session information.

Here, for example, is a scriptlet that uses the `response` object to set various headers for preventing the page from being cached by a browser:

```
<% response.setDateHeader("Expires", 0);
   response.setHeader("Pragma", "no-cache");
   if (request.getProtocol().equals("HTTP/1.1")) {
     response.setHeader("Cache-Control", "no-cache");
   }
%>
```

The scriptlet first sets the `Expires` header to a date in the past. This indicates to the recipient that the page's contents have already expired, as a hint that its contents should not be cached.

NOTE   For the `java.util.Date` class, Java follows the tradition of the UNIX operating system in setting time zero to midnight, December 31, 1969 (GMT). That moment in time is commonly referred to as the UNIX *epoch*.

The `no-cache` value for the `Pragma` header is provided by version 1.0 of the HTTP protocol to further indicate that browsers and proxy servers should not cache a page. Version 1.1 of HTTP replaces this header with a more specific `Cache-Control` header, but recommends including the `Pragma` header as well for backward compatibility. Thus, if the request indicates that the browser (or its proxy server) supports HTTP 1.1, both headers are sent.

Out object

This implicit object represents the output stream for the page, the contents of which will be sent to the browser as the body of its response. The `out` object is an instance of the `javax.servlet.jsp.JspWriter` class. This is an abstract class that extends the standard `java.io.Writer` class, supplementing it with several of the methods provided by the `java.io.PrintWriter` class. In particular, it inherits all of the standard `write()` methods provided by `java.io.Writer`, and also implements all of the `print()` and `println()` methods defined by `java.io.PrintWriter`.

For example, the `out` object can be used within a scriptlet to add content to the generated page, as in the following page fragment:

```
<P>Counting eggs
<% int count = 0;
   while (carton.hasNext()) {
     count++;
     out.print(".");
   }
%>
<BR>
There are <%= count %> eggs.</P>
```

The scriptlet in this fragment, in addition to counting the elements in some hypothetical iterator named `carton`, also has the effect of printing a period for each counted element. If there are five elements in this iterator, this page fragment will produce the following output:

```
Counting eggs.....
There are 5 eggs.
```

By taking advantage of this implicit object, then, output can be generated from within the body of a scriptlet without having to temporarily close the scriptlet to insert static page content or JSP expressions.

In addition, the `javax.servlet.jsp.JspWriter` class defines a number of methods that support JSP-specific behavior. These additional methods are summarized in table 4.11, and are primarily used for controlling the output buffer and managing its relationship with the output stream that ultimately sends content back to the browser. The full set of methods for this class appears in appendix E.

Table 4.11   JSP-oriented methods of the `javax.servlet.jsp.JspWriter` interface

Method	Description
`isAutoFlush()`	Returns `true` if the output buffer is automatically flushed when it becomes full, `false` if an exception is thrown.
`getBufferSize()`	Returns the size (in bytes) of the output buffer.
`getRemaining()`	Returns the size (in bytes) of the unused portion of the output buffer.
`clearBuffer()`	Clears the contents of the output buffer, discarding them.
`clear()`	Clears the contents of the output buffer, signaling an error if the buffer has previously been flushed.
`newLine()`	Writes a (platform-specific) line separator to the output buffer.
`flush()`	Flushes the output buffer, then flushes the output stream.
`close()`	Closes the output stream, flushing any contents.

Here is a page fragment that uses the `out` object to display the buffering status:

```
<% int total = out.getBufferSize();
   int available = out.getRemaining();
   int used = total - available; %>
Buffering Status:
<%= used %>/<%= total %> = <%= (100.0 * used)/total %>%
```

Local variables are created to store the buffer size parameters, and expressions are used to display the values of these local variables. This page fragment is particularly useful when tuning the buffer size for a page, but note that the values it prints are only approximate, because the very act of displaying these values on the page uses up some of the output buffer. As written, the displayed values are accurate for all of the content that precedes this page fragment, but not for the fragment itself (or any contents that follow it, of course). Given, however, that this code would most likely be used only during page development and debugging, this behavior is not only acceptable, but also preferable: the developer needs to know the buffer usage of the actual page content, not of the debugging message.

The methods provided for clearing the buffer are also particularly useful. In the discussion of exception handling, recall that it was necessary to rewrite our original example in order to make the output more user-friendly when an error condition arose. More specifically, it was necessary to introduce a local variable and pre-compute the result we were interested in. Consider, instead the following approach:

```
<% out.flush();
   try { %>
   <p align=center> <%= x %>! = <%= fact(x) %></p>
<% } catch (IllegalArgumentException e) {
          out.clearBuffer(); %>
   <p>Sorry, factorial argument is out of range.</p>
<% } %>
```

In this version, the `flush()` method is called on the `out` object to empty the buffer and make sure all of the content generated so far is displayed. Then the `try` block is opened and the call to the `fact()` method, which has the potential of throwing an `IllegalArgumentException`, is made. If this method call successfully completes, the code and content in the `catch` block will be ignored.

If the exception is thrown, however, then the `clearBuffer()` method is called on the `out` object. This will have the effect of discarding any content that has been generated since the last time the output buffer was flushed. In this particular case, the output buffer was flushed just before opening the `try` block. Therefore, only the content generated by the `try` block before the exception occurred would be in the output buffer, so only that content will be removed when the output buffer is cleared. The output buffer will then be overwritten with the error message indicating that the argument was out of range.

WARNING There is, of course, a down side to this approach. Recall from the discussion of buffered output in chapter 2, that once the output buffer has been flushed, it is no longer possible to change or add response headers, or forward to another page. The call to the `flush()` method at the beginning of this page fragment thus limits your options for processing the remainder of the page.

4.1.3 Contextual objects

The implicit objects in this category provide the JSP page with access to the context within which it is being processed. The session object, for example, provides the context for the request to which the page is responding. What data has already been associated with the individual user who is requesting the page? The application object provides the server-side context within which the page is running. What other resources are available, and how can they be accessed? In contrast, the page-Context object is focused on the context of the JSP page itself, providing programmatic access to all of the other JSP implicit objects which are available to the page, and managing their attributes.

Session object

This JSP implicit object represents an individual user's current session. As described in the section on session management in chapter 2, all of the requests made by a user that are part of a single series of interactions with the web server are considered to be part of a session. As long as new requests by that user continue to be received by the server, the session persists. If, however, a certain length of time passes without any new requests from the user, the session expires.

The session object, then, stores information about the session. Application-specific data is typically added to the session by means of attributes, using the methods in table 4.2. Information about the session itself is available through the other methods of the javax.servlet.http.HttpSession interface, of which the session object is an instance. The most commonly used methods of this interface are summarized in table 4.12, and the full API appears in appendix E.

Table 4.12 Relevant methods of the javax.servlet.http.HttpSession interface

Method	Description
getId()	Returns the session ID.
getCreationTime()	Returns the time at which the session was created.
getLastAccessedTime()	Returns the last time a request associated with the session was received.
getMaxInactiveInterval()	Returns the maximum time (in seconds) between requests for which the session will be maintained.
setMaxInactiveInterval(t)	Sets the maximum time (in seconds) between requests for which the session will be maintained.
isNew()	Returns true if user's browser has not yet confirmed the session ID.
invalidate()	Discards the session, releasing any objects stored as attributes.

One of the primary uses for the `session` object is the storing and retrieving of attribute values, in order to transmit user-specific information between pages. As an example, here is a scriptlet that stores data in the session in the form of a hypothetical `UserLogin` object:

```
<% UserLogin userData = new UserLogin(name, password);
   session.setAttribute("login", userData); %>
```

Once this scriptlet has been used to store the data via the `setAttribute()` method, another scripting element—either on the same JSP page or on another page later visited by the user—could access that same data using the `getAttribute()` method, as in the following:

```
<% UserLogin userData = (UserLogin) session.getAttribute("login");
   if (userData.isGroupMember("admin")) {
     session.setMaxInactiveInterval(60*60*8);
   } else {
     session.setMaxInactiveInterval(60*15);
   }
%>
```

Note that when this scriptlet retrieves the stored data, it must use the casting operator to restore its type. This is because the base type for attribute values is `java.lang.Object`, which is therefore the return type for the `getAttribute()` method. Casting the attribute value enables it to be treated as a full-fledged instance of the type to which it has been cast. In this case, a hypothetical `isGroupMember()` method is called to determine whether or not the user is a member of the administrator group. If so, the session timeout is set to eight hours. If not, the session is set to expire after fifteen minutes of inactivity. The implication is that administrators (who are presumably more responsible about restricting access to their computers) should not be required to log back in after short periods of inactivity during the workday, while access by other users requires stricter security.

Note that JSP provides a mechanism for objects to be notified when they are added to or removed from a user's session. In particular, if an object is stored in a session and its class implements the `javax.servlet.http.HttpSessionBindingListener` interface, then certain methods required by that interface will be called whenever session-related events occur. Details on the use of this interface are presented in chapter 6.

Finally, mention must be made that, unlike most of the other JSP implicit objects which can be accessed as needed from any JSP page, use of the `session` object is restricted to pages that participate in session management. This is indicated via the `session` attribute of the `page` directive, as described earlier in this chapter. The default is for all pages to participate in session management. If the `session` attribute of the `page` directive is set to `false`, however, any references to the `session` implicit object will result in a compilation error when the JSP container attempts to translate the page into a servlet.

Application object

This implicit object represents the application to which the JSP page belongs. It is an instance of the `javax.servlet.ServletContext` interface. JSP pages are grouped into applications according to their URLs. JSP containers typically treat the first directory name in a URL as an application. For example, http://server/games/index.jsp, http://server/games/matrixblaster.jsp, and http://server/games/space/paranoids.jsp are all considered part of the same `games` application. Alternatively, complete control over application grouping can be obtained by use of Web Application Descriptor files, as described in chapter 10.

The key methods of the `javax.servlet.ServletContext` interface can be grouped into five major categories. First, the methods in table 4.13 allow the developer to retrieve version information from the servlet container. Next, table 4.14 lists several methods for accessing server-side resources represented as filenames and URLs. The `application` object also provides support for logging, via the methods summarized in table 4.15. The fourth set of methods supported by this interface are those for getting and setting attribute values, presented in table 4.2. A final pair of methods (identical to those in table 4.3) provides access to initialization parameters associated with the application as a whole (as opposed to the page-specific initialization parameters accessed via the `config` implicit object). For the full API of the `javax.servlet.ServletContext` interface, see appendix E.

Table 4.13   Container methods of the `javax.servlet.ServletContext` interface

Method	Description
getServerInfo()	Returns the name and version of the servlet container.
getMajorVersion()	Returns the major version of the Servlet API for the servlet container.
getMinorVersion()	Returns the minor version of the Servlet API for the servlet container.

As indicated in tables 4.13–4.15, the `application` object provides a number of methods for interacting with the HTTP server and the servlet container in an implementation-independent manner. From the point of view of JSP development, however, perhaps the most useful methods are those for associating attributes with an application. In particular, a group of JSP pages that reside in the same application

Table 4.14   Methods of the `javax.servlet.ServletContext` **interface for interacting with server-side paths and files**

Method	Description
`getMimeType(filename)`	Returns the MIME type for the indicated file, if known by the server.
`getResource(path)`	Translates a string specifying a URL into an object that accesses the URL's contents, either locally or over the network.
`getResourceAsStream(path)`	Translates a string specifying a URL into an input stream for reading its contents.
`getRealPath(path)`	Translates a local URL into a pathname in the local filesystem.
`getContext(path)`	Returns the application context for the specified local URL.
`getRequestDispatcher(path)`	Creates a request dispatcher for the indicated local URL.

Table 4.15   Methods of the `javax.servlet.ServletContext` **interface for message logging**

Method	Description
`log(message)`	Writes the message to the log file.
`log(message, exception)`	Writes the message to the log file, along with the stack trace for the specified exception.

can use application attributes to implement shared resources. Consider, for example, yet another version of the example `jspInit()` method used in a previous section:

```
<%! static private DbConnectionPool pool = null;
    public void jspInit () {
      pool = (DbConnectionPool)application.getAttribute("dbPool");
      if (pool == null) {
        String username = config.getInitParameter("username");
        String password = config.getInitParameter("password");
        pool = DbConnectionPool.getPool(this, username, password);
        application.setAttribute("dbPool", pool);
      }
    } %>
```

In this case, the connection pool is constructed in the same manner, and continues to be stored in a class variable named `pool`. Before constructing the connection pool, however, an application attribute is first checked for a pool that has already been constructed.

If a pool is not available via this application attribute, a new connection pool must be constructed. In this case, construction proceeds as before, with the added step of assigning this pool to the application attribute. The only significant difference is that, in this version, the initialization parameters are retrieved from the `application` object, rather than from the `config` object. Initialization parameters associated with the application can be accessed by any of the application's JSP pages. Such parameters need only be specified once, using the aforementioned Web Application Descriptor file (see chapter 10), whereas the initialization parameters associated with the `config` object must be specified on a page-by-page basis.

Reliance on application initialization parameters enables reuse of this code across multiple JSP pages within the application, without having to specify the initialization parameters multiple times. Such reuse can be facilitated by making use of the JSP `include` directive, and enables you to ensure that the connection pool will only be constructed once, and then shared among all of the pages.

TIP   Like session attributes, the base type for application attributes is `java.lang.Object`. When attribute values are retrieved from an application, they must be cast back to their original type in order to access their full functionality. Initialization parameters take the form of `string` objects.

As indicated in table 4.13, the `application` implicit object also provides access to information about the environment in which the JSP page is running, through the `getServerInfo()`, `getMajorVersion()`, and `getMinorVersion()` methods. Keep in mind, however, that the data returned by these methods is with respect to the servlet container in which the JSP page is running. To obtain the corresponding information about the current JSP container, the JSP specification provides an abstract class named `javax.servlet.jsp.JspEngineInfo` that provides a method for retrieving the JSP version number. Since this is an abstract class, a somewhat convoluted path is necessary in order to access an actual instance. The required steps are implemented by the following JSP page fragment:

```
<%@ page import="javax.servlet.jsp.JspFactory" %>
<% JspFactory factory = JspFactory.getDefaultFactory(); %>
JSP v. <%= factory.getEngineInfo().getSpecificationVersion() %>
```

For further details on the `JspEngineInfo` and `JspFactory` classes, see appendix E.

PageContext object

The `pageContext` object provides programmatic access to all other implicit objects. For the implicit objects that support attributes, the `pageContext` object also provides methods for accessing those attributes. In addition, the `pageContext` object implements methods for transferring control from the current page to another page, either temporarily to generate output to be included in the output of the current page, or permanently to transfer control altogether.

The `pageContext` object is an instance of the `javax.servlet.jsp.PageContext` class. The full API for this class in presented in appendix E, but the important methods of this class fall into four major groups. First, there is a set of methods for programmatically accessing all of the other JSP implicit objects, as summarized in table 4.16. While these methods are not particularly useful from a scripting perspective (since these objects are already available as scripting variables), we will discover their utility in chapter 13 when we look at how JSP custom tags are implemented.

The second group of `javax.servlet.jsp.PageContext` methods enables the dispatching of requests from one JSP page to another. Using these methods—listed in table 4.17—the handling of a request can be transferred from one page to another either temporarily or permanently. Further details on the application of this functionality will be provided when we look at the `<jsp:forward>` and `<jsp:include>` actions toward the end of this chapter.

Table 4.16 Methods of the `javax.servlet.jsp.PageContext` class for programatically retrieving the JSP implicit objects

Method	Description
getPage()	Returns the servlet instance for the current page (i.e., the page implicit object).
getRequest()	Returns the request that initiated the processing of the page (i.e., the request implicit object).
getResponse()	Returns the response for the page (i.e., the response implicit object).
getOut()	Returns the current output stream for the page (i.e., the out implicit object).
getSession()	Returns the session associated with the current page request, if any (i.e., the session implicit object).
getServletConfig()	Returns the servlet configuration object (i.e., the config implicit object).
getServletContext()	Returns the context in which the page's servlet runs (i.e., the application implicit object).
getException()	For error pages, returns the exception passed to the page (i.e., the exception implicit object).

Table 4.17 Request dispatch methods of the `javax.servlet.jsp.PageContext` class

Method	Description
forward(path)	Forwards processing to another local URL.
include(path)	Includes the output from processing another local URL.

The remaining two groups of methods supported by the `pageContext` object deal with attributes. This implicit object is among those capable of storing attributes. Its class therefore implements all of the attribute access methods listed in table 4.2. In keeping with its role as an avenue for programmatically accessing the other JSP implicit objects, however, the `javax.servlet.jsp.PageContext` class provides a set of methods for managing their attributes, as well. These methods are summarized in table 4.18.

Table 4.18   Methods of the `javax.servlet.jsp.PageContext` class for accessing attributes across multiple scopes

Method	Description
`setAttribute(key, value, scope)`	Associates an attribute value with a key in a specific scope.
`getAttributeNamesInScope(scope)`	Retrieves the names of all attributes in a specific scope.
`getAttribute(key, scope)`	Retrieves the attribute value associated with the key in a specific scope.
`removeAttribute(key, scope)`	Removes the attribute value associated with the key in a specific scope.
`findAttribute(name)`	Searches all scopes for the named attribute.
`getAttributesScope(name)`	Returns the scope in which the named attribute is stored.

As indicated earlier in this chapter, four different implicit objects are capable of storing attributes: the `pageContext` object, the `request` object, the `session` object, and the `application` object. As a result of this ability, these objects are also referred to as *scopes*, because the longevity of an attribute value is a direct result of the four objects in which it is stored. Page attributes, stored in the `pageContext` object, only last as long as the processing of a single page. Request attributes are also short-lived, but may be passed between pages as control is transferred. Session attributes persist as long as the user continues interacting with the web server. Application attributes are retained as long as the JSP container keeps one or more of an application's pages loaded in memory—conceivably, as long as the JSP container is running.

NOTE   Only a single thread within the JSP container can access attributes stored with either page or request scope: the thread handling the processing of the associated request. Thread safety is more of a concern, then, with session and application attributes. Because multiple requests for an application's pages will be handled simultaneously, objects stored with application scope must be robust with respect to access by these multiple threads. Similarly, because a user may have multiple browser windows accessing a server's JSP pages at the same time, it must be assumed that objects stored with session scope may also be accessed by more than one thread at a time.

In conjunction with the methods listed in table 4.18 whose parameters include a scope specification, the `javax.servlet.jsp.PageContext` class provides static variables for representing these four different scopes. Behind the scenes, these are just symbolic names for four arbitrary integer values. Since the actual values are hidden though, the symbolic names are the standard means for indicating attribute scopes, as in the following page fragment:

```
<%@ page import="javax.servlet.jsp.PageContext" %>
<% Enumeration atts =
    pageContext.getAttributeNamesInScope(PageContext.SESSION_SCOPE);
  while (atts.hasMoreElements()) { %>
  Session Attribute: <%= atts.nextElement() %><BR>
<% } %>
```

These variables are summarized in table 4.19.

Table 4.19   Class scope variables for the `javax.servlet.jsp.PageContext` class

Variable	Description
PAGE_SCOPE	Scope for attributes stored in the `pageContext` object.
REQUEST_SCOPE	Scope for attributes stored in the `request` object.
SESSION_SCOPE	Scope for attributes stored in the `session` object.
APPLICATION_SCOPE	Scope for attributes stored in the `application` object.

The last two methods listed in table 4.18 enable developers to search across all of the defined scopes for an attribute with a given name. In both cases, the `pageContext` object will search through the scopes in order—first page, then request, then session, and finally application—to either find the attribute's value, or identify in which scope (if any) the attribute is defined.

WARNING   The `session` scope is accessible only to `pageContext` methods on pages that actually participate in session management.

4.1.4 *Error handling*

This last category of JSP implicit objects has only one member, the `exception` object. As its name implies, this implicit object is provided for the purpose of error handling within JSP.

Exception object

The ninth and final JSP implicit object is the `exception` object. Like the `session` object, the `exception` object is not automatically available on every JSP page. Instead, this object is only available on pages that have been designated as error pages using the `isErrorPage` attribute of the `page` directive. On those JSP pages that are error pages, the `exception` object will be an instance of the `java.lang.Throwable` class corresponding to the uncaught error that caused control to be transferred to the error page. The methods of the `java.lang.Throwable` class that are particularly useful in the context of JSP are summarized in table 4.20.

Table 4.20   Relevant methods of the `java.lang.Throwable` class

Method	Description
`getMessage()`	Returns the descriptive error message associated with the exception when it was thrown.
`printStackTrace(out)`	Prints the execution stack in effect when the exception was thrown to the designated output stream.
`toString()`	Returns a string combining the class name of the exception with its error message (if any).

Here is an example page fragment demonstrating the use of the `exception` object:

```
<%@ page isErrorPage="true" %>
<H1>Warning!</H1>
The following error has been detected:<BR>
<B><%= exception %></B><BR>
<% exception.printStackTrace(out); %>
```

In this example, the `exception` object is referenced in both an expression and a scriptlet. As you may recall, expression values are converted into strings for printing. The expression here will therefore call `exception` object's `toString()` method in order to perform this conversion, yielding the results described in table 4.20. The scriptlet is used to display the stack trace for the exception, by supplying the `out` implicit object as the argument to the `printStackTrace()` method.

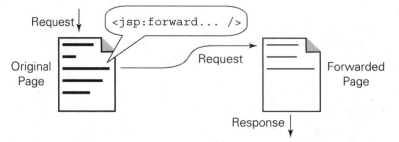

Figure 4.1 Effect of the <jsp:forward> action on the processing of a request

4.2 *Actions*

In chapter 3 we examined three types of JSP tags, directives, scripting elements, and comments. Actions are the fourth and final major category of JSP tags, and themselves serve three major roles. First, JSP actions allow for the transfer of control between pages. Second, actions support the specification of Java applets in a browser-independent manner. Finally, actions enable JSP pages to interact with JavaBeans component objects residing on the server.

In addition, all custom tags defined via tag libraries take the form of JSP actions. The creation and use of custom tags is described in chapter 13. Finally, note that unlike directives and scripting elements, actions support only a single, XML-based syntax.

4.2.1 *Forward*

The <jsp:forward> action is used to permanently transfer control from a JSP page to another location on the local server. Any content generated by the current page is discarded, and processing of the request begins anew at the alternate location. The basic syntax for this JSP action is as follows:

```
<jsp:forward page="localURL" />
```

The page attribute of the <jsp:forward> action is used to specify this alternate location to which control should be transferred, which may be a static document, a CGI, a servlet, or another JSP page. Note that the browser from which the request was submitted is not notified when the request is transferred to this alternate URL. In particular, the location field at the top of the browser window will continue to display the URL that was originally requested. The behavior of the <jsp:forward> action is depicted in figure 4.1.

For added flexibility, the `<jsp:forward>` action supports the use of request-time attribute values (as described in chapter 2) for the `page` attribute. Specifically, this means that a JSP expression can be used to specify the value of the `page` attribute, as in the following example:

```
<jsp:forward page='<%= "message" + statusCode + ".html" %>' />
```

Every time the page is processed for a request and the `<jsp:forward>` action is to be taken, this expression will be evaluated by the JSP container, and the resulting value will be interpreted as the URL to which the request should be forwarded. In this particular example, the URL value is constructed by concatenating two constant `String` values with the value of some local variable named `statusCode`. If, for example, the value of `statusCode` were 404, then this action would forward control to the local URL, `message404.html`.

As mentioned above, the `<jsp:forward>` action can be used to transfer control to any other document on the local server. For the specific case when control is transferred to another JSP page, the JSP container will automatically assign a new `pageContext` object to the forwarded page. The `request` object and the `session` object, though, will be the same for both the original page and the forwarded page. Sharing of the `application` object depends upon whether or not the two pages are both part of the same application, as described earlier in this chapter. As a result, some but not all of the attribute values accessible from the original page will be accessible on the forwarded page, depending upon their scope: page attributes are not shared, request and session attributes are, and application attributes may or may not be shared. If you need to transfer data as well as control from one page to another, the typical approach is to store this data either in the request or in the session, depending upon how much longer the data will be needed. (Recall, however, that the `session` object is available only on pages which are marked as participating in session management.)

TIP   All of the objects in which JSP pages can store attribute values are also accessible via the servlet API. As a result, this approach can also be used to transfer data when forwarding from a JSP page to a servlet.

Since the `request` object is common to both the original page and the forwarded page, any request parameters that were available on the original page will also be accessible from the forwarded page. It is also possible to specify additional request parameters to be sent to the forwarded page through use of the

`<jsp:param>` tag within the body of the `<jsp:forward>` action. The syntax for this second form of the `<jsp:forward>` action is as follows:

```
<jsp:forward page="localURL">
  <jsp:param name="parameterName1"
             value="parameterValue1"/>
     ...
  <jsp:param name="parameterNameN"
             value="parameterValueN"/>
</jsp:forward>
```

For each `<jsp:param>` tag, the `name` attribute identifies the request parameter to be set and the `value` attribute provides the corresponding value. This value can be either a static character string or a request-time attribute value (i.e., a JSP expression). There is no limit on the number of request parameters that may be specified in this manner. Note also that the passing of additional request parameters is independent of the type of document to which control is transferred; the `<jsp:param>` tag can thus be used to set request parameters for JSP pages, servlets, CGI scripts, and so forth.

NOTE   As you might infer from the inclusion of `getParameterValues()` among the methods of the `request` implicit object listed in table 4.4, HTTP request parameters can actually have multiple values. The effect of the `<jsp:param>` tag when used with the `<jsp:forward>` and `<jsp:include>` actions is to add a value to a particular parameter, rather than simply set its value.

This means that if a request parameter has already been assigned one or more values by some other mechanism, the `<jsp:param>` tag will simply add the specified value to those already present. Note, however, that this new value will be added as the first (or primary) value of the request parameter, so subsequent calls to the `getParameter()` method, which returns only one value, will in fact return the value added by the `<jsp:param>` tag.

If the `<jsp:param>` tag is applied to a request parameter that does not already have any values, then the value specified in the tag becomes the parameter's first and only value. Again, subsequent calls to `getParameter()` will return the value set by the tag.

Given that the `<jsp:forward>` action effectively terminates the processing of the current page in favor of the forwarded page, this tag is typically used in conditional code. Although the `<jsp:forward>` action could be used to create a page which generates no content of its own, but simply uses the `<jsp:param>` tag to set request parameters for some other page, scenarios such as the following are much more common:

```
<% if (! database.isAvailable()) { %>
    <% Notify the user about routine maintenance. %>
    <jsp:forward page="db-maintenance.html"/>
<% } %>
<%-- Database is up, proceeed as usual... --%>
```

Here, a method is called to check whether or not a hypothetical database server is available. If not, control is forwarded to a static HTML page which informs the user that the database is currently down for routine maintenance. If the server is up and running, then processing of the page continues normally, as indicated in the comment following the conditional code.

One factor that you need to keep in mind when using this tag is its interaction with output buffering. When the processing of a page request encounters the `<jsp:forward>` tag, all of the output generated thus far must be discarded by clearing the output buffer. If the output buffer has already been flushed at least once, however, some of the output from the page will already have been sent to the user's browser. In this case, it is impossible to discard that output. Therefore, if the output buffer associated with the current page request has ever been flushed prior to the `<jsp:forward>` action, the action will fail, and an `IllegalStateException` will be thrown.

As a result, any page that employs the `<jsp:forward>` action should be checked to make sure that its output buffer is large enough to ensure that it will not be flushed prior to any calls to this action. Alternatively, if output buffering is disabled for the page, then any code which might call the `<jsp:forward>` action must appear on the page before any static or dynamic elements that generate output.

The final consideration in the use of this tag is the issue of cleanup code. If a JSP page allocates request-specific resources, corresponding cleanup code may need to be run from the page once those resources are no longer needed. If such a page makes use of the `<jsp:forward>` tag, then processing of that page will end if and when this tag is reached. Any cleanup code that appears in the JSP file after the `<jsp:forward>` tag will therefore not be run if processing of the page causes this action to be taken. Dependent upon the logic in the page, then, it may be necessary to include a call to the cleanup code just before the `<jsp:forward>` tag, in order to make sure that resources are managed properly.

4.2.2 *Include*

The `<jsp:include>` action enables page authors to incorporate the content generated by another local document into the output of the current page. The output from the included document is inserted into the original page's output in place of the `<jsp:include>` tag, after which processing of the original page resumes. In contrast to the `<jsp:forward>` tag, then, this action is used to *temporarily* transfer control from a JSP page to another location on the local server.

The `<jsp:include>` action takes the following form:

```
<jsp:include page="localURL" flush="true" />
```

The `page` attribute of the `<jsp:include>` action is used to identify the document whose output is to be inserted into the current page, and is specified as a URL on the local server (i.e., there is no host or protocol information in the URL, just directories and a filename). The included page can be a static document, a CGI, a servlet, or another JSP page. As with the `<jsp:forward>` action, the `page` attribute of the `<jsp:include>` action supports request-time attribute values (i.e., specifying its value via a JSP expression).

The `flush` attribute of the `<jsp:include>` action controls whether or not the output buffer for the current page (if any) is flushed prior to including the content from the included page. As of version 1.1 of the JSP specification, it is required that the `flush` attribute be set to `true`, indicating that the buffer is flushed before processing of the included page begins. This is a result of current limitations in the underlying servlet API; as such, this requirement may be relaxed in subsequent versions of the specification.

Note that because the output buffer is flushed as the first step in performing the `<jsp:include>` action, the standard restrictions on the behavior of JSP pages after the buffer has been flushed apply. In particular, forwarding to another page—including an error page—is not possible. Likewise, setting cookies or other HTTP headers will not succeed if attempted after processing a `<jsp:include>` tag. For similar reasons, attempting to forward requests or set headers or cookies in the included page will also fail (in fact, an exception will be thrown), although it is perfectly valid for an included page to itself include other pages via the `<jsp:include>` action.

As with pages accessed via the `<jsp:forward>` action, JSP pages processed via the `<jsp:include>` tag will be assigned a new `pageContext` object, but will share the same `request` and `session` objects as the original page, and may or may not share the same `application` object. As was also the case with the `<jsp:forward>` action, then, the best way to transfer information from the original page to an included JSP page (or servlet) is by storing the data as an attribute of either the `request` object or the `session` object, depending upon its expected longevity.

Another element of functionality that the `<jsp:include>` action has in common with the `<jsp:forward>` action is the ability to specify additional request parameters for the included document. Again, this is accomplished via use of the `<jsp:param>` tag within the body of the `<jsp:include>` action, as follows:

```
<jsp:include page="localURL" flush="true">
  <jsp:param name="parameterName1"
             value="parameterValue1"/>
    ...
  <jsp:param name="parameterNameN"
             value="parameterValueN"/>
</jsp:include>
```

As before, the `name` attribute of the `<jsp:param>` tag identifies the request parameter to be set and the `value` attribute provides the corresponding value (which may be a request-time attribute value), and there is no limit on the number of request parameters that may be specified in this manner, or on the type of document to which the request parameters will be passed.

As indicated in figure 4.2, the `<jsp:include>` action works by passing its request on to the included page, which is then handled by the JSP container as it would handle any other request. The output from the included page is then folded into the output of the original page, which resumes processing. This incorporation of content takes place at the time the request is handled. In addition, because the JSP container automatically generates and compiles new servlets for JSP pages that have changed, if the text in a JSP file included via the `<jsp:include>` action is changed, the changes will automatically be reflected in the output of the including file. When the request is directed from the original file to the included JSP page, the standard JSP mechanisms—that is, translation into a stand-alone servlet, with automatic recompilation of changed files—are employed to process the included page.

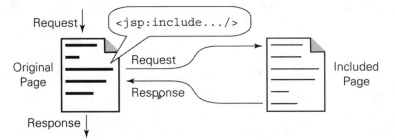

Figure 4.2 Effect of the `<jsp:include>` action on the processing of a request

In contrast, the JSP `include` directive, described in the previous chapter, does not automatically update the including page when the included file is modified. This is because the `include` directive takes effect when the including page is translated into a servlet, effectively merging the base contents of the included page into those of the original. The `<jsp:include>` action takes effect when processing requests, and merges the output from the included page, rather than its original text.

There are a number of tradeoffs, then, that must be considered when deciding whether to use the action or the directive. The `<jsp:include>` action provides the benefits of automatic recompilation, smaller class sizes (since the code corresponding to the included file is not repeated in the servlets for every including JSP page), and the option of specifying additional request parameters. The `<jsp:include>` action also supports the use of request-time attribute values for dynamically specifying the included page, which the directive does not. Furthermore, the `include` directive can only incorporate content from a static document (e.g., HTML) or another JSP page. The `<jsp:include>` action, since it includes the output from an included URL rather than the contents of an included source document, can be used to include dynamically generated output, such as from a servlet or a CGI script.

On the other hand, the `include` directive offers the option of sharing local variables, as well as slightly better run-time efficiency, since it avoids the overhead of dispatching the request to the included page and then incorporating the response into the output of the original page. In addition, because the `include` directive is processed during page translation and compilation, rather than during request handling, it does not impose any restrictions on output buffering. As long as the output buffer is sufficiently large, pages which utilize the `include` directive are not limited with respect to setting headers and cookies or forwarding requests.

4.2.3 *Plug-in*

The `<jsp:plugin>` action is used to generate browser-specific HTML for specifying Java applets which rely on Sun Microsystem's Java plug-in. As the primary focus of this book is the use of JSP for server-side Java applications rather than client-side applications, details on the use of this action may be found in appendix B.

4.2.4 *Bean tags*

JSP provides three different actions for interacting with server-side JavaBeans: `<jsp:useBean>`, `<jsp:setProperty>`, and `<jsp:getProperty>`. Because component-centric design provides key strengths with respect to separation of presentation and application logic, the next two chapters are devoted to the interaction between JSP and JavaBeans.

Using JSP components

5

This chapter covers

- The JSP component model
- JavaBean fundamentals
- Interacting with components through JSP

111

JSP scriptlets and expressions allow developers to add dynamic elements to web pages by interleaving their HTML pages with Java code. While this is a great way for Java programmers to create web-based applications and expressive sites, in general this approach lacks an elegant separation between presentation and implementation, and requires the content developer to be well versed in the Java programming language. Along with scripting, JSP provides an alternative, component-centric approach to dynamic page design. JSP allows content developers to interact with Java components not only though Java code, but through HTML-like tags as well. This approach allows for a cleaner division of labor between application and content developers.

5.1   *The JSP component model*

The JSP component model is centered on software components called JavaBeans. Before we can explain the specifics of JavaBeans and how they relate to JSP development we must first understand the role of software components in the development process. Once we have an understanding of component based design principles we will learn how to apply these techniques to web page design in JSP.

5.1.1   *Component architectures*

Components are self-contained, reusable software elements that encapsulate application behavior or data into a discrete package. You can think of

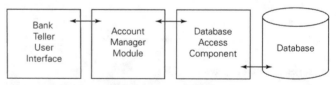

Figure 5.1   **A component-based application**

components as black box devices that perform specific operations without revealing the details of what's going on under the hood. Because they abstract their behavior from their implementation, they shield their user from messy details—providing added functionality without increased complexity. Components are stand-alone and not bound tightly to any single application or use. This allows them to be used as building blocks for multiple, potentially unrelated projects. These two principles, abstraction and reusability, are the cornerstones of component-centric design. Figure 5.1 illustrates how a collection of independent software components is assembled to form a complete solution.

Think of components as reusable software elements that we can glue together to construct our applications. A good component model allows us to eliminate or greatly reduce the amount of glue code necessary to build our applications. Component architectures work by employing an interface that allows our components to work together in a more integrated fashion. It is this commonality that binds components together and allows them to be used by development tools that understand the interface to further simplify development.

5.1.2 *Benefits of a component architecture*

Let's look at an example of component-centric design that's a little more concrete. When an architect designs a new home he or she relies on components to save time, reduce complexity, and cut costs. Rather than design every wall unit, window frame, and electrical system from scratch he or she uses existing components to simplify the task. Architects don't design a custom air-conditioning system; they select an existing unit that will fit their requirements from the many models available on the market. There's a good chance that the architect doesn't have the skills or resources to design an air-conditioning system anyway. And conversely the designer of the air-conditioning system probably couldn't build a house. Because of this component-based approach the architect and contractor can concentrate on building what they know best—houses, and the air-conditioning company can build air-conditioners. Component architectures allow us to hide a component's complexity behind an interface that allows it to interact with its environment or other components. It isn't necessary to know the details of how a component works in order to access its functionality.

We can use this real world example to illustrate another important feature of component design—reusability. The construction company can select an off-the-shelf air-conditioner because it supports standard connectors, fastens with standard screws, and runs off a standard electric voltage. Later, if the homeowner decides to replace the unit with a new and improved model, there is no need to rebuild the house—simply swap out the old component for the new. Standardized environments and design specifications have allowed for a flexible system that is easily maintained. Software components are designed to operate in specific environments, and interact in predetermined ways. The fact that components must follow a certain set of rules allows us to design systems that can accept a wide array of components.

Component development

While it would be nice if we could design our entire application from preexisting components, that's an approach that's rarely practical for real application design. Usually an application developed with a component approach involves a combination of general purpose and application specific components. The benefits of component reuse surface not only by sharing components among differing applications, but through reuse of components across several segments of the same or related applications.

A banking application, for example, might have several different customer interfaces, an employee access module, and an administrative screen. Each of these related applications could make use of a common component that contained all of the knowledge necessary to display the specifics of a particular bank account. With luck, and good forethought during component design, this banking component might be useful to anyone developing financial management applications.

Once a component has been designed, the component's author is relatively free to change its inner-workings without having to track down all of the component's users. The key to achieving this high level of abstractness is defining an interface that shields any application relying on the component from the details of its implementation.

5.1.3 *Component design for web projects*

A component-based approach is ideal for the design of web applications. JSP lets web designers employ the same component design principles that other software developers have been using for years. Rather than having to embed complex logic directly into pages through scripting code, or building page content into the programming logic, they can simply employ HTML layout around components. The component model's ability to reuse common components can reduce development time and project complexity.

Isolating application logic from presentation layout is a necessity for web development organizations that are built around teams whose members have a diverse set of complementary skill sets. In many enterprises the web team is composed of both application developers and web developers. Java application developers are skilled in tasks such as exchanging information with a database and optimizing back-end server code for performance, while web developers are good with the presentation aspects like interface design and content layout. In a componentized JSP development project, application developers are free to concentrate on developing components that encapsulate program logic, while web developers build the application around these components, focusing their energies on its presentation. As illustrated in figure 5.2, clearly defined boundaries between an application's core functionality and its presentation to its user allow for a clearer separation of responsibilities between development teams.

In some cases a single person may handle both aspects of design, but as project complexity grows, splitting up the tasks of the development process can yield a number of benefits. Even for web projects being handled by a small, unified team of developers, a component-based architecture makes sense. The flexibility offered by components allows a project to handle the sudden changes in requirements that often seem to accompany web projects.

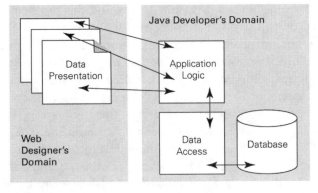

Figure 5.2   Division of labor in a web application's development

5.1.4   *Building applications from components*

So how can we use these component design principles in the design of web applications? Let's look at how we might develop a web shopping application with such an approach. As is typical for an enterprise application, this example involves collecting information from a database based on user input, performing some calculations on the data, and displaying the results to the user. In this case we will display a catalog of items, allow the user to select some for purchase, and calculate tax and shipping costs, before sending the total back to the user.

What we want to end up with is an online form that allows us to enter the customer's purchases, and, upon submitting the form, returns a new page with a nicely formatted invoice that includes shipping fees and tax. Our page designers should have no problem creating an attractive input form and invoice page, and our developers can easily calculate shipping and tax costs. It is only the interaction between the two worlds that gets a little sticky. What technologies are best utilized in the design of such an application?

Since our product catalog is stored in a database, that portion of the application has to be tied to the server, but where should the tax and shipping calculations take place? We could use a client-side scripting approach with something like JavaScript. However, JavaScript isn't supported in every browser, and would reveal our calculations in the source of our page. Important calculations like shipping and tax should be confined to the server for security purposes; we certainly don't want the client browser performing the task.

A server-side approach using JSP scripts would get around this problem. We can access back-end resources with the code running safely on the server. While this approach works well for smaller projects, it creates a number of difficulties for a project such as this one. Directly imbedding JSP scripts into all of our pages introduces a high degree of intermingling between our HTML page design and our business logic. Our web designers and application developers will require a detailed understanding of each other's work in order to create the application. We could choose to have the developers create a bare-bones implementation, then let our designers polish it up. Or, we could let the designers develop a nice page layout with no logic in it and then have the application developer punch in the code to calculate tax and shipping. Does that provide the division of labor we're looking for? Not quite.

A problem with this approach surfaces when we deploy and maintain our application. Consider, for example, what happens when our catalog sales application (originally developed for use by a single location of the company) becomes so wildly successful our bosses decide to deploy it companywide to all twenty-eight branches. Of course the sales tax is different at each branch so we make twenty-eight copies of our page and find an application developer familiar with the code to make the necessary changes to the JSP scripts. Then, we have to get our web developers to change the HTML of each page to correct any branch-specific design or branding issues. Over the course of the application's lifetime we will constantly have to fiddle with calculations, fix bugs, increase shipping rates, update the design, and add new features. All of this work must happen across twenty-eight different versions of the code. Why should we need two groups of people doing the same job twenty-eight times over?

A web application developed around components offers a better approach. With the ability to deploy components into our HTML pages we can allow our application developers to design tax and shipping calculating components that can be configured at run time with determining factors like the local tax rate. Our web page developers can then rely on these components without having to involve the application developers each time some HTML needs to be changed or a new version of the page created. On the application development side any bug fixes or updates would be isolated to the components themselves and would not affect our web page developer's duties. So how do components fit in with JSP? JSP leverages the JavaBeans component model, which we'll explore next.

5.2   *JavaBean fundamentals*

JavaBeans are software components written in Java. The components themselves are called *Beans* and must adhere to specifications outlined in the JavaBeans API. The JavaBeans API was created by Sun with the cooperation of the industry and dictates the rules that software developers must follow in order to create stand-alone, reusable software components. Like many other software components, Beans encapsulate both state and behavior. By using JSP's collection of Bean-related tags in their web pages, content developers can leverage the power of Java to add dynamic elements to their pages without writing a single line of Java code. Before delving into the specifics of working with Beans in JSP, we need to learn more about the Beans themselves.

Bean containers

A *Bean container* is an application, environment, or programming language that allows developers to call up Beans, configure them, and access their information and behavior. Applications that use Beans are composed purely of Java code, but Bean containers allow developers to work with it at a higher conceptual level. This is possible because JavaBeans expose their features and behavior to the Bean container, allowing the developer to work with the Bean in a more intuitive fashion. The Bean container defines its own way of presenting and interacting with the Bean and writes the resulting Java code itself.

If you have used Sun's Bean Box, IBM's Visual Age for Java, Visual Café, or other Java development tools you've already had some experience with Beans. These applications include Bean containers that work with Beans in a visual format. With these tools you can build an application by simply dragging Bean icons into position and defining the specifics of their behavior and their connections to other Beans. The application then generates all of the necessary Java code. Like these visual tools, JSP containers allow developers to create web-based Java applications without needing to write Java. In JSP we interact with Beans through a collection of tags that we can embed inside our HTML.

Bean properties

Bean containers allow you to work with Beans in terms of *properties*—named attributes of the Bean that maintain its state and control its behavior. A Bean is defined by its properties, and would be pretty much useless without them. Bean properties can be modified at run time by the Bean container to control specifics of the Bean's behavior. These property values are the sole mechanism the Bean container uses to expose Beans to the developer.

As an example, let's suppose we have a Bean called `WeatherBean` that knows various things about the current weather conditions and forecasts. The Bean could collect current weather information from the National Weather Service computers, or extract it from a database—the point being that as the Bean's user we do not need to understand the specifics of how the Bean gets its information. All we care about as developers is that the `WeatherBean` is able to give us information like the current temperature, the projected high, or the chances for rain. Each of these bits of information is exposed to the Bean container as a property of the Bean whose value we can access for our web page or application.

Each Bean will have a different set of properties depending on the type of information it contains. We can customize a Bean by setting some its property values ourselves. The Bean's creator will impose restrictions on each property of the Bean, controlling our access to it. A property can be read-only, write-only, or readable and writable. This concept of accessibility allows the Bean designer to impose limits on how the Beans can be used. In our `WeatherBean`, for example, it doesn't make any sense to allow developers to modify the value of the Bean's property representing today's high temperature. That information is managed by the Bean itself and should be left read-only. On the other hand, if the Bean had a property controlling the ZIP code of the region in whose weather we are interested, it would certainly make sense to allow developers to specify it. Such a property would be writable, and probably readable as well.

NOTE   As we'll learn in detail in chapter 6, behind the scenes JavaBeans are merely Java objects. A JavaBean's properties map to the methods of a Java object that manipulates its state. So when you set a property of a Bean, it's like a shortcut for calling object methods through Java. Likewise, viewing the current value of a Bean's property is essentially calling a method of an object and getting its results. We'll learn how a Java object's methods map into Bean properties in the next chapter.

Trigger and linked properties

Some properties are used to trigger behavior as well as report information and are thus called *trigger properties*. Reading from or writing to a trigger property signals the Bean to perform an activity on the back end. These triggers, once activated, can either update the values of other properties or cause something to happen on the back end. Changing the value of our ZIP code property for example might cause the Bean to run off to the National Weather Service, request weather conditions in the new ZIP code, and update its other weather related properties accordingly. In that case the weather properties and the ZIP code property are considered *linked properties* because changing the value of one updates the values of others.

Indexed properties

It is also possible for a single property to store a collection of values. These properties are known as *indexed properties* because each value stored in the property is accessed through an index number, which specifies which particular value you want. For example you can request the first value in the list, the third, or the twenty-seventh. Our `WeatherBean` could have a property that holds forecasted temperatures for the next five days, for example. Not every Bean container provides a simple mechanism for working with these multivalue properties directly, however. The JSP Bean tags, for example, do not recognize indexed properties. Instead, you must use JSP scriptlets, JSP expressions, or custom JSP tags (discussed in chapters 13 and 14) to access them.

Property data types

Bean properties can be used to hold a wide array of information. `WeatherBean`'s properties would need to store everything from temperatures to rainfall odds, forecasts, ZIP codes, and more. Each property of a Bean can hold only one specific type of data such as text or a number. Bean property values are assigned a Java data type, which is used internally by the Bean and in the Java code generated by the Bean container. As you might expect, properties can hold any of the Java primitives like `int` or `double`, as well as Java objects like `Strings` and `Dates`. Properties can also store user-defined objects and even other Beans. Indexed properties generally store an array of values, each of the same data type.

The Bean container determines how we work with the property values of a Bean. With JSP scriptlets and expressions we reference property values by their Java data type. If a property stores integer values we get integer values out of it and must put integer values into it. With Bean tags, however, we treat every property as if it were stored text, or in Java parlance, a `String`. When you set the value of a Bean property, you pass it text. Likewise, when you read the contents of a property you get back text, regardless of the internal data type used inside the Bean. This text-only strategy keeps JSP Bean tags simple to work with and fits in nicely with HTML.

The JSP container automatically performs all of the necessary type conversions. When you set an integer property, for example, it performs the necessary Java calls to convert the series of numeric characters you gave it into an actual integer value. Of course this conversion process requires you to pass in appropriate text values that Java can correctly covert into the native data type. If a property handles floating point values, for example, it would throw an error if you attempted to set the value to something like banana bread, one hundred, or (3,9).

Clever Bean designers can control property values themselves by accepting string values for nonstring properties and performing the conversions themselves. For any value which is neither a string nor a Java primitive type, this technique must be used. Therefore it might be perfectly legal to set an integer property to one hundred, provided the Bean's designer had prepared it for such input.

Bean property sheets

A Bean's capabilities are documented in a table called a property sheet which lists all of the properties available on the Bean, their level of access afforded to the users, and their Java type. Property sheets may also specify example or valid values for each property of the Bean. Table 5.1 shows the property sheet for the WeatherBean component that we have been using.

Table 5.1   Property sheet examples

Name	Access	Java Type	Example Value
zipCode	read/write	String	77630
currentTemp	read-only	int	87
todaysHigh	read-only	int	101
todaysLow	read-only	int	85
rainOdds	read-only	float	0.95
forecasts	read-only	String[]	Sunny, Rainy, Cloudy, Sunny, Hot
iconURL	read-only	URL	http://imageserver/weather/rainy.gif

Property sheets allow Bean designers to describe the features of a Bean to its users, such as JSP developers, servlet programmers, and the like. From the property sheet a developer can determine what type of information the Bean can contain and what behavior it can provide. Of course, the property sheet alone may not be enough to adequately explain the behavior of a Bean to the end user. In this case additional information can be communicated through the Bean's documentation.

5.2.1   The different types of JavaBeans

For purposes of discussion we can think of Beans as falling into three general categories: *visual component Beans* used as elements of graphical user interfaces (GUI), *data Beans* that provide access to a collection of information, and *service Beans* (also known as *worker* Beans) that can perform specific tasks or calculations. Of course some Beans can be classified in more than one category.

Visual component Beans

The development of visual components has been one of the most common uses of JavaBeans. Visual components are elements such as text fields, selectors, or other widgets useful for building user interfaces. By packaging GUI components into Beans, Java development environments can take advantage of JavaBean's support for visual programming. This allows developers to create their interfaces by simply dragging the desired elements into position. Since visual Beans have been designed to run as part of graphical Java applications, they are not compatible with JSP, which is intended for text-based applications such as HTML interface design.

Data Beans

Data Beans provide a convenient way to access data that a Bean itself does not necessarily have the capability to collect or generate. The calculation or collection of the data stored inside Data Beans is the responsibility of some other, more complex component or service. Data Beans are typically read-only, allowing you to fetch data from them but not allowing you to modify their values on your own.

However, some Data Beans allow you to set some of their properties in order to control how data is formatted or filtered before being returned through other properties. For example, an `AccountStatusBean` might also have a `currencyType` property that controls whether the balance property returned data in dollars, pounds, or Swiss francs. Because of their simplicity, Data Beans are useful to standardize access to information by providing a stable interface.

Service Beans

Service Beans, as you might expect, provide access to a behavior or particular service. For this reason they are sometimes referred to as worker Beans. They can retrieve information from a database, perform calculations, or format information. Since the only way that we can interact with a Bean is through its properties, this is how we will access a Bean's services. In a typical design, we will set the value of certain properties that control the Bean's behavior, and then read the results of the request through other properties. A Bean designed to access a database of employee phone numbers, for example, might have a property called `employee`, which we could set to the name we wish to look up. Setting this property triggers the database search and sets the `phone` and `email` properties of the Bean to reflect the information of the requested employee.

Not all service Beans collect data from a back-end source. Some simply encapsulate the logic necessary to perform calculations, conversions, or operations. A `StatisticsBean` might know how to calculate averages, medians, and standard deviations, for example. A `UnitConversionBean` might allow the page designer to specify some distance in inches and get it back in feet, yards, miles, or furlongs.

Some service Beans will not return any information. Their service may be to store information in a database or log file, for example. In this case, you might set a property's value not to get results of the service, but simply for its side-effect behavior—what happens on the back end. Service Beans allow for a clear separation of responsibility and for teams to have separate knowledge domains. The web designer doesn't need to understand statistical calculations and the programmer doesn't need to understand subtleties of page layout. A change in either the presentation or the program logic will not affect the others, provided the Bean's interface does not change.

5.3   JSP Bean tags

Now that we have a good understanding of the principles of component architecture and JavaBeans we can get into the nitty-gritty of building web pages around them. JSP has a set of Bean tags which can be used to place Beans into a page, then access their properties. Unlike JSP scriptlets and expressions we explored in the previous chapter, you do not need to be a Java programmer in order to design pages around Beans. In fact, you don't need to be any type of programmer at all because JSP does a pretty good job of eliminating the need for messy glue between our HTML and components.

5.3.1   Tag-based component programming

JSP needs only three simple tags to enable interaction with JavaBeans. These tags allow you to place Beans into the page as well as alter and access their properties. Some people complain about the simplicity of the JSP tag set, preferring an approach that embeds more functionality into the tags themselves similar to PHP or ColdFusion. It is important to understand that the limited set of functionality afforded to JSP Bean tags is intentional. They are not meant to provide a full-featured programming language; programmers can use JSP scriptlets for that. Instead, the Bean tags enable the use of component design strategies in HTML documents without the need for the page author to learn a programming language or to understand advanced programming concepts.

As always, there is a fine line in determining the trade-off between the power of a language and its complexity. As a good compromise, the JSP designers elected to keep the core functionality very simple, defining only a few tags for working with Beans and establishing a specification that allows for the development of new, custom tags that solve specific problems. The standard tags allow you to create references to Beans you need to use, set the values of any configurable properties they might have, and read information from the Bean's properties. Custom tags with more complex levels of functionality can be developed by individuals and organizations and integrated into any JSP environment through an extension mechanism known as custom tag libraries. Through custom tags the JSP language can be extended to support additional programming constructs, like conditionals and loops, as well as provide additional functionality such as direct access to databases. We'll learn about custom tags and tag libraries in chapters 13 and 14.

An illustrative example

Let's whet our appetite by looking at JSP code built around components, rather than scriptlets. This example shows some of the things we can accomplish with the component-centric design model, and will serve as a kick off to our discussion of JSP's component features.

```
<jsp:useBean id="user" class="RegisteredUser" scope="session"/>
<jsp:useBean id="news" class="NewsReports" scope="request">
  <jsp:setProperty name="news" property="category" value="financial"/>
  <jsp:setProprety name="news" property="maxItems" value="5"/>
</jsp:useBean>
<html>
<body>
Welcome back <jsp:getProperty name="user" property="fullName"/>,
your last visit was on
<jsp:getProperty name="user" property="lastVisitDate"/>.
Glad to see you again!
<P>
There are <jsp:getProperty name="news" property="newItems"/> new articles
available for your reading pleasure. Please enjoy your stay and come back soon.
</body>
</html>
```

Notice how straightforward the page design has become? We have used a few special JSP tags to eliminate all of the Java code from our page. Even though we have not yet discussed the specifics of any of the Bean tags, you probably already have a good idea of what the code does just by looking at it. It uses two components, user and news. The first allows us to greet visitors personally, and the second stores news items in which they might be interested. JSP Bean tags allow us to more clearly understand the page's layout because we are writing HTML, not code. Figure 5.3 shows what the page looks like on the browser.

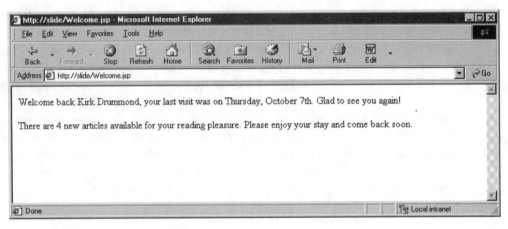

Figure 5.3   Dynamic content with JSP

5.3.2   Accessing JSP components

To interact with a Bean we first tell the page where to find the Java class file that defines the Bean and assign it a name. We can then use this name to access the values stored in the Bean's properties. By mastering just three simple JSP tags you can add component-based web page design to your repertoire. We will look at each of these tags in-depth.

The <jsp:useBean> tag

The <jsp:useBean> tag tells the page that we want to make a Bean available to the page. The tag is used to create a Bean or fetch an existing one from the server. Attributes of the tag specify the type of Bean you wish to use and assign it a name we can use to refer to it. The <jsp:useBean> tag comes in two forms, a single empty tag and a matching pair of start and end tags that contain the body of the tag which can be used to specify additional configuration information. In its simplest and most straightforward form the <jsp:useBean> tag requires only two attributes, id and class. Like all of the JSP tags, you must enclose each attribute value in quotes. The basic syntax for the tag's two forms is:

```
<jsp:useBean id="bean name" class="class name"/>

<jsp:useBean id="bean name" class="class name">
   initialization code
</jsp:useBean>
```

Table 5.2 shows all of the possible attribute values supported by the `<jsp:use-Bean>` tag. We will discuss the purpose of each throughout the chapter, but for now we will concentrate on understanding the basic Bean tag attributes.

Table 5.2 Attributes of the `<jsp:useBean>` tag

Attribute	Value	Default	Example Value
id	Java identifier	none	`myBean`
scope	page, request, session, application	page	`session`
class	Java class name	none	`java.util.Date`
type	Java class name	same as class	`com.manning.jsp.AbstractPerson`
beanName	Java class or serialized Bean	none	`com.manning.jsp.USCurrency.ser`

The ID attribute

The `id` attribute specifies a name for the Bean—a unique value that will refer to this particular Bean throughout the page and over the course of its lifetime (we'll learn how to extend the Bean's life beyond the current page later). We can use multiple `<jsp:useBean>` tags to define more than one Bean within a page, even multiple instances of the same Bean class, as long as there is a unique identifier associated with each individual Bean. The name we select for our Bean is arbitrary, but it must follow some simple rules:

- It must be unique to the page
- It is case sensitive
- The first character must be a letter
- Only letters, numbers, and the underscore character (_) are allowed (no spaces!)

The class attribute

The value of the `class` attribute specifies the class name of the JavaBean itself. To help better organize code and avoid conflicts, Java classes are usually organized into *packages*. Packages are collections of individual Java class files organized inside a single directory. Package names are usually composed of multiple, period-separated names where each name is a directory in the package hierarchy. Unless you have used the `<%@ page %>` tag to give your page access to the Bean's package through its `import` attribute you must specify the fully qualified name of the Bean class. A fully qualified class name consists of the name of the class's package and the class name itself. By convention, packages begin with the Internet domain name of their creator, and usually include more levels of hierarchy to help better organize collections of classes into logical collections. The Bean's developer will determine the actual package and class name of the Bean. Some fully qualified Bean class names might look something like the following:

```
com.manning.RegisteredUserBean
com.deepmagic.beans.database.logging.LogBean
com.blokware.MagicPizzaBean
com.taglib.wdjsp.arch.EmployeeBean
```

The actual Bean class is the last part of the fully qualified name, so in the first example we are talking about a `RegisteredUserBean` inside the `com.manning` package. We can include this Bean with or without the package name, provided we first import all of the package's classes:

```
<% @page import="com.taglib.wdjsp.*" %>
<jsp:useBean name="user" class="RegisteredUserBean" />
```
    or just...
```
<jsp:useBean name="user" class="com.taglib.wdjsp.RegisteredUserBean" />
```

The type attribute

In practice you won't use this attribute too much. The `<jsp:useBean>` tag's `class` attribute determines which Java class is used to create our Bean, but JSP offers a way of fine-tuning the JSP container's interpretation of the Bean's type which is sometimes needed when Beans exist on the server and are not being instantiated by the current page. By default, the Bean is referenced by the class type corresponding directly to the underlying object's class. However, if you need to refer to the Bean as another type, for example a base class or an interface that the Bean implements, you can use the `type` attribute of the `<jsp:useBean>` tag to do so. The class type you specify is used to represent the Bean object in the Java resulting from the JSP compilation phase. The Bean's actual class must, of course, be assignable to the class type specified. If you specify both `class` and `type` attributes, the Bean will be created using the given class, then cast to the given type. The `type` attribute can only be used alone (that is without a corresponding `class` attribute) in cases where the Bean already exists on the server, a feature known as *scope* which we'll cover in the last section of this chapter.

The tag body

The tag's optional body portion can be used to initialize any user configurable properties of the Bean. This lets us configure a Bean specifically for this page or our particular application. We will discuss Bean initialization in detail later. For now, we'll look at Beans that do not require any special initialization at the time they are created.

<jsp:useBean> in action

Enough background, let's get into using the Bean tags. Here's an example of the `<jsp:useBean>` tag in action.

```
<jsp:useBean id="myclock" class="com.manning.jsp.ClockBean"/>
<html>
<body>
There is a Bean hiding in this page!
</body>
</html>
```

We've told the page that we will be using a Bean that is defined in the Java class file `ClockBean` in the `com.manning.jsp` package and we've named the Bean `myclock` for use in the page. In practice we like to put all of our `<jsp:useBean>` tags at the beginning of the HTML document, but syntactically it is valid to use the tag anywhere in the page. However, keep in mind that Beans are only available to portions of the page following the `<jsp:useBean>` tag in which they were defined. Portions of the page before the `<jsp:useBean>` tag will have no reference to the Bean, and attempting to access the Bean will cause an error.

The `<jsp:useBean>` tag creates an instance of the Bean and assigns its ID as specified by the `id` attribute. When the new Bean is created it performs any tasks or data processing as designed by the Bean's author. For example, the `ClockBean` sets its internal state to reflect the current time and date, while another Bean might look up information in a database. This is part of the normal Java instantiation process and happens without any help from you. Once a Bean has been given a name and been made available to the page we can begin using its properties. Depending on the Bean design, the properties may simply provide information such as the time of day or the name of the current user, or they might also execute complex transactions or look up information in a database. Whichever the case, the results are accessible through the Bean's properties.

It is important to understand the difference between a Bean's class and its instance. The Bean's class controls what type of Bean will be created, its properties, and capabilities. It is used like an object template to create a unique instance of the Bean with each call of the `<jsp:useBean>` tag. For example, consider the following tags:

```
<jsp:useBean id="clock1" class="com.manning.jsp.ClockBean" />
<jsp:useBean id="clock2" class="com.manning.jsp.ClockBean" />
```

This creates two independent, that is, completely separate, Beans with their own names: `clock1` and `clock2`. They are instances of the same class, but any changes made to one Bean will have no effect on the other. Later in this chapter we will talk about how other attributes of the `<jsp:useBean>` tag can allow a Bean to be reused between visits to a single page or across multiple pages throughout the site. In the examples above, our Beans are there, but we aren't actually using them to do anything. The next Bean tag, `<jsp:getProperty>` allows us to retrieve the information stored inside the Bean.

Accessing Bean properties with <jsp:getProperty>

The primary way to access a Bean's properties in JSP is through the `<jsp:getProperty>` tag. Unlike the `<jsp:useBean>` tag which performs some work behind the scenes but doesn't produce any output, the `<jsp:getProperty>` tag actually produces content that we can see in the HTML generated by the page. The `<jsp:getProperty>` tag is empty with no body element and expects two attributes, *name* and *property*. Its syntax is:

```
<jsp:getProperty name="bean name" property="property name"/>
```

The `name` attribute specifies the Bean we are evaluating, and should correspond to the name we selected for the Bean in the `<jsp:useBean>` tag's `id` attribute. Don't forget that the `<jsp:useBean>` tag refers to the Bean with the `id` attribute, and that other tags refer to the Bean through a `name` attribute. It is a JSP convention that the `id` attribute is used to define a new object, while the `name` attribute is used to reference an existing object. Be careful, it can be easy to confuse the two.

In the resulting HTML that is displayed at run time, the tag is replaced with the value of the property of the Bean you request. Of course, since we are creating an HTML document, the property is first converted into text by the JSP container. This tag is very easy to use. Let's look at the `ClockBean` example again, but this time we'll use the `<jsp:getProperty>` tag to ask the Bean to tell us what time it is:

```
<jsp:useBean id="myclock" class="com.manning.jsp.ClockBean"/>
<html>
<body>
The Bean says that the time is now:
<jsp:getProperty name="myclock" property="time"/>
</body>
</html>
```

This should display HTML that looks something like:

```
<html>
<body>
The Bean says that the time is now: 12:33 pm
</body>
</html>
```

You'll use this tag a lot, as it's the key to component-based dynamic output with JSP. You can use as many `<jsp:getProperty>` tags in your page as you need. You can intersperse them with HTML to not only dynamically generate single values and blocks of text, but to control attributes of the HTML as well. It is perfectly legal to nest JSP tags inside HTML attributes. A Bean's property could be used to control the page's background color, the width of a table, or the source of an image. For example, a Bean reflecting a standardized corporate style might have a property that exposes the URL location of the latest version of the corporate logo and the corporate color scheme. We can display this image in our HTML as shown below without hard coding the URL value in each page.

```
<jsp:useBean id="style" class="beans.CorporateStyleBean"/>
<html>
<body bgcolor="<jsp:getProperty name="style" property="color"/>">
<center>
<img src="<jsp:getProperty name="style" property="logo"/>">
Welcome to Big Corp!
</center>
</body>
</html>
```

This would generate HTML like this:

```
<html>
<body bgcolor="pink">
<center>
<img src="http://imageserver/logo.gif">
Welcome to Big Corp!
</center>
</body>
</html>
```

If the logo changes next week when the company replaces the corporate branding director, or is acquired, all of your pages will instantly reflect the new value built into the `CorporateStyleBean`. Another advantage here is that application programmers might be relying on the same Bean to brand their interfaces, and the change would be reflected there as well.

TIP   According to the specifications, white space in a document is not significant to the JSP parser, but should be preserved by the JSP processor. In some implementations that we have encountered, however, the parser does not properly preserve white space characters between JSP Bean tags when no other (non-white space) characters are present. For example, you would expect the following JSP code to display something like "Firstname Lastname", but instead you might get "FirstnameLastname":

```
<jsp:getProperty name="user" property="firstName"/>
<jsp:getProperty name="user" property="lastName"/>
```

This might happen because the JSP parser ignored the newline, which would normally be treated as a whitespace character. If this happens, adding blank lines probably won't help as the JSP parser would simply ignore them too, assuming that there was nothing relevant between the two Bean tags.

If your JSP container suffers from this annoyance, you can work around it by placing meaningful, but empty content, such as an HTML comment, which should force it to preserve the newline character in the page output.

```
<jsp:getProperty name="user" property="firstName"/>
<!-- insert a space -->
<jsp:getProperty name="user" property="lastName"/>
```

The <jsp:setProperty> tag

We use `<jsp:setProperty>` to modify the properties of Beans. The `<jsp:set-Property>` tag can be used anywhere within the page to modify a Bean's properties, provided that the property has been made writable by the Bean developer. We modify property values of a Bean either to control specifics of the Bean's operation or access its services. The exact behavior of changing a property's value is Bean specific. The Bean's author might, for example, provide a `query` property that specifies a database query whose results are reflected in other properties. In that case you might call `<jsp:setProperty>` several times in the page, reading the results properties again and again, since they would return new values after each change to the `query` property.

Most service Beans will require some amount of run-time configuration to be useful, because they depend on user-configurable properties that control some aspect of their behavior. This allows the same Bean to be used over and over again to encapsulate different sets of information. For example, if a developer needed a Bean to provide information about a registered user it would not be necessary to create a different type of Bean for each user——`BobBean`, `SueBean`, `JoeBean`, and so forth. The developer would instead design the Bean's properties to abstractly refer to properties of any user, and then make one of the Bean's properties control which user's information is stored in the Bean

The `<jsp:setProperty>` tag is relatively straightforward. It requires three attributes: `name`, `property`, and `value`. Just as in the `<jsp:getProperty>` tag, the `name` attribute specifies the Bean you are working with; the `property` attribute specifies which of the Bean's properties you wish to set; the `value` attribute is text that you want to set the property to.

```
<jsp:setProperty name="bean name" property="property name"/>
```

The `<jsp:setProperty>` tag can be used anywhere inside the JSP document after the Bean has been defined with the `<jsp:useBean>` tag. At run time JSP evaluates the tags in a page in the order they were defined, from top to bottom. Any property values that you set will only affect tags in the page that follow the `<jsp:setProperty>` tag. The `value` attribute can be specified as text or calculated at run time with JSP expressions. For example, here are a couple of ways that we can set the days since a user's last visit by setting the value of a property. Both examples are functionally equivalent, they set the `daysLeft` property to a value of `30`.

```
<jsp:setProperty name="user" property="daysLeft" value="30"/>
<jsp:setProperty name="user" property="daysLeft" value="<%= 15 * 2 %>"/>
```

Indexed properties

As we mentioned earlier, indexed properties contain a whole collection of values for the property. To access a value, you must pass the Bean an index to indicate which value you are interested in. The standard JSP Bean tags cannot deal with indexed properties; they can only be accessed through JSP scriptlets, expressions, and custom tags. For example, let's look at `WeatherBean`'s `forecasts` property, which holds five `String` values, a forecast for each of the next five days. To view tomorrow's forecast we must specify the first element, which is referenced in array style notation as element `0`, the next day's is element `1`, and so forth. You access an indexed property through a JSP scriptlet or expression simply by calling the method behind the property and passing it an index value. To read from an indexed property, prefix it with the word `get`; to write to it use the prefix `set`. (We'll explain how properties are mapped to method names in detail later in chapter 6.) To read from the `forecasts` property we would call the method `getForecasts()`. For example,

```
<B>Tomorrow's Forecast</B>: <%= weather.getForecasts(0) %> <BR>
<B>The Rest of the Week</B>
<UL>
<% for (int index=1; index < 5; index++) { %>
<LI><%= weather.getForecasts(index) %> (maybe)
<% } %>
</UL>
```

In the above example we use JSP scriptlets and expressions to access the indexed forecasts property of our WeatherBean, which has been loaded into the page with an id of weather. To display the forecast for tomorrow, we use a JSP expression to get the first element of the forecasts property by calling its access method, get-Forecasts(), with an argument of 0. We then use a scriptlet to loop through elements 1, 2, 3, and 4 to display a list of the forecasts for the rest of the week.

Beans with indexed properties can be designed to work more easily with JSPs so that the JSP developer doesn't have to resort to scriptlets in order to access them. A Bean can include a convenience property that allows you to treat an indexed property as a single string value by separating each value with a comma or other delimiter.

5.3.3 Initializing Beans

When a Bean is first created it can be initialized by setting the value of its configurable properties. This initialization happens only the first time the Bean is created. By default, this initialization phase will take place each time the page is accessed, since a Bean is being created for each request. As we will see later when we discuss the Bean life cycle, Beans can also be stored in and retrieved from the environment of the web server, in which case they will not need to be reinitialized.

When a Bean is first created it may be necessary to initialize it by setting the value of any properties that control its operation before we attempt to read any Bean properties. We could simply use the <jsp:setProperty> tag in the page, but as we will learn later on, it is possible for Beans to exist beyond the scope of a single page request, and thus it becomes important to define a separate block of initialization code for the Bean.

Bean configuration

The body tag version of the <jsp:useBean> tag allows you to configure the Bean before using it by setting any necessary properties with the <jsp:setProperty> tag. This form of the <jsp:useBean> has both start and end tags enclosing a body area as follows:

```
<jsp:useBean id="myBean" class="com.manning.jsp.MyBean">
<%- This is the body area --%>
</jsp:useBean>
```

Any commands inside the body are processed immediately after the Bean is instantiated and before it is made available to the rest of the page. For example:

```
<jsp:useBean id="clock" class="com.manning.jsp.ClockBean">
  <jsp:setProperty name="clock" property="timezone" value="CST"/>
</jsp:useBean>
```

You can think of the `<jsp:useBean>` tag's body elements as a run-once configuration phase. It is a useful way to configure the Bean with page-specific configuration data or to prepare the Bean for use later in the page. You can even set properties of other Beans, as long as they have been created earlier in the page.

The body of the `<jsp:useBean>` tag can also contain JSP scriptlets and arbitrary HTML markup. This HTML will be displayed as part of the page only if the Bean must be instantiated. (Be sure that you place such text after your opening HTML tag!) If the Bean already exists in the environment, then subsequent page requests will not display this initialization HTML. For example:

```
<html>
<body>
<jsp:useBean id="clock" class="com.manning.jsp.ClockBean">
  The <b>ClockBean</b> is initializing...
</jsp:useBean>
The main page follows…
</body>
</html>
```

Initializing Beans from the request

A key feature of the `<jsp:setProperty>` tag is its ability to set a Bean's properties dynamically at run time using information retrieved from the page request. This allows us to dynamically configure our Beans based on user input or other events by embedding the configuration information into the page request itself. The request information typically comes from an HTML form, or from request parameters hard coded into the URL. It can also be populated with values—and even entire Beans— from a servlet. HTML forms provide a natural way to get input from users, fitting well into the name/value pair's associated with JavaBean properties. Like a CGI program, a JSP page can be used as a form handler by specifying its URL in the form tag's `action` attribute. Any data in the form will be accessible to the JSP page and can be used to provide information to the Bean.

Example: a compound interest calculator

Listing 5.1 shows how to build a simple application that can calculate the value of compounded interest for an investment. We'll first create an HTML page with a form that will collect the necessary information to perform our calculation:

Listing 5.1   CompoundInterest.htm

```
<html>
<body>
<form action="CompoundInterestResults.jsp">
Principal: <input type="text" name="principal">
Interest Rate: <input type="text" name="interestRate">
Years: <input type="text" name="years">
<input type="submit" value="Calculate Future Value">
</form>
</body>
</html>
```

We can then create a handler for our form called `CompoundInterestResults.jsp`, which will use the values specified in the form fields to configure a Bean that can calculate compounded interest. We'll actually create this Bean in the next chapter, but for now let's concentrate on using this Bean as a service for our page. Let see the `CompoundInterestBean`'s property sheet, shown in table 5.3.

Table 5.3   `CompoundInterestBean` property sheet

Name	Access	Java Type	Example
principal	read/write	double	100.50
interestRate	read/write	double	.10
years	read/write	int	10
futureValue	read-only	String	155.21

The `futureValue` property is linked to the other properties. Its value is calculated using the values of the `principal`, `interestRate`, and `years` properties. To use this Bean we must therefore first set the values of these three properties, then read the results from the `futureValue` property. Let's look at the JSP that will be the form's handler. First we must create a reference to the `CompoundInterestBean`.

```
<%@page import="com.taglib.wdjsp.components.*"%>
<jsp:useBean id="calculator" class="CompoundInterestBean"/>
```

In the body of our `<jsp:useBean>` tag we need to map each of the Bean's configuration properties to the appropriate data from the form field. The `<jsp:setProperty>` tag looks for an incoming request parameter matching the value specified in the `param` attribute of the tag. If it finds one, it tells the Bean to set the corresponding property, specified via the `property` attribute, to that value, performing any necessary type conversion. We'll add the following three lines to the body of our `<jsp:useBean>` tag:

```
<jsp:setProperty name="calculator" property="principal" param="principal"/>
<jsp:setProperty name="calculator" property="interestRate"
  param="interestRate"/>
<jsp:setProperty name="calculator" property="years" param="years"/>
```

The `param` attribute of the `<jsp:setProperty>` tag is the equivalent of the JSP scriptlet `<% request.getParameter("something") %>`. So, the above block of code is functionally equivalent to the following, which uses scriptlets instead of the `param` attribute to initialize the Bean's values:

```
<jsp:setProperty name="calculator" property="principal"
  param="<%= request.getParameter("principal") %>"/>
<jsp:setProperty name="calculator" property="interestRate"
  param="<%= request.getParameter("interestRate") %>"/>
<jsp:setProperty name="calculator" property="years"
  param="<%= request.getParameter("years") %>"/>
```

When the request comes in from the form, the Bean's properties will be set to the form values specified by the user. Since this is such a common way of configuring Beans in JSP, a shortcut has been provided. If a property name is the same as the name of the parameter passed in through the form, we can omit the `param` attribute. Therefore the body of our `<jsp:useBean>` tag could be simplified to:

```
<jsp:setProperty name="calculator" property="principal"/>
<jsp:setProperty name="calculator" property="interestRate"/>
<jsp:setProperty name="calculator" property="years"/>
```

When multiple form field names map directly to Bean properties you can also use the special wild card character "`*`" in the place of a property name. Using a wild card indicates that you wish to set the value of any Bean property whose name corresponds to the name of a request parameter. The names must match exactly as there is no way to map parameters to properties with different names when the wild card is used. For each property of the Bean, a matching request parameter is looked for. Extra request parameters are ignored, though they can be accessed through scriptlets and the implicit `request` object. You can, of course, issue additional `<jsp:setProperty>` commands to pick up any request parameters whose names don't map directly to Bean properties. There is no way to determine or specify the order in which the Bean's properties are changed. If there are interdependencies, one property depending on another, you will want to explicitly set them by specifying a `<jsp:setProperty>` tag for each one. If we are careful to match up all of the form field names with our Bean's property names, we can configure all of the Bean's properties with a single statement. Using the wild card, our Bean could be configured with a single line, like this:

```
<jsp:setProperty name="calculator" property="*">
```

Now that the Bean has been configured, we can read the results of the Bean's calculation in the `futureValue` property. We can also verify the input by reading the values of the properties that we just configured.

```
If you invest $<jsp:getProperty name="calculator" property="principal"/>
for <jsp:getProperty name="calculator" property="years"/> years
at an interest rate of
<jsp:getProperty name="calculator" property="interestRate"/>%
compounding monthly, you will have
$<jsp:getProperty name="calculator" property="futureValue"/>
```

The output of our JSP form handler will produce results like this:

```
If you invest $1000 for 30 years at an interest rate of 15% compounding
monthly, you will have $87,541.99
```

The JSP page is shown in its entirety in listing 5.2.

Listing 5.2 CompoundInterestResults.jsp

```
<%@ page import="com.taglib.wdjsp.components.CompoundInterestBean" %>
<jsp:useBean id="myBean" class="CompoundInterestBean"/>
  <jsp:setProperty name="myBean" property="principal"/>
  <jsp:setProperty name="myBean" property="years"/>
  <jsp:setProperty name="myBean" property="interestRate"/>
</jsp:useBean>
<html>
<body>
If you invest $<jsp:getProperty name="calculator" property="principal"/>
for <jsp:getProperty name="calculator" property="years"/> years
at an interest rate of
<jsp:getProperty name="calculator" property="interestRate"/>%
compounding monthly, you will have
$<jsp:getProperty name="calculator" property="futureValue"/>

</body>
</html>
```

JSP does not care if you are using GET or POST requests for form submission. If desired, you can also use hidden form elements to add configuration information to a form without requiring the user to enter it. You can also encode directives into the request URL directly by following standard URL encoding conventions. For example the following URL will calculate interest for us, no form needed:

```
http://host/InterestCalculator.jsp?interestRate=0.10&years=15&principal=1000
```

The properties in the URL are exactly the same as if they came from a form using the GET method of data delivery. You will need to escape any special characters of course, but you will not need to decode them in the JSP, because the JSP container handles this automatically. A word of warning on form values: do not rely on hidden fields for the storage of sensitive information like database passwords. Any form data fields in your HTML, hidden or otherwise, can be viewed quite easily by anyone viewing the source of the HTML page that contains the form data. It is all right to store sensitive information inside your JSP however, provided it is part of a Bean tag or JSP scriptlets, because this data will be processed on the server and will never be seen by the client code.

WARNING You cannot use request parameters that begin with java., javax., sun. and com.sun. They are reserved for the JSP container's own use and may conflict with request parameters assigned to the request by the container itself.

Specifying default initialization values

If you are attempting to initialize a Bean property from a request parameter that does not exist or is defined as an empty value then the <jsp:setProperty> command has no effect. The property does not get set to a null value, the <jsp:setProperty> tag is just ignored. You can provide a default value for a property by first setting it explicitly, then attempting to set it from the request as shown:

```
<jsp:setProperty name="calculator" property="interestRate" value="0.10"/>
<jsp:setProperty name="calculator" property="interestRate" param="interestRate"/>
```

In this example, the interestRate property is set to 10 percent, but can be overwritten by the value of the interestRate request parameter if it exists. This allows you to supply appropriate default values for critical properties and to create flexible pages that might be accessed through several means.

A security consideration

The wild card notation introduced earlier, `<jsp:setProperty property="*">`, is a very powerful shortcut for initializing Bean properties from a request. It is particularly convenient for mapping the input values from a form into a set of Bean properties that perform some computation. Because it is very easy for a user to construct his or her own requests, you need to be careful about using this shorthand notation when the properties of the Bean control sensitive information.

For example, consider an online banking application that represents account information via a JavaBean class named `AccountBean`. The `AccountBean` class provides properties for accessing information about the account, such as `accountNumber` and `balance`, as well as properties corresponding to account transactions, such as `withdrawalAmount` and `transferAmount`. Given a form that allows a user to specify a withdrawal amount, this form might then point to a JSP page such as the following that actually performs the transaction (as a side effect of setting the property values) and reports the result:

```
<jsp:useBean id="myAccount" class="AccountBean">
  <jsp:setProperty name="myAccount" property="*"/>
</jsp:useBean>
<html>
<head><title>Cash Withdrawal</title></head>
<body>
<p>
$<jsp:getProperty name="myAccount" property="withdrawalAmount"/>
has been withdrawn from Account
#<jsp:getProperty name="myAccount" property="withdrawalAmount"/>.
Your new balance is $<jsp:getProperty name="myAccount" property="balance"/>.
Thank you for patronizing us at the First Bank of Orange.
```

At first glance, the code seems benign. Assuming, however, that both getters and setters are available for the Bean's properties, the potential is very real. If the URL for this page were withdraw.jsp, consider the effect of a user submitting a request for:

```
http://server/account/withdraw.jsp?accountNumber=PH1L31N&balance=1000000
```

Normally, this page would be accessed as the target of a form, but there is nothing to prevent a user from manually constructing his or her own request. No withdrawal amount is specified in this URL, which presumably is not a problem, but the presence of a request parameter named `balance` seems a bit troublesome. When processing the page's `<jsp:setProperty>` tag, the JSP container will map this parameter to the Bean's like-named `balance` property, and attempt to set it to $1,000,000!

One must hope the Java developer responsible for the `AccountBean` implementation will have put safeguards in place to prevent this sort of tampering, but the bottom line is that care must be taken when using the `<jsp:setProperty>` wild card. If the Bean whose properties are to be set contains properties whose access must be carefully controlled (such as a bank account balance), then the Bean must enforce that access control itself. Otherwise, the Bean will be subject to the sort of request spoofing described here if it is ever used in conjunction with a `<jsp:set-Property>` tag employing the wildcard shortcut.

5.3.4 *Controlling a Bean's scope*

Up to now we've been talking about using Beans as ways to encapsulate data or behavior over the life span of a single page. Each time the page is requested, a new instance of a Bean is created and possibly modified via `<jsp:setProperty>` tags. However JSP has a very powerful feature that allows you to specify that a Bean should continue to exist beyond the scope of a single page request. Such Beans are stored in the server environment and reused on multiple pages, or across multiple requests for the same page. This allows us to create a Bean once and then access it throughout a user's visit to our site. Any properties that we set will remain set throughout the lifetime of the Bean.

Bean accessibility and life span

A Bean's accessibility and life span are controlled through the `scope` attribute of the `<jsp:useBean>` tag. The `scope` attribute can have a value of `page`, `request`, `session`, or `application`. The accessibility of a Bean determines which pages or parts of a web application can access the Bean and its properties. A Bean's life span determines how long a particular Bean exists before it is no longer accessible to any page. A summary of how each scope value affects the accessibility and life span of a Bean is shown in table 5.4.

Table 5.4   Possible Bean scopes

Scope	Accessibility	Life span
`page`	current page only	until page is displayed or control is forwarded to a new page
`request`	current page and any included or forwarded pages	until the request has been completely processed and the response has been sent back to the user
`session`	the current request and any subsequent request from the same browser window	life of the user's session
`application`	the current and any future request that is part of the same web application	life of the application

When a Bean is created on the server for reuse between pages it is identified by the name specified by the `id` attribute of its `<jsp:useBean>` tag. Any time you attempt to create a Bean with the `<jsp:useBean>` tag, the server memory is searched for a Bean with the same `id` as specified in the tag. If one is found, and it is accessible by the current request, that Bean is used instead of creating a new one. If any configuration commands have been specified in the body of the `<jsp:useBean>` tag, they will be ignored because the Bean has already been initialized. The syntax of the `scope` attribute is shown below. A Bean can have only one `scope` value. You cannot combine them in any fashion; they are by definition mutually exclusive.

```
<jsp:useBean id="beanName" class="class"
scope="page|request|session|application"/>
```

Page Beans

If you do not specify a scope for a Bean at the time it is created through the `<jsp:useBean>` tag, it is assigned the default scope value of `page`. A Bean with a page-level scope is the least accessible and shortest lived of all JSP Beans. Each time the page is requested, either from a new visitor or a return visitor, an instance of the Bean is created. If there are any initialization tags or scriptlets in the body of the `<jsp:useBean>` tag, these will be executed each time.

Essentially, Beans with a page-level scope are transient—they are not persistent between requests. For that matter, such Beans are not accessible outside of the page itself. If you use the `<jsp:include>` or `<jsp:forward>` tags, any Beans with only page-level scope will not be available within the new or included page. If a page referenced by one of these tags contains `<jsp:useBean>` tags specifying a Bean with the same id as a Bean created on the parent page, they will ignore the original Bean because it is out of scope, and will be forced to create their own new instance of the Bean instead. Since the default scope of the `<jsp:useBean>` tag is page-level, there is no difference between these two tags:

```
<jsp:useBean id="bean1" class="com.manning.jsp.ClockBean"/>
<jsp:useBean id="bean2" class="com.manning.jsp.ClockBean scope="page"/>
```

If a Bean does not need to persist between requests, or its information is of no use after the request has been completed, it's probably a good candidate for page-level scope. For example, if our `ClockBean` is initialized to the current time and date the first time it is created then it probably doesn't do any good to keep it around for very long. If you are using the `<jsp:include>` or `<jsp:forward>` tags however, you may need to set the scope of your Bean to request-level so it can be accessed from within these supplemental pages.

Request Beans

If you specify a value of `request` for the scope attribute of a `<jsp:useBean>` tag the JSP container will attempt to retrieve the Bean from the request itself. Since the HTTP protocol does not provide a mechanism that would allow a web browser to store anything other than simple name value pairs into the request, a Bean can only be stored in the request by a servlet or another JSP page on the local server. Beans are stored in the request as request attributes, a feature of the Java Servlet 2.2 API which we cover in chapter 8. If the Bean is not initially found in the request it will be created and placed there.

The life span for a Bean with request-level scope is essentially the same as one with page scope except that the Bean's accessibility will be extended to pages referenced with the `<jsp:include>` and `<jsp:forward>` tags. This gives the request scope a dual purpose. First, it allows you to use Java servlets to create a Bean and forward it to your JSP page. Second, it gives you a way to extend the reach of Bean to pages that are included in or forwarded from the original page.

For example, consider the situation where you include a footer at the bottom of each page via the `<jsp:include>` tag, and want to include page specific data. If you place the data into the `page` scope however, it will not be accessible by the included footer. The desired effect can be accomplished by storing your information in a Bean with request scope, assuring that if present it will be seen by the footer, as well as the current page. In this example, we associate a contact name with each page, which appears in the footer.

```
<jsp:useBean id="contact" class="jsp.ContactBean" scope="request">
  <jsp:setProperty name="contact" property="name" value="Kris DeHart"/>
</jsp:useBean>
<html>
<body>
Welcome to our web site!
<jsp:include file="/footers/standardFooter.jsp" flush="true"/>
</body>
</html>
```

In this example, `contact` will be accessible from both the current page and `standardFooter.jsp`, which is an HTML excerpt which looks like this:

```
<HR>
To request changes to this page contact
<jsp:getProperty name="contact" property="name"/>
```

This example of building up a page by including smaller, component pages to build a larger composite one is a useful technique for designing complex pages. It will be discussed in detail in chapter 8.

Session Beans

The session scope introduces component persistence to JSP, and is one of its most powerful constructs. Unlike the request and page scopes, a Bean with a scope attribute value of session exists beyond the life of a single request because it is placed into the user's session object. Recall from our discussion of JSP session management in chapter 2 that the JSP container maintains a unique session object for each user visiting the site. Placing a Bean into session scope stores it in this session object, using the value of the id attribute as its identifier.

A Bean does not have to do anything special to support such persistence; the JSP container itself will handle the necessary state maintenance whenever you place a Bean into the session through the scope attribute. Once the Bean is stored in a user's session it will be available to any other JSP on the server. If you call up a Bean with the <jsp:useBean> tag that already exists in the session, the identifier that you specify will refer to the existing instance of the Bean, rather then creating a new one.

Since it is the JSP container that determines the length of time a session Bean exists, its lifetime might be minutes, hours, or days. Some JSP containers, like IBM's WebSphere, can write session data to disk when the server is shut down, and restore the sessions upon restart. A container with such a capability effectively gives the Beans an infinite life span. Not all containers exhibit this behavior so it's not currently a feature you can rely on. If you need to store information for an indefinite length of time, or the session will be used to store critical data, you should consider storing your information in a database instead. Typically, most containers will let session data expire after it hasn't been accessed for a few hours.

TIP   If you have used the <%@ page session="false" %> to indicate that your page does not require session support you will be unable to add Beans to or fetch them from the current session! The default value of the session attribute is true, enabling session support. If you have no need for session support however, you set this attribute to false to prevent the servlet container from creating needless, wasteful session objects in memory.

Sessions are useful for storing information collected through a user's visit to the site and for caching information that is frequently needed at the page level. Sessions can be used to pass information from page to page without each one needing to include the logic or additional processing time required to access information stored in a database or external resource. A shopping cart is a good example of session-oriented data. A user would like a shopping cart's contents to be accessible throughout the JSP application, so we create a ShoppingCartBean and store it in the user's session. At each page we can include a reference to the shopping cart, allowing us to display a running total if we wish.

As a simple example, let's look at how we would use a `TimerBean` to report to us how long a user's session has been active. We can use such a Bean to log the person out after a period of inactivity or to record time-sensitive visits like completing an online survey or exam. Our `TimerBean` has one basic function: to report the difference between its creation time and the current time. This Bean, which we'll develop in chapter 6, has the properties shown in its property sheet, table 5.5.

Table 5.5   TimerBean properties

Name	Access	Java Type	Example
elapsedMillis	read-only	long	180000
elapsedSeconds	read-only	long	180
elapsedMinutes	read-only	long	3
startTime	read/write	long	857374234

The `startTime` property is intended to provide a way to affect the Bean's start time by either setting it to a particular time (expressed in milliseconds since the epoch), or the current time by passing it a zero or negative value.

Here's a simple use of the Bean that on the first load will start the clock, and display the elapsed time every subsequent load. (Providing of course that the time between visits does not exceed the JSP container's session timeout value.)

```
<%@ page import="com.taglib.wdjsp.components.*" %>
<jsp:useBean id="timer" class="TimerBean" scope="session"/>
<html>
<body>
Elapsed Time:
<jsp:getProperty name="timer" property="elapsedMinutes"/> minutes
</body>
</html>
```

If we wanted to add this functionality to a whole series of pages, we could include the appropriate Bean tags in their own file, which we then call with the `<jsp:include>` tag. This example, taken from a web based quiz application, uses the `TimerBean` through an included file to display the elapsed time in the footer of each page:

```
<html>
<body>
<form action="/servlet/processQuestions/6">
<b>Question 6</b><br>
What is the airspeed velocity of an unlaiden European swallow?
<br> <input type="text" name="answer">
<br> <input type="submit" value="Submit Answer">
</form>
<jsp:include page="/footers/ElapsedTimeFooter.html" flush="true"/>
</body>
</html>
```

Here are the contents of the TimedFooter.html file:

```
<%@ page import="com.taglib.wdjsp.components.*" %>
<jsp:useBean id="timer" class="TimerBean" scope="session"/>
<hr>
Remember, speed is a factor in this exam!<BR>
Time Used: <jsp:getProperty name="timer" property="elapsedSeconds"/> seconds
```

We can even have several different instances of `TimerBean` running at once, as long as they have different identifiers. It is the `id` attribute of the `<jsp:useBean>` tag that is important in distinguishing between different instances of a Bean, whether referencing it from within the page or searching for it in the session.

TIP   The default lifetime of a session is determined by the JSP container (or more accurately, the servlet container). New to the Servlet API 2.2, the `HttpSession` interfaces's `getMaxInactiveInterval()` and `setMaxInactiveInterval()` methods can be used to view or set the timeout variables. The `getLastAccessedTime()` method of this interface can tell you how long it has been since the data in the session was last accessed.

Application Beans

A Bean with a scope value of `application` has an even broader lifecycle and further reaching availability then a session Bean. Beans with `application` scope are associated with a given JSP application on the server. A JSP application is a collection of JSP pages, HTML pages, images, applets, and other resources that are bundled together under a particular URL hierarchy. Application Beans exist throughout the life of the JSP container itself, meaning that they are not reclaimed until the server is shut down—they do not expire after a few hours or days. Unlike session Beans that are available only to subsequent requests from a given user, application Beans are shared by all users of the application they are associated with. Any JSP page that is part of an application can access application Beans created by other pages within that application. We will explain how to create the packaged JSP applications themselves in chapter 10.

The application scope is used to store information that is useful throughout the application and not specific to the individual page requesting access to the Bean. Once a Bean is placed into application scope it will be used by pages throughout the site. If the Bean requires any configuration information it must be page independent. If you expect configuration information to change between page requests or between users, it is probably not a good candidate for application scope.

When a Bean is stored in application scope there is only one instance of the Bean per server. You should be very cautious about changing an application Bean's property once it has been stored in the application because any changes you make to the properties will instantly affect all of the JSP pages which reference the Bean.

Another good use of the `application` scope is the ability to cache application information that would be too computationally expensive to generate for each individual page request. For example, say that all of the pages of your online catalog needed access to a table of shipping rates. This information can be encapsulated into a Bean and placed into the application scope. This would mean that the data would have to be collected from the database only once, conserving not only database access time but server memory as well. In each page you simply reference the Bean as normal, if it has not yet been instantiated and placed into the session, the server will handle it:

```
<jsp:useBean id="ship" class="ShipRateBean" scope="application"/>
<html>
<body>
Current shipping charges are:
<jsp:getProperty name="ship" property="baseCharge"/>
per shipment plus
<jsp:getProperty name="ship" property="perItemCharge"/>
per each item shipped.
</body>
</html>
```

If the Bean requires any configuration you should use the body of the `<jsp:use-Bean>` tag to set your initial property values. Since you would have to do this on each and every page users might enter you will probably want to seek alternatives in this situation. First, you could use application-specific Beans which require no special configuration or whose constructor's collect configuration information from another source (such a property file). Second, you could take steps to assure that the necessary Bean is placed into the application scope prior to the time any of the dependent pages would need to access the Bean. Or, you can serialize your preconfigured Beans off to disk, and restore them as needed.

Scope and the type attribute

The `type` attribute of the `<jsp:useBean>` tag is generally only used when dealing with Beans that expected to be in scope and that are subclasses of some higher base class. If the Bean exists in the current scope (say in the request or session), but you have no way of knowing its exact type, you can simply specify its base class through the type attribute. For example, a servlet or other JSP page placed a collection of objects into your session. You know that the objects are in some derivative of Java's `Collection` interface, but have no way of knowing if the other pages used a `List`, a `Set`, a `ListArray`, or anything else. In this case you simply reference the common `Collection` interface as the Bean's type; there is no need to specify a class in this case. For example:

```
<jsp:useBean id="elements" type="java.util.Collection" scope="session"/>
```

Developing JSP components

6

This chapter covers
- The JavaBeans API
- Developing your own JSP components
- Mixing scriptlets and Beans

This chapter will help developers create their own JavaBeans for use as JSP components, and teach web designers how they are implemented behind the scenes. Fortunately, it is not necessary to understand all of the details of JavaBeans development to work with JSP. As component architectures go, the interface between JavaServer Pages and JavaBeans is quite simple, as we will see.

6.1   What makes a Bean a Bean?

So what makes a Bean so special? A Bean is simply a Java class that follows a set of simple naming and design conventions outlined by the JavaBeans specification. Beans are not required to extend a specific base class or implement a particular interface. If a class follows these Bean conventions, and you treat it like a Bean—then it is a Bean. A particularly good thing about the Bean conventions is that they are rooted in sound programming practices that you may already be following to some extent.

6.1.1   Bean conventions

The JavaBean conventions are what enable us to develop Beans because they allow a Bean container to analyze a Java class file and interpret its methods as properties, designating the class as a Java Bean. The conventions dictate rules for defining a Bean's constructor and the methods that will define its properties.

The JavaBeans API

Following the conventions specified by the JavaBeans API allows the JSP container to interact with Beans at a programmatic level, even though the containing application has no real understanding of what the Bean does or how it works. For JSP we are primarily concerned with the aspects of the API that dictate the method signatures for a Bean's constructors and property access methods.

Beans are just objects

Like any other Java class, instances of Bean classes are simply Java objects. As a result, you always have the option of referencing Beans and their methods directly through Java code in other classes or through JSP scripting elements. Because they follow the JavaBeans conventions, we can work with them a lot easier than by writing Java code. Bean containers, such as a JSP container, can provide easy access to Beans and their properties. Following the JavaBeans API coding conventions, as we will see, means creating methods that control access to each property we wish to define for our Bean. Beans can also have regular methods like any other Java object. However,

JSP developers will have to use scriptlets, expressions, or custom tags to access them since a Bean container can manipulate a Bean only through its properties.

Class naming conventions

You might have noticed that in most of our examples Bean classes often include the word Bean in their name, such as `UserBean`, `AlarmClockBean`, `DataAccessBean`, and so forth. While this is a common approach that lets other developers immediately understand the intended role of the class, it is not a requirement for a Bean to be used inside a JSP page or any other Bean container. Beans follow the same class-naming rules as other Java classes: they must start with an alphabetic character, contain only alphanumeric and underscore characters, and be case sensitive. Additionally, like other Java classes it is common, but not required, to start the name of a Bean class with a capital letter.

The magic of introspection

How can the JSP container interact with any Bean object without the benefit of a common interface or base class to fall back on? Java manages this little miracle through a process called *introspection* that allows a class to expose its methods and capabilities on request. The introspection process happens at run time, and is controlled by the Bean container. It is introspection that allows us to rely on conventions to establish properties.

Introspection occurs through a mechanism known as *reflection,* which allows the Bean container to examine any class at run time to determine its method signatures. The Bean container determines what properties a Bean supports by analyzing its public methods for the presence of methods that meet criteria defined by the Java-Beans API. For a property to exist, its Bean class must define an access method to return the value of the property, change the value of the property, or both. It is the presence of these specially named access methods alone that determine the properties of a Bean class, as we will soon see.

6.1.2 The Bean constructor

The first rule of JSP Bean building is that you must implement a constructor that takes no arguments. It is this constructor that the JSP container will use to instantiate your Bean through the `<jsp:useBean>` tag. Every Java class has a constructor method that is used to create instances of the class. If a class does not explicitly specify any constructors, then a default zero-argument constructor is assumed. Because of this default constructor rule the following Java class is perfectly valid, and technically satisfies the Bean conventions:

```
public class DoNothingBean { }
```

This Bean has no properties and can't do or report anything useful, but it is a Bean nonetheless. We can create new instances of it, reference it from scriptlets, and control its scope. Here is a better example of a class suitable for Bean usage, a Bean which knows the time. This class has a zero-argument constructor that records the time of its instantiation:

```
package com.taglib.wdjsp.components;
import java.util.*;

public class CurrentTimeBean {
  private int hours;
  private int minutes;

  public CurrentTimeBean() {
    Calendar now = Calendar.getInstance();
    this.hours = now.get(Calendar.HOUR_OF_DAY);
    this.minutes = now.get(Calendar.MINUTE);
  }
}
```

We've used the constructor to initialize the Bean's instance variables `hours` and `minutes` to reflect the current time at instantiation. The constructor of a Bean is the appropriate place to initialize instance variables and prepare the instance of the class for use. Of course to be useful within a JSP page we will need to define some properties for the Bean and create the appropriate access methods to control them.

6.1.3 *Defining a Bean's properties*

As we've mentioned, a Bean's properties are defined simply by creating appropriate access methods for them. Access methods are used either to retrieve a property's value or make changes to it. A method used to retrieve a property's value is called a *getter* method, while a method that modifies its value is called a *setter* method. Together these methods are generally referred to as *access methods*—they provide access to values stored in the Bean's properties.

To define properties for a Bean simply create a `public` method with the name of the property you wish to define, prefixed with the word `get` or `set` as appropriate. Getter methods should return the appropriate data type, while the corresponding setter method should be declared void and accept one argument of the appropriate type. It is the `get` or `set` prefix that is Java's clue that you are defining a property. The signature for property access methods, then, is:

```
public void setPropertyName(PropertyType value);
public PropertyType getPropertyName();
```

For example, to define a property called `rank`, which can be used to store text, and is both readable and writable, we would need to create methods with these signatures:

```
public void setRank(String rank);
public String getRank();
```

Likewise, to create a property called `age` that stores numbers:

```
public void setAge(int age);
public int getAge();
```

NOTE   Making your property access methods `public` is more than a good idea, it's the law! Exposing your Bean's access methods by declaring them `public` is the only way that JSP pages will be able to call them. The JSP container will not recognize properties without `public` access methods.

Conversely, if the actual data being reflected by the component's properties is stored in instance variables it should be purposely hidden from other classes. Such instance variables should be declared `private` or at least `protected`. This helps ensure that developers restrict their interaction with the class to its access methods and not its internal workings. Otherwise, a change to the implementation might negatively impact code dependent on the older version of the component.

Let's revisit our previous example and make it more useful. We will add a couple of properties to our `CurrentTimeBean` called `hours` and `minutes`, that will allow us to reference the current time in the page. These properties must meet the getter method signatures defined by the JavaBeans design patterns. They therefore should look like this:

```
public int getHours();
public int getMinutes();
```

In our constructor we store the current time's hours and minutes into instance variables. We can have our properties reference these variables and return their value where appropriate. The source for this Bean is shown in listing 6.1.

Listing 6.1   CurrentTimeBean.java

```java
package com.taglib.wdjsp.components;
import java.util.*;

public class CurrentTimeBean {
  private int hours;
  private int minutes;

  public CurrentTimeBean() {
    Calendar now = Calendar.getInstance();
    this.hours = now.get(Calendar.HOUR_OF_DAY);
    this.minutes = now.get(Calendar.MINUTE);
  }

  public int getHours() {
    return hours;
  }

  public int getMinutes() {
    return minutes;
  }
}
```

That's all there is to it. These two methods simply return the appropriate values as stored in the instance variables. Since they meet the JavaBean rules for naming access methods, we have just defined two properties that we can access through JSP Bean tags. For example:

```
<jsp:useBean id="time" class="CurrentTimeBean"/>
<html><body>
It is now <jsp:getProperty name="time" property="minutes"/>
minutes past the hour.
</body></html>
```

Properties should not be confused with instance variables, even though instance variables are often mapped directly to property names but properties of a Bean are not required to correspond directly with instance variables. A Bean's properties are defined by the method names themselves, not the variables or implementation behind them. This leaves the Bean designer free to alter the inner workings of the Bean without altering the interface and collection of properties that you expose to users of the Bean.

As an example of dynamically generating property values, here is a Bean that creates random numbers in its property access methods rather than simply returning a copy of an instance variable. Its code is shown in listing 6.2.

Listing 6.2   DiceBean.java

```java
package com.taglib.wdjsp.components;
import java.util.*;

public class DiceBean {
  private Random rand;
  public DiceBean() {
    rand = new Random();
  }

  public int getDieRoll() {
    // return a number between 1 and 6
    return rand.nextInt(6) + 1;
  }

  public int getDiceRoll() {
    // return a number between 2 and 12
    return getDieRoll() + getDieRoll();
  }
}
```

In this example, our `dieRoll` and `diceRoll` properties are not managed by instance variables. Instead, we create a `java.util.Random` object in the constructor and call its random number generator from our access methods to dynamically generate property values. In fact, nowhere in the Bean are any static values stored for these properties—their values are recomputed each time the properties are requested.

You are not required to create both getter and setter methods for each property you wish to provide for a Bean. If you wish to make a property read-only then define a getter method without providing a corresponding setter method. Conversely creating only a setter method specifies a write-only property. The latter might be useful if the Bean uses the property value internally to affect other properties but is not a property that you want clients manipulating directly.

Property name conventions

A common convention is that property names are mixed case, beginning with a lowercase letter and uppercasing the first letter of each word in the property name. For the properties `firstName` and `lastName` for example, the corresponding getter methods would be `getFirstName()` and `getLastName()`. Note the case difference between the property names and their access methods. Not to worry, the JSP container is smart enough to convert the first letter to uppercase when constructing the target getter method. If the first two or more letters of a property name are uppercased, for example `URL`, then the JSP container assumes that you really mean it, so its corresponding access methods would be `getURL()` and `setURL()`.

6.1.4   *Indexed properties*

Bean properties are not limited to single values. Beans can also contain multivalued properties. For example, you might have a property named `contacts` that is used to store a list of objects of type `Contact`, containing phone and address information. Such a property would be used in conjunction with scriptlets or a custom iteration tag to step through the individual values. Each value must be of the same type; a single indexed property cannot contain both string and integer elements, for example.

To define an indexed valued property you have two options. The first style is creating an access method that returns the entire set of properties as a single array. In this case, a JSP page author or iterative custom tag can determine the size of the set and iterate through it. For example:

```
public PropertyType[] getProperty()
```

In the second option, you can access elements of the set by using an index value. This allows you additional flexibility. For example you might want to access only particular contacts from the collection.

```
public PropertyType getProperty(int index)
```

While not specifically required by JavaBean conventions, it is useful to implement both styles for a multivalued property. It's not much more work and it adds a good deal more flexibility in using the Bean.

To set multivalue properties there are setter method signatures analogous to the getter method naming styles described earlier. The syntax for these methods is:

```
public void setProperty(int index, PropertyType value)
public void setProperty(PropertyType[])
```

Another type of method commonly implemented and recognized by Bean containers is the `size()` method that can be used to determine the size of an indexed property. A typical implementation would be:

```
public int getPropertySize()
```

This is another method that is not required but increases the flexibility of the design to give page developers more options with which to work.

Example: a Bean with indexed properties

In this example we will build a component that can perform statistical calculations on a series of numbers. The numbers themselves are stored in a single, indexed property. Other properties of the Bean hold the value of statistical calculations like the average or the sum. This StatBean's source code is shown in listing 6.3:

Listing 6.3   StatBean.java

```java
package com.taglib.wdjsp.components;
import java.util.*;

public class StatBean {
  private double[] numbers;

  public StatBean() {
    numbers = new double[2];
    numbers[0] = 1;
    numbers[1] = 2;
  }

  public double getAverage() {
    double sum = 0;
    for (int i=0; i < numbers.length; i++)
      sum += numbers[i];
    return sum/numbers.length;
  }

  public double[] getNumbers() {
    return numbers;
  }

  public double getNumbers(int index) {
    return numbers[index];
  }

  public void setNumbers(double[] numbers) {
    this.numbers = numbers;
  }

  public void setNumbers(int index, double value) {
    numbers[index] = value;
  }

  public void setNumbersList(String values) {
    Vector n = new Vector();
    StringTokenizer tok = new StringTokenizer(values, ",");
    while (tok.hasMoreTokens())
      n.addElement(tok.nextToken());
```

```
    numbers = new double[n.size()];
    for (int i=0; i < numbers.length; i++)
      numbers[i] = Double.parseDouble((String) n.elementAt(i));
  }

  public String getNumbersList() {
    String list = new String();
    for (int i=0; i < numbers.length; i++) {
      if (i != numbers.length)
        list += numbers[i] + ",";
      else
        list += "" + numbers[i];
    }
    return list;
  }

  public int getNumbersSize() {
    return numbers.length;
  }
}
```

Since the JSP Bean tags deal exclusively with scalar properties, the only way to interact with indexed properties such as these is through JSP scriptlets and expressions. In this JSP page we'll use a JSP scriptlet in the body of the `<jsp:useBean>` tag to pass an array of integers to the Bean's `numbers` property. We'll have to use a scriptlet to display back the numbers themselves, but we can use a `<jsp:getProperty>` tag to display the average. The page is shown in listing 6.4:

Listing 6.4   stats.jsp

```
<jsp:useBean id="stat" class="com.taglib.wdjsp.StatBean">
  <%
  double[] mynums = {100, 250, 150, 50, 450};
  stat.setNumbers(mynums);
  %>
</jsp:useBean>
<html>
<body>
The average of
<%
double[] numbers = stat.getNumbers();
for (int i=0; i < numbers.length; i++) {
  if (i != numbers.length)
    out.print(numbers[i] + ",");
  else
    out.println("" + numbers[i]);
}
```

```
%>
is equal to
<jsp:getProperty name="stat" property="average"/>
</body>
</html>
```

The use of custom tags, a technique that we will discuss in chapters 13 and 14, can greatly aid in working with indexed properties by eliminating the need for inline code by encapsulating common functionality into simple tag elements. With custom tags, we could eliminate the need for Java code in this example. We can also move this code inside the Bean, which is what we'll do for now.

Accessing indexed values through JSP Bean tags

We might also want to include a method that will enable us to pass in the array of numbers through a standard Bean tag. Since Bean tags deal exclusively with single values, we will have to perform the conversion ourselves in the property access methods. We'll create another pair of access methods that treat the array as a list of numbers stored in a comma delimited string. To differentiate between these two approaches, we will map the String versions of our new access methods to a new property we will call numbersList. Note that even though we are using a different property name, it is still modifying the same internal data, and will cause changes in the average and numbers properties. (Another example of this technique can be found in the Whois example of chapter 12.)

```
public void setNumbersList(String values) {
  Vector n = new Vector();
  StringTokenizer tok = new StringTokenizer(values, ",");
  while (tok.hasMoreTokens())
    n.addElement(tok.nextToken());
  numbers = new double[n.size()];
  for (int i=0; i < numbers.length; i++)
    numbers[i] = Double.parseDouble((String) n.elementAt(i));
}

public String getNumbersList() {
  String list = new String();
  for (int i=0; i < numbers.length; i++) {
    if (i != numbers.length)
      list += numbers[i] + ",";
    else
      list += "" + numbers[i];
  }
  return list;
}
```

Now we can access this Bean through JSP tags alone, as shown in listing 6.5.

Listing 6.5   stats2.jsp

```
<jsp:useBean id="stat" class="com.taglib.wdjsp.components.StatBean">
  <jsp:setProperty name="stat" property="numbersList" value="100,250,150,50,450" />
</jsp:useBean>
<html>
<body>
The average of <jsp:getProperty name="stat" property="numbersList" />
is equal to
<jsp:getProperty name="stat" property="average" />
</body>
</html>
```

The resulting display is shown in figure 6.1.

6.1.5 *Boolean properties*

For boolean properties, that hold only true or false values, you can elect to use another Bean convention for getter methods. This convention is to prefix the property name with the word `is` and return a boolean result. For example, consider these method signatures:

```
public boolean isProperty();
public boolean isEnabled();
public boolean isAuthorized();
```

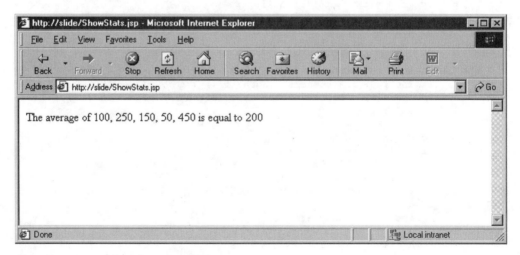

Figure 6.1   The ShowStat's page in action

The container will automatically look for this form of method if it cannot find a property access method matching the getter syntax discussed earlier. Setting the value of a boolean property is no different then the setter methods for other properties.

```
public void setProperty(boolean b);
public void setEnabled(boolean b);
public void setAuthorized(boolean b);
```

6.1.6 *JSP type conversion*

A JSP component's properties are not limited to `String` values, but it is important to understand that all property values accessed through the `<jsp:getProperty>` tag will be converted into a `String`. A getter method need not return a `String` explicitly, however, as the JSP container will automatically convert the return value into a `String`. For the Java primitive types, conversion is handled by the methods shown in table 6.1

Table 6.1   Type conversions for `<jsp:getProperty>`

Property Type	Conversion to String
`boolean`	`java.lang.Boolean.toString(boolean)`
`byte`	`java.lang.Byte.toString(byte)`
`char`	`java.lang.Character.toString(char)`
`double`	`java.lang.Double.toString(double)`
`int`	`java.lang.Integer.toString(int)`
`float`	`java.lang.Float.toString(float)`
`long`	`java.lang.Long.toString(long)`

Likewise, all property setter methods accessed with a `<jsp:setProperty>` tag will be automatically converted from a `String` to the appropriate native type by the JSP container. This is accomplished via methods of Java's wrapper classes as shown in table 6.2.

Table 6.2   Type conversions for `<jsp:setProperty>`

Property Type	Conversion from String
`boolean` or `Boolean`	`java.lang.Boolean.valueOf(String)`
`byte` or `Byte`	`java.lang.Byte.valueOf(String)`
`char` or `Character`	`java.lang.Character.valueOf(String)`

Table 6.2 Type conversions for `<jsp:setProperty>` (continued)

Property Type	Conversion from String
double or Double	java.lang.Double.valueOf(String)
int or Integer	java.lang.Integer.valueOf(String)
float or Float	java.lang.Float.valueOf(String)
long or Long	java.lang.Long.valueOf(String)

Properties are not restricted to primitive types. For objects, the JSP container will invoke the object's `toString()` method, which, unless you have overloaded it, will probably not be very representative of the data stored in the object. For properties holding objects rather than a `String` or native Java type you have several strategies. You can perform the conversion between simple and complex types yourself, or you can overload your getter and setter methods to accept the appropriate object type. This latter strategy requires that you use custom tags or JSP scripting elements to access them since the `<jsp:setProperty>` and `<jsp:getProperty>` tags work exclusively with `Strings`. You can also set the property indirectly, for example allowing the user to set the hours and minutes separately through a pair of write-only properties and having a single read-only property called `time`.

Handling properties with null values

Property getter methods for Java's primitive types like `int` and `double` cannot return a `null` value, which is only valid for methods that return objects. Sometimes however, a property really is undefined. For example, if a property represents a user's age, and a call to the database reveals that we don't know their age, what do we return? While not that critical in many applications, it may be important to some. In this case, we can simply establish a convention for this property, which says if the age is a negative number then we don't have any idea what the age is—it is undefined. It is up to the JSP developer in this case to understand the convention and react to such a situation accordingly.

Unfortunately, it's not always that easy. How would we handle a temperature reading, where negative numbers are perfectly valid? We could still pick an unreasonable number, like -999, as an indicator that this particular value is unknown. However, such an approach is not only messy—requiring too much in-depth understanding by the JSP designer—it is also dangerous. Who knows what will be a reasonable value for this application (or its decedents) ten years from now? A better approach to this problem is to add a boolean property which can verify the legitimacy of the property in question. In that case, it doesn't matter what the property is actually set to. For example we would define both a `getTempReading()` and `isValidTempReading()` methods.

6.1.7 *Configuring Beans*

Many times a Bean will require run-time configuration by the page initializing it before it can properly perform its tasks. Since we can't pass information into the Bean's constructor we have to use the Bean's properties to hold configuration information. We do this by setting the appropriate property values immediately after the container instantiates the Bean in the body of the `<jsp:useBean>` tag or anywhere in the page before the Bean's properties are accessed. It can be useful to set a flag in your class to indicate whether or not an instance is in a useful state, toggling the flag when all of the necessary properties have been set.

Even though the Bean tags do not allow you to pass any arguments into a Bean's constructor, you can still define constructors that take arguments. You will not however, be able to call them through Bean tags. You can only instantiate an object requiring arguments in its constructor through a JSP scriptlet. For example:

```
<% Thermostat t = new Thermostat(78); %>
The thermostat was set at a temperature
of <%= t.getTemp() %> degrees.
```

One technique we have found useful is to provide a single method that handles all configuration steps. This method can be called by your constructors that take arguments, for use outside of Bean tags, as well as by your property access methods once all the necessary properties have been configured. In this example we'll provide two constructors for this `Thermostat` class, as well as an `init()` method which would handle any necessary internal configuration. The zero argument constructor is provided for Bean compatibility, calling the constructor which takes an initial temperature argument with a default value. Our `init()` method is then called through this alternate constructor.

```
public class Thermostat {
  private int temp;
  private int maxTemp;
  private int minTemp;
  private int fuelType;

  public Thermostat() {
    // no argument constructor for Bean use
    this(75);
  }
```

```
public Thermostat(int temp) {
  this.temp = temp;
  init();
}

public void setTemp(int temp) {
  this.temp = temp;
  // initialize settings with this temp
  init();
}

public int getTemp() {
  return temp;
}

private void init() {
  maxTemp = this.temp + 10;
  minTemp = this.temp - 15;
  if (maxTemp > 150)
    fuelType = Fuels.DILITHEUM;
  else
    fuelType = Fuels.NATURALGAS;
}
```

6.2   Some Examples

In this section we will present a number of more detailed examples of creating Java-Beans for use in JSP. These examples are more in depth than the ones we've been looking at so far, and they will help give you the feel for developing more complex components. For additional examples, see the Beans we develop in chapters 9 and 11.

6.2.1   Example: a TimerBean

In the previous chapter we used a TimerBean to track the amount of time a user has been active in the current browsing session. In the Bean's constructor we simply need to record the current time, which we will use as our starting time, into an instance variable:

```
long private start;

public TimerBean() {
  start = System.currentTimeMillis();
}
```

The elapsedMillis property should return the number of milliseconds that has elapsed since the session began. The first time we place a TimerBean into the session with a <jsp:useBean> tag, the JSP container will create a new instance of the Bean, starting our timer. To calculate the elapsed time we simply compute the difference between the current time and our starting time:

```
public long getElapsedMillis() {
  long now = System.currentTimeMillis();
  return now - start;
}
```

The other property access methods are simply conversions applied to the elapsed milliseconds. We have chosen to have our minutes and seconds properties return whole numbers rather than floating points to simplify the display of properties within the JSP page and eliminate the issues of formatting and precision. If the application using our Bean needs a finer degree of resolution, it can access the milliseconds property and perform the conversions themselves. You are often better off reducing component complexity by limiting the properties (and corresponding methods) you provide with the component. We have found it helpful to focus on the core functionality we are trying to provide, rather than attempt to address every possible use of the component.

```
public long getElapsedSeconds() {
  return (long)this.getElapsedMillis() / 1000;
}

public long getElapsedMinutes() {
  return (long)this.getElapsedMillis() / 60000;
}
```

For convenience we will add a method to restart the timer by setting our start to the current time. We'll then make this method accessible through the JSP Bean tags by defining the necessary access methods for a startTime property and interpreting an illegal argument to setStartTime() as a request to reset the timer.

```
public void reset() {
  start = System.currentTimeMillis();
}

public long getStartTime() {
  return start;
}

public void setStartTime(long time) {
  if (time <= 0)
    reset();
  else
    start = time;
}
```

The complete source for the Bean is shown in listing 6.6.

Listing 6.6   Timer Bean

```
package com.taglib.wdjsp.components;
public class TimerBean {
  private long start;
  public TimerBean() {
    start = System.currentTimeMillis();
  }

  public long getElapsedMillis() {
    long now = System.currentTimeMillis();
    return now - start;
  }

  public long getElapsedSeconds() {
    return (long)this.getElapsedMillis() / 1000;
  }

  public long getElapsedMinutes() {
    return (long)this.getElapsedMillis() / 60000;
  }

  public void reset() {
    start = System.currentTimeMillis();
  }

  public long getStartTime() {
    return start;
  }

  public void setStartTime(long time) {
    if (time <= 0)
      reset();
    else
      start = time;
  }
}
```

Here's an example of a JSP page that pulls a `TimerBean` from the user's session (or instantiates a new Bean, if necessary) and resets the clock, using the approach described above:

```
<jsp:useBean id="timer" class="TimerBean" scope="session">
  <jsp:setProperty name="timer" property="startTime" value="-1"/>
</jsp:useBean>
<html><body>
Your online timer has been restarted...
</body></html>
```

6.2.2 A Bean that calculates interest

As a more complex example let's create a JSP component that knows how to calculate the future value of money that is accumulating interest. Such a Bean would be useful for an application allowing the user to compare investments. The formula for calculating the future value of money collecting compounding interest is:

```
FV = principal(1 + rate/compounding periods)^(years * compounding periods)
```

This Bean will require:

- The sum of money to be invested (the principal)
- The interest rate
- The number of years for the investment
- How often interest is compounded

This gives us the list of properties that the user must be able to modify. Once all of these properties have been initialized, the Bean should be able to calculate the future value of our principal amount. In addition, we will need to have a property to reflect the future value of the money after the calculation has been performed. Table 6.3 defines the Bean's properties.

Table 6.3   Properties of a Bean that calculates interest

Property Name	Mode	Type
principal	read/write	double
years	read/write	int
compounds	read/write	int
interestRate	read/write	double
futureValue	read-only	double

Since users will probably want to display the input values in addition to configuring them, they have been given both read and write access. The futureValue property is designated read-only because it will reflect the results of the calculation. Retrieving the value of the futureValue property uses the other properties to calculate our results. (If you wanted to get fancy, you could write a Bean that, given any four of the properties, could calculate the remaining property value.) We'll store our initialization properties in instance variables:

```
public class CompoundInterestBean {
  private double interestRate;
  private int years;
  private double principal;
  private int compounds;
```

It is a good practice to make your instance variables `private` since we plan to define access methods for them. This assures that all interaction with the class is restricted to the access methods allowing us to modify the implementation without affecting code that makes use of our class. Following the Bean conventions, we must define a constructor that has no arguments. In our constructor we should set our initialization properties to some default values that will leave our Bean property initialized. We cannot calculate the future value without our initialization properties being set to appropriate, legal values.

```
public CompoundInterestBean() {
  this.compounds = 12;
  this.interestRate = 8.0;
  this.years = 1;
  this.principal = 1000.0;
}
```

Since investments are generally compounded monthly (that is twelve times a year) it might be handy to provide a shortcut that allows the Bean user to not specify the `compounds` property and instead use the default. It would also be nice if we could provide other clients of the Bean with a more robust constructor that would allow them to do all their initialization through the constructor. This can be accomplished by creating a constructor that takes a full set of arguments and calling it from the zero-argument constructor with the default values we have selected for our Bean's properties:

```
public CompoundInterestBean() {
  this(12, 8.0, 1, 1000.0);
}

public CompoundInterestBean(int compounds, double interestRate,
  int years, double principal) {
  this.compounds = compounds;
  this.interestRate = interestRate;
  this.years = years;
  this.principal = principal;
}
```

This is a good compromise in the design. The Bean is now useful to both traditional Java developers as well as JSP authors. We must now define access methods for our initialization properties. For each one we will verify that they have been passed valid information. For example, money cannot be invested into the past, so the `year` property's value must be a positive number. Since the access methods are all similar, we'll just look at those for the `interestRate` property.

```
public void setInterestRate(double rate) {
  if (rate > 0)
    this.interestRate = rate;
  else
    this.interestRate = 0;
}

public double getInterestRate() {
  return this.interestRate;
}
```

When we catch illegal arguments, such as negative interest rates, we have to decide the appropriate way of handling it. We can pick a reasonable default value, as we did here for example, or take a stricter approach and throw an exception.

We chose to initialize our properties with a set of legitimate, but hard-coded values to keep our Bean in a legal state. Of course, this approach might not be appropriate in every situation. Another technique for handling uninitialized data is setting up boolean flags for each property which has no legal value until it is initialized, and tripping them as each setter method is called. Another method could then be used to check the status of the flags to determine if the component had been initialized yet or not. For example, we could have defined our `futureValue` access method like this:

```
public double getFutureValue() {
  if (isInitialized())
    return principal * Math.pow(1 + interestRate/compounds,
      years * compounds);
  else
    throw new RuntimeException("Bean requires configuration!");
}

private boolean isInitialized() {
  return (compoundsSet && interestRateSet && yearsSet && principalSet);
}
```

In such as case, the Bean is considered initialized if and only if the flags for each property are set to `true`. We would initialize each flag to `false` in our constructor and then define our setter methods as:

```
public void setYears(int years) {
  yearsSet = true;
  if (years >=1 )
    this.years = years;
  else
    this.years = 1;
}
```

Here is the complete code, shown in listing 6.7:

Listing 6.7 CompoundInterestBean.java

```
package com.taglib.wdjsp.components;
public class CompoundInterestBean {
  private double interestRate;
  private int years;
  private double principal;
  private int compounds;

  public CompoundInterestBean() {
    this(12);
  }

  public CompoundInterestBean(intcompounds) {
    this.compounds = compounds;
    this.interestRate = -1;
    this.years = -1;
    this.principal = -1;
  }

  public double getFutureValue() {
    if ((compounds != -1) &&
        (interestRate != -1 ) &&
        (years != -1))
      return principal * Math.pow(1+interestRate/compounds, compounds*12);
    else
      throw new RuntimeException("Bean requires configuration!");
  }

  public void setInterestRate(double rate) {
    if (rate > 0)
      this.interestRate = rate;
    else
      this.interestRate = 0;
  }

  public double getInterestRate() {
    return this.interestRate;
  }
```

```
public void setYears(int years) {
  if (years >=1 )
    this.years = years;
  else
    this.years = 1;
}

public int getYears() {
  return this.years;
}

public void setPrincipal(double principal) {
  this.principal = principal;
}

public double getPrincipal() {
  return this.principal;
}

public static void main(String[] args) {
  CompoundInterestBean bean = new CompoundInterestBean();
  bean.setInterestRate(0.06);
  bean.setYears(30);
  bean.setPrincipal(1200.00);
  System.out.println("FutureValue = " + bean.getFutureValue());
}
}
```

6.3 Bean interfaces

While not specifically required, there are a number of interfaces that you may choose to implement with your Beans to extend their functionality. We'll cover them briefly in this section.

6.3.1 The BeanInfo interface

We learned about reflection earlier, but another way that a Bean class can inform the Bean container about its properties is by providing an implementation of the BeanInfo interface. The BeanInfo interface allows you to create a companion class for your Bean that defines its properties and their corresponding levels of access. It can be used to adapt existing Java classes for Bean use without changing their published interface. It can also be used to hide what would normally be accessible properties from your client, since sometimes Java's standard reflection mechanism can reveal more information than we would like.

To create a `BeanInfo` class use your Bean's class name with the suffix `BeanInfo` and implement the `java.beans.BeanInfo` interface. This naming convention is how the Bean container locates the appropriate `BeanInfo` class for your Bean. This interface requires you to define methods that inform the container about your Bean's properties. This explicit mapping eliminates the introspection step entirely.

There is also a `java.beans.SimpleBeanInfo` class that provides default, do-nothing implementations of all of the required BeanInfo methods. This often provides a good starting point when designing a `BeanInfo` class for a JSP Bean, because many of the Bean features designed for working with visual Beans are irrelevant in the context of JavaServer Pages, and are ignored by the JSP container.

One area where the `BeanInfo` approach is particularly useful is in visual, or WYSIWYG, JSP editors. JSP was designed to be machine-readable in order to support visual editors and development tools. By applying the `BeanInfo` interface to existing Java classes, developers can construct their own JSP components for use in such editors, even if the original component class does not follow the Java Bean conventions. Using `BeanInfo` classes you can designate which methods of an arbitrary class correspond to Bean properties, for use with the `<jsp:setPropety>` and `<jsp:getProperty>` tags.

6.3.2 *The Serializable interface*

One of the Java Bean requirements that JSP does not mandate is that Beans should implement the `Serializable` interface. This will allow an instance of the Bean to be *serialized*, turning it into a flat stream of binary data that can be stored to disk for later reuse. When a Bean is serialized to disk (or anywhere else for that matter), its state is preserved such that its property values remained untouched. There are several reasons why you might want to "freeze-dry" a Bean for later use.

Some servers support indefinite, long-term session persistence by writing any session data (including Beans) to disk between server shutdowns. When the server comes back up, the serialized data is restored. This same reasoning applies to servers that support clustering in heavy traffic environments. Many of them use serialization to replicate session data among a group of web servers. If your Beans do not implement the `Serializable` interface, the server will be unable to properly store or transfer your Beans (or other classes) in these situations.

Using a similar tactic, you might choose to store serialized copies of your Beans to disk, an LDAP server, or a database for later use. You could, for example, implement a user's shopping cart as a Bean, which you store in the database between visits.

If a Bean requires particularly complicated configuration or setup it may be useful to fully configure the Beans' properties as required, then serialize the configured

Bean to disk. This snapshot of a Bean can then be used anywhere you would normally be required to create and configure the Bean by hand, including the `<jsp:useBean>` tag via the `beanName` attribute.

The `beanName` attribute of the `<jsp:useBean>` tag is used to instantiate serialized Beans rather than creating new instances from a class file. If the Bean doesn't exist in the scope, then the `beanName` attribute is passed on to `java.beans.Bean.instantiate()`, which will instantiate the Bean for the class loader. It first assumes that the name corresponds to a serialized Bean file (identified by the .ser extension) in which case it will bring it to life, but if it can't find or invoke the serialized Bean it will fall back to instantiating a new Bean from its class.

6.3.3 *The HttpSessionBindingListener interface*

Implementing the Java Servlet API's `HttpSessionBindingListener` interface in your Java Bean's class will enable its instances to receive notification of session events. The interface is quite simple, defining only two methods.

```
public void valueBound(HttpSessionBindingEvent event)
public void valueUnbound(HttpSessionBindingEvent event)
```

The `valueBound()` method is called when the Bean is first bound (stored into) the user's session. In the case of JSP, this will typically happen right after a Bean is instantiated by a `<jsp:useBean>` tag that specifies a `session` scope, thus assigning the Bean to the user's session.

The `valueUnbound()` method is called, as you would expect, when the object is being removed from the session. There are several situations that could cause your Bean to be removed from the session. When the JSP container plans to expire a user's session due to inactivity, it is required to first remove each item from the session, triggering the `valueUnbound` notification. The JSP container will automatically recognize that the Bean is implementing the `HttpSessionBindingListener` interface, hence there is no need to register the Bean with the container as a listener. Alternatively, this event would be triggered if a servlet, scriptlet, or other Java code specifically removed the Bean from the session for some reason.

Each of these events is associated with an `HttpSessionBindingEvent` object, which can be used to gain access to the session object. Implementing this interface will allow you to react to session events by, for example, closing connections that are no longer needed, logging transactions, or performing other maintenance activities. If you are implementing your own session persistence, such as saving a shopping cart, this would be where you would move your data off to disk or database.

6.3.4 *Other features of the Bean API*

In addition to the access methods and constructor conventions that we have examined here, the JavaBeans Specification defines several other features. When writing Beans for use with JSP we do not generally need to concern ourselves with these remaining elements of the specification because they are more oriented toward visual Beans, such as GUI components. While most of this extra functionality is not reflected into the Bean tags, it can be useful working with Beans through JSP scriptlets or as part of a larger system. For clarity and for the sake of completeness we will quickly point out these other features. For full details on these aspects of JavaBeans, see the JavaBeans Specification or Manning's *The Awesome Power of Java Beans*.

JavaBean event model

The JavaBeans API supports Java 1.1 style event handling, a feature intended primarily for visual components. Events allow visual Beans to communicate with one another in a standard way, without each Bean having to be too tightly coupled to other Beans. However, JSP containers do not support the JavaBeans event model directly. Any Bean-to-Bean communication is the responsibility of the Bean designer.

Bound properties

A Bean can be designed to generate events any time changes are made to its properties. This allows users of the Bean to be notified of the changes and react accordingly. If, for example, a Bean contained information about the status of a radio button on a user interface which was modified by one of the Bean's users, any other users of the Bean would be notified and could update their displays accordingly.

Constrained properties

Constrained properties are properties whose values must fall within specific limits. For example a property representing a percentage value must be greater than or equal to zero, and less than or equal to one hundred. The only difference between the design patterns for setting a constrained versus an unconstrained property is that it must declare that it throws the `java.beans.PropertyVetoException`. Objects that want to support constrained properties must also implement methods that allow other objects to register with the Bean so that they can play a part in the change approval process. Constrained property functionality is not directly implemented through the Bean tags, although Beans can still take advantage of this functionality internally. If a Bean throws an exception in response to an illegal property value, the normal JSP error handling will take place.

6.4 *Mixing scriptlets and Bean tags*

Since JSP Bean tags, scriptlets, and expressions eventually are translated into the same single Java servlet class on the server, you can combine any of the elements. This allows you to take advantage of component-centric design while not being bound by the limits of the built-in tag commands. Using the `<jsp:useBean>` tag to create objects puts them into the scope of the page, making them available to both scriptlets and `<jsp:getProperty>` and `<jsp:setProperty>` tags.

6.4.1 *Accessing Beans through scriptlets*

Since the `<jsp:useBean>` tag creates an object reference behind the scenes, you are free to access that object through scriptlets and expressions, using the Bean's name as the object identifier. For example, it is perfectly valid to do either of these snippets, both of which produce the same results:

```
<jsp:useBean id="stocks" class="StockMarketBean" scope="page"/>
The Dow is at <jsp:getProperty name="stocks" property="dow"/> points
```

or

```
<jsp:useBean id="stocks" class="StockMarketBean" scope="page"/>
The Dow is at <%= stocks.getDow() %> points
```

Calling Bean properties through an expression rather than the somewhat lengthy `<jsp:getProperty>` tag can be a handy shortcut if you aren't afraid of a little Java code in your page. A word of caution however! You can't always assume that a Bean's property returns a String or maps directly to the method you expect. It may return a different type of data than you expect (which is all right if you are calling the method in an expression), or a `BeanInfo` class may be redirecting you to a completely different method—one for which you may not even know the name.

6.4.2 *Accessing scriptlet created objects*

The reverse of this operation is not true. Objects created through scriptlets are not guaranteed to be accessible through the Bean tags, because there is no guarantee that these objects will become part of the page context. Consider the following JSP code for example, which is not valid in most JSP containers.

```
<html><body>
Auto-Shop 2000<br>
<% Car car = (Car)request.getAttribute("car"); %>
<% car.updateRecords(); %>
This car has <jsp:getProperty name="car" property="milage"/> miles on it…
</body></html>
```

In this example we have attempted to pull an object reference, car, out of the request and use it in the page. However, the <jsp:getProperty> tag will not have a reference to the object because it was not scoped into the page through a <jsp:useBean> tag. The corrected code is:

```
<html><body>
Auto-Shop 2000<br>
<jsp:useBean id="car" class="Car" scope="request"/>
<% car.updateRecords(); %>
This car has <jsp:getProperty name="car" property="milage"/> miles on it…
</body></html>
```

Notice that we can access the object through both scriptlets and JSP tags, allowing us to call the updateRecords() method directly. We can even change the object referenced by the named identifier specified by <jsp:useBean>—it is the identifier that's important, not the actual object reference.

Handling indexed properties

This technique is particularly useful in handling indexed properties, which JSP doesn't provide any easier way to deal with (other than custom tags, as we'll learn in chapters 13 and 14). We apply the same principles as before, creating objects with the <jsp:useBean> tag and referencing them through scriptlets and expressions. For example, to loop through an indexed property we write code similar to that which follows. The exact syntax will depend on your Bean's properties and associated methods. In this example, MusicCollectionBean contains an array of Album objects, nested in its albums property. Each Album object in turn has a number of Bean properties. Note however, that we must declare the Album object reference through a Bean tag as a placeholder, or it will not be available to our page context and therefore inaccessible through the Bean tags.

```
<jsp:useBean id="music" class="MusicCollectionBean"/>
<jsp:useBean id="album" class="Album"/>
<%
Album[] albums = music.getAlbums();
for (int j=0; j < albums.length; j++) {
  album = albums[a];
%>
Title: <jsp:getProperty name="album" property="title"/><BR>
Artist: <jsp:getProperty name="album" property="artist"/><BR>
Year: <jsp:getProperty name="album" property="year"/><BR>
<% } %>
```

This code will loop through each of the albums in the array returned by the `getAlbums()` method of `MusicCollectionBean`, assigning each to the variable `album` in turn. We can then treat `album` as a Bean, accessing it through the `<jsp:getProperty>` tags. You can use this technique to create tables, lists, and other sequences of indexed properties.

Other Bean methods

Since Beans are just objects, they may also have methods that are accessible through JSP scripting elements. While it is desirable to create Beans that can be used entirely through the tags, sometimes it is useful to create Beans with two levels of complexity. These extra methods are not Bean-related, but allow you to treat the Bean as any other Java object for more benefits or advanced functionality.

Not all of your methods need to follow the Bean conventions, although only those methods that can be found by introspection will be made available through the Bean container. It is sometimes useful to provide basic functionality accessible through the Bean container, such as JSP tags, and more advanced functionality only accessible through scriptlets or direct programmer intervention.

Removing a Bean when done with it

At the end of a Bean's life span, which is determined by its scope, all references to the Bean will be removed and it will become eligible for garbage collection. Beans in the page or request scopes are automatically reclaimed at the end of the HTTP request, but session and application Beans can live on. The life of a session Bean is, as discussed, dependent on the JSP container while the application scope is tied to the life of the server. There are several situations where you might want to prematurely end the life of a Bean. The first involves removing it from memory for performance reasons. When you have no more use for the Bean, especially one in session or application scope, it's a good idea to get rid of it. Eliminating unused Bean objects will improve the performance of your server-side applications by freeing as many of the JVM's resources as soon as possible.

Another reason you want to remove a Bean is to eliminate it from the user's session for security reasons. A good example of this would be removing a user's login information from the session when the user has specifically advised that they are logging off. A typical approach to user authentication with JSP is to place the user's login credentials into the session following a successful login. The presence of these credentials in the session satisfies the login requirements for future visits to protected pages until the session expires. For security reasons however it is desirable to offer the visitor the ability to eliminate their login information from the session when they have completed their visit. We can accomplish this by simply removing their credentials from the session, returning them to their unauthenticated state. The methods available to you are summarized in table 6.4.

Table 6.4   Discarding a used Bean from various scopes

Scope	Scriptlet	Servlet
session	`session.removeAttribute(name)`	`HttpSession.removeAttribute(name)`
request/page	`pageContext.remove-Attribute(name)`	`ServletRequest.remove-Attribute(name)`
application	`application.remove-Attribute(name)`	`ServletContext.remove-Attribute(name)`

The request Bean

As discussed in previous chapters, JSP defines a number of implicit objects that reflect information about the environment. The request object encapsulates information about the request and has several properties that are accessible through the Bean tags. Like other Beans, we can access the properties of the request objects through `<jsp:getProperty>`. The `id` value assigned to the implicit request object is, as you probably guessed, `request`. For example, we can display the remote user name as follows:

```
<jsp:getProperty name="request" property="remoteUser"/>
```

Table 6.5 summarizes some of the more useful methods of the request object, which can be exposed as properties to the Bean tags.

Table 6.5 Properties of the request Bean

Name	Access	Use
`authType`	read	Gets the authentication scheme of this request or null if unknown. Same as the CGI variable `AUTH_TYPE`
`method`	read	Gets the HTTP method (for example, `GET`, `POST`, `PUT`) with which this request was made. Same as the CGI variable `REQUEST_METHOD`.
`pathInfo`	read	Gets any optional extra path information following the servlet path of this request's URI, but immediately preceding its query string. Same as the CGI variable `PATH_INFO`
`pathTranslated`	read	Gets any optional extra path information following the servlet path of this request's URI, but immediately preceding its query string, and translates it to a real path. Same as the CGI variable `PATH_TRANSLATED`
`queryString`	read	Gets any query string that is part of the HTTP request URI Same as the CGI variable `QUERY_STRING`
`remoteUser`	read	Gets the name of the user making this request. The user name is set with HTTP authentication. Whether the user name will continue to be sent with each subsequent communication is browser-dependent. Same as the CGI variable `REMOTE_USER`.
`requestURI`	read	Gets the URI corresponding to the original request
`characterEncoding`	read	Gets the character set encoding for the input of this request.
`contentType`	read	Gets the Internet media type of the request entity data, or null if not known. Same as the CGI variable `CONTENT_TYPE`.
`protocol`	read	Gets the protocol and version of the request as a string of the form <protocol>/<major version>.<minor version>. Same as the CGI variable `SERVER_PROTOCOL`.
`remoteAddr`	read	Gets the IP address of the agent that sent the request. Same as the CGI variable `REMOTE_ADDR`.
`serverName`	read	Gets the host name of the server that received the request. Same as the CGI variable `SERVER_NAME`.
`serverPort`	read	Gets the port number on which this request was received. Same as the CGI variable `SERVER_PORT`.
`scheme`	read	Gets the scheme of the URL used in this request, for example "http," "https," or "ftp."
`remoteHost`	read	Gets the fully qualified host name of the agent that sent the request. Same as the CGI variable `REMOTE_HOST`

Working with databases

7

While long a bastion of large, well-funded enterprises, databases have found their way into a much wider range of web sites in recent years. Along with their traditional role as back office data sources, most large-scale web sites employ databases for at least some portion of the content. Ad management, users registration information, community services, and contact lists are just some of the features commonly managed through a database. JSPs and relational databases make a good combination. The relational database gives us the organizational capabilities and the performance necessary to manage large amounts of dynamic data, while JSP gives us a convenient way to present it. By combining the power of a relational database with the flexibility of JSP for content presentation and front-end design you can quickly develop rich, interactive web applications.

7.1 *JSP and JDBC*

Unlike other web scripting languages such as ColdFusion, Server Side JavaScript, and PHP, JSP does not define its own set of tags for database access. Rather than develop yet another mechanism for database access, the designers of JSP chose to leverage Java's powerful, popular, database API—JDBC.

When a JSP application needs to communicate with a database, it does so through a vendor-provided driver class written to the JDBC API. Accessing a database in JSP then is nothing new; it sticks to this tried and true workhorse from Sun. In practice, as we'll learn in chapter 8, we'll often isolate database access inside a servlet or a Bean, keeping the details hidden from the presentation aspects of the JSP page. Both of these approaches are illustrated in figure 7.1

Learning JDBC is beyond the scope of this book, and a wealth of valuable information already exists on the topic. If you aren't familiar with Java's JDBC API, a number of online tutorials can be found on Sun's JDBC web site, http://java.sun.com/products/jdbc. Check online or at your favorite bookstore if you need more information. In this chapter we'll focus instead on the relationship between JSP and JDBC.

NOTE The JDBC classes are part of the `java.sql` package, which must be imported into any Java class from which you wish to access JDBC, including your JSP pages. Additional, optional extensions for the 2.0 version of the JDBC API can be found in the `javax.sql` package, if it is installed on your system. If your JDBC driver is not in your JSP container's class path, you will have to either import it into your page or refer to it through its fully qualified class name.

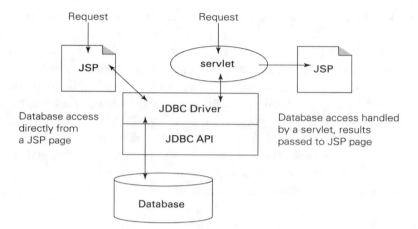

Figure 7.1 Database access options in JSP

7.1.1 *JNDI and data sources*

In ColdFusion and other template/scripting systems you access a database through a single identifier that corresponds to a preconfigured database connection (or connection pool) assigned by the system's administrator. This allows you to eliminate database connection information from your code, referring to your database sources by a logical name such as EmployeeDB or SalesDatabase. The details of connecting to the database are not exposed to your code. If a new driver class becomes available, the database server moves, or the login information changes, only the resource description needs to be reconfigured. Any components or code referencing this named resource will not have to be touched.

JSP does not define its own database resource management system; instead you can rely on JDBC 2.0's Datasource interface and Java's Naming and Directory Interface (JNDI) technology for naming and location services. JNDI can be used to shield your application code from the database details such as the driver class, the username, password, and connection URI. To create a database connection with JNDI, specify a resource name which corresponds to an entry in a database or naming service, and receive back the information necessary to establish a connection with your database. This shields your JSP code and supporting components from changes to the database's configuration. More information on using JNDI is available from Sun, at http://java.sun.com/products/jndi. Here's an example of creating a connection from a data source defined in the JNDI registry:

```
Context ctx = new InitialContext();
DataSource ds = (DataSource)ctx.lookup("jdbc/SalesDB");
Connection con = ds.getConnection("username", "password");
```

We can further improve upon this abstraction, and further simplify database access, through custom tags, which use JNDI to allow simple access to named database resources in a manner familiar to ColdFusion and other tag-style languages.

7.1.2 *Prepared statements*

Prepared statements allow us to develop an SQL query template that we can reuse to handle similar requests with different values between each execution. Essentially we create the query, which can be any sort of SQL statement, leaving any variable values undefined. We can then specify values for our undefined elements before executing the query, and repeat as necessary. Prepared statements are created from a Connection object, just like regular Statement objects. In the SQL, replace any variable values with a question mark.

```
String query = "SELECT * FROM GAME_RECORDS WHERE SCORE > ? AND TEAM = ?";
PreparedStatement statement = connection.prepareStatement(query);
```

Before we can execute the statement we must specify a value for all of our missing parameters. The `PreparedStatement` object supports a number of methods, each tied to setting a value of a specific type—int, long, String, and so forth. Each method takes two arguments, an index value indicating which missing parameter you are specifying, and the value itself. The first parameter has an index value of 1 (not 0) so to specify a query that selects all high scores > 10,000 for the "Gold" team we use the following statements to set the values and execute the query:

```
statement.setInt(1, 10000);     // Score
statement.setString(2, "Gold"); // Team
ResultSet results = statement.execute();
```

Once you have defined a prepared statement you can reuse it simply by changing parameters, as needed. There is no need to create a new prepared statement instance as long as the basic query is unchanged. So, we can execute several queries without having to create a statement object. We can even share a single prepared statement among an application's components or a servlet's users. When using prepared statements, the RDBMS engine has to parse the SQL statement only once, rather than again and again with each new request. This results in more efficient database operations.

Not only is this more efficient in terms of database access, object creation, and memory allocation but the resulting code is cleaner and more easily understood.

Consider this example again, but this time the queries are not hard coded, but come from a Bean, `userBean`, which has been initialized from an input form.

```
statement.setInt(1, userBean.getScore());  // Score
statement.setString(2, userBean.getTeam(); // Team
ResultSet results = statement.execute();
```

The alternative is to build each SQL statement from strings, which can quickly get confusing, especially with complex queries. Consider the following example again, this time without the benefit of a prepared statement:

```
Statement statement = connection.getStatement();
String query = "SELECT * FROM GAME_RECORDS WHERE SCORE > " +
userBean.getScore() + " AND TEAM = '" + user.getTeam() +
userBean.getTeam() + "'";
ResultSet results = Statement.executeQuery(query);
```

Another, perhaps even more important, benefit of using prepared statements is evidenced here. When you insert a value into a prepared statement with one of its setter methods you do not have to worry about proper quoting of strings, escaping of special characters, and conversions of dates and other values into the proper format for your particular database. This is particularly important for JSPs that are likely to be collecting search terms input directly from users through form elements and are particularly vulnerable to special characters and unpredictable input. Since each database might have its own formatting peculiarities, especially for dates, using prepared statements can help further distance your code from dealing with any one particular database.

7.2 Database driven JSPs

There are a number of ways to develop database driven applications through JSP. In this chapter, we're concentrating on the database interaction itself, and less on program architecture. JSP application design will be covered in chapter 8 and again in chapter 9 which will feature a walk-through example of a database driven JSP project.

7.2.1 Creating JSP components from table data

You may have recognized a similarity between the tables of a relational database and simple JavaBean components. When building your applications think of tables as being analogous to JavaBeans. While JavaBeans have properties, data from a table has columns. A table's schema is like the class that defines a JavaBean—defining the names and types data that instances will hold. Like Java classes, tables are templates for storing a specific set of information like the data from a purchase order or details about inventory items and by themselves are not particularly useful.

It is only when we create instances of a JavaBean class or add rows to a table that we have something worthwhile. Each row is an instance of what the table represents, just as a Bean is an instance of its class. Both classes and tables then serve as data models, a useful container for managing information about some real world object or event. Keep this relationship in mind as we learn about JSP database development. It will form the basis for many of our applications.

One of the most common areas for utilizing databases with JSP applications is to retrieve data stored in a table to create a Bean for use within the page. The configuration of JSP components from information in the database is pretty straightforward if your table schema (or the results of a join between tables) closely corresponds to your Bean's properties. We simply use the row access methods of the `ResultSet` class to configure the Bean's properties with the values in the table's corresponding columns. If there is more than a single row in the result set we must create a collection of Beans, one for each row of the results.

Database Beans from scriptlets

You can use JSP scriptlets to configure a Bean's properties when it is created. After establishing the connection, set its properties as appropriate through the data carried in the `ResultSet`. Don't forget to import the `java.sql` package into the page with the `<%@ page import="java.sql.*" %>` directive.

In this example we will use an `ItemBean` class used to represent a particular item from inventory, taking the item number from the request object.

```
<%@ page import="java.sql.*" %>
<jsp:useBean id="item" class="ItemBean">
<%
Connection connection = null;
Statement statement = null;
ResultSet results = null;
ItemBean item = new ItemBean();
try {
  Class.forName("oracle.jdbc.driver.OracleDriver");
  String url = "jdbc:oracle:oci8@dbserver";
  String id = request.getParameter(id);
  String query = "SELECT * FROM PRODUCTS_TABLE WHERE ITEM_ID = " + id;
  connection = DriverManager.getConnection(url, "scott", "tiger");
  statement = connection.createStatement();
  results = statement.executeQuery(query);
  if (results.next()) {
    item.setId(results.getInteger("ITEM_ID"));
    item.setDesc(results.getString("DESCRIPTION"));
```

```
    item.setPrice(results.getDouble("PRICE"));
    item.setStock(results.getInteger("QTY_AVAILABLE"));
  }
  connection.close();
}
catch (ClassNotFoundException e) {
  System.err.println("Could not load database driver!");
}
catch (SQLException e) {
  System.err.println("Could not connect to the database!");
}
finally {
  try { if (connection != null) connection.close(); }
  catch (SQLException e) { }
}
%>
</jsp:useBean>
<html>
<body>
<table>
<tr><td>Item Number</td><td>
<jsp:getProperty name="item" property="id"/></td></td>
<tr><td>Description</td><td>
<jsp:getProperty name="item" property="desc"/></td></td>
<tr><td>Price $</td><td>
<jsp:getProperty name="item" property="price"/></td></tr>
<tr><td>On hand</td><td>
<jsp:getProperty name="item" property="stock"/></td></tr>
</table>
</body>
</html>
```

When this code finishes we will have an ItemBean that is either empty (if the SELECT found no matches) or is populated with data from the PRODUCTS_TABLE. After creating our Bean and using the database to populate it we then display its properties. In this approach we've ended up with a lot of Java code, supporting a small amount of HTML presentation. If we have several pages with similar needs, we'll end up rewriting (or using the cut and pasting operation, then maintaining) all of this code again. In chapter 8, we'll learn about architectures that help eliminate these problems. In the meantime, we could wrap the code into the Bean, creating one that is self-populating.

Self-populating Beans
You can use a similar technique to that used in the JSP page example earlier to create Beans that populate themselves. In the Bean's constructor, you can establish the database connection, perform the query, set your property values, close the connection, and be ready for business. You can also define some of your Bean's properties

as triggers that cause the Bean to retrieve data from the database by including the database access code inside your property method. For example, changing the ID property of our `ItemBean` could cause it to fetch that row of data from the database and build up the other properties.

Outside influence

As we will learn in chapter 8, it is often desirable to keep the actual Java code in the JSP page to a minimum. Instead we can rely on servlets to package data from the database into the Beans needed by the JSP page. The same approach that applies to database access still applies, but with a servlet we can share and reuse our database connection. We can move the management of database connections and the collection of data out of the page, and into a servlet.

7.2.2 JSPs and JDBC data types

Each database supports its own set of internal data types, which vary significantly among vendors. JDBC provides a layer of abstraction between Java's data types and those of the database. The JDBC layer frees a Java developer from having to worry about subtle type distinctions and proper formatting. JDBC deals with the difference in data types in two ways. It defines a set of SQL types that logically map back to native database types and it maps Java data types to the SQL types, and vice-versa.

When dealing with the database directly, such as setting up a table's schema, you must deal with SQL types. However, when retrieving or storing data through JDBC, you work in Java's type system—the JDBC method calls you make determine how to convert the data into the appropriate SQL type. When building JSP components that interact with the database it is important to understand how such data is handled. The following information will give you a good feel for some of the more important SQL types and their handling by JDBC.

Integer data

JDBC defines four SQL types for handling integer data, but the major database vendors commonly support only two. The SMALLINT type represents 16-bit signed integers and is treated as a Java `short`. The INTEGER type is mapped to Java's `int` type and holds a 32-bit signed integer value. The remaining two types, TINYINT and BIGINT, represent 8-bit and 64-bit integers and are not commonly supported.

Floating-point numbers

There are two floating-point data types specified by JDBC, DOUBLE and FLOAT. For all practical purposes they are essentially the same, the latter being included for consistency with ODBC. Sun recommends that programmers generally stick with the DOUBLE type, which is analogous to Java's double type.

Textual data

JDBC defines two primary SQL types for handling text: CHAR and VARCHAR. Each is treated as a String object by JDBC. CHAR is widely supported by most databases, and holds text of a fixed length. VARCHAR, on the other hand, holds variable length text, up to a maximum specified width. Because CHAR is a fixed length data type, if the data placed into a CHAR column contains fewer characters than the specified width it will be padded with spaces by JDBC. While HTML browsers will ignore extra spaces in JSP output data, you can call String's trim() method before acting on the data to remove trailing spaces. A third text type defined by JDBC is LONG-VARCHAR, which holds especially large amounts of text. Because vendor support for LONGVARCHAR differs wildly, you probably won't use it much.

Dates and times

To handle date and time information JDBC defines three distinct types: DATE, TIME, and TIMESTAMP. DATE holds day, month, and year values only. TIME holds hours, minutes, and seconds. TIMESTAMP combines the information held in DATE and TIME, and adds a nanoseconds field. Unfortunately, none of these corresponds exactly to java.util.Date, which falls somewhere between each of these, due to its lack of a nanoseconds field.

All of these SQL types are handled in Java by one of three subclasses of java.util.Date: java.sql.Date, java.sql.Time, and java.sql.Timestamp. Since they are subclasses of java.util.Date, they can be used anywhere a java.util.Date type is expected. This allows you to treat them as you might normally treat date and time values, while retaining compatibility with the database. Understanding how each of these specialized subclasses differs from its common base class is important. For example, the java.sql.Date class zeros out the time values, while java.sql.Time zeros out the date values. Don't forget about these important distinctions when exchanging data between the database and your JSP components. If you need to convert a java.sql.Timestamp object into its closest approximate java.util.Date object, you can use the following code:

```
Timestamp t = results.getTimestamp("MODIFIED");
java.util.Date d;
d = new java.util.Date(t.getTime() + (t.getNanos()/1000000));
```

Some of the most common data type mappings you will encounter are listed in table 7.1, along with the recommended `ResultSet` access method for retrieving data of that type.

Table 7.1 Common Java-to-JDBC type mappings

Java type	JDBC type	Recommended JDBC access method
short	SMALLINT	getShort()
int	INTEGER	getInt()
double	DOUBLE	getDouble()
java.lang.String	CHAR	getString()
java.lang.String	VARCHAR	getString()
java.util.Date	DATE	getDate()
java.sql.Time	TIME	getTime()
java.sql.Timestamp	TIMESTAMP	getTimestamp()

Handling undefined column data

If a column in the database is not assigned a value it will be set to null. The problem is that there is no good way to represent an empty value with Java's primitive types like `int` and `double`, which are not objects and cannot be set to null. For example, a call to `getInt()` might return 0 or −1 to indicate null, but those are both valid values. The problem exists for `String`s as well. Some drivers return an empty string (`""`), some return null, and still others return the string value `null`. The solution, which isn't particularly elegant but does work, is the `ResultSet`'s `wasNull()` method. This method returns true or false, depending on whether or not the last row access method called should have returned an actual null value.

We have this same problem when creating JSP components from Java Beans. The interpretation of a null value by the `<jsp:getProperty>` tag is not consistent among vendors, so if we can't use a literal value to represent null we have to design an approach similar to that of JDBC. What we can do is define a boolean property that will indicate the validity of the property value in question. When we encounter a null value in the database, we set the property to some non-null value, then make sure the validity check will return false. In the following code we set the value of our quantity property using the `QTY_AVAILABLE` column of our `ResultSet`. We also set a flag to indicate whether or not the value was actually valid.

```
init() {
  . . .
  myQuantity = results.getInt("QTY_AVAILABLE");
  if (results.wasNull()) {
    myQuantity = 0;
    validQuantity = false;
  }
  else {
    validQuantity = true;
  }
  . . .
}

  isValidQuality() {
    return validQuantity;
}
```

Of course, that means that in our JSP code we will have to check the validity of the value before using it. We have to call our boolean check method:

```
Quantity Available:
<% if (item.isValidQuantity()) %>
<jsp:getProperty name="item" property="quantity"/> units
<% else %>
Unknown
```

An alternative, if the value were being used by the JSP only for display, would be to define a `String` property that would return an appropriate value, no matter the state of the property. While this approach would limit the flexibility of the Bean, it might be worth it to gain simplicity in your JSP code.

```
getQuantityString() {
  if (validQuantity)
    return new Integer(quantity).toString();
  else
    return "Unknown";
  }
```

The most popular way to avoid this irritating problem is to not allow null values in the database. Most databases even allow you to enforce this at the schema level by flagging a column as not being allowed to have null values.

7.2.3 *Maintaining persistent connections*

Sometimes you may want to keep your database connection across several requests by the same client. You must be careful when you do this because the number of database connections that a single server can support is limited. While continuing the connection is all right for a few simultaneous users, if you have high traffic you will not want each request to have its own connection to the database. Unfortunately, establishing a connection to a database is probably one of the slowest parts of your application, so it is something to be avoided where possible.

There are a number of solutions to this. Connection pools—implemented either by the database driver or through connection pool classes—maintain a fixed number of live connections, and loan them as requested by your JSP pages or Beans. A connection pool is a good compromise between having too many open connections and paying the penalty for frequent connections and disconnections.

The following code (listing 7.1) creates a Bean which encapsulates a database connection. Using this `ConnectionBean` allows us to easily shield our JSP page from database connection details, as well as enables us to keep our connection across several pages by storing it in the session. That way we needn't reconnect to the database each time. We've also included some convenience methods that call the corresponding methods on the wrapped connection object. (Note: To keep things simple here, we've hard coded our database access parameters. You would probably want to make these configurable.)

Listing 7.1   Source Code: ConnectionBean.java

```
package com.taglib.wdjsp.databases;

import java.sql.*;
import javax.servlet.http.*;


public class ConnectionBean implements HttpSessionBindingListener {
  private Connection connection;
  private Statement statement;

  private static final String driver="postgresql.Driver";
  private static final String dbURL="jdbc:postgresql://slide/test";
  private static final String login="guest";
  private static final String password="guest";

  public ConnectionBean() {

    try {
      Class.forName(driver);
      connection=DriverManager.getConnection(dbURL,login,password);
      statement=connection.createStatement();
    }
    catch (ClassNotFoundException e) {
      System.err.println("ConnectionBean: driver unavailable");
      connection = null;
    }
```

```
   catch (SQLException e) {
     System.err.println("ConnectionBean: driver not loaded");
     connection = null;
   }
}

public Connection getConnection() {
  return connection;
}

public void commit() throws SQLException {
  connection.commit();
}

public void rollback() throws SQLException {
  connection.rollback();
}

public void setAutoCommit(boolean autoCommit)
  throws SQLException {
  connection.setAutoCommit(autoCommit );
}

public ResultSet executeQuery(String sql) throws SQLException {
  return statement.executeQuery(sql);
}

public int executeUpdate(String sql) throws SQLException {
  return statement.executeUpdate(sql);
}

public void valueBound(HttpSessionBindingEvent event) {
  System.err.println("ConnectionBean: in the valueBound method");
  try {
    if (connection == null || connection.isClosed()) {
      connection =
        DriverManager.getConnection(dbURL,login,password);
      statement = connection.createStatement();
    }
  }
  catch (SQLException e) { connection = null; }
}

public void valueUnbound(HttpSessionBindingEvent event) {
  try {
    connection.close();
  }
  catch (SQLException e) { }
  finally {
    connection = null;
```

```
      }
    }

  protected void finalize() {
    try {
      connection.close();
    }
    catch (SQLException e) { }
  }
}
```

This `ConnectionBean` class implements `HttpSessionBindingListener`, disconnecting itself from the database if the Bean is removed from the session. This keeps the connection from living too long after we are done with it, and before it actually gets garbage collected.

This Bean has been designed to shield our application from the database connection details, but we could also create a more generic Bean which accepts the necessary configuration values (`url`, `username`, `password`, and `driver`) as properties that the JSP page would have to set to activate the connection.

7.2.4 *Handling large sets of results*

If your query to the database returns a large number of rows, you probably don't want to display all of them at once. A 15,000-row table is hard to read and the HTML resulting from your JSP can take a considerable amount of time to download and display. If your application design allows, enforce a limit on the amount of rows a query can return. Asking the user to restrict his or her search further can be the quickest way to eliminate this problem.

A better solution is to present results a page at a time. There are a number of approaches to solving this problem with JSPs. The `RowSet` interface was introduced in JDBC 2.0 to define a standard way to access cached data through a JavaBeans component, or across distributed systems.

Creating a persistent ResultSet

When you retrieve a `ResultSet` object from a query, not all of the results are stored in memory. The database actually maintains a connection to the database and doles out rows as needed. This result buffering behavior keeps traffic and memory requirements low, but means you will remain connected to the database longer—which might be an issue in high traffic environments where you want to recycle database connections quickly. The database driver will determine the optimum number of rows to fetch at a time, or, in JDBC 2.0, you can offer your own suggestion to the driver. Fetching a new set of rows occurs automatically as you advance through the ResultSet; you don't have to keep track of state yourself.

One strategy then is to page through the ResultSet a page at a time, say twenty rows per page. We simply loop through twenty rows, then stick the ResultSet into our session, and visit twenty more. The cursor position internal to the ResultSet won't change between requests; we'll pick up right where we left off when we pull it out of the user's session. You don't need to explicitly keep a reference to the original Connection object, the ResultSet itself does that. When your ResultSet goes out of scope and is garbage collected your Connection will be shut down. You might want to wrap your ResultSet in a Bean and implement HttpSessionBindingListener to shut down your database connections as soon as they are no longer needed, or expose a cleanup method and call it at the bottom of your JSP page. One problem with this approach is you're keeping the database connection open for so long. We'll look at a couple of approaches that don't hold the connection open while the user browses from page to page.

Performing the query multiple times

In this technique we re-execute the search for each page of results we wish to show, storing our current window position in the user's session. At each step, we reissue the original query, then use the ResultSet's next() method (or JDBC 2.0's absolute() method) to skip forward in order to start our listing at the appropriate position. We then display the next, say, twenty rows and stop. We skip ahead twenty rows the second time the JSP is loaded, forty rows on the third, and so on. If we wish to provide additional feedback as to where the user is in the ResultSet, simply note its size. Now that you know the number of rows you can display the appropriate status information such as "page 1 of 5." One potential drawback to this technique is that each page represents a new look at the database. Should the data be modified between requests, the user's view could change from page to page.

Use a self-limiting query

This technique is less general then the others we've looked at, and can't be used in every situation. The strategy here is to show a page of data, then record the primary key of the last item you displayed. Then for each page you issue a new query, but fine-tune the search through your query's WHERE clause to limit the results of the search to those you have not shown the user.

This method works great in situations where your data is listed in sequence, say a series of product IDs. If the last product ID shown was 8375, store that number in the session, and modify your next query to use this number in the WHERE clause. For example:

```
SELECT * FROM PRODUCTS WHERE ID > 8357
```

The CachedRowSet Bean

An alternative way of handling more manageable query results—those that are bigger than a screen full, but not so big as to be a memory hog—is through Cached-RowSet. At the time of this writing Sun was providing an early implementation of the JDBC 2.0 RowSet interface, which encapsulates a database connection and associated query results into a JavaBean component, called the CachedRowSet. This Bean provides a disconnected, scrollable container for accessing result set style data in your JSP page, or other JavaBean container. This is a very useful tool for working with database information from within JSP. Sun may eventually add this class to the JDBC 2.0 optional extensions; you can find out more at Sun's JDBC web page, http://java.sun.com/products/jdbc. Unlike ResultSet, CachedRowSet is an offline connection that caches all of the rows in your query into the object. No active connection is required because all of the data has been fetched from the database. While convenient, if the results of your database query are so large that memory usage is a problem, you will probably want to stick to a persistent result set.

CachedRowSet is very easy to use. Simply configure the appropriate properties— like username, password, and the URL of your database—then set the command property to your SQL query. Doing so populates the rowset with results you can then browse through. You can also populate CachedRowSet using a RowSet object, created from another query.

Example: paging through results with a CachedRowSet

Let's build an example of paging through a series of results using Sun's Cached-RowSet Bean and JSP. We'll pull in the data, then allow the user to browse through it five rows at a time, or jump back to the first row if desired. The same technique applies to using a persistent ResultSet, although we'd have to resort to JSP scriptlets or wrap our live ResultSet object into our own Bean. In this example we'll page through a set of results five rows at a time. In figure 7.2 you can see a screen shot of our example in action.

And here in listing 7.2 is the source code:

Listing 7.2   Source code for CachedResults.jsp

```
<%@ page import="java.sql.*,javax.sql.*,sun.jdbc.rowset.*" %>
<jsp:useBean id="crs" class="CachedRowSet" scope="session">
```

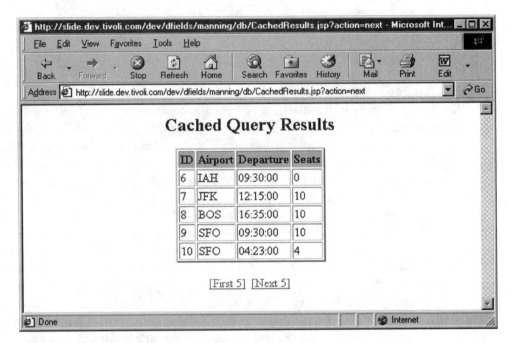

Figure 7.2   Browsing through data with a CachedRowSet

```
<%
try { Class.forName("postgresql.Driver"); }
catch (ClassNotFoundException e) {
  System.err.println("Error" + e);
}
%>
<jsp:setProperty name="crs" property="url"
   value="jdbc:postgresql://slide/test" />
<jsp:setProperty name="crs" property="username" value="guest" />
<jsp:setProperty name="crs" property="password" value="apple" />
<jsp:setProperty name="crs" property="command"
   value="select * from shuttles order by id" />
<%
  try { crs.execute(); }
  catch (SQLException e) { out.println("SQL Error: " + e); }
%>
</jsp:useBean>

<html>
<body>
<center>
<h2>Cached Query Results</h2>
<P>
```

```
<table border="2">
<tr bgcolor="tan">
<th>id</th><th>Airport</th><th>Departure</th><th>Seats</th></tr>
<%
try {
  if ("first".equals(request.getParameter("action")))
    crs.beforeFirst();
  for (int i=0; (i < 5) && crs.next(); i++) {
%>
<tr>
<td><%= crs.getString("id") %></td>
<td><%= crs.getString("airport") %></td>
<td><%= crs.getString("time") %></td>
<td><%= crs.getString("seats") %></td>
</tr>
<% } %>
</table>
</p>
<%
if (crs.isAfterLast()) {
  crs.beforeFirst(); %>
<br>At the end of the result set<br>
<% } }
catch (SQLException e) { out.println("SQL Error" + e); }
%>

<a href="<%= HttpUtils.getRequestURL(request) %>?action=first">
[First 5]</a> 
<a href="<%= HttpUtils.getRequestURL(request) %>?action=next">
[Next 5]</a> 
</center>
</body>
</html>
```

In this example, we create a session scoped `CachedRowSet` in our `<jsp:useBean>` tag, and use the body of that tag to configure it and execute our query. It is important to note that we must call attention to the database driver *before* we set the `url` property of our Bean. If we don't, the database `DriverManager` class will not recognize the URL as being associated with our driver, resulting in an error.

If the user clicks either link at the bottom of the page, a request parameter is set to indicate the desired action. So if the user clicks the "First Five" link, we move the cursor back to its starting position just before the first row of the `CachedRowSet`.

If the user selects the next five, the default, we don't have to do anything special. Since the `CachedRowSet` set is stored inside our session the cursor position will not change, and we'll simply pick up where we left off at the end of the previous viewing. We loop through the result with a `for` loop.

If more than five rows are left in the `CachedRowSet` the loop iterates through them. In each step we are advancing the cursor one position and making sure we don't go off the end of the results. The loop stops after five iterations or when `crs.next()` returns `false`—whichever occurs first. Inside the loop we simply display the data from the database. After the loop, we must move the cursor back to the beginning as if we had run out of data, essentially looping back through the data. Note the following code, near the end of the example:

```
<a href="<%= HttpUtils.getRequestURL(request) %>?action=next">
```

The `getRequestURL()` method of `HttpUtils` (part of `javax.servlet`, which is automatically imported by the JSP page) creates a link back to the current page, rather than hard coding our own URL. We include the `action` request necessary to indicate the user's selection by tacking it onto the end of the request in GET encoding syntax.

7.2.5 *Transaction processing*

Most of the JSP/database interactions we've been studying involve single step actions. That is, one SQL statement is executed and we are done. Oftentimes however, a single action is actually composed of a series of interrelated SQL statements that should succeed or fail together. For example, transferring money between two accounts is a two-step process. You have to debit one account and credit the other. By default, the database will process each statement immediately, an irrevocable action. In our funds transfer example, if the credit action went through but the debit one didn't, we would be left with accounts that don't balance.

Databases provide a mechanism known as *transactions* that help avoid such problems. A transaction is a block of related SQL statements treated as a single action, and subsequently recalled in the event that any one of the individual statements fails or encounters unexpected results. It is important to understand that to each statement in the transaction, the database will show any changes made by the previous statements in the same transaction. Anyone looking at the database outside the scope of the transaction will either not see the changes until the entire transaction has completed, or will be blocked from using the database until it is done. The behavior of the database during the transaction is configurable, but limited to the capabilities of the database with which you are working. This ability to block access to data you are working with lets you develop transactions composed of a complex series of steps without having to worry about leaving the database in an invalid state.

When you are satisfied with the results of your database statements, signal the database to accept the changes as final through the `commit()` method of your `Connection` object. Likewise, to revoke any changes made since the start of the transaction simply call your `Connection` object's `rollback()` method, which returns the database to the state it was after the last transaction was committed.

By default, JDBC assumes that you want to treat each SQL statement as its own transaction. This feature is known as *autocommit*, where each statement is committed automatically as soon as it is issued. To begin a block of statements under transaction control, you have to turn off the autocommit feature, as shown in the example which follows—a transaction where we'll swap funds between Bob's and Sue's accounts. When we've completed all of the steps in our transaction, we'll re-enable the auto-commit feature.

```
connection.setAutoCommit(false);
try {
  Statement st = connection.createStatement();
  st.executeUpdate(
    "UPDATE ACCTS SET BALANCE=(BALANCE-100) WHERE OWNER = "Bob");
  st.executeUpdate(
    "UPDATE ACCTS SET BALANCE=(BALANCE + 100) WHERE OWNER = "Sue");
  connection.commit();
}
catch (SQLException e) { connection.rollback(); }
finally { connection.setAutoCommit(true); }
```

In the example we roll back the transaction if a problem occurs, and there are a number of reasons one could. Bob and Sue might not exist, or their account may not be accessible to our program, Bob's account may not have enough funds to cover the transaction, the database could explode between the first and second statements. Wrapping them into a transaction ensures that the entire process either completes, or the whole thing fails—not something in between.

7.3 *Example: JSP conference booking tool*

We'll wrap up this chapter with an example that ties together much of what we've learned about JSP database access: data retrieval, persistent connections, and multi-page transaction processing. Here we'll concentrate on the database code rather than the application architecture, which is covered in chapter 8.

7.3.1 Project overview

In this project we must build an application to support an upcoming JSP conference, which is being held in several major cities across the U.S. First, we must determine which conference (city) the user plans to attend and reserve a slot for him or her, as seating is very limited. Secondly, we must also reserve a seat for the user on one of the several shuttle buses which will transport participants from the airport to the conference. The tricky part is making sure that once the user has secured a ticket to the conference he or she doesn't lose it to other users while picking a shuttle option. This becomes a very real possibility when you consider thousands of users registering across the globe simultaneously.

7.3.2 Our database

Our database backend already exists and is populated with the relevant data in two tables, CONFERENCES (table 7.2) and SHUTTLES (table 7.3). The tables are related through their respective AIRPORT column, which holds the three-character identifier for each airport associated with each conference city. Once the user has selected a city, we can use the airport identifier to locate appropriate shuttle service.

Table 7.2   Schema for the Conferences table

Column	Type
ID	int
CITY	varchar(80)
AIRPORT	char(3)
SEATS	int

Table 7.3   Schema for the Shuttles table

Column	Type
ID	int
AIRPORT	char(3)
TIME	time
SEATS	int

7.3.3 Design overview

There are four basic steps in this process: picking a city, choosing a shuttle, reviewing selections, and confirming the transaction. A user will be presented a list of cities where the conference will be held and may select any one of them where space is available. Doing so should hold his or her seat in the database by starting a transaction. This will ensure that the user doesn't lose his or her seat while selecting the shuttle in the second step. The third and fourth steps in the process are to have the user review his or her selections and confirm them—committing the changes to the database—or abort the process, rolling back the selections to free them for other, less fickle attendees.

To maintain a transaction across several pages like this we'll need to use JSP's session management capabilities to store our connection to the database, which we'll wrap in the `Connection Bean` we built earlier in this chapter. This will allow our transaction to span each page in the process. The pages, in order of application flow, are shown in figure 7.3. As you can see, we've also created a separate error page we can use to report any problem with the database or other element of the application.

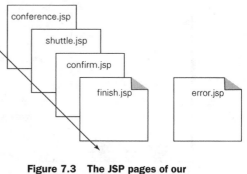

Figure 7.3   The JSP pages of our registration application

Step 1: conference.jsp

The responsibilities of the conference selection page (figure 7.4) are to present the user with a list of conference cities, pulled from the database, and allow him/her to select any of them which have openings. The source code is shown in listing 7.3.

Listing 7.3   Source code for conference.jsp

```
<%@ page import="java.sql.*,com.taglib.wdjsp.databases.*" errorPage="error.jsp" %>
<jsp:useBean id="connection" class="ConnectionBean" scope="session"/>
<html>
<body>
<center>
<font size="+2" face="arial"><b>Conference Registration</b></font>
<form action="shuttle.jsp" method="post">
<table border=1 bgcolor="tan" width="50%" align="center">
<tr><td>
<table border="0" bgcolor="white" cellspacing=0 width="100%">
<tr bgcolor="tan">
<th> </th><th>City</th><th>Tickets Remaining</th></tr>
<%
String sql = "SELECT * FROM CONFERENCES";
```

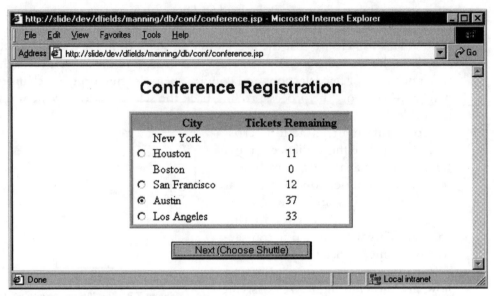

Figure 7.4   The conference selection page

```
ResultSet results = connection.executeQuery(sql);
while (results.next()) {
  if (results.getInt("seats") > 0) {
%>
<td>
<input type="radio" name="show"
value="<%= results.getString("id") %>">
</td>
<% } else { %>
<td> </td>
<% } %>
<td><%= results.getString("city") %></td>
<td align="center"><%= results.getString("seats") %></td>
</tr>
<% } %>
</table>
</td></tr></table>

<p>
<input type="submit" value="Next (Choose Shuttle)">
</form>
</center>

</body>
</html>
```

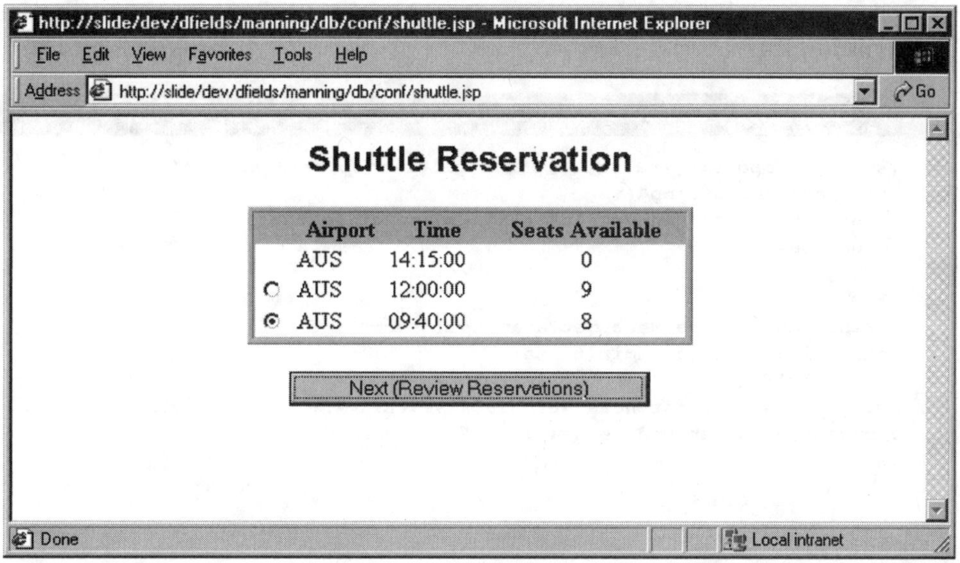

Figure 7.5 The shuttle selection page

This is the entry point into our application, but because our simple `Connection-Bean` shields the database information from the page, we needn't do anything special to configure it. In fact, each page in our application starts with a block of code to import our database classes and reference the `ConnectionBean` from the session, or—in this case—create a `ConnectionBean` and place it into the session.

Once we have a connection to the database we can simply build our form using data from the `CONFERENCE` table by executing the appropriate query and looping through it with a `while` loop. For each row in the table, we verify that there are seats available before adding a radio button for this city, ensuring that we don't allow the user to pick a conference that is full. We use the ID of each conference as the value of the radio button, to which we have given the name `show`. We'll use that in the next page to hold their seat at the conference. The rest of the code is pretty straightforward HTML. Clicking the Next button directs the user to the next page of the application, shuttle.jsp (figure 7.5).

Step 2: shuttle.jsp

The shuttle selection page has a double duty. First it has to act on the information gathered on the conference selection page. We have to reserve the user a seat at the selected conference. Secondly, we have to allow the user to pick a conference shuttle selection based on which conference city he/she will be visiting. The source appears in listing 7.4.

Listing 7.4   Source code for shuttle.jsp

```jsp
<%@ page import="java.sql.*,com.taglib.wdjsp.databases.*"
errorPage="error.jsp" %>
<jsp:useBean id="connection" class="ConnectionBean"
scope="session"/>

<%
String showID = request.getParameter("show");
connection.setAutoCommit(false);
String sql;
sql = "UPDATE conferences set seats=seats-1 where id=" + showID;
connection.executeUpdate(sql);
%>

<html>
<body>
<center>
<font size="+2" face="arial"><b>Shuttle Reservation</b></font>
<form action="confirm.jsp" method="post">
<table border=1 bgcolor="tan" width="50%" align="center">
<tr><td>
<table border="0" bgcolor="white" cellspacing=0 width="100%">
<tr bgcolor="tan"><th> </th>
<th>Airport</th><th>Time</th><th>Seats Available</th></tr>
<%
sql = "SELECT s.* from shuttles s, conferences c where c.id=" +
showID + " and s.airport = c.airport";
ResultSet results = connection.executeQuery(sql);
while (results.next()) {
  if (results.getInt("seats") > 0) {
%>
<td>
<input type="radio" name="shuttle"
value="<%= results.getString("id") %>">
</td>
<% } else { %>
<td> </td>
<% } %>
<td><%= results.getString("airport") %></td>
<td><%= results.getTime("time") %></td>
<td align="center"><%= results.getString("seats") %></td>
</tr>
<% } %>
</table>
</td></tr></table>
```

```
<p>
<input type="hidden" name="show" value="<%= showID %>">
<input type="submit" value="Next (Review Reservations)">
</form>
</center>

</body>
</html>
```

Now, after grabbing a reference to the `ConnectionBean` from the session, we grab the selected show ID from the request and stash it in a local variable. We'll need it to update the database, plus we'll pass it on to the pages that follow so we can summarize the user's selections on the last page.

```
String showID = request.getParameter("show");
```

We now actually reserve the user a seat at his or her selected conference, by reducing the open seat count by one. Before we do this however, we turn off the auto-commit feature of the database, thereby starting a transaction.

Generating our input form is no different than on the first page of the application, though the database query is more complicated.

```
"SELECT s.* from shuttles s, conferences c WHERE c.id=" +
showID + " and s.airport = c.airport"
```

That translates into a statement something like this:

```
SELECT s.* from shuttles s, conferences c
WHERE c.id=12 and s.airport = c.airport
```

Which, in English, means "perform a join on the tables shuttles and conferences, keeping only the shuttle table's columns, and select only those rows where the conference ID is 12 and the conference and shuttle are associated with the same airport." This gives us a subset of the available shuttles, showing only those available for our selected city. (Note that we can specify a table alias after each table's name (the s and c values) which keeps us from having to spell out the full table name each time we use it in the application.)

We then loop through the result set as before, again not allowing the user to select an entry that is already full. We'll still need the `showID` selected in the original page later in the application, so we'll carry that on through a hidden form field.

```
<INPUT TYPE="HIDDEN" NAME="show" VALUE="<%= showID %>">
```

We could have placed it into the session, but this is just as easy for now and involves fewer steps. Figure 7.6 shows how the user confirms his/her reservation.

Figure 7.6   The confirmation request page

Step 3: confirm.jsp

On this page we must reserve the user's seat on the selected shuttle, display a summary of his/her selections from the first two screens, and then ask the user to either commit or cancel the reservation. Here in listing 7.5 is source code for the page:

Listing 7.5   Source code for confirm.jsp

```
<%@ page import="java.sql.*,com.taglib.wdjsp.databases.*" errorPage="error.jsp" %>
<jsp:useBean id="connection" class="ConnectionBean" scope="session"/>
<%
String sql;
String shuttleID = request.getParameter("shuttle");
String showID = request.getParameter("show");
sql = "UPDATE shuttles set seats=seats-1 where id=" + shuttleID;
connection.executeUpdate(sql);
sql = "SELECT c.city, c.airport, s.time from conferences c, " +
  "shuttles s where c.id=" + showID + " and s.id=" + shuttleID;
ResultSet results = connection.executeQuery(sql);
results.next();
%>
<html>
<body>
<center>
```

```
<font size="+2" face="arial"><B>Reservation Confirmation</b></font>
<form action="finish.jsp" method=post>
<table border=1 bgcolor="tan" width="50%" align="center">
<tr><td>
<table border="0" bgcolor="white" cellspacing=0 width="100%">
<tr bgcolor="tan"><th>Summary</th></tr>
<tr><td>
Reservations have been requested for
the <b><%= results.getString("city") %></b>
show, with a complimentary shuttle from
the <b><%= results.getString("airport") %></b> airport
departing at <b><%= results.getTime("time") %></b>.
<p>
To confirm your reservations select commit below.
</td></tr>
</table>
</td></tr></table>

<p>
<input type="submit" name="commit" value="Commit Reservation">
<input type="submit" name="rollback" value="Cancel Reservations">
</body>
</html>
```

Again, there's not much new here. We decrement the appropriate shuttle seat count, just as we did earlier with the conference. We've now made all the changes we plan to make to the database, but remember we are still under transaction control since we turned off autocommit earlier. We have to disable autocommit only once, because it is a property of our connection, which we have stored in our session via the ConnectionBean.

```
sql = "UPDATE shuttles set seats = seats - 1 where id = " + shuttleID;
connection.executeUpdate(sql);
```

The query to get the summary information is a little complicated; we could have broken it into a couple of separate queries, extracting the appropriate data from each. However, it's not necessary.

```
sql = "SELECT c.city, c.airport, s.time from conferences c, shuttles s where
  c.id=" + showID + " and s.id=" + shuttleID;
```

This selects the columns we are interested in from the intersection of the CONFERENCE and SHUTTLES table where the corresponding ID values match the two selections the user already made. At that point, we are ready to move on to the final page (figure 7.7), which, depending on which button the user clicks, will commit the transaction or roll it back.

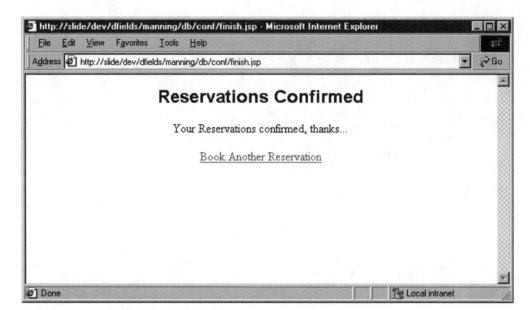

Figure 7.7   The final page

Step 4: finish.jsp

Listing 7.6 is the final segment of our application.

Listing 7.6   Source code for finish.jsp

```
<%@ page import="java.sql.*,com.taglib.wdjsp.databases.*"
errorPage="error.jsp" %>
<html>
<body>
<%
ConnectionBean connection =
(ConnectionBean)session.getValue("connection");
if (request.getParameter("commit") != null)
  connection.commit();
else
  connection.rollback();
session.removeAttribute("connection");
%>
<center>
<% if (request.getParameter("commit") != null) { %>
<font size="+2" face="arial"><b>Reservations Confirmed</b></font>
<p>
Your Reservations confirmed, thanks...
```

```
<% } else { %>
<font size="+2" face="arial"><b>Reservations Canceled</b></font>
<p>
Your reservations have been canceled.
<% } %>

<p>
<a href="conference.jsp">Book Another Reservation</a>

</body>
</html>
```

If the user selected the Commit button, it will show up as a request parameter. If we detect this we'll commit the transaction. Otherwise, we'll call rollback:

```
if (request.getParameter("commit") != null)
  connection.commit();
else
  connection.rollback();
```

After saving our changes, we must get rid of that `ConnectionBean` to free its resources, including the database we've been holding. So, we simply remove the connection object from the session.

```
session.removeAttribute("connection");
```

The last step is to give the user feedback, with an if block, based on his/her decision. All in all the flow through this example is straightforward and linear. To wrap this example up, let's look at the error page.

The error.jsp page

This page (see listing 7.7) is referenced as an error handler for each page in the application. If any exception occurs in the course of communicating with the database, it will be forwarded to this page.

Listing 7.7   Source code for error.jsp

```
<%@ page import="java.sql.*,com.taglib.wdjsp.databases.*"
isErrorPage="true" %>
<html>
<body>
<%
if (exception instanceof SQLException) {
  try {
    ConnectionBean connection = (ConnectionBean)session.getAttribute("connection");
    connection.getConnection().rollback();
```

```
    session.removeAttribute("connection");
  }
  catch (SQLException e) { }
}
%>
<center>
<font size="+2" face="arial"><b>Application Error</b></font>
<p>
An error has occurred: <tt><%= exception %></tt>
<p>
<a href="conference.jsp">Book Another Reservation</a>
</center>
</body>
</html>
```

On this page we try to clean up some things and let the user know what has happened. In the code we abort our transactions and remove the connection object from our session when an error occurs. We'll see more detailed discussion on creating error pages in chapter 11.

Architecting JSP applications

Now that we have covered the better portion of material on how to use JSP to build dynamic web pages, we will look at how we can construct complete web applications with this technology. In this chapter we will discuss several architectural models useful for developing JSP applications. We will examine architectural options available to us when we combine JSP pages with servlets, Enterprise JavaBeans, HTML, and other software elements to create web-based applications.

8.1 *Web applications*

When designing a web application of any complexity, it helps to think of its high-level architecture in terms of three logical areas:

- The *presentation layer*, the front end which controls the look and feel and delivers results, also known as the view
- The *control layer*, which controls application flow, also known as the controller
- The *application logic* layer, which manages application data, performs calculations and communicates with back-end resources, also known as the model

The three layers (figure 8.1) aren't necessarily separate software elements or components (though as we shall see they can be), but rather useful constructs to help us

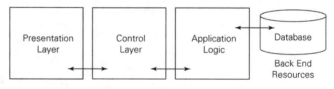

Figure 8.1 Web application layers

understand our application's requirements. If you are familiar with design patterns, a collection of common strategies used in software development, you might recognize this three-part architecture as an implementation of the Model-View-Controller, or MVC, pattern. The MVC pattern is concerned with separating the information (the model) from its presentation (the view), which maps nicely into our strategy.

Each layer plays an important role in an application's architecture and will be discussed briefly in the sections which follow. It is often advantageous to treat each tier as an independent portion of your application. Isolating the logical portions of the application helps ensure that you've covered all the bases in the design, focuses attention on creating a robust architecture, and lays the groundwork for the implementation.

Do not confuse logical separation of responsibilities with actual separation of components. Each tier does not necessarily need to be implemented by separate components. Some or all of the tiers can be combined into single components to reduce application complexity, at the expense of modularity and high-level abstraction.

The presentation layer

This tier includes the client side display elements, such as HTML, XML, or Java Applets. The presentation layout tier can be thought of as the user interface for the application because it is used to get input from the end user and display the application's results. In the MVC paradigm, the presentation layout tier fills the role of the view. It is an application specific presentation of the information owned by the application logic, or model in MVC terms.

The presentation layout tier is not concerned with how the information was obtained, or from where. Its responsibilities lie only in displaying the information itself, while delegating any other activity up the chain to other tiers. For example, in an application which involves submitting a search query through a web form only the form itself and the corresponding results are the responsibility of the presentation layer. What happens in between, the processing of the request and the retreival of the results, is not.

Application logic

The application logic layer is the heart of the application, responsible for actually doing whatever it is the application is supposed to do. It is responsible for performing queries against a database, calculating sales tax, or processing orders. This layer models the data and behavior behind the business process for which we are developing the application. It is an encapsulation of data and behavior that is independent of its presentation.

Unlike the presentation layer, this tier cares only about storing, manipulating, and generating data, not displaying it. For this reason, components designed to work as application logic can be relocated outside web-based applications, since the behavior they encapsulate isn't web-centric.

Control layer

The control layer determines the application's flow, serving as an intermediary between the presentation layer and the application logic. This tier serves as the logical connection between the user's interaction with the front-end and business services on the back end. In the MVC pattern this tier is acting as the controller. It delivers the model to the view and regulates communication between the two.

This tier is also responsible for making decisions among multiple presentations, when available. If a user's language, locale, or access level dictates a different presentation, this decision is made in the control layer. For example, an administrator might see all of the data from a database query, while an end user might see an alternate, more restrictive results page.

Each request enters the application through the control layer, which decides how the request should be handled and what information should be returned. Several things could happen at this point, depending on the circumstances of the request and the application.

For example, the control layer might determine that the requested URL is protected by access control, in which case it would forward the request to a logon page if the user has not yet been authenticated. This is an example of presentation logic controlling the application's flow from screen to screen. If any application work needs to be done, the application's presentation logic will collect data from the request, if necessary, and deliver it to the application logic tier for processing. When the application logic has completed its operation, the controller directs the request back to the user via the presentation layer.

8.1.1   *Web application flow*

Applications, no matter the platform, are designed with a particular flow in mind. Operations are expected to unfold in a series of steps, each with a specific purpose and each in an order anticipated by the application's designer. For example, to edit a user's profile you might prompt for a username whose profile you wish to edit, display that user's current profile information, ask for changes, process those changes, and then display or confirm the results of the operation. As programmers, we expect the user—indeed require the user—to proceed through each part of the application in a certain, predetermined order. We can't, for example, display user profile details without first selecting the username. The nature of the web however, can disrupt the rigid flow we've come to expect from applications.

Unlike traditional applications, web-based programs are forced to deal with strange interruptions that may occur in the expected flow of a program due to the inherent stateless request/response behavior of the HTTP protocol. The user can hit the Back button on the browser, hit reload, prematurely abort an in-process request, or open new browser windows at any time. In an application involving transactions, the application may require that certain activities happen under very specific circumstances or after certain prerequisites have been met. For example, you can't save a modified entry until you have first retrieved the original from the database, you can't delete an item until you have confirmed your selection, you can submit an order twice, and so forth.

In a traditional, off-line application, the developer has full control over the program flow. Each step in the application's process logically flows through the program. A JSP application is a different story all together. Web applications are vulnerable to irregularities in the program flow. We're not talking malicious intent; it's a perfectly innocent action on the part of users, conditioned to browsing traditional web pages. They may bookmark the application halfway through the process, or may click the back button in an attempt to go back to a step in the application. Or, they may abort the request prematurely or attempt to reload the page. In any case, they break the program flow we might normally expect. It is the responsibility of the JSP application to ensure that proper program state and application flow is maintained.

8.1.2 Architectural approaches

Possibly the biggest choice you face in designing a JSP application is determining how to separate the responsibilities of presentation, control, and application logic. There are two basic approaches to take when architecting a JSP application: page-centric and servlet-centric.

In the first approach, control and application logic responsibilities are handled by the JSP pages themselves; in the second, an intermediate servlet (or servlets) are used. Cleanly separating a JSP application into presentation, control, and application logic subsystems makes it easier to develop, understand, and maintain.

8.2 Page-centric design

In the page-centric approach an application is composed solely of a series of interrelated JSP pages that handle all aspects—the presentation, control, and the application logic. In this approach client requests are handled directly by JSP pages that perform whatever tasks are necessary, including communicating with back-end data sources, performing operations, and generating dynamic content elements.

All of the application logic and control decisions about which page to visit next will be hard coded into the page itself or expressed through its Beans, scriptlets, and expressions at run time. Commonly, the next page visited would be determined by a user clicking on a hyperlink anchor, for example <A HREF="checkout.jsp">, or through the action of submitting a form, <FORM ACTION="processSearch.jsp">.

8.2.1 Role-based pages

In the page-centric design model, each JSP page has a very specific role to play in the application. One page might display a menu of options, another might provide a form for selecting items from the catalog, and another would be needed to complete the shopping process. How a typical application might flow between these different pages is illustrated in figure 8.2.

We've combined the application logic and program flow layers of our applications at the page level. This doesn't mean that we lose our separation of presentation and content. We can still use the dynamic nature of JSP and its support for JavaBeans components to keep things squared away. We've just elected to use the JSP pages as containers for the application's control and logic, which ideally would still be encapsulated into discrete components wherever possible.

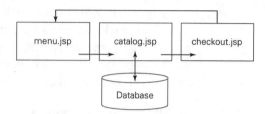

Figure 8.2   Page-centric program flow

A simple page-centric application

Here's a simple example of a trivial, two-page application using scriptlets for the application logic. In this application (and we are using the term very loosely) we are creating a system for rebel command to help sign up new recruits for Jedi training. Perhaps the most important part of the process is determining the Jedi name given to new recruits. This highly scientific calculation involves manipulating the letters of the user's first and last names with that of the hometown and mother's maiden name. This is a pretty typical two-step form application. The first page, `jediform.html`, contains an HTML form, which collects the information needed to perform processing, while the second screen, `jediname.jsp`, calculates and displays the recruit's new name (figure 8.3). The source codes for the operations are in listings 8.1 and 8.2.

Listing 8.1   Source for jediform.html

```
<html>
<body>
<b>Jedi Registration Center</b>
<form action="jediname.jsp" method="post">
<input type="text" name="firstName"> First Name<BR>
<input type="text" name="lastName"> Last Name<BR>
<input type="text" name="mother"> Mother's Maiden Name<BR>
<input type="text" name="hometown"> Hometown<BR>
<p>
<input type="submit" value="Signup Now!">
</form>
</body>
</html>
```

Figure 8.3 A page-centric application

Listing 8.2 Source for jediname.jsp

```
<html>
<body>
<%
  String firstName = request.getParameter("firstName");
  String lastName = request.getParameter("lastName");
  String mother = request.getParameter("mother");
  String hometown = request.getParameter("hometown");

  String newFirst = lastName.substring(0,3) + "-" +
    firstName.substring(0,2);
  String newLast = mother.substring(0,2) +
    hometown.substring(0,3).toLowerCase();
  String jediname = newFirst + " " + newLast;
%>
<b>Jedi Registration Center</b>
<p>
<blockquote>
<%= firstName %> <%= lastName %> of <%= hometown %>,
house of <%= mother %>, your Jedi name is <i><%= jediname %></i>.
<p>
Thank you for signing up to fight the empire.
Your training will begin soon. May the force be with you...
```

```
</blockquote>
<a href="jediform.html">Sign up another recruit</a>
</body>
</html>
```

Application flow is maintained through the form action in the first page, and through the anchor tab on the results page. The pages are tightly coupled in this case. Not only do they need to sync up request parameters, but they must be aware of each other's URLs.

8.2.2 Building composite pages

The idea of creating composite pages expands on the single page approach illustrated earlier but doesn't change the fact that application presentation, logic, and control systems are confined to a series of JSP pages. However in this design style we combine a collection of small component pages, containing either HTML or JSP, to create each screen in the application. This is accomplished through the use of the `<jsp:include>` action and the `<%@ include>` directive.

Reducing complexity through decomposition

The composite page structure is a good approach when the pages that make up your application (or web site) are composed of a number of complex dynamic elements. For example, to display details of a catalog item we might break the page into several elements—a site standard header containing navigational elements and branding, the details of the item itself, and a footer to close the page. Each of these elements can be either static, such as a snippet of HTML code, or dynamic—another JSP file. We can take this strategy a step further by building our composite page of elements

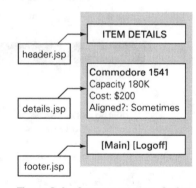

Figure 8.4   Component page design

which are also composite pages themselves—iteratively breaking down each element into more manageable structures. Each portion of the page comes from a separate JSP or HTML file, as shown in figure 8.4.

As illustrated, the header and footer files might be static HTML elements. We would then use the `<%@ include %>` directive to load the contents of the files in at run time. The item we wish to display however, might apply a boilerplate approach, by creating a JSP template, which we reuse throughout the site. This gives us the ability to isolate the presentation of an item's details (which might involve complex

HTML code) from the higher-level layout of its containing page. The page designer could choose to include the item information anywhere on the page, and in any context desired.

At run time, the primary page and any of its dynamic elements will not have to be recompiled by the JSP engine unless they themselves have changed—static content is included dynamically and not through the compilation process. For example, a change to the header file will show up at run-time, but will not compile a new version of its containing JSP page each time. An excerpt from such a compound catalog page code might look like this:

```
<html>
<body>
<jsp:include page="/headers/support_section.jsp" flush="true"/>
<center><h2>Catalog Item 7423</h2></center>
<jsp:include page="/catalog/item7423.jsp" flush="true"/>
<hr>
<jsp:include page="/footers/standard.html" flush="true"/>
</html>
</body>
```

We can concentrate on the design of each portion of the page independently of the system as a whole. This also gives us the ability to change the design at any time, from a single point.

Constructing dynamic page components

Let's not overlook the fact that you can pass information to your composite page elements through the request to provide page-specific or dynamic behaviors. For example, when we call the page we specify the title through a request parameter:

```
<jsp:include page="/headers/basic.jsp" flush="true">
  <param name="title" value="About Our Company"/>
  <param name="bgcolor" value="#FFFFFF"/>
</jsp:include>
```

And then in the /headers/basic.jsp file we retrieve the request parameters, and use JSP expressions to include their contents as part of the content we return through the include tag:

```
<html>
<head><title><%= request.getParameter("title") %></title></head>
<body bgcolor="<%= request.getParameter("bgcolor") %>">
<HR>
```

Or, revisiting our catalog item example, we might provide a more complex page component that allows you to pass in parameters to determine which catalog item to display.

```
<jsp:include page="/catalog/fetchItem.jsp" flush="true">
  <param name="item" value="7423"/>
</jsp:include>
```

We could of course configure the item parameter at run time, based on input parameters, giving us an even more useful dynamic page.

```
<param name="item" value="<%= request.getParameter("item") %>"/>
```

Any Beans or other objects that have been loaded into request or application level scope will be available to pages included through the `<jsp:include>` action. Objects created in the default page level scope will not be available however.

Component architecture, revisited

In many ways, the composite page view pattern mirrors the component architectural strategies we discussed in the chapter 5. We have broken out various content elements from our page design in order to improve the reusability and ease the process of presentation design and development. The approach we have used here, factoring out the dynamic portions of the page, is a good way to build up a composite page and reduce the complexity of any given JSP page.

The composite page approach provides some excellent benefits among collections of pages that can share common elements. By factoring out reusable, redundant information and isolating it to its own files, we get two advantages. First, we reduce the number of files involved by reusing common code. Second, we improve our ability to manage site and application design by gaining the ability to delegate engineering and design resources to discrete subsections of the application—without the potential for stepping on each other's toes.

8.2.3 *Limitations of the page-centric approach*

A page-centric design is very simple from an architectural perspective. Because there are few moving parts, little abstraction, and a minimum of layers it can be a good approach for individuals and small teams of developers savvy in both HTML design and Java development to quickly create dynamic web pages and simple JSP applications. Because a page-centric approach requires less overall code it may also be a good choice for developing prototypes. However, for an application of any complexity, the page-centric approach suffers from a number of problems.

Maintainability

Because the JSP pages that compose the application contain both presentation and logic/control code, the application can be difficult to maintain. Significant mingling between HTML and JSP code blurs the distinction between web page designer and Java coder, often requiring a high degree of interaction between developers.

Flow contol

The inherent flow control issues of web applications can lead to a number of problems unless you take the proper steps, coding your JSP pages defensively to be prepared for receiving requests out of sequence. Since each segment of a page-centric JSP application is its own page represented by its own URL, there is really nothing to stop a user from executing the pages out of order. Each page of your application must check for valid request parameters, verify open connections, watch for changing conditions, and generally take an assume-nothing approach with regards to the order of operations of your pages. As you can imagine, this quickly becomes unmanageable for all but the simplest applications. A servlet-centric approach, which we discuss next, helps centralize flow control and reduce the complexity of the individual pages.

8.3 Servlet-centric design

Another, often more manageable approach to application design with JSPs is to use its pages only for presentation, with the control and application logic aspects of the application handled by a servlet, or group of servlets, on the back end. In this approach, requests are indirectly routed to the JSP front-end pages via a servlet, which performs whatever actions are needed by the application. A servlet can do any or all of three things for the application:

- Perform actions on behalf of the JSP, such as submitting an order
- Deliver data for display, such as a database record, do a JSP
- Control flow between related JSP pages in an application

After performing the task the servlet forwards the request on to the appropriate JSP, or, for that matter, a static HTML page. This approach is illustrated in figure 8.5.

If you are familiar with the mediator design pattern, this is the same approach only applied to the JSP pages and other components of our application rather than Java objects. In the mediator pattern we create a centralized component, in this case a servlet, whose job it is to control how the other components of the application interact with each other and the application's data resources. This approach loosens the coupling between the pages—allowing them to interact without having to be directly aware of each other, and improves the abstraction between presentation and application logic.

The goal in this approach to application design is to minimize the amount of work being done in the pages themselves, relying instead on application dedicated servlets to handle such aspects. This approach eliminates complexity from the front-end JSP code, reducing them to pure data display and input collection activities.

Likewise, we eliminate the need for embedding presentation information inside the servlets. The servlets in this case should be concerned only with application flow and generating the data needed by the JSP pages for presentation to the user.

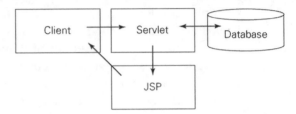

Figure 8.5   Program flow in a servlet-centric application

8.3.1 *Hello, World—with servlets*

Like any good programming book we started this one off with a couple of "Hello, World" examples—using JSPs with scriptlets and Beans. We'll now add another one, using a servlet-centric approach. The request will actually come in to the servlet, which will in turn forward it on to this JSP page (helloFromservlet.jsp):

```
<% String msg = (String)request.getAttribute("message"); %>
<html>
<body>
<%= msg %>
</body>
</html>
```

As you'll notice we aren't creating any Beans here. The getAttribute() method of the request here is the key. It's similar to getParameter()—it pulls information from the request—but deals with any object rather than just simple Strings. Later in this chapter we'll learn more about how we can use getAttribute() (and its companion the setAttribute() method) to pass Beans from servlets to JSP pages. For now though, just understand that it's looking for an object with an identifer of message and retrieving it from the request. How did it get there? The servlet put it there! Remember that this page is not designed to be called directly, but rather pass through our servlet first. The code for our servlet is:

```
package com.taglib.wdjsp.arch;

import java.io.*;
import javax.servlet.*;
import javax.servlet.http.*;

public class HelloWorldServlet extends HttpServlet {
  public void service(HttpServletRequest req,
          HttpServletResponse res)
    throws ServletException, IOException {
    String theMessage = "Hello, World";
    String target = "helloFromServlet.jsp";
    req.setAttribute("message", theMessage);
    RequestDispatcher rd;
    rd = getServletContext().getRequestDispatcher(target);
    rd.forward(req, res);
  }
}
```

When this servlet is called, it creates a "Hello, World" String object, places it into the request with the identifier of "message", creates a RequestDispatcher (a mechanism for finding servlets and JSP pages) for our JSP page, and forwards the request on to it. Notice that the servlet hasn't done any presentation. There is not a single out.println() in there! The dynamic information is generated by the servlet, but it's the JSP page that is in charge of displaying it. We've taken all of the application logic from the JSP and moved it to the servlet. While you should be familiar with the basics of Java servlets for this section, don't worry if you aren't familiar with the new Servlet API features that JSP uses. We will cover those next.

8.3.2   JSP and the servlet API

There are a number of recent additions to the Servlet API with releases 2.1 and 2.2 that enable the combination of JSPs and servlets. We'll quickly cover the relevant editions and explain how they enable a servlet-centric approach to JSP application design. Visit Sun's site (http://java.sun.com/products/servlets) for more details.

Controlling flow: the RequestDispatcher

We've talked about passing control from the servlet to the JSP, but we've haven't explained how to do this. Servlet API 2.1 introduced the RequestDispatcher interface that allows you to forward processing of a request to a JSP or another servlet, or call and include the output from a local document (a JSP, a servlet, an HTML page) into the existing output stream. A RequestDispatcher object is created by passing the URI of either the JSP page or the destination servlet to the getRequest-Dispatcher() method of either the incoming request object, or the servlet's

`ServletContext`. The `ServletContext`'s method requires an absolute URI, while the request object's method allows you use relative paths. The path is assumed relative to the servlet's request object. If the servlet that calls the methods below is mapped to the URI /store/fetchOrderServlet, then the following methods are equivalent.

```
req.getRequestDispatcher("showOrders.jsp")
getServletContext().getRequestDispatcher("/store/showOrders.jsp");
```

Why go through a `RequestDispatcher` if you already have the URI? Many things could affect the actual destination of the request—a web application, servlet mappings, and other server configuration settings. For example, the absolute path is rooted at the application level (which we will learn more about in chapter 10), which is not necessarily the same as your web server's document root. Once you have a `RequestDispatcher` object you can forward the request on, or include the output of the specified servlet JSP page in the output of the current servlet.

Once you have created a `RequestDispatcher` object corresponding to your JSP page (or another servlet for that matter) you have two choices. You can either hand control of processing the current request over to the page associated with the `RequestDispatcher` with the `forward()` method, or you can include its contents in your servlet's response via the `include()` method. The `include()` method can be called at any time, but if you have done anything in your servlet to generate output, such as written to the output stream, trying to call `forward()` will generate an exception. Both methods need a reference to the current request and response object. The signatures of these two methods of the `RequestDispatcher` class are:

```
public void include(HttpServletRequest, HttpServletResponse)
public void forward(HttpServletRequest, HttpServletResponse)
```

As we will soon see, it is the RequestDispatcher that allows us to use servlets in the role of application controller. If the servlet code needs to perform any sort of output at all, it simply does its job, then forwards the request for handling by the JSP page. You will notice that this is not a browser redirect—the browser's view of the URL will not change. The processing of the page is handled entirely by the server and the user will not experience a page reload or even see the URL of the JSP page.

Passing data: request attributes

Request attributes are objects that are associated with a given request. Unlike String values, which can be expressed through request parameters, request attributes can be any Java object. They are placed into the request by the servlet container—usually to pass information between the servlet and another servlet or JSP page.

WARNING   Attribute names beginning with `java.`, `javax.`, `sun.`, and `com.sun.` are reserved for internal usage by the servlet container and should not be used in your application. A good way to avoid attribute collisions between applications running on the same server is to use your package identifier as a prefix to your attribute name. The same approach applies for storing attributes in the session as well. If you need to maintain a consistent set of attribute names throughout a number of classes, consider defining them in a common interface that can be implemented by your servlets or other classes which need to refer to them.

Setting and getting request attributes is quite straightforward; simply use these two methods of the `ServletRequest` object, and remember that when retrieving an object stored as a request attribute, you'll have to cast it to the appropriate class.

```
public void setAttribute(String name, Object o)
public Object getAttribute(String name)
```

It is request attributes that enable servlets to hand application logic by providing a portable mechanism to exchange data between servlets and JSP pages. The data resulting from an operation, such as a database lookup, can be packaged into a Bean or other object and placed directly into the request, where the JSP page can retrieve it for presentation. We'll discuss this concept in more detail later.

Effects of dispatching on the request

It is important to understand that when the RequestDispatcher transfers the request to a JSP page it modifies the path information in the request object to reflect the URL of the destination page. If you attempt to read the path information (such as with `HttpUtils.getRequestURL()` or `getServletPath()`) you will see only the JSP page URL, not the servlet URL as originally requested. There are a few exceptions to this rule. If you use the `include()` method rather than the `forward()` method, the servlet container will create the following request attributes to reflect the original path requested:

```
javax.servlet.include.request_uri
javax.servlet.include.context_path
javax.servlet.include.servlet_path
javax.servlet.include.path_info
javax.servlet.include.query_string
```

You can retrieve these request attributes if you need to determine the original request. For this reason, if your JSP pages need to connect back to the original servlet targeted request, and you want to determine the servlet's path at run time, you will have to use `RequestDispatcher.include()` in your servlet, rather than forwarding control on to the JSP directly.

There is another type of RequestDispatcher called the `NamedRequestDis-patcher` that allows you to reference servlets by a logical name assigned to them at deployment time. A `NamedRequestDispatcher` can be obtained by calling the `get-NamedRequestDispatcher()` method of the `ServletContext`. When using the `NamedRequestDispatcher` the request information is left intact, and is not modified to map to the new servlet. Servlets are named for these purposes as part of the Servlet API's web application packaging process—which we'll introduce in chapter 10.

8.3.3 *Servlets for application control*

One important role servlets in this architecture can play is to proxy transactions between the individual JSP pages that compose the front end of the application. By making certain that each HTTP request is first handled by a centralized controlling servlet, we can better tie the pages together by performing tasks that span the scope of any single page, such as authentication, and ensure that the application maintains proper state and expected flow between components.

Enforcing application level requirements

For example, we could use our con-trolling servlet to enforce proper authentication for accessing any portion of our application. Unau-thenticated users would be detoured through a logon subsystem, which must be successfully completed, before arriving at their destination. Rather than try to build this com-plexity into each JSP page making up our application, we handle each

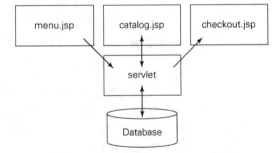

Figure 8.6   A servlet-centric catalog application

request that comes in through the mediation servlet.

In this architecture the servlet is managing flow through the application, rather than the flow being driven by HTML anchor links and forms hard coded into each JSP page. This eliminates some of the flow control problems inherent to HTTP based communications as we find in a page-centric application. The page-centric application design we built earlier could be redesigned with a servlet-centric approach to JSP application development as shown in figure 8.6.

Directing application flow

Directing application requests through a servlet shields JSP presentation code from the complexities of application flow. We can use a servlet to provide a single URL that will serve as our application's entry point and encode the logical program flow into the servlet. After being called, the servlet determines the appropriate action to take, then uses a `RequestDispatcher` to route data to the appropriate JSP page. A `submitFeedback.jsp` page delivers its data to our controlling servlet, and doesn't have to know that the next step is to send the user back to the main web page. Compare this to one JSP page calling another. This approach not only leaves our pages free of application logic, but allows us to reuse them for several purposes, even across applications, because they have been reduced to their essence—as presentation devices.

One technique for managing this flow is by employing a *screen mapper*, a data structure that can associate a logical name with each of the screens that make up your application. Then, your servlet deals with application flow as a series of logical screen names, rather than actual filenames. For example, a page featuring an input form asking for information for a new employee, might be logically mapped to the ID `NewEmployeeForm` and might refer to the URL /forms/employees/new.jsp. If you place your mappings into a property file, or even a database, you can make changes to the program's configuration without having to edit your servlet code. Although centralized storage permits sharing between applications, even something as simple as a hash table, initialized in your servlet's `init()` method will help better manage your logical to physical file mapping.

8.3.4 Servlets for handling application logic

Servlets provide an excellent mechanism for creating reusable services for your JSP pages. Provided with the inputs (such as a purchase order number or customer ID) it can deliver your page the data it needs, via request attributes. You can create as many servlets for your application as needed: one that fetches purchase orders, one that grabs customer data, and so forth. Alternatively, you can wrap up all of your application's functionality into a single servlet, and use request parameters to direct the action to be taken.

Servlets provide services

In the case of an application displaying an item's detail information from the database, the servlet might get the item's ID from the request, perform the lookup, and package the item information into a Bean. This Bean could then be added to the request before forwarding control on to the JSP page containing the item presentation

HTML. In the JSP page, we would be able to retrieve the Bean from the request, and display its information accordingly. For example, we'll grab a `PurchaseOrderBean` and place into the request object under the name `po`. In this example assume that `getPurchaseOrder()` uses the ID passed in from the JSP form to retrieve a record from the database. The `service()` method of our servlet would look like this:

```
String id = request.getParameter("id");
PurchaseOrderBean bean = getPurchaseOrder(id);
request.setAttribute("po", bean);
RequestDispatcher rd;
rd = getServletContext().getRequestDispatcher("/DisplayOrder.jsp");
rd.forward(req, res);
```

To get a reference to the `PurchaseOrderBean` we can either use the `<jsp:useBean>` tag, specifying `request` scope, or we can use the `getAttribute()` method of the request object to reference the object in as a scriptlet, casting it to the appropriate type.

```
<jsp:useBean name="po" class="PurchaseOrderBean" scope="request"/>
Purchase Order Number: <jsp:getProperty name="po" property="number"/>
```

or

```
<% jsp:useBeanname="po" class="PurchaseOrderBean"/>
<% po = (PurchaseOrderBean)request.getAttribute("po"); %>
Purchase Order Number: <jsp:getProperty name="po" property="number"/>
```

The servlet in this case is acting as a service for the JSP page.

8.3.5 *Servlets as single entry points*

If we send all of our requests through a single servlet we must encode action information into the request to declare our intentions—such as adding an item to the database or retrieving an existing one. We can do this through request parameters, using hidden form elements, URL encoding, or appending extra information after the base servlet path. For example, if the URI for the servlet controlling your application were /servlet/catalog, you could signal the desire to look up item 123 as follows by encoding request parameters:

```
/servlet/catalog?action=lookup&item=123
```

Another way to accomplish the same thing is by tacking additional information onto the end of the URI, which the servlet can pick up through the `getPathInfo()` method of its request object.

```
/servlet/catalog/lookup/123
```

The scheme by which you choose to communicate your progress is irrelevant, as long as you can easily retrieve the request information. Using request parameters makes it easy, since the servlet has built-in support for processing them. On the servlet side, we use these request parameters to determine where we are next headed in the application and to pass along any relevant information (such as the item code in the previous two examples). Once the desired action has been determined in the servlet, it can decide what needs to happen next.

Utilizing the command pattern

Many servlet-centric JSP applications involve command-oriented architecture. Requests from each JSP page include some sort of command identifier, which triggers behavior in the servlet or otherwise directs program flow. The command pattern, a design pattern (a commonly understood programming technique) familiar to GUI programmers, can help us better structure our servlet, by reducing complexity and improving the separation between control and application logic.

Using this design pattern, we encapsulate each command our servlet can handle into its own class—allowing us to break their functionality out of the main servlet code. When a request comes in from the JSP page, the servlet dispatches the request to the particular object associated with performing that command. The knowledge of how that command corresponds to application logic is the domain of the command object only; the servlet merely mediates the request between the JSP and the command object. Consider this simple excerpt from a servlet's `service()` method which can dispatch a command request to our command class based on the command identified through the request.

```
String cmd = req.getParameter("cmd");
if (cmd.equals("save")) {
  SaveCommand saver = new SaveCommand();
  saver.save(); // do its thing
}
if (cmd.equals("edit")) {
  EditCommand editor = new EditCommand();
  editor.edit(); // do its thing
}
if (cmd.equals("remove")) {
  RemoveCommand remover = new RemoveCommand();
  remover.remove(); // do its thing
}
```

Without utilizing the command pattern, each `if` block of our servlet would have to contain all of the logic necessary to perform the command as requested. Instead, we now have a reusable, encapsulated set of behavior that makes our code clearer and more easily understood and has the added benefit of being able to be developed and tested independently of the web application itself. While the code above is an incremental improvement, what if our application has dozens of commands? We'll end up with a huge cascading group of `if/then/else` blocks.

We can improve on the example by eliminating the servlet's need to understand the exact relationship between a request command and the command object itself. If we create a common way to handle all command objects, the servlet can treat them all the same, in a single command-processing loop. Through an interface we can create a common way to perform each command, without having to understand its specifics. We treat the request command string as a unique identifier to obtain the particular type of command object we require. Once we get a reference to the appropriate command, we can call the methods defined in its interface to actually perform the command. Consider the following code excerpt, where `Command` is a common interface implemented by all command objects, and the `CommandFactory` class maps command identifiers to specific command objects, returning the appropriate object as type `Command`.

```
Command cmd = CommandFactory.getCommand(request.getParameter("command"));
cmd.execute();
```

This code is the heart of our servlet, and can handle any command with just those few lines. In the event that an unknown command comes through, we can have `CommandFactory` return a valid command object that doesn't actually do anything, throw an exception, or perform some default behavior. There are a number of strategies for mapping command identifiers to `Command` classes. We can employ a simple `HashMap` for example. Another useful technique is utilizing the `Class.forName()` method to create a `Command` instance dynamically using the command identifier itself. Consider the following code snippet:

```
String cmdID = request.getParameter("command");
Command cmd = Class.forName(cmdID + "Command").newInstance();
```

In the example we combine the command identifier in the request with the string `Command`, and attempt to locate the appropriate class. For example, if the command passed in were `GetUser` then we would try to create an instance of the `GetUserCommand` class. This technique requires you to establish a naming convention among your command handlers, and can get more complicated if you need to support several different types of constructors. The command pattern is an excellent way to simplify JSP/servlet interaction. In chapter 9 we will use the command pattern in a full length JSP application.

Ensuring transaction integrity

As we discussed earlier, web applications suffer somewhat from the stateless request/response nature of the HTTP protocol. Reloading a page or clicking the Back button can reissue requests or call them out of sequence—something we want to be sure to catch in a mission-critical application.

One way to solve this continuity problem is by recording a token in the user's session upon completion of activity prerequisites and requiring this token in the second step. When a request comes in to perform the second step of the transaction, the servlet can first verify that the prerequisite has been met by retrieving the token from the session. Once completed, the token is removed from the session. A token then gives the servlet the ability to perform an action, but only once. Secondary requests will find no matching token and can raise an exception. Depending on your application's requirements you can maintain either a list of tokens—which would simultaneously support multiple browser windows from the same user—or a single token, which is overwritten each time.

Let's say your transaction is purchasing an item from your store. The final steps of your checkout process are handled by checkout.jsp, a page that contains a form requesting the selections and asks for final confirmation. Clicking Confirm places an order for each item on the page, and then shows `thankyou.jsp` which thanks the visitor for the order. What happens if the user hits Reload at this point, or the Back button? Remember that as far as the browser is concerned it is submitting the contents of a form. It doesn't matter if a servlet or another JSP is receiving the action, the browser will remember the request parameter contained in the form and deliver it to its handler. Clicking Reload essentially repeats the process—resulting in the placement of a duplicate order.

To add our transaction token scheme to this example, we have to have both pages fall under the control of servlets (or the same servlet). When the user goes to check out, the servlet should first generate a single-use token and store it in the session before directing the request to checkout.jsp where we include the token as a hidden form element. When the form is submitted, the servlet verifies that the token in the form and the token on the server match. It then performs the action, and revokes the token before proceeding on to thankyou.jsp.

If the user were to click Reload on the thank-you page, the form action would be resubmitted, but this time there would be no corresponding token indicating to the servlet that it was all right to proceed with the transaction. The servlet could then decide to just ignore the duplicate request and reload thankyou.jsp. This process is illustrated in figure 8.7.

One technique for generating a simple transaction token that is both unique to each session and non-repeatable throughout the application is by computing a message digest from the user's unique session ID and the current system time. In chapter 9 we will apply this technique as part of our example application.

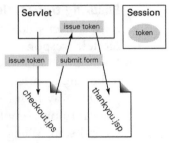

Figure 8.7   Transaction validation

8.3.6   *Handling errors in the servlet*

If in the course of normal application events your servlet encounters an unexpected error, you have the option of passing the error on to a JSP error page. This keeps all of your exception handling and error processing consistent throughout the application, regardless of whether errors crop up in the JSP pages themselves or your servlets. Simply catch the Exception (which can be any subclass of `Throwable`) and put it into the request object under the name `javax.servlet.jsp.jspException`. Then use an instance of `RequestDispatcher` to forward your request on to your error handling page. For example:

```
String username = req.getParameter("user");
if (username == null)
  req.setAttribute("javax.servlet.jsp.jspException", new Exception("no user-
    name!"));
RequestDispatcher rd = getServletContext().getRequestDispatcher("/error.jsp");
rd.forward(req, res);
```

The errorHandler.jsp page in this example should be defined as a JSP error page as normal. When we stuff an exception object into the request with that attribute name (`javax.servlet.jsp.JspException`) the error page will automatically create the implicit exception object, and error handling can proceed. There is no difference between an exception created by our servlet in this example and one being generated by an error in another JSP page.

8.3.7   *Example: servlet-centric employee browser*

In this example we will develop an application that browses through personnel records of an existing database (figure 8.8). To keep things simple the user will not be allowed to modify or add records to the database, which will be treated as read-only. We'll build a more complex database application later in this book.

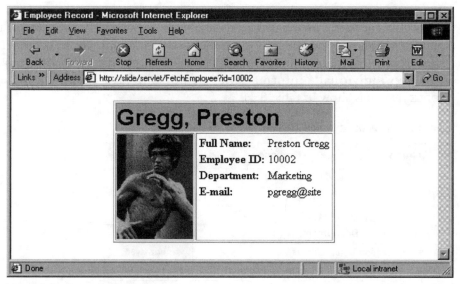

Figure 8.8   An employee's ID card

Design considerations

The employee database we are accessing may also be used by the payroll department, the logon security system, and who knows what—or who—else. It is a good idea therefore to design the components of this application to be as independent from the application as possible.

We'll need two main interfaces in this example, one to list all of the available employees, and another that can view the details about the employee selected from the list. The core component of our application will be a Bean, `EmployeeBean`, which will encapsulate the information we are interested in. It will be the job of our central servlet to handle all of the database interaction. The application model can be seen in figure 8.9.

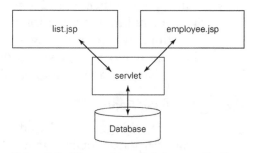

Figure 8.9   The employee database application

The database

We will be accessing an existing database that is accessible through JDBC. Thanks to the JDBC API, the Java code itself is database independent and should apply to whatever particular database you favor. The information we wish to access, employee records, is contained in a single table called PEOPLE_TABLE. While this was done for simplicity's sake in this example, spreading employee information across several tables would only complicate the discussion and the SQL query required to collect an individual's information, but not our Java code. The schema for PEOPLE_TABLE is show in table 8.1:

Table 8.1   The PEOPLE_TABLE scheme

Column	Purpose	Type
ID	Unique Employee ID	int
FNAME	First Name	varchar(80)
LNAME	Last Name	varchar(80)
DEPARTMENT	Department	varchar(80)
EMAIL	Email Address	varchar(80)
IMAGE	URL of personal photo	varchar(80)

To access a particular employee's record, say employee #1000, we can use the following SQL query, which should return a single record since each ID number is unique to a single employee.

```
SELECT * FROM PEOPLE_TABLE WHERE ID = 1000
```

We can wrap the results of this query into an EmployeeBean that encapsulates all of the information we have about an employee. We can then use this Bean inside a JSP page to display the information, but we will also have a reusable component that we can apply to other applications that deal with employees and our database. Rather than including the code for accessing information from the database inside the functionality of our EmployeeBean or the JSP pages composing the front end, we have chosen to create a servlet that is responsible for dealing with the database and controlling the application.

8.3.8   *EmployeeBean*

The first thing we need to do is to define the Java Bean that will represent the employee data contained in each record of the table. To do this we simply map each column of the table to a Bean property of the appropriate type. The property sheet for a Bean designed to hold a record from our PEOPLE_TABLE is shown in table 8.2.

The decision on what level of access to afford each property depends on how you expect the Bean to be used in the application. The id property for example is

Table 8.2   An EmployeeBean

Name	Access	Java Type	Example
id	read-only	int	1000
firstName	read/write	String	Arlon
lastName	read/write	String	Fields
department	read/write	String	Engineering
email	read/write	String	afields@headquarters
image	read/write	String	http://server/1000.gif

unique to each record and will generally not be changed, even if we are editing an employee's details, so we will make it read-only to emphasize this fact. We still need to be able to specify the `id` value at some point however—as it needs to be reflected through the read-only property. To do so we will pass it in through the constructor. The constructor will also set all of the instance variables, which are used to store property data, to empty strings.

```
public EmployeeBean(int id) {
  this.id = id;
  firstName = "";
  lastName = "";
  image = "";
  email = "";
  department = "";
}
```

Of course a JSP page will not be able to pass arguments to a constructor, and indeed won't be able to instantiate a Bean without a zero argument constructor. We'll provide one that simply passes a dummy, impossible `id` value to the primary constructor. In this application however, we shouldn't need to create a Bean in our JSP page anyway.

```
public EmployeeBean() {
  this(0);
}
```

This way we can create the Bean and leave it in a state that tells us that we don't have a valid identifier for this Bean yet, such as when we are creating a record. If we needed to construct a new database record from the data contained in the Bean we will need to create a valid identifier, usually by asking the database for the next unique identifier. The `EmployeeBean` code (listing 8.3) is straightforward:

Listing 8.3   Source code for EmployeeBean

```java
package com.taglib.wdjsp.arch;

public class EmployeeBean {
  private int id;
  private String firstName;
  private String lastName;
  private String image;
  private String email;
  private String department;

  public EmployeeBean(int id) {
    this.id = id;
    firstName = "";
    lastName = "";
    image = "";
    email = "";
    department = "";
  }

  public EmployeeBean() {
    this(0);
  }

  public int getId() {
    return this.id;
  }

  public void setFirstName(String firstName) {
    this.firstName = firstName;
  }

  public String getFirstName() {
    return this.firstName;
  }

  public void setLastName(String lastName) {
    this.lastName = lastName;
  }

  public String getLastName() {
    return this.lastName;
  }

  public void setImage(String image) {
    this.image = image;
  }
```

```
  public String getImage() {
    return this.image;
  }

  public void setEmail(String email) {
    this.email = email;
  }

  public String getEmail() {
    return this.email;
  }

  public void setDepartment(String department) {
    this.department = department;
  }

  public String getDepartment() {
    return this.department;
  }
}
```

8.3.9 *FetchEmployeeServlet*

The FetchEmployeeServlet knows how to do only two things. It can, given an employee ID number, retrieve that employee's information from the database and forward it to the employee.jsp page for display, or return a Vector containing a Bean representing each employee in the database to the list.jsp page. The coding is in listing 8.4.

Listing 8.4   Source code for FetchEmployeeServlet.java

```
package com.taglib.wdjsp.arch;

import javax.servlet.*;
import javax.servlet.http.*;
import java.io.*;
import java.sql.*;
import java.util.*;

public class FetchEmployeeServlet extends HttpServlet {
  private final static String driver = "postgresql.Driver";
  private final static String url =
    "jdbc:postgresql://slide.dev/emp";
  private final static String user = "guest";
  private final static String password = "guest";
  private final static String sql =
    "select * from people_table where id = ?";
```

```java
private Connection connection = null;
private PreparedStatement statement = null;
private ServletContext context;

public void init(ServletConfig config) throws ServletException {
  super.init(config);
  context = config.getServletContext();
  try {
    Class.forName(driver);
    connection = DriverManager.getConnection(url, user, password);
    statement = connection.prepareStatement(sql);
  }
  catch (ClassNotFoundException e) {
    System.err.println("Unable to load database driver");
    throw new ServletException("Unable to load database driver");
  }
  catch (SQLException e) {
    System.err.println("Unable to connect to database");
    throw new ServletException("Unable to connect to database");
  }
}

public void service(HttpServletRequest req,
          HttpServletResponse res)
  throws ServletException, IOException {
  String jsp;
  String cmd = req.getParameter("cmd");
  String idString = req.getParameter("id");
  int id;
  try { id = Integer.parseInt(idString); }
  catch(NumberFormatException e) { id=0; };

  if ("get".equals(cmd)) {
    EmployeeBean bean = fetchEmployee(id);
    req.setAttribute("employee", bean);
    jsp = "/employee.jsp";
  }
  else {
    Vector list = fetchAll();
    req.setAttribute("list", list);
    jsp = "/list.jsp";
  }
  RequestDispatcher dispatcher;
  dispatcher = context.getRequestDispatcher(jsp);
  dispatcher.forward(req, res);
}

public EmployeeBean makeBean(ResultSet results)
  throws SQLException {
  EmployeeBean bean = new EmployeeBean(results.getInt("id"));
```

```
    bean.setFirstName(results.getString("fname"));
    bean.setLastName(results.getString("lname"));
    bean.setEmail(results.getString("email"));
    bean.setDepartment(results.getString("department"));
    bean.setImage(results.getString("image"));
    return bean;
  }

  public EmployeeBean fetchEmployee(int id) {
    try {
      ResultSet results;
      synchronized (statement) {
  statement.clearParameters();
  statement.setInt(1, id);
  results = statement.executeQuery();
      }
      EmployeeBean bean = null;
      if (results.next()) {
  bean = makeBean(results);
      }
      if (results != null)
  results.close();
      return bean;
    }
    catch (SQLException se) { return null; }
  }

  public Vector fetchAll() {
    try {
      Vector list = new Vector();
      ResultSet results;
      Statement st = connection.createStatement();
      results = st.executeQuery("select * from people_table");
      while (results.next())
  list.add(makeBean(results));
      return list;
    }
    catch (SQLException se) { return null; }
  }

  public void destroy() {
    try {
      if (connection != null)
  connection.close();
    }
    catch (SQLException e) { }
  }
}
```

In the `init()` method of our servlet we establish a connection to the database that will remain throughout the life of the servlet. In the `destroy()` method, which will be called by the servlet container just prior to shutdown, we close this connection. Each time the servlet is requested, `service()` will be called. It is here that we encode our application's logic and flow control. We basically support two commands, `get` to fetch a specific employee, or anything else to create a `Vector` containing all possible employees.

```
String cmd = req.getParameter("cmd");
if ("get".equals(cmd)) {
  EmployeeBean bean = fetchEmployee(id);
  req.setAttribute("employee", bean);
  jsp = "employee.jsp";
}
else {
  Vector list = fetchAll();
  req.setAttribute("list", list);
  jsp = "list.jsp";
}
```

After processing, we've set the variable `jsp` to the URI of the JSP page which should be visited next by the application. We use a `RequestDispatcher` to transfer control to that page.

```
RequestDispatcher dispatcher = context.getRequestDispatcher(jsp);
dispatcher.forward(req, res);
```

Both `fetchEmployee()` and `fetchAll()` rely on the `makeBean()` method, which takes the current row of the `ResultSet` sent to it and extracts the appropriate columns to populate a newly created `EmployeeBean`.

```
public EmployeeBean makeBean(ResultSet results) throws SQLException {
  EmployeeBean bean = new EmployeeBean(results.getInt("id"));
  bean.setFirstName(results.getString("fname"));
  bean.setLastName(results.getString("lname"));
  bean.setEmail(results.getString("email"));
  bean.setDepartment(results.getString("department"));
  bean.setImage(results.getString("image"));
  return bean;
}
```

8.3.10 *JSP employee list*

This page receives the list of employees from the servlet in the form of a `Vector` filled with `EmployeeBean` objects. It simply uses scriptlets to extract each one, then builds a link back to the servlet to provide the user with a detail view of each entry.

We pass each employee's ID number in through the link, which will allow our servlet to pick the proper one. The source code is in listing 8.5.

Listing 8.5   Source code for list.jsp

```
<%@ page import="java.util.*,com.taglib.wdjsp.arch.EmployeeBean" %>
<jsp:useBean id="employee" class="EmployeeBean"/>
<html>
<body>
<b>Current Employees</b>
<ul>
<%
  Vector v = (Vector)request.getAttribute("list");
  Iterator i= v.iterator();
  while (i.hasNext()) {
      employee = (EmployeeBean)i.next();
%>
<li>
<a href="/servlet/FetchEmployeeServlet?cmd=get&id=
<jsp:getProperty name="employee" property="id"/>">
<jsp:getProperty name="employee" property="lastName"/>,
<jsp:getProperty name="employee" property="firstName"/></a>
<% } %>
</ul>
</body>
</html>
```

8.3.11 JSP page viewer

The JSP code needed to view the information stored inside the Bean is fairly straightforward. After we have a reference to the Bean we simply display the values of the appropriate properties needed for our interface. To grab the Bean, which has been placed into the request by our servlet, we specify a scope value of request and an ID with the same identifier value used by the servlet.

```
<jsp:useBean id="employee" class="EmployeeBean" scope="request" />
```

If the id value that we specify is not the same identifier used by the servlet when placing the Bean into the request, or if the page is requested directly rather than through the servlet, the Bean will not be found. If the Bean is not found, the `<jsp:useBean>` tag will, of course, create an empty EmployeeBean and place it into the request. Once we have a reference to the Bean we can use it to display the fields extracted from the database, as we do with any other Bean.

```
<B>Department:</B> <jsp:getProperty name="employee" property="department"/>
```

We have in essence encapsulated a database record into a JSP accessible Bean without muddying our page with database code. This solution also provides a high degree of abstraction for the page designer. As far as the JSP code is concerned it doesn't matter where the data came from—flat file, database, input form, or an LDAP server—the page still displays the record's fields. This not only allows the back-end implementation to change over time without affecting the front end, it allows this front-end code (listing 8.6) to be reused throughout the system.

Listing 8.6   Souce code for employee.jsp

```
<%@page import="com.taglib.wdjsp.arch.EmployeeBbean"%>
<jsp:useBean id="employee" class="EmployeeBean" scope="request" />
<html>
<head><title>employee record</title></head>
<body>
<table border="1" align="center">
<tr bgcolor="tan"><td colspan=2><font size=+3 face=arial><b>
<jsp:getProperty name="employee" property="lastname"/>,
<jsp:getProperty name="employee" property="firstname"/>
</b></font></td></tr>
<tr><td align=left valign=top>
<img height="150"
src="<jsp:getProperty name="employee" property="image"/>"></td>
<td align=left valign=top>
<table border=0>
<tr><td><b>full name:</b></td><td>
<jsp:getProperty name="employee" property="firstname"/>
<jsp:getProperty name="employee" property="lastname"/>
</td></tr>
<tr><td><b>employee id:</b></td><td>
<jsp:getProperty name="employee" property="id"/>
</td></tr>
<tr><td><b>department:</b></td><td>
<jsp:getProperty name="employee" property="department"/>
</td></tr>
<tr><td><b>e-mail:</b></td><td>
<jsp:getProperty name="employee" property="email"/>
</td></tr>
</table>
</td>
</tr>
</table>
</body>
</html>
```

8.4   *Enterprise JavaBeans*

The previous two JSP architectures we've discussed easily do not directly support complicated transaction management and distributed architectures. The introduction of the Enterprise JavaBeans (EJBs) specification by Sun Microsystems and its adoption by major application server companies like Netscape and IBM promises to ease and speed the development of mission-critical applications. EJBs are positioned to play an increasingly important role in Java applications and pair up excellently with JSPs and servlets. However, teaching you the details of EJBs is beyond the scope of this book. We can only hope to introduce them to you, and leave you with an understanding of how they fit into JSP application design.

8.4.1   *What are Enterprise JavaBeans?*

EJBs are reusable business logic components for use in distributed, multitier application architectures. You can get up and running quickly by building applications around EJBs you have created or by leveraging the growing number of off-the-shelf components. The EJB framework provides functionality that traditionally has represented the biggest challenge to creating web-based applications.

For example, if you were developing a high-end e-commerce application, you might purchase one EJB component that performed real-time credit card approval, another that managed your customers, and another that calculated shipping costs. You would then tie these together within your application server by customizing the run-time properties of the EJBs, and there you would have it—an order processing system. The application server would automatically handle sticky issues like balancing loads, maintaining security, monitoring transaction processes, sharing resources, ensuring data integrity, and so on.

8.4.2   *JavaBeans vs. EJBs*

How do EJBs and JavaBeans relate? They actually don't have much in common from a technical perspective, even if the philosophy behind them—enabling developers to take advantage of reusable components in their applications—is the same.

Like the Beans we have been studying, EJBs are a Java-based software component. However these Beans follow a completely different set of conventions and interfaces and are not accessible directly through Bean containers or JSP tags (at least the standard tags). The purpose of EJBs is to encapsulate business logic (for example, the steps involved in depositing money into an account, calculating income tax, or selecting which warehouse to ship an order from) into reusable server-side components. In the EJB paradigm, an application is implemented as a set of business-logic-controlling components that have been configured in application-specific ways inside an EJB container such as an application server. Clients are then written to communicate with the EJB components and handle the results. The standardized interfaces exist to allow the EJB container to manage security and transactional aspects of the Bean. We can use EJBs to create JavaBeans for use in our JSP page.

8.4.3 *Application servers and EJB containers*

Like JSPs, Enterprise JavaBeans are designed to work in concert with a container, typically integrated into an application server such as Netscape Application Server (NAS) or IBM's WebSphere. An EJB container and a JSP container are different things, but many application servers offer support for both. EJB containers must support Sun's EJB specification, which details the interface between application server elements. Enterprise JavaBeans can be used with any application server or other system providing an EJB container that implements these interfaces. EJB containers can also exist as part of other systems such as transaction monitors or database systems.

Application servers in particular are excellent environments to host EJB containers because they automate the more complex features of multitier computing. Application servers manage scarce resources on behalf of the components involved in the design. They also provide infrastructure services such as naming, directory services, and security. And they provide Bean-based applications with the benefit of scalability—most application server environments will let you scale your application through the addition of new clusters of machines.

EJB containers transparently provide their EJBs with a number of important services. While you may not deal with these services directly since they're conveniently kept under the covers, EJBs couldn't function without them. These services are:

- **Life cycle management:** enables initialization and shutdown of EJBs.
- **Load management:** automatically distributes EJB objects across a cluster of servers.
- **Security management:** enables EJBs to work with a wide variety of authentication schemes and approval processes.
- **Transaction support:** manages such things as rolling back transactions that didn't fully complete and handling final commitment of transactions, plus transactions across multiple databases.
- **Persistence and state management:** enables EJBs to keep information between sessions and individual requests, even if the container's server must be rebooted.

The EJB container also provides a communications channel to and from its Beans, and it will handle all of its EJBs multithreading issues. In fact, the EJB specification explicitly forbids an EJB from creating its own threads. This ensures thread-safe operation and frees the developer from often-complicated thread management concerns.

8.4.4 *Application design with EJBs*

Now let's examine how we would build a JSP application employing EJBs. Because the role of an EJB is to handle only the core business logic of your application, you will still need JSPs to deal with presentation issues like generating web pages to communicate results and servlets for control. While you can build your application from JSPs and EJBs alone, either through scriptlets or JSP JavaBeans, we don't generally recommend it. An application complex enough to benefit from EJBs would almost certainly employ a servlet-centric design. Similar to the use of the command pattern we described ealier, EJBs handle processing command requests or other application logic, freeing the servlet from direct responsibility over command execution.

For example, in a banking application a servlet might use the services of an EJB component to determine whether users are business or consumer customers and use a servlet to direct them to an appropriate JSP-controlled web page to show them their account balance. The application logic has been moved out of the servlet, in favor of the EJB, which might be better able to handle it (figure 8.10).

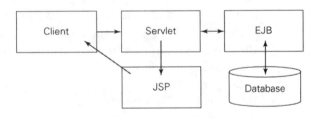

Figure 8.10   An EJB handling application logic

In such an approach, we'd want to shield the JSP pages themselves from the EJB's inner workings as much as possible. If the servlet's calls to the EJB server return particularly complex objects, we might be better off wrapping the results of the call into simpler Data Beans, which contain a view of the data relevant to the JSP page. For example, consider this excerpt from a servlet where we extract account information from an EJB and place it into a JavaBean before forwarding control on to our presentation page:

```
Context initial = new InitialContext();
Object objref = initial.lookup("AccountStatus");
AcctHome home;
home = (AcctHome)PortableRemoteObject.narrow(objref, AcctHome.class);
AccountStatus accountStatus = home.create();
AccountViewBean bean = new AccountViewBean();
bean.setBalance(accountStatus.getBalance());
bean.setLastUpdate(accountStatus.getLastModifiedTimeStamp());
request.setAttribute("accountview", bean);
RequestDispatcher rd;
rd = getServletContext().getRequestDispatcher("/AccountStatus.jsp");
rd.forward(req, res);
```

8.5   *Choosing an appropriate architecture*

So when is it appropriate to use each of these different architectures for your JSP application? Like most architectural decisions, it depends. It depends on a number of factors, including your own team's skills, experiences, personal preferences and biases. Sophisticated, multitier architectures provide a larger degree of abstraction and modularity, but only at the cost of complexity and increased development time. In practice, large multifaceted JSP applications tend to make use of more than one single architectural model, using different models to fill different sets of requirements for each aspect of the application. When making your architectural selection there are several important aspects to consider, each with its own advantages, disadvantages, and tradeoffs.

8.5.1   *Application environment*

A JSP application's environment plays an important role in determining the best-fit architecture for a project. Every environment is different, but each places its own unique pressures on JSP application design and deployment.

Firewalls and the DMZ

Today's enterprise networks are pretty complicated places. Combined with the fact that many applications cross the firewall we must be aware of the different zones of accessibility in most enterprise situations. There are three basic access zones inside most enterprises: intranet (the networks inside the inner firewall); DMZ or no man's land (the area between the intranet firewall and the public web); and the public web or Internet (the network outside all firewalls).

Firewalls divide the corporate network into a series of distinct zones (figure 8.11), each of which is afforded a different level of accessibility. Of course in practice there are generally several different levels of accessibility within each zone, but for purposes of discussion these definitions will suffice.

The public web

Machines on the public web, with the exception of corporate public web servers are generally restricted from any access to internal networks, including the DMZ. You can think of the public web as "the rest of the world,"

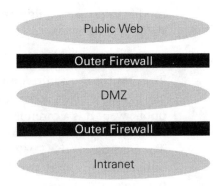

Figure 8.11 **A typical enterprise network**

since it literally includes everyone on the Internet. This is the area that will host the web servers and JSP containers that the general public will connect to. While systems in this zone may include various levels of authentication designed to restrict access to information on the server, the important thing to remember is that the general public is given direct network connectivity to these systems, at least to some degree. Applications running in this segment of the network generally experience more traffic, and are more concerned with scalability and performance.

If a company runs an extranet for its business partners, it will generally be deployed from this network zone. While we often think of an extranet as being private, from a network connectivity point of view it still falls into the domain of public access, at least for the front end. On the other hand, *virtual private networks* (VPNs) created by corporations for their partners, employees, or field offices do not fall into this category. Although they carry information across the Internet they have been designed to map into the company's network in a transparent matter. For this reason, we treat VPNs as simply another segment of our intranet, or internal corporate network.

The intranet

The intranet is composed of internal networks and systems. Traditionally, systems on the intranet can access machines inside the DMZ and on the public web. JSP applications designed to run in the intranet can be entirely self-contained internal applications, relying totally on resources local to the intranet they run on. Or, JSP applications on the intranet may be acting on back-end data sources located in the DMZ or the public web. For example, a JSP application might let a content manager modify information ultimately displayed on the corporate web server, which lives in the public web.

The DMZ

The DMZ is the name commonly given to the area between public and private networks and is given some level of access to machines on both the intranet and the public web. It is a carefully restricted network zone. For this reason the DMZ can be used to host back-end databases and support services for front-end JSP services. The purpose of the DMZ is to provide the connectivity to communicate between public and private network zones, while establishing a buffer zone where you can better control access to information. Generally, the firewall is designed to let only web traffic into the DMZ.

Back-end resources

Back-end resources (also known as enterprise information systems) are databases, LDAP servers, legacy applications, and other sources of information that we will need to access through our JSP application. Projects for the enterprise generally require access to some sort of information system on the back end. Where are your databases located? What sort of access is granted between your JSP container and your information systems?

8.5.2 *Enterprise software requirements*

If you are building JSP applications for the enterprise, your choice of JSP application architecture is largely influenced by the requirements placed on it by the very nature and requirements of the enterprise itself. While every project is different, of course, any JSP application we might develop for use in the enterprise shares some common characteristics that are worth exploring.

8.5.3 *Performance, scalability, and availability*

Enterprise applications are particularly sensitive to performance and availability issues, especially in mission-critical situations and heavily loaded web servers. One strategy commonly employed to address scalability issues is web server clustering, using groups of machines to distribute the load across a single web site. If you will be deploying JSP applications into a clustered environment you must understand how your web servers, JSP containers, and application servers (if present) will handle requests. Distributed transactions, sessions, and object persistence will vary differently by vendor and program design. Some configurations will place restrictions on your JSP components, such as support for object serialization, while others may limit your use of persistence. If you are using JSP's session management services you must understand how your environment manages sessions across cluster nodes.

Maintenance and updates

Unlike retail software, which is developed around fixed schedules of release, applications designed for use within an enterprise are typically evolving constantly. If an application is critical to the success of the business it will certainly be the target of frequent bug fixes, improvements, and enhancements. In such a situation, modularity and design flexibility will be critical to the ongoing success of the project. One of JSPs big strengths is its ability to separate the presentation aspects of your application, allowing you to alter it independently of the application logic itself.

Understand risk factors

What task is your application performing? How much time should you spend ensuring transaction integrity and bulletproofing each step of the process? If you are building mission-critical applications, count on spending more time designing transaction-processing code and developing an architecture that reduces the risk of interruptions in the program flow, as this can often be the most complicated and time-consuming aspect of application design and testing.

8.5.4 *Technical considerations*

The technical nature of a JSP project will play a large role in determining the best architectural approach. The complexity and number of moving parts should, in a very real way, affect the project direction.

Complexity and scope

How complex and interrelated are the activities surrounding your application? If your application must deal with multiple data sources, resource pooling, or complex transaction management, a fairly sophisticated architecture will certainly be in order. It is very likely that you will want to employ servlets, and possibly EJBs to shield your JSP front-end from a complicated back end. On the other hand, if there are very few steps involved, placing all of your application logic directly into JSP pages in a page-centric approach eliminates complexity and will likely reduce the amount of development time required to complete the project

Potential for reuse

Could your application make use of components that already exist or would be useful in other applications? If the JSP application you are developing is part of a larger series of projects, the extra time involved in focusing on the development of components may pay off in the long run. If you can develop JavaBeans to model your domain objects you can reuse them throughout related applications—even if they are not JSP based.

Expected lifetime and propensity for change

How likely is it that requirements will change over the life of the application? A long life with an expectation for frequent change points to the need for a more modular architecture with a higher degree of flexibility. However, an application that you expect to use briefly and then discard would probably not benefit from the increased complexity of a loosely coupled component-based architecture.

8.5.5 *Organizational considerations*

Every organization's situation is different. What worked for you in your last job won't necessarily work in this one. The talents of your team and your organization's work style will play a big role in determining the most appropriate JSP architecture.

Team size and capabilities

How big is your team? Is it just you or are you lucky enough to have a large corporate development team at your command? Is your Java development team composed of beginners or seasoned veterans? Is there a high degree of variance in skill levels? Larger teams with a range of complementary skill sets tend to favor the more distributed models incorporating servlets and EJBs.

The ability to divide your application into discrete components promotes division of labor, developer specialization, and better manageability in the team. Less experienced developers can work on Data Beans and other less complicated aspects while your senior members can worry about the more complicated aspects of the architecture and application logic. If necessary you can even hire contractors to develop individual components beyond the area of expertise of your own developers, then integrate them into your project. Such a modular approach becomes less important if a single small team will handle the JSP project alone.

Removing the Java from the front-end code frees your design team to concentrate on the application interface rather than its implementation. On the other hand, if you are a lone wolf coding commando, then you will probably benefit from the simplicity of single source, JSP-only style applications. The makeup of your team will, in part play a role in determining the best architecture for your application.

Time and money

How much time and money has been allocated to your project? Increased levels of complexity generally mean more time and, in the case of EJB's, more money. Complexity and time are trade-offs, but you have to consider maintenance expenses as well. It doesn't do much good to create a rigid, hard to maintain design in an effort to save time and money up front if you are continually forced to devote development resources to maintaining the project in the future.

Control of assets and resources

How much control do you have over corporate resources that are important to your project? If your application will be accessing databases or other information sources that already exist or are beyond your control, you will probably want to select an architecture with the additional layers of abstraction necessary to shield your developers from a disparate and possibly variant interface.

An example JSP project

## 9

This chapter covers

- Building a servlet-centric application.
- Component-based JSP development.
- JSP/Database interaction.
- Utilizing the command pattern
- Maintaining transaction integrity

In this chapter, we will apply the JSP programming techniques covered in previous chapters toward the design and development of a real-world enterprise application more complex then would be allowed as part of another chapter. We will develop a database driven system for creating, managing, and displaying a list of frequently asked questions (FAQs) and making them available through a web site. We hope it will help tie together all the concepts we have discussed so far.

9.1   Introduction

We selected an FAQs system as the example for this chapter for several reasons. It is a nontrivial application that illustrates many of the principals of JSP application design such as command handling, form element processing, database interaction, and transaction management. It was also important to present an application simple enough that it could be constrained to a readable number of pages.

Lastly, we wanted to end up with a web application that could be useful in its own right. While we will approach this project from an FAQ perspective, the project itself is applicable to maintaining and displaying any collection of information managed by a database through a browser with JSP. Just to show you where we are heading, a screen shot of the finished application in action is shown in figure 9.1.

9.1.1   Project motivations

A recent client of ours has been maintaining a list of FAQs to address common customer product issues. As the list has grown over the years it had became increasingly difficult to maintain and it had become necessary to maintain several different versions—a table of contents view, the whole list view, a list of new entries sorted by date, and so forth. Each version was maintained by hand from the master list. The web content team was responsible for updating the HTML based on the input of product management, technical support, the documentation team, and a host of others.

The combination of frequent updates and the need to maintain multiple views of the list was the driving force behind the desire to automate the FAQ administration process. This chapter-length example is based on this project, which we recently completed with the help of JSP technology.

9.1.2   Application requirements

The FAQ system we will build in this example is designed to allow the company's internal content owners (product managers, technical support, etc.) to add, update, and delete entries from the list without needing to enlist the help of the content team, and without having to edit individual HTML files. We'll use a simple

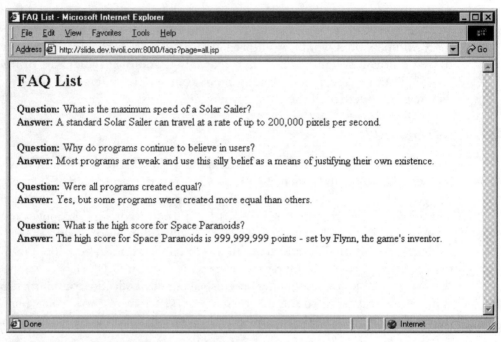

Figure 9.1   Viewing FAQs through our JSP application

web-based interface to allow them to manipulate the FAQ entries. FAQ information created by this process will be stored inside a database, and will be viewable in several forms and contexts through the company web site in place of the old, static pages.

After devising the concept and establishing our basic application goals, we must devise a list of specific features we expect the application to support. The goal here is not to dive into the details of the implementation behind each feature of the application, but rather to list activities and events that the application will be required to support:

- Each entry in the list will have a question, and an answer
- When an entry is modified we need to record the modification date
- FAQ entries should have a unique identifier that does not change, even if the wording of the question itself changes, so that it is possible to link a user to a particular FAQ
- FAQs must be visible in a variety of formats on the web—by title, by modification date, and so forth

- The FAQ lists on the web site should be generated dynamically, without the need for content engineers to perform production work
- Users need to view single FAQ or multiple FAQs as presentation dictates

Another important requirement was to fit into the client's network architecture. In this case, they had database servers in the DMZ accessible from both the public web servers and the intranet. We therefore decided that the most logical deployment scheme would be to let intranet users manage FAQs stored on the DMZ databases, and have the web servers access those same databases in order to display the FAQs.

9.1.3 Application modules

In order to start coding on this project we'll first separate the application into discrete modules which can then be built individually, without being burdened by the details of the implementation of the others. To accomplish this we looked for common areas of functionality that we could separate out from the project as a whole. An important goal in this process was to create modules that were more or less independent of each other. After studying the different areas, functions, and requirements we had identified we defined three modules:

- Storage—stores and retrieves FAQs in the database
- Administration—lets administrators create and edit entries
- Web access—displays the FAQs on the public web site

Decomposing our FAQ system into three modules gave us a number of benefits—before, during, and after development. First, it allowed us to divide development tasks among our development team resources. As long as the requirements for interaction between modules were clear it was possible for each team to work more or less independently—at least until we were ready to integrate the modules.

This approach also tends to encourage abstraction and promotes looser coupling between modules and gives the ability to make changes to the implementation of one module without having to rewrite the supporting ones. In other words, future enhancements to one module can be made without involving the design teams of the others.

Storage module

The storage module manages access to the database where each FAQ entry is stored. We created it to shield the administration and web access modules from the complexities of dealing with the database, and provide a layer of abstraction in case we decided to make changes to the underlying storage mechanism as requirements changed. In this case we are using a relational database, but may in the future need to move to an object database or perhaps a simple flat file format.

Administration module

The administration module is the tool that product managers, support staff, and other internal users would use to create and maintain the database of FAQs. It includes a JSP-based user interface allowing them to add, delete, and update FAQs in the database. This module is designed to be used within the enterprise exclusively, and will not be exposed to the public web.

Web access module

This module is pretty much the reason we started this project. It allows us to retrieve FAQs from the database and display them on the web dynamically. The purpose of this module is to give our content team the JSP components and Java classes they need to easily include individual or whole collections of FAQs into web pages without having to constantly update them. It turns out that this module is pretty simple; building off of components created for use in the other modules, but is infinitely flexible in its capabilities. It essentially becomes a new service (fetching an FAQ from the database) available to the content designers.

9.1.4   Building an FAQ component

It is clear that each module will need to exchange data at some point. To do so, we'll create a class to represent each FAQ. This class will be the building block from each of our related modules, since, after all, it's the FAQs we are building this whole thing for in the first place. Since servlets and JSPs can both deal in terms of objects, a FaqBean object gives a common unit of exchange that will greatly simplify interaction between components. The FaqBean class defines a simple set of properties, as shown in table 9.1.

Table 9.1   FaqBean properties

Property	Java Type
ID	int
question	String
answer	String
lastModified	java.util.Date

Creating the Bean is straightforward; we simply provide the getter and setter methods for each of the Bean's properties as shown in chapter 3. The source code is shown in listing 9.1.

Listing 9.1   Source code for the FaqBean

```
package com.taglib.wdjsp.faqtool;

import java.util.Date;

public class FaqBean {
  private int id;
  private String question;
  private String answer;
  private Date lastModified;

  public FaqBean() {
    this.id = 0;
    this.question = "";
    this.answer = "";
    this.lastModified = new Date();
  }

  public void setQuestion(String question) {
    this.question = question;
    this.lastModified = new Date();
  }

  public String getQuestion() {
    return this.question;
  }

  public void setAnswer(String answer) {
    this.answer = answer;
    this.lastModified = new Date();
  }

  public String getAnswer() {
    return this.answer;
  }

  public void setID(int id) {
    this.id = id;
  }

  public int getID() {
    return this.id;
  }
```

```
public Date getLastModified() {
  return this.lastModified;
}

public void setLastModified(Date modified) {
  this.lastModified = modified;
}

public String toString() {
  return "[" + id + "] " + "Q: " + question + "; A: " +
    answer + "\n";
}
}
```

Modifying any property of the Bean through a setter method triggers an update in the value of the `lastModified` property, which was initialized in the constructor to match its creation date. You may be wondering why we created setter properties for properties you might not expect the user to manipulate, such as `lastModified` and `ID`. Since we'll be constructing Beans out of data from the database (and using them in our JSPs), we need to be able to manipulate all the properties of our Bean in order to completely mirror their state in the database. The `ID` property for new Beans is assigned by the storage module, rather than the Bean itself, as we'll soon learn.

9.2   *The storage module*

The storage module must be accessible by several application components. We wanted to isolate all database activity into a single module—hiding database code behind a series of access methods that dependent components could use to add, remove, and update FAQ objects in the database.

The goal is to provide a single point of access into and out of the database. In fact, we decided that the other modules should not even need to know that there is a database; they simply request or deliver FAQs to the storage module, which magically handles the transaction. Likewise, we wanted the storage module to be application independent. It does not need to be concerned about how the information it manages is used by the other two modules, or any future modules for that matter.

The design we came up with was to create a Java class designed to handle any requests for access to FAQs stored in the database. This code is independent of the other modules in our database, but its interface would provide the necessary methods to manage FAQs. By isolating database specific code in this manner, we are able to pursue development of this module independently of the other two. It also restricts database or schema specific operations to a single module.

9.2.1 *Database schema*

For this application we created a single table, FAQS, with four columns. The table is used to store data for our FAQ objects. Each row of the table represents an FAQ (and its answer) and is identified by a unique ID value. The schema is summarized in table 9.2.

Table 9.2   The FAQ database schema

Column	SQL Type
id	int
question	varchar(255)
answer	varcar(4096)
modified	timestamp

Most of these mappings between database columns and FaqBean properties are pretty straightforward. The modified column is used to store the date the FAQ was last modified. The ID of each FAQ will be kept unique by maintaining a sequence on the database, which is incremented automatically with each new Bean we add to the table.

9.2.2 *The FaqRepository class*

The FaqRepository class is an example of the singleton pattern, a class which allows only one instance of itself to be created and provides clients with a means to access that instance. In this case, the singleton object provides a number of methods for manipulating FAQs stored in the database. All of the methods in this class deal with FaqBean objects, not strings or SQL data, improving the abstraction between this and its companion classes which will use it. We can build and debug this class independently of the other modules because, while the repository lets us manipulate Beans in the database, it does so with no direct ties to the main application. The FaqRepository class is shown in listing 9.2.

Listing 9.2   Source code for the FaqRepository

```java
package com.taglib.wdjsp.faqtool;

import java.util.*;
import java.sql.*;

public class FaqRepository {
  private static FaqRepository instance;

  private static final String driver = "postgresql.Driver";
  private static final String user= "guest";
  private static final String pass = "guest";
  private static final String dbURL =
    "jdbc:postgresql://slide/test";

  private Connection connection;
  private PreparedStatement getStmt;
  private PreparedStatement putStmt;
  private PreparedStatement remStmt;
  private PreparedStatement getAllStmt;
  private PreparedStatement updStmt;

  public static FaqRepository getInstance()
    throws FaqRepositoryException {
    if (instance == null)
      instance = new FaqRepository();
    return instance;
  }

  private FaqRepository() throws FaqRepositoryException {
    String get="SELECT * FROM FAQS WHERE ID=?";
    String put=
      "INSERT INTO FAQS VALUES (NEXTVAL('faqid_seq'), ?, ?, ?)";
    String rem="DELETE FROM FAQS WHERE ID=?";
    String upd=
      "UPDATE FAQS SET QUESTION=?, ANSWER=?, MODIFIED=? WHERE ID=?";
    String all="SELECT * FROM FAQS ORDER BY ID";

    try {
      Class.forName(driver);
      connection = DriverManager.getConnection(dbURL, user, pass);
      getStmt = connection.prepareStatement(get);
      putStmt = connection.prepareStatement(put);
      remStmt = connection.prepareStatement(rem);
      getAllStmt = connection.prepareStatement(all);
      updStmt = connection.prepareStatement(upd);
    }
    catch (ClassNotFoundException e) {
```

```
        throw new FaqRepositoryException("No Driver Available!");
      }
    catch (SQLException se) {
        throw new FaqRepositoryException(se.getMessage());
      }
  }

  private FaqBean makeFaq(ResultSet results)
    throws FaqRepositoryException {
    try {
      FaqBean faq = new FaqBean();
      faq.setID(results.getInt("ID"));
      faq.setQuestion(results.getString("QUESTION"));
      faq.setAnswer(results.getString("ANSWER"));
      Timestamp t = results.getTimestamp("MODIFIED");
      java.util.Date d;
      d = new java.util.Date(t.getTime() + (t.getNanos()/1000000));
      faq.setLastModified(d);
      return faq;
    }
    catch (SQLException e) {
      throw new FaqRepositoryException(e.getMessage());
    }
  }

  public FaqBean getFaq(int id)
    throws UnknownFaqException, FaqRepositoryException {
    try {
      ResultSet results;
      synchronized (getStmt) {
        getStmt.clearParameters();
        getStmt.setInt(1, id);
        results = getStmt.executeQuery();
      }
      if (results.next())
        return makeFaq(results);
      else
        throw new UnknownFaqException("Could not find FAQ# " + id);
    }
    catch (SQLException e) {
      throw new FaqRepositoryException(e.getMessage());
    }
  }

  public FaqBean[] getFaqs()
    throws FaqRepositoryException {
    try {
      ResultSet results;
      Collection faqs = new ArrayList();
      synchronized(getAllStmt) {
```

```
        results = getAllStmt.executeQuery();
      }
      FaqBean faq;
      while (results.next()) {
        faqs.add(makeFaq(results));
      }
      return (FaqBean[])faqs.toArray(new FaqBean[0]);
    }
  catch (SQLException e) {
    throw new FaqRepositoryException(e.getMessage());
  }
}

public void update(FaqBean faq)
  throws UnknownFaqException, FaqRepositoryException {
  try {
    synchronized(updStmt) {
      updStmt.clearParameters();
      updStmt.setString(1, faq.getQuestion());
      updStmt.setString(2, faq.getAnswer());
      Timestamp now;
      now = new Timestamp(faq.getLastModified().getTime());
      updStmt.setTimestamp(3, now);
      updStmt.setInt(4, faq.getID());
      int rowsChanged = updStmt.executeUpdate();
      if (rowsChanged < 1)
        throw new UnknownFaqException("Could not find FAQ# " +
        faq.getID());
    }
  }
  catch (SQLException e) {
    throw new FaqRepositoryException(e.getMessage());
  }
}

public void put(FaqBean faq) throws
  FaqRepositoryException {
  try {
    synchronized(putStmt) {
      putStmt.clearParameters();
      putStmt.setString(1, faq.getQuestion());
      putStmt.setString(2, faq.getAnswer());
      Timestamp now;
      now = new Timestamp(faq.getLastModified().getTime());
      putStmt.setTimestamp(3, now);
      putStmt.executeUpdate();
    }
  }
  catch (SQLException e) {
    throw new FaqRepositoryException(e.getMessage());
```

```
      }

   }

   public void removeFaq(int id)
      throws FaqRepositoryException {
      try {
         synchronized(remStmt) {
            remStmt.clearParameters();
            remStmt.setInt(1, id);
            int rowsChanged = remStmt.executeUpdate();
            if (rowsChanged < 1)
               throw new UnknownFaqException("Can't delete FAQ# "+ id);
         }
      }
      catch (SQLException e) {
         throw new FaqRepositoryException(e.getMessage());
      }
   }

   public void destroy() {
      if (connection != null) {
         try { connection.close(); }
         catch (Exception e) { }
      }
   }

}
```

The Constructor

The constructor for a singleton class like this one is `private` to prevent outside classes from instantiating it. The only way to obtain an instance of the `FaqReposi-tory` class then is through a `static` method of the `FaqRepository` itself. In the constructor we establish a connection to the database. For brevity, we've hard coded all of our database connection information, but in practice we would employ a `ResourceBundle`, a properties file, JNDI, or some other means of externally configuring this information. In the constructor we also create a number of prepared statements to support the various operations we require—adding FAQs, removing FAQs, and so forth.

Using prepared statements not only improves the performance, it keeps our database access particulars in one place. While we've hard coded the database connection and the SQL code for simplicity, we could pull database access and schema related statements out of the code, retrieving them from a properties file at run time, allowing us some more flexibility. Remember, we'll only have to go through this prepared statement setup process once, since the constructor will be called only once, when we create the sole instance of the class.

Referencing the instance

A `static` member of the class itself maintains a reference (`instance`) to a single instance of the class that will be passed to anyone calling the `getInstance()` method. The `getInstance()` method also takes care of creating the instance the first time it is called. Note that if there is a problem, we throw a `FaqRepositoryEx-cpeption` in the constructor and rethrow it here. This way we can alert the calling class that, for whatever reason, we are unable to create a `FaqRepository`.

To use the `FaqRepository` then, the calling class just calls `getInstance()` (within a try block of course), and then calls the appropriate `public` methods. For example, to get an FAQ from the database, we would use code such as this:

```
try {

  FaqRepository faqDatabase = FaqRepository.getInstance();
  FaqBean faq = faqDatabase.getFaq(10005);
  System.out.println("The Question Is: " + faq.getQuestion()");
}
catch (UnknownFaqException e1) {
  System.out.println("Could not find Faq 10005");
}
catch (FaqRepositoryException e2) {
  System.out.println("Could not get access to Faqs!");
}
```

We can use the code to write a test harness for this module and test each method of our `FaqRepository` class, even though the other modules may still be in development. Very handy.

Prepared statements

Note that our access methods all contain synchronized blocks around the prepared statements. This is necessary because we are reusing `PreparedStatement` objects. Because there is only a single instance of this class, there may be several threads executing these methods simultaneously. Without synchronization, one thread could be manipulating elements of the `PreparedStatement` object while another is attempting to use it. Not a good thing.

Each prepared statement handles a different type of operation and each works with the data stored inside the `FAQS` table of the database. As a typical example, notice the prepared statement we are using to add FAQs to the database:

```
String put="INSERT INTO FAQS VALUES (NEXTVAL('faqid_seq'), ?, ?, ?)";
```

This statement says that the first value (which maps to the ID of the FAQ) is determined by incrementing a sequence, faqid_seq, on the database. The operation nextval() is a built-in method of our database server. This keeps us from having to manage id allocation ourselves. Most, but not all, databases provide some sort of managed sequences. If necessary you can create your own table of sequence values and manage them yourself.

Access methods

Our FAQ access methods getFaq() and getFaqs() have a common operational requirement. Given a ResultSet as output from executing the appropriate prepared statement they need to turn each row into a FaqBean object. This is accomplished by creating an empty FaqBean object, and populating it with data from the appropriate columns of the current row of the result set. Take a look at the getFaq() method in the previous section. As you can see, we simplify things by delegating this common task off to a utility method, getFaq(), which takes the ResultSet as its argument, and builds a Bean mirroring the data in the ResultSet. Also note the conversion from the database Timestamp to the Bean's java.util.Date type.

9.2.3 Storage module exceptions

In our methods that need to access execute JDBC calls, we trap any SQLExceptions that arise and rewrap them into FaqRepositoryExceptions. We could have simply thrown them back, but since the decision was made to make the interface to FaqRepository independent of its implementation—meaning that calling classes shouldn't have to know that FaqRepository is accessing a database, and thus shouldn't have to deal with SQLExceptions. Besides, if they can't access the FaqRepository, there's not much the calling class can do about it, other than reporting it. Failure in this case is fatal. We do pass the message along in any case, to make things easier to debug.

We've created two simple exceptions classes to handle various error conditions that may arise inside the storage module. The first, FaqRepositoryException is the base class. The second, UnknownFaqException is a more specific exception that is thrown when a requested FAQ cannot be located. They are very simple classes. Their source is shown in listings 9.3 and 9.4.

Listing 9.3   Source code for FaqRepositoryException

```
package com.taglib.wdjsp.faqtool;

public class FaqRepositoryException extends Exception {

  public FaqRepositoryException() {
    super();
  }

  public FaqRepositoryException(String msg) {
    super(msg);
  }
}
```

Listing 9.4   Source code for UnknownFaqException

```
package com.taglib.wdjsp.faqtool;

public class UnknownFaqException extends FaqRepositoryException {

  public UnknownFaqException() {
    super();
  }

  public UnknownFaqException(String msg) {
    super(msg);
  }
}
```

9.3   *The administration module*

The administration module is a tool allowing administrators to add, delete, and update FAQs in the system. It is composed of a series of interconnected screens that form the user interface to our application. The application's screens are a function of the various steps the user can take along the way. Transitioning between each step causes activity—such as adding an FAQ to the database or deleting an existing one—and results in different outcomes that lead us to new screens.

At each screen, we'll want to give the user a chance to go back to the main menu (aborting the current step), as well as perform the appropriate activity for that page. Therefore, from each screen in our application different choices take the user to different parts of the program. This is a typical tree-style application flow (figure 9.2). (For brevity and clarity in the diagram, we've left out the abort path from each screen which just takes the user back to the main menu.) Each path through the application adds another branch to the tree.

In developing the administration portion of our FAQ management system we decided to create one central servlet, `FaqAdminServlet`, to handle the application logic and direct each request to the appropriate screen, depending on the state of the application and information specified in the request. The screens themselves are a series of JSP pages, which make use of data provided by the servlet. The servlet will be a mediator between the various pages that make up the user interface screens, and will direct requests to the appropriate application logic, which deals with the FAQ data itself.

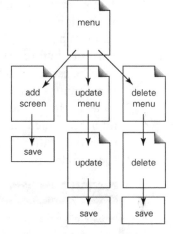

Figure 9.2 Flow through the administration application

9.3.1 The administration servlet

A servlet is at the heart of our application. We will direct each request to this servlet, and have it determine the actions to take and the next appropriate page to display. Our goal here is to use the JSPs for display and presentation purposes only, and have the servlet managing flow through the application and handling the application logic. We created an implementation of the command pattern approach discussed in chapter 8 to help better separate the application logic from the program control aspects of our servlet.

Utilizing the command pattern

In the command pattern, we associate application activities (such as adding an FAQ or editing an entry) with instances of classes that know how to perform the requested function. Each activity will be represented by a specific command. The implementation we elected to use for this project packages the application logic into a collection of independent command handler classes, all of which implement a common interface called `Command`. The `Command` interface specifies a single method, `execute()`:

```
package com.taglib.wdjsp.faqtool;
import javax.servlet.*;
import javax.servlet.http.*;

public interface Command {
  public String execute(HttpServletRequest req)
    throws CommandException;
}
```

The execute() method of each command handler takes an HttpServletRequest, allowing it to pull out from the request any parameters it needs to perform its operation. When complete, the command handler can then store its results as a request attribute before returning control to the servlet. The results of the operation can then be retrieved from the request by the JSP page ultimately handling the request. If anything goes wrong, an instance of CommandException, (listing 9.5), is thrown to alert the servlet to the problem. The big idea here is that we have created an interface which allows the servlet to delegate the handling of a command to a handler class, without having to know any details about the handler class itself, even its specific class name.

Listing 9.5 Source code for CommandException

```
package com.taglib.wdjsp.faqtool;

public class CommandException extends Exception {

  public CommandException() {
    super();
  }

  public CommandException(String msg) {
    super(msg);
  }
}
```

Mapping actions to commands

Each JSP screen will indicate the user's desired action to the servlet by passing in a value through the request parameter cmd. The value of cmd serves as a command identifier, telling us what to do next. So to delete an FAQ, the JSP page would simply pass in the appropriate identifier, say delete, signaling the servlet to hand the request off to the command handler for deletion. Each action we want to support in our application needs its own unique identifier that the JSP pages can use to request different actions to be performed.

However, processing a command is more than just calling the appropriate command handler's execute() method. We must also direct the request to the appropriate JSP page following successful completion of the action. We didn't want the pages themselves to have to be bound to specific pages or understand flow control issues. Therefore we've designed each of our command handlers to accept a Stringvalue in its constructor to specify the next page in the process. This String value is passed back to the controlling servlet from the `execute()` method as a return value, identifying the JSP page that should now receive the request.

In our servlet, we associate each command identifier with a separate instance of one of our command classes (each of which we'll discuss in a bit), which has been preconfigured with the file name of the destination screen we should visit next. We store each command class instance in a `HashMap`, using the command identifier used by our JSP pages as the key. We'll do this in the `init()` method of the servlet, which is run only the first time the servlet is started by the server. This operation is performed in the `initCommands()` utility method:

```
private void initCommands() {
  commands = new HashMap();
  commands.put("main-menu", new NullCommand("menu.jsp"));
  commands.put("abort", new AbortCommand("menu.jsp"));
  commands.put("add", new NullCommand("add.jsp"));
  commands.put("do-add", new AddCommand("menu.jsp"));
  commands.put("update-menu", new GetAllCommand("upd_menu.jsp"));
  commands.put("update", new GetCommand("update.jsp"));
  commands.put("do-update", new UpdateCommand("menu.jsp"));
  commands.put("delete-menu", new GetAllCommand("del_menu.jsp"));
  commands.put("delete", new GetCommand("delete.jsp"));
  commands.put("do-delete", new DeleteCommand("menu.jsp"));
}
```

As you can see we've created ten different commands, each with its own unique identifier, which form the keys to our `HashMap`. Each command activity involves more than just mapping a command identifier to a command handler; it's a combination of command identifier, command handler class, and destination screen. Some command handlers can be used to handle several different command identifiers, by being configured with different destination pages. For example, both the update menu and delete menu JSP pages will need a list of the FAQs in the database to allow the user to make their selection. Collecting all of the FAQs for retrieval by the JSP page is the job of the `GetAllCommand` class. Creating two different instances of the `GetAllCommand` class with different destinations allows us to reuse the application logic isolated inside of the command handler We aren't required to create a unique class for each identifier, since only the destination screens are different in this case.

Processing commands

The implementation behind each command handler is, as we'll see, independent of the operations inside the servlet itself. We'll discuss each of these in turn. The `service()` method of our servlet is extremely simple in this design. We simply fetch the

appropriate command handler from our list, call its execute() method, then redirect the request to the appropriate page. The lookupCommand() method simply
pulls the appropriate object from the HashMap and provides sane defaults—sort of a
factory method. The CommandToken.set() method creates a special token to help
maintain transaction integrity, which will be explained soon.

```
public void service(HttpServletRequest req, HttpServletResponse res)
  throws ServletException, IOException {
  String next;
  try {
    Command cmd = lookupCommand(req.getParameter("cmd"));
    next = cmd.execute(req);
    CommandToken.set(req);
  }
  catch (CommandException e) {
    req.setAttribute("javax.servlet.jsp.jspException", e);
    next = error;
  }
  RequestDispatcher rd;
  rd = getServletContext().getRequestDispatcher(jspdir + next);
  rd.forward(req, res);
}
```

If executing the command throws an exception, we catch it and store it as a request
attribute before forwarding the request on to our error-handling page. This allows
us to handle both servlet originated exceptions and JSP exceptions in the same
place. The complete source code for the servlet is shown in listing 9.6.

Listing 9.6   Source code for FaqAdministrationServlet

```
package com.taglib.wdjsp.faqtool;

import java.io.*;
import javax.servlet.*;
import javax.servlet.http.*;
import java.util.*;

public class FaqAdminServlet extends HttpServlet {
  private HashMap commands;
  private String error = "error.jsp";
  private String jspdir = "/jsp/";

  public void init(ServletConfig config) throws ServletException {
    super.init(config);
    initCommands();
  }
```

```
public void service(HttpServletRequest req,
          HttpServletResponse res)
   throws ServletException, IOException {
   String next;
   try {
     Command cmd = lookupCommand(req.getParameter("cmd"));
     next = cmd.execute(req);
     CommandToken.set(req);
   }
   catch (CommandException e) {
     req.setAttribute("javax.servlet.jsp.jspException", e);
     next = error;
   }
   RequestDispatcher rd;
   rd = getServletContext().getRequestDispatcher(jspdir + next);
   rd.forward(req, res);
}

private Command lookupCommand(String cmd)
   throws CommandException {
   if (cmd == null)
     cmd = "main-menu";
   if (commands.containsKey(cmd.toLowerCase()))
     return (Command)commands.get(cmd.toLowerCase());
   else
     throw new CommandException("Invalid Command Identifier");
}

private void initCommands() {
   commands = new HashMap();
   commands.put("main-menu", new NullCommand("menu.jsp"));
   commands.put("abort", new AbortCommand("menu.jsp"));
   commands.put("add", new NullCommand("add.jsp"));
   commands.put("do-add", new AddCommand("menu.jsp"));
   commands.put("update-menu", new GetAllCommand("upd_menu.jsp"));
   commands.put("update", new GetCommand("update.jsp"));
   commands.put("do-update", new UpdateCommand("menu.jsp"));
   commands.put("delete-menu", new GetAllCommand("del_menu.jsp"));
   commands.put("delete", new GetCommand("delete.jsp"));
   commands.put("do-delete", new DeleteCommand("menu.jsp"));
   }
}
```

Transaction integrity

Now to explain the meaning of that CommandToken.set() call following a successful command execution. As explained in chapter 8, some actions in a JSP application

are vulnerable to accidental re-execution due to the user reloading a page or clicking the Back button.

Take for example the steps involved in adding a new FAQ to the database. In the first step, we collect information for the new FAQ through a form. In the second step it takes the question and answer from the request, and instructs the `FaqRepository` to process it, adding it to the database. The FAQ is added and the user ends up back at the main menu. However, the URL that the browser has stored in memory for the current page request now includes the add request and the appropriate question and answer variables. If the user clicks Reload, the request is resubmitted, all the request parameters are resent, and another instance is added to the database. A similar problem can also happen with Delete and Update. We need to trap each of these cases and act accordingly. Something has to alert the servlet to the fact that we've already performed this operation once and that we should not do it again a second or third time.

In our servlet we will apply the command token technique discussed in chapter 8 to assure that sensitive commands are performed only once. To issue and manage our tokens we'll use an application independent utility class we've designed called `CommandToken`, which has two public methods, both of which are static:

```
public static void set(HttpServletRequest req)
public static boolean isValid(HttpServletRequest req)
```

The first method, `set()`, creates a unique transaction token and stores it (as a string of hex characters) in the user's session and in the request as an attribute. The second method, `isValid()`, can be used to validate a request, and will search for the existence of a token in the request and the session and compare them for equality. If they are equal, it returns true—otherwise it returns false indicating that there is either a missing or mismatched token. The token itself is an MD5 message digest (a kind of checksum) generated from the combination of the user's session ID and the current system time. This assures that each token is unique to the user and will not be repeated. The code for the `CommandToken` class is in listing 9.7:

Listing 9.7   Source code for CommandToken

```
package com.taglib.wdjsp.faqtool;

import javax.servlet.http.*;
import java.security.*;

public class CommandToken {
  public static void set(HttpServletRequest req) {
    HttpSession session = req.getSession(true);
```

```
      long systime = System.currentTimeMillis();
      byte[] time  = new Long(systime).toString().getBytes();
      byte[] id = session.getId().getBytes();
      try {
        MessageDigest md5 = MessageDigest.getInstance("MD5");
        md5.update(id);
        md5.update(time);
        String token = toHex(md5.digest());
        req.setAttribute("token", token);
        session.setAttribute("token", token);
      }
      catch (Exception e) {
        System.err.println("Unable to calculate MD5 Digests");
      }
    }

    public static boolean isValid(HttpServletRequest req) {
      HttpSession session = req.getSession(true);
      String requestToken = req.getParameter("token");
      String sessionToken = (String)session.getAttribute("token");
      if (requestToken == null || sessionToken == null)
        return false;
      else
        return requestToken.equals(sessionToken);
    }

    private static String toHex(byte[] digest) {
      StringBuffer buf = new StringBuffer();
      for (int i=0; i < digest.length; i++)
        buf.append(Integer.toHexString((int)digest[i] & 0x00ff));
      return buf.toString();
    }
}
```

To make use of this class, we need to set a new token after the successful completion of each command. That's the reason for the call to `CommandToken.set()` in our servlet's `service()` method. We are essentially creating a single-use token each time to help regulate flow between pages. On pages that precede flow-critical commands we must include the token as a hidden element of our form data by retrieving it from the request. Then, we'll have each sensitive command pass the request object to the `isValid()` method to verify that this is a valid request before handling it. We'll see this in practice in the `AddCommand`, `UpdateCommand`, and `DeleteCommand` classes and their respective front-end JSP pages.

9.3.2   *The main menu*

This screen is the main interface for managing the FAQ list. Here the user can select to add, modify, or delete an entry. Selecting an action for an FAQ will lead to other screens. The user will be returned to this screen after completing any operations from the other screens, and should have a status message area that can be used to report the results of each operation.

You are taken to the main menu via the main-menu command. Visiting the main menu is also the default activity if no command identifier is specified. In either case, no action is required, and so the command is handled by a very simple implementation of the Command interface called NullCommand.

The NullCommand class

The simplest of our commands, as you might expect, is the NullCommand class (listing 9.8). It simply returns its next URL value, performing no operation. This class is used for commands that are simply requests to visit a particular page, such as visiting the main menu and collecting the information necessary to add an FAQ to the database.

Listing 9.8   Source code for NullCommand

```
package com.taglib.wdjsp.faqtool;

import javax.servlet.*;
import javax.servlet.http.*;

public class NullCommand implements Command {
  private String next;

  public NullCommand(String next) {
    this.next = next;
  }

  public String execute(HttpServletRequest req)
    throws CommandException {
    return next;
  }
}
```

The AbortCommand class

We also created an AbortCommand class to handle the case where the user wants to abort the current operation and return to the main menu from any page. Abort-Command differs from NullCommand in only one way: it adds a message to the request in the form of a request attribute—creating a simple page-to-page communication system. This message is retrieved by the main menu JSP page, and used to update the status area of the main menu interface (figure 9.3.) This gives us a way to give feedback to the user about the status of the last operation. We'll use this technique in several other commands as well. The AbortComand code is shown in listing 9.9.

Listing 9.9   Source Code for AbortCommand

```java
package com.taglib.wdjsp.faqtool;

import javax.servlet.*;
import javax.servlet.http.*;

public class AbortCommand implements Command {
  private String next;

  public AbortCommand(String next) {
    this.next = next;
  }

  public String execute(HttpServletRequest req)
    throws CommandException {
    req.setAttribute("faqtool.msg", "Operation Aborted");
    return next;
  }
}
```

The main menu JSP page

The operation of this page is straightforward. The main menu page allows the user to add, update, or delete an FAQ from the database. That is the page's only job. The source code for the main menu page, menu.jsp is shown in listing 9.10.

Listing 9.10   Source code for menu.jsp

```jsp
<%@ page import="com.taglib.wdjsp.faqtool.*" errorPage="/jsp/error.jsp" %>
<html>
<head>
<title>Main Menu</title>
<script language="JavaScript">
function setCmd(value) {
  document.menu.cmd.value = value;
}
</script>
</head>
<body bgcolor="white">
<form name="menu" action="/faqtool" method="post">
```

```
<input type="hidden" name="cmd" value="">
<table bgcolor="tan" border="0" align="center" cellpadding="10">
<tr><th>FAQ Administration: Main Menu</th></tr>
<tr><td align="center">
<input type="submit" value="Create New FAQ"
onClick="setCmd('add')"></td></tr>
<tr><td align="center">
<input type="submit" value="Update An Exiting FAQ"
onClick="setCmd('update-menu')"></td></tr>
<tr><td align="center">
<input type="submit" value="Delete An Existing FAQ"
onClick="setCmd('delete-menu')"></td></tr>
<tr><td bgcolor="white"><font size="-1">
<% if (request.getAttribute("faqtool.msg") != null) { %>
<i><%= request.getAttribute("faqtool.msg") %></i>
<% } %>
</font></td></tr>
</table>
</form>
</body>
</html>
```

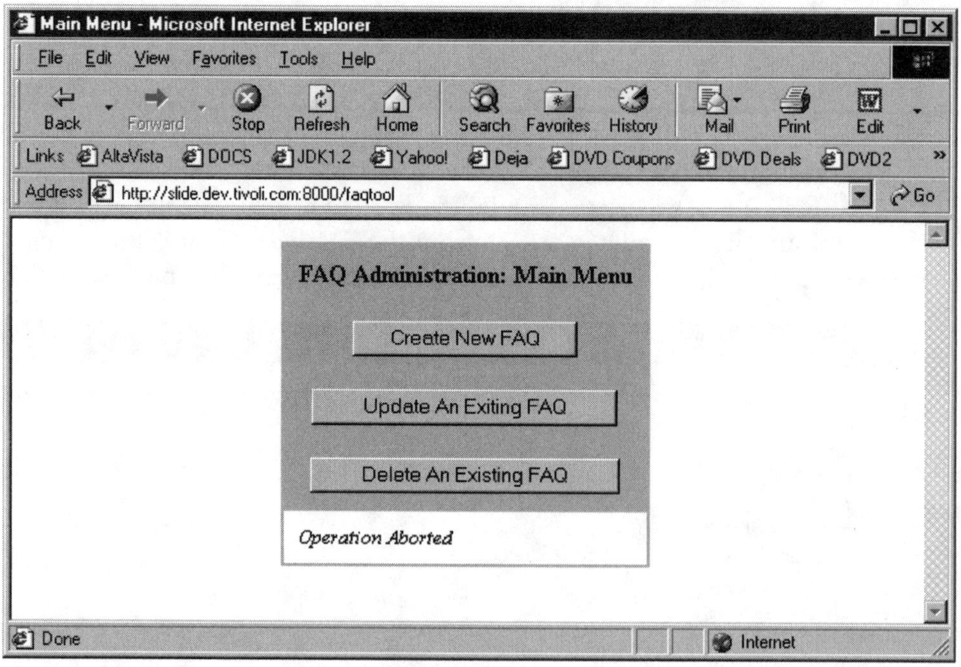

Figure 9.3   A status message on the main menu

We've created a simple form, which upon submittal posts the form data back to the URL /faqtool, which we've mapped to the FaqAdminServlet in our JSP container. The command action will be specified through the request parameter cmd, which must be set by our form. There are a number of different ways to include this request parameter into our form submission. We could have three separate forms on the page each with its own appropriate values assigned to the hidden element called cmd, and the three selection buttons would be the submit buttons for each form. We could also have named our submit buttons cmd, and set the value of each to the appropriate command identifiers. We could have even used anchor tags with URLs such as the following, which encode the cmd identifier into the URL as a parameter:

```
<a href="/faqtool?cmd=add">Create New FAQ</a>
<a href="/faqtool?cmd=update-menu">Create New FAQ</a>
<a href="/faqtool?cmd=delete-menu">Create New FAQ</a>
```

The point is that the servlet and application logic classes don't care how the front end code works, as long as it sets the appropriate request parameters. We chose to set the command identifier through a hidden element (cmd) by using JavaScript to change the value depending on the user's selection. Each of the buttons on the page is a submit button—all for the same, single form. However, each has its own JavaScript onClick event handler which sets the value of our cmd element to the appropriate value upon the user selecting the button. This approach gives us more flexibility in how we describe each button, and lets us stick to POST style form processing rather than mucking up our URLs by tacking on parameters as we did in the hypothetical example above. If you change the form handler's method type to GET it will still work, and you will see that the resulting request looks exactly like those shown. We are just setting the same request parameters after all. The POST approach keeps our URLs nice and clean and avoids tempting the user to bookmark deep into the application.

At the bottom of our little interface we check for the presence of a status message, and display it if necessary. As we talked about in the discussion of the Abort-Command, feedback messages may be placed into the request by our other commands to update us as to the status of things.

9.3.3 *Adding an FAQ*

Adding an FAQ to the database involves two steps, but only one screen. The users first choose to create an FAQ from the main menu. We don't need to do anything database related at this point, so in our servlet we use the NullCommand (which does nothing, remember) to handle this activity, forwarding us to the add.jsp page, which collects the question and the answer information that make up an FAQ. From this form the user selects to either abort the action, which simply takes them back to the main menu courtesy of the `AbortCommand` class, or commit the new FAQ to the database via a `do-add` request, which calls the `AddCommand` class to add the FAQ to the database, ending back at the main menu once it has been added successfully.

The add page

We must remember our earlier discussion on transaction integrity for sensitive, flow-dependent commands which we do not want to inadvertently process multiple times. Adding an FAQ to the database definitely qualifies as a sensitive command, and it will be looking for a token in the request it receives which matches the one stored in the session. We therefore need to include the single use token, which was stored as a request attribute following the successful completion of the command that brought us to this page. This is simple enough to include in our form.

```
<input type="hidden" name="token"
value="<%= request.getAttribute("token") %>">
```

which turns into something like this at request processing time:

```
<input type="hidden" name="token" value="485a4b73c03ef8149e6a438b6aa749e3">
```

This value, along with input from the user detailing the new question and answer will be sent to `FaqAdminServlet` for processing by an instance of the `AddCommand` class, which we will discuss in a moment. The source for `add.jsp` is shown in listing 9.11 and the page shown in figure 9.4

Listing 9.11   Souce code for add.jsp

```
<%@ page import="com.taglib.wdjsp.faqtool.*" errorPage="/jsp/error.jsp" %>
<html>
<head><title>Add FAQ</title></head>
<body bgcolor="white">
<form name="menu" action="/faqtool" method="post">
<table bgcolor="tan" border="0" align="center" cellpadding="10">
<tr><th colspan="2">FAQ Administration: Add FAQ</th></tr>
<tr><td><b>Question:</b></td>
<td><input type="text" name="question" size="41" value=""></td>
</td></tr>
<tr><td><b>Answer:</b></td>
<td>
<textarea name="answer" cols="35" rows="5">
</textarea>
</td></tr>
<tr><td colspan="2" align="center">
<input type="submit" value="Abort Addition">
```

```
<input type="submit" value="Add This FAQ"
  onClick="document.menu.cmd.value='do-add'">
</td></tr>
</table>
<input type="hidden" name="token"
value="<%= request.getAttribute("token") %>">
<input type="hidden" name="cmd" value="abort">
</form>
</body>
</html>
```

As with the main menu, we use some JavaScript to manipulate the value of the hidden form field `cmd`, which directs our action within the controller servlet, which defaults to the `abort` directive, changing its value to `do-add` if the user indicates he or she wishes to add the FAQ to the database. If you refer to the `FaqAdminServlet`'s `initCommands()` method you will see that the `do-add` directive is handled by an instance of the `AddCommand` class.

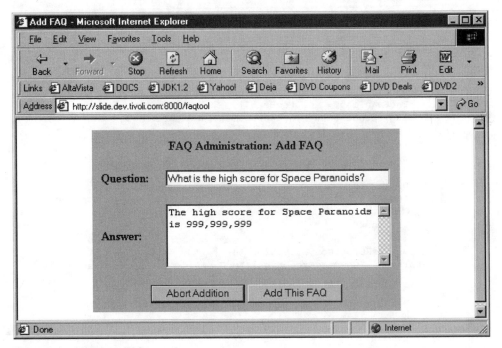

Figure 9.4 Adding an FAQ

The AddCommand class

The source for the AddCommand class is relatively straightforward, because most of the hard work is done inside the FaqRepository class we described earlier. We merely have to use the information placed into the request through the JSP form to build an FaqBean object to pass to the put method of FaqRepository, and do some sanity checks. The code is shown in listing 9.12:

Listing 9.12   Source code for AddCommand

```
package com.taglib.wdjsp.faqtool;

import javax.servlet.*;
import javax.servlet.http.*;

public class AddCommand implements Command {
  private String next;

  public AddCommand(String next) {
    this.next = next;
  }

  public String execute(HttpServletRequest req)
    throws CommandException {
    try {
      if (CommandToken.isValid(req)) {
        FaqRepository faqs = FaqRepository.getInstance();
        FaqBean faq = new FaqBean();
        faq.setQuestion(req.getParameter("question"));
        faq.setAnswer(req.getParameter("answer"));
        faqs.put(faq);
        req.setAttribute("faqtool.msg", "FAQ Added Successfully");
      }
      else {
        req.setAttribute("faqtool.msg", "Invalid Reload Attempted");
      }
      return next;
    }
    catch (FaqRepositoryException fe) {
      throw new CommandException("AddCommand: " + fe.getMessage());
    }
  }
}
```

Before we process the request, we must check that we received a valid token in the request by passing the request to the CommandToken.isValid() method. This command validator will expect to find a token in the user's session that matches the token passed in through the JSP form's hidden token field. If it does, we can add the FAQ to the database. If there is an error, we catch the appropriate exception and rethrow it as an exception of type `CommandException`. This allows the servlet that called the command to handle it—in this case `FaqAdminServlet` bundles it up as a request attribute and forwards the whole request to our error page. If it succeeds, it inserts an appropriate status message in the form of a request attribute to indicate what happened before returning the user to the main menu.

9.3.4 Deleting an FAQ

Deleting an FAQ takes three steps spread over two screens. After selecting delete from the main menu, the user is given a list of FAQs to select for removal. Before anything is deleted however, the FAQ's information is displayed and the user is asked for confirmation and given a final chance to abort the process and return to the main menu. Like adding an FAQ, deleting one is considered a sensitive operation, so we'll be checking that token again.

The GetAllCommand class

The first step in the deletion process, as you can see from the command mapping for the delete directive, is handled by the `GetAllCommand` class whose job is to retrieve the entire collection of FAQs from the database, wrap them into an array, and store them as a request attribute under the attribute name `faqs`. This allows the JSP page following this command to display a listing of all of the FAQs in the database. As before, most of the work is done inside the already covered `FaqReposi-tory`. The source for this class is shown in listing 9.13.

Listing 9.13   Source code for GetAllCommand

```
package com.taglib.wdjsp.faqtool;

import javax.servlet.*;
import javax.servlet.http.*;

public class GetAllCommand implements Command {
  private String next;

  public GetAllCommand(String next) {
    this.next = next;
  }

  public String execute(HttpServletRequest req)
    throws CommandException {
```

```
try {
  FaqRepository faqs = FaqRepository.getInstance();
  FaqBean[] faqList = faqs.getFaqs();
  req.setAttribute("faqs", faqList);
  return next;
}
catch (FaqRepositoryException fe) {
  throw new CommandException("GetCommand: " + fe.getMessage());
}
}

}
```

The deletion selection screen

The `del_menu.jsp` page is responsible for displaying the available FAQs and allowing the user to select one for deletion. It is delivered after `GetAllCommand` has retrieved the FAQs from the database and stored them as an array in request. We simply have to pull them out one by one, and build up our form. The end result is shown in figure 9.5, the source code is in listing 9.14. There are a few tricky parts, which we'll discuss.

Listing 9.14   Source code for del_menu.jsp

```
<%@ page import="com.taglib.wdjsp.faqtool.*"
 errorPage="/jsp/error.jsp" %>
<jsp:useBean id="faq" class="FaqBean"/>
<%
  FaqBean[] faqs = (FaqBean[])request.getAttribute("faqs");
%>
<html>
<head><title>Delete Menu</title></head>
<form name="menu" action="/faqtool" method="post">
<table bgcolor="tan" border="1" align="center" cellpadding="10">
<tr><th colspan="2">FAQ Administration: Delete Menu</th></tr>
<%
for (int i=0; i < faqs.length; i++) {
  faq = faqs[i];
%>
<tr>
<td><input type="radio" name="id"
value="<jsp:getProperty name="faq" property="ID"/>">
<jsp:getProperty name="faq" property="ID"/></td>
<td><jsp:getProperty name="faq" property="question"/></td>
</tr>
<% } %>
<tr><td colspan=2>
```

```
<input type="submit" value="Abort Delete">
<input type="submit" value="Delete Selected FAQ"
   onClick="document.menu.cmd.value='delete'">
<input type="hidden" name="cmd" value="abort">
</td></tr>
</table>
</form>
</html>
```

Looping through the array of `FaqBean` objects we pulled from the request seems straightforward, but there's a tricky part here. We wanted to use the Bean tags inside our loop, but remember that there are no standard tags for handling indexed properties or elements of an array like this. Therefore, we have to pull each item out of the array and create a reference to it accessible by the `PageContext` object, most importantly for the Bean tag `<jsp:getProperty>`. We simply declare the reference, `faq`, at the top of the page via `<jsp:useBean>`, even though we actually assign a

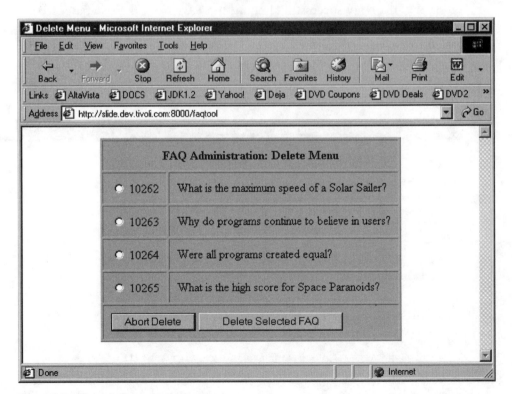

Figure 9.5 The deletion selection screen

`FaqBean` object to the reference through a scriptlet. Leaving out the `<jsp:use-Bean>` tag would cause an error when the page tried to use `<jsp:getProperty>` on the `faq` variable.

The form itself is straightforward. We need to obtain the ID number of the FAQ that is to be deleted, as well as give the user the abort option. The submit buttons are handled as before, through JavaScript, and radio buttons give us an easy way to pick up the selected ID. If the user chooses to continue on to the second of the three steps, we set the `cmd` identifier to the delete action, which is handled by the `GetCommand` class to ask for confirmation.

The GetCommand class

The `GetCommand` class can retrieve a single FAQ from the database by its ID value. It looks in the request for the `id` parameter, then uses the `FaqRepository` class we created in our storage module to retrieve the matching FAQ from the database. We use the `id` value pulled from the request to call the `getFaq()` method of our `FaqRepository`. If we are successful fetching the FAQ from the database, we store in the request under the attribute name `faq`. This allows the destination screen, in this case `delete.jsp`, to retrieve it from the request to make sure the user really wants to delete this FAQ. The only thing new here is that we have to catch several different exceptions and react accordingly. When we're done we return the next screen to the servlet. The source for the `GetCommand` class is shown in listing 9.15.

Listing 9.15   Source code for GetCommand

```
package com.taglib.wdjsp.faqtool;

import javax.servlet.*;
import javax.servlet.http.*;

public class GetCommand implements Command {
  private String next;

  public GetCommand(String next) {
    this.next = next;
  }

  public String execute(HttpServletRequest req)
    throws CommandException {
    try {
      FaqRepository faqs = FaqRepository.getInstance();
      int id = Integer.parseInt(req.getParameter("id"));
      FaqBean faq = faqs.getFaq(id);
      req.setAttribute("faq", faq);
```

```
      return next;
    }
    catch (NumberFormatException e) {
      throw new CommandException("GetCommand: invalid ID");
    }
    catch (UnknownFaqException uf) {
      throw new CommandException("GetCommand: " + uf.getMessage());
    }
    catch (FaqRepositoryException fe) {
      throw new CommandException("GetCommand: " + fe.getMessage());
    }
  }

}
```

The delete confirmation screen

This page allows the user to confirm the selection and triggers the deletion on the server. We simply need to retrieve the FAQ from the request, display its properties, and get the user's decision. Because the handler class for the `do-delete` action, `DeleteCommand`, is vulnerable we must include the current command token in our request, just as we did on the screen where we were creating an FAQ entry. The source for this page is shown in listing 9.16 and a screen is shown in figure 9.6

Listing 9.16   Source code for delete.jsp

```
<%@ page import="com.taglib.wdjsp.faqtool.*" errorPage="/jsp/error.jsp" %>
<jsp:useBean id="faq" class="FaqBean" scope="request"/>
<html>
<head><title>Delete FAQ</title></head>
<form name="menu" action="/faqtool" method="post">
<table bgcolor="tan" border="0" align="center" cellpadding="10">
<tr><th colspan="2">FAQ Administration: Delete FAQ</th></tr>
<tr><td><b>ID:</b></td>
<td><jsp:getProperty name="faq" property="ID"/></td>
</tr>
<tr><td><b>Question:</b></td>
<td><jsp:getProperty name="faq" property="question"/></td>
</tr>
<tr><td><b>Answer:</b></td>
<td><jsp:getProperty name="faq" property="answer"/></td>
</tr>
<tr>
<td colspan="2">
<input type="submit" value="Abort Deletion">
<input type="submit" value="Delete This FAQ"
onClick="document.menu.cmd.value='do-delete'">
```

```
</td></tr>
</table>
<input type="hidden" name="token"
value="<%= request.getAttribute("token") %>">
<input type="hidden" name="id"
value="<jsp:getProperty name="faq" property="id"/>">
<input type="hidden" name="cmd" value="abort">
</form>
</html>
```

The DeleteCommand class

Another straightforward command handler, `DeleteCommand` requires an FAQ ID, which it obtains from the request. It simply calls the appropriate `FaqRepository` method, catching exceptions where appropriate. This is a sensitive command, so we check the token before proceeding.

```
package com.taglib.wdjsp.faqtool;

import javax.servlet.*;
import javax.servlet.http.*;
```

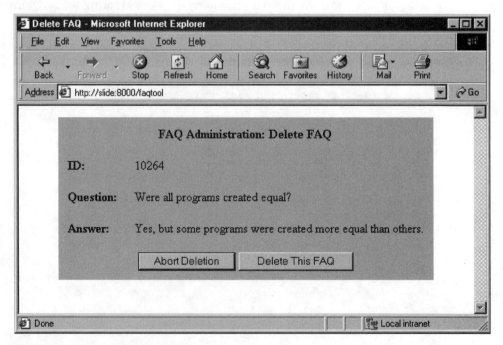

Figure 9.6   The deletion confirmation screen

```
public class DeleteCommand implements Command {
  private String next;

  public DeleteCommand(String next) {
    this.next = next;
  }

  public String execute(HttpServletRequest req)
    throws CommandException {
    try {
      if (CommandToken.isValid(req)) {
        FaqRepository faqs = FaqRepository.getInstance();
        int id = Integer.parseInt(req.getParameter("id"));
        faqs.removeFaq(id);
        req.setAttribute("faqtool.msg", "FAQ Deleted Successfully");
      }
      else {
        req.setAttribute("faqtool.msg", "Invalid Reload Attempted");
      }
      return next;
    }
    catch (NumberFormatException e) {
      throw new CommandException("DeleteCommand: invalid ID");
    }
    catch (UnknownFaqException u) {
      throw new CommandException("DeleteCommand: "+u.getMessage());
    }
    catch (FaqRepositoryException fe) {
      throw new CommandException("DeleteCommand: "+fe.getMessage());
    }
  }

}
```

9.3.5 *Updating an FAQ*

Updating an FAQ—that is, editing its question and answer values—is a three-step process. In the first step, just as with deleting an FAQ, the user picks an FAQ from the list in the database. The next step is a screen which looks like the add screen we built earlier, but this time has default values equal to the current values for the selected FAQ in the database. Committing changes on this screen updates the database with the new values.

Update selection screen

This screen is nearly identical to the one we created for the Delete menu. Its source is shown in listing 9.17 and its screen shot in figure 9.7. Submitting the form on the page causes the servlet to execute the `GetCommand` on the selected servlet, in preparation for the update screen.

Listing 9.17 Source code for upd_menu.jsp

```jsp
<%@ page import="com.taglib.wdjsp.faqtool.*" errorPage="/jsp/error.jsp" %>
<jsp:useBean id="faq" class="FaqBean"/>
<%
  FaqBean[] faqs = (FaqBean[])request.getAttribute("faqs");
%>
<html>
<head><title>Update Menu</title></head>
<form name="menu" action="/faqtool" method="post">
<table bgcolor="tan" border="1" align="center" cellpadding="10">
<tr><th colspan="2">FAQ Administration: Update Menu</th></tr>
<%
for (int i=0; i < faqs.length; i++) {
  faq = faqs[i];
%>
<tr>
<td><input type="radio" name="id"
value="<jsp:getProperty name="faq" property="ID"/>">
<jsp:getProperty name="faq" property="ID"/></td>
<td><jsp:getProperty name="faq" property="question"/></td>
</tr>
<% } %>
<tr><td colspan=2>
<input type="submit" value="Abort Updating">
<input type="submit" value="Update Selected FAQ"
  onClick="document.menu.cmd.value='update'">
<input type="hidden" name="cmd" value="abort">
</td></tr>
</table>
</form>
</html>
```

Update screen

This page operates nearly identically to the page for adding FAQs. The only difference (other than passing a different command identifier) is that we have to prepopulate the form fields with the current values for the selected FAQ. The `GetCommand` has placed a `FaqBean` corresponding with the selection into the request, so all we

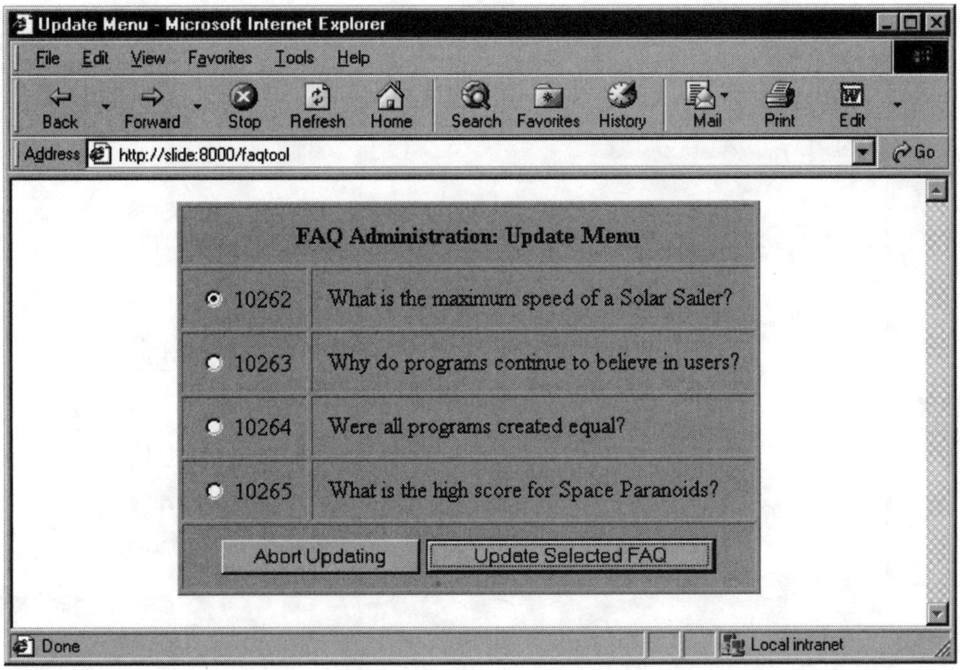

Figure 9.7   The Update menu

have to do is retrieve its values and place them into the form fields. More detailed information on populating forms—including radio buttons, select lists, and other elements—with JSP can be found in chapter 11. The listing for this page is shown in listing 9.18, and the screenshot in figure 9.8.

Listing 9.18   Source code for update.jsp

```
<%@ page import="com.taglib.wdjsp.faqtool.*" errorPage="/jsp/error.jsp" %>
<jsp:useBean id="faq" class="FaqBean" scope="request"/>
<html>
<head><title>Update FAQ</title></head>
<body bgcolor="white">
<form name="menu" action="/faqtool" method="post">
<table bgcolor="tan" border="0" align="center" cellpadding="10">
<tr><th colspan="2">FAQ Administration: Update FAQ</th></tr>
<tr><td><b>Question:</b></td>
<td><input type="text" name="question" size="41"
value="<jsp:getProperty name="faq" property="question"/>">
</td></tr>
<tr><td><b>Answer:</b></td>
```

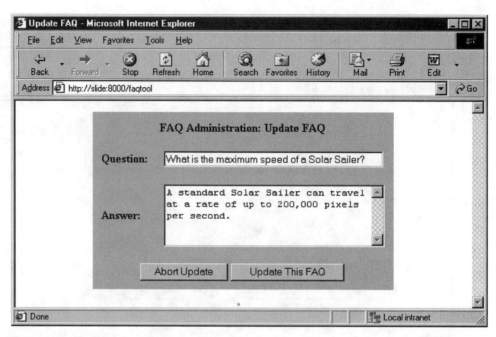

Figure 9.8 The update screen

```
<td>
<textarea name="answer" cols="35" rows="5">
<jsp:getProperty name="faq" property="answer"/>
</textarea>
</td></tr>
<tr><td colspan="2" align="center">
<input type="submit" value="Abort Update">
<input type="submit" value="Update This FAQ"
onClick="document.menu.cmd.value='do-update'">
</td></tr>
</table>
<input type="hidden" name="cmd" value="abort">
<input type="hidden" name="token"
value="<%= request.getAttribute("token") %>">
<input type="hidden" name="id"
value="<jsp:getProperty name="faq" property="ID"/>">
</form>
</body>
</html>
```

The UpdateCommand class

The operation of this command is very similar to that of AddCommand discussed earlier. We take elements of the request to populate a FaqBean object which is passed to the update() method of the FaqRepository class. Again, we catch the appropriate exceptions. The source is shown in listing 9.19.

Listing 9.19   Source code for the UpdateCommand

```
package com.taglib.wdjsp.faqtool;

import javax.servlet.*;
import javax.servlet.http.*;

public class UpdateCommand implements Command {
  private String next;

  public UpdateCommand(String next) {
    this.next = next;
  }

  public String execute(HttpServletRequest req)
    throws CommandException {
    try {
      if (CommandToken.isValid(req)) {
        FaqRepository faqs = FaqRepository.getInstance();
        FaqBean faq = new FaqBean();
        faq.setID(Integer.parseInt(req.getParameter("id")));
        faq.setQuestion(req.getParameter("question"));
        faq.setAnswer(req.getParameter("answer"));
        faqs.update(faq);
        req.setAttribute("faqtool.msg", "FAQ Updated Successfully");
      }
      else {
        req.setAttribute("faqtool.msg", "Invalid Reload Attempted");
      }
      return next;
    }
    catch (NumberFormatException e) {
      throw new CommandException("UpdateCommand: invalid ID");
    }
    catch (UnknownFaqException uf) {
      throw new CommandException("UpdateCommand: "+uf.getMessage());
    }
    catch (FaqRepositoryException fe) {
      throw new CommandException("UpdateCommand: "+fe.getMessage());
    }
  }
}
```

Error screen

This application has a single, very simple error screen, as shown in listing 9.20.

Listing 9.20   Source code for error.jsp

```
<%@ page isErrorPage="true" %>
<html>
<body>
The ERROR : <%= exception.getMessage() %>
<% exception.printStackTrace(); %>
</body>
</html>
```

9.4   The web access module

When we started thinking about how the FAQs would be represented on the web, we realized that with a JSP solution, it was less important to know how they would look (which would be determined by our content team), and more important to know what type of information they would need to convey. From talking with the content team we knew that they would need a way to access the information pertaining to a single FAQ in the database as well as a way to access the entire list of FAQs at once. With these capabilities, they could use JSP to design any number of displays. The decision then was to concentrate on providing them these necessary components (through JavaBeans), and leaving the details of the page design up to them. We also wanted to allow them to create pages in additional styles of formats without the development team having to modify any servlets.

An important consideration that went into the design of this module is that the exact requirements of how the FAQs will be displayed on the web will never be nailed down. We have some basic ideas, but in implementation it is limited only by the creativity of the design team and will certainly change over time and with each site redesign. The goal was to provide the content team with a collection of flexible JSP components that would allow them to fill just about whatever content needs might arise now, or in the future. We'll implement several possible FAQ presentations that work with the components we create.

9.4.1   The FaqServlet

For the web access module we created `FaqServlet` which can be used to retrieve either a single FAQ or all of the FAQs from the database. Its operation depends on the information passed into the servlet through request parameters. The servlet stores the FAQ (or FAQs) as a request attribute before forwarding it to the front-end JSP page, which, unlike our administration servlet, is also specified by the user through the request at run time. The source code for this servlet is shown in listing 9.21.

Listing 9.21   Source code for FaqServlet

```
package com.taglib.wdjsp.faqtool;

import java.io.*;
import javax.servlet.*;
import javax.servlet.http.*;
import java.util.*;

public class FaqServlet extends HttpServlet {
  private String jspdir = "/jsp/";
  private String error = "error.jsp";

  public void service(HttpServletRequest req, HttpServletResponse res)
    throws ServletException, IOException {
    String next;
    Command cmd;
    try {
      next = req.getParameter("page");
      if (next == null)
        throw new CommandException("Page not specified");
      if (req.getParameter("id") != null)
        cmd = new GetCommand(next);
      else
        cmd = new GetAllCommand(next);
      cmd.execute(req);
    }
    catch (CommandException e) {
      req.setAttribute("javax.servlet.jsp.jspException", e);
      next = error;
    }
    RequestDispatcher rd;
    rd = getServletContext().getRequestDispatcher(jspdir + next);
    rd.forward(req, res);
  }

}
```

We were able to reuse the `GetCommand` and `GetAllCommand` classes that were developed for the administration module in this servlet. However, since there are only a couple of possible actions in this servlet, we eliminated the command identifiers and instead base our actions on what parameters were present in the request. If a single

FAQ is to be retrieved its ID values should be passed in through the id request parameter. If this parameter doesn't exist, we'll default to fetching all of the FAQs. In either case, we need to know which JSP page will be ultimately handling the request, and this should be indicated through the page request parameter. If this parameter is missing we have no choice but to throw an exception and visit the error page. We mapped the servlet to /faqs/ on the external web server. So, for example, to retrieve FAQ number 1437 and display it in the JSP page showfaq.jsp we would use a URL such as this:

```
/faqs?page=showfaq.jsp&id=1437
```

This simple servlet is quite flexible; it is basically an FAQ lookup service for JSP pages. It allows the web team to develop many different pages that display FAQs in a variety of formats and styles without having to modify the application or control logic. They can have a hundred different versions if they want to. This simple core service can serve them all. Let's look at a couple of examples of how this service can be used to display FAQs.

9.4.2 Viewing a single FAQ

To view a single FAQ we simply pass in the page name, in this case single.jsp, and the ID number of the FAQ we want to display. We then retrieve the FAQ from the request and display its properties. The source for the page is shown in listing 9.22 and a screen shot in figure 9.9.

Listing 9.22   Source code for single.jsp

```jsp
<%@ page import="com.taglib.wdjsp.faqtool.*" errorPage="/jsp/error.jsp" %>
<jsp:useBean id="faq" class="FaqBean" scope="request"/>
<html>
<head>
<title>FAQ <jsp:getProperty name="faq" property="ID"/></title>
</head>
<body bgcolor="white">
<b>Question:</b> <jsp:getProperty name="faq" property="question"/>
<br>
<b>Answer:</b> <jsp:getProperty name="faq" property="answer"/>
<p>
<font size=-1>Last Modified:
<i><jsp:getProperty name="faq" property="lastModified"/></i>
</font>
</body>
</html>
```

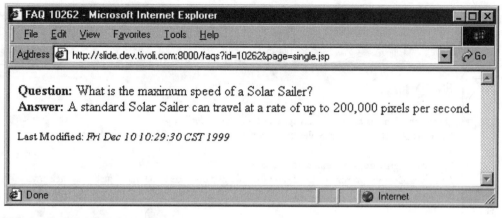

Figure 9.9   Viewing a single FAQ

9.4.3   *Viewing all the FAQs*

Showing the contents of all of the FAQs on a single page is not much different. We use the same looping constructs we developed for the delete and update menus in the Administration module to cycle through the FAQs. The source code is shown in listing 9.23, and a screen shot is shown in figure 9.10.

Listing 9.23   Source code for all.jsp

```
<%@ page import="com.taglib.wdjsp.faqtool.*"
 errorPage="/jsp/error.jsp" %>
<jsp:useBean id="faq" class=" FaqBean"/>
<% FaqBean[] faqs = (FaqBean[])request.getAttribute("faqs"); %>
<html>
<head><title>FAQ List</title></head>
<body bgcolor="white">
<h2>FAQ List</h2>
<%
for (int i=0; i < faqs.length; i++) {
  faq = faqs[i];
%>
<b>Question:</b> <jsp:getProperty name="faq" property="question"/>
<br>
<b>Answer:</b> <jsp:getProperty name="faq" property="answer"/>
<p>
<% } %>
</body>
</html>
```

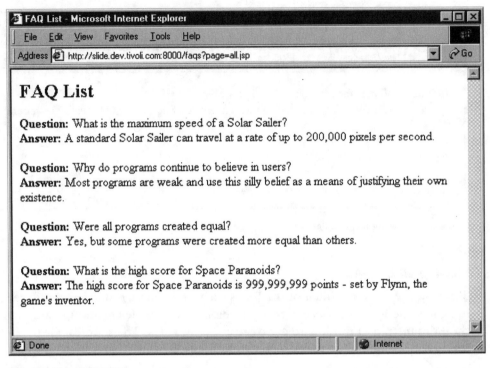

Figure 9.10   All the FAQs

9.4.4   A table of contents view

A more imaginative use of the FAQ lookup servlet is to create a table of contents view of the FAQs in the database. To do this we need to reference all of the FAQs, just as we did in the above view. This time, however, we only display the questions as a link to our single FAQ view. This dynamically generates links to each individual FAQ. The source for this page is shown in listing 9.24, and a screen shot in figure 9.11.

Listing 9.24   Source code for toc.jsp

```
<%@ page import="com.taglib.wdjsp.faqtool.*"
 errorPage="/jsp/error.jsp" %>
<jsp:useBean id="faq" class="FaqBean"/>
<% FaqBean[] faqs = (FaqBean[])request.getAttribute("faqs"); %>
<html>
<head><title>FAQ Index</title></head>
```

```
<body bgcolor="white">
<h2>FAQ Index</h2>
<%
for (int i=0; i < faqs.length; i++) {
  faq = faqs[i];
%>
<b>Q:</b>
<a href="/faqs?page=single.jsp&id=
<jsp:getProperty name="faq" property="ID"/>">
<jsp:getProperty name="faq" property="question"/></a>
<p>
<% } %>
</body>
</html>
```

Figure 9.11   The FAQ index page

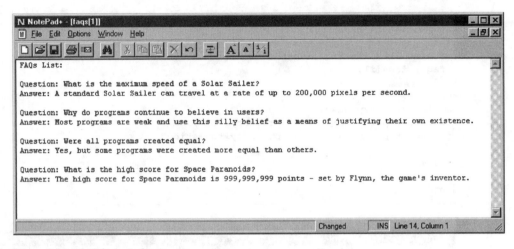

Figure 9.12   A plain text view

9.4.5   *Plain text view*

As an alternative view of the FAQs we create a plain text version of the list by simply changing the content type and omitting HTML code. This view is shown in listing 9.25 and can be seen in action (loaded into a text viewer) in figure 9.12.

Listing 9.25   Source code for plain.jsp

```
<%@ page import="com.taglib.wdjsp.faqtool.*" errorPage="/jsp/error.jsp" %>
<jsp:useBean id="faq" class=" FaqBean"/>
<% FaqBean[] faqs = (FaqBean[])request.getAttribute("faqs"); %>
FAQs List:
<%
for (int i=0; i < faqs.length; i++) {
  faq = faqs[i];
%>
Question: <jsp:getProperty name="faq" property="question"/>
Answer: <jsp:getProperty name="faq" property="answer"/>
<% } %>
```

Deploying JSP applications

10

Whatever architecture you have selected for your JSP's development, a web-based application can't be used until it has been successfully deployed on a web server. Whereas desktop applications are often packaged with customized installation programs that walk the user through the required configuration and deployment steps, the installation of applications targeted toward the server environment has historically been somewhat less user-friendly.

In an effort to remedy this situation, at least for Java-based web applications, the servlet and JSP specifications support the bundling of an application's files into a single *web archive*, which can be deployed as is to a Java-enabled web server. All of the resources required for a given web application—JSP files and servlets, as well as associated content such as HTML documents, images, applets, and JavaBeans—are deposited in a web archive, along with an XML-based configuration file. This archive can then be placed into a designated directory on the web server and, after customizing the included configuration file as necessary, the associated application is run straight from the archive file. When requests are received for URLs corresponding to the contents of the archive, the JSP container extracts those resources as needed. Processing then resumes as if the extracted resources were part of the server's normal document hierarchy.

10.1 *This means WAR*

Web archives take the form of JAR files, the standard file archive format for the Java platform. Each web archive also contains a special descriptor file describing how the files in the archive are used to implement a web-based application. So that tools can easily distinguish between web archives and other JAR files, web archives are assigned the extension .war, and for this reason are commonly referred to as WAR files.

As mentioned in chapters 3 and 4, a Java web application is mapped to a directory hierarchy, rooted in a single top-level directory. The URLs for all of the elements of the application will therefore all begin with the same initial directory, the name of which also serves as the name of the application. In an application named clu, for example, its resources are all accessed in or below a top-level directory named clu, using URLs such as http://server/clu/index.jsp, http://server/clu/servlet/dashboard, and http://server/clu/images/reticle.gif.

As also described in chapters 3 and 4, all Java-based resources in an application (i.e., servlets and JSPs) share the same javax.servlet.ServletContext instance, which is made available to the application's JSP pages via the application implicit object. This object, by means of the standard attribute methods outlined in table 4.2, provides a simple data-sharing mechanism for use within an application, which serves as the foundation for storing objects (e.g., Beans) with `application` scope.

WAR files are designed to store the contents of a single application. The hypothetical `clu` application introduced previously would therefore be stored in a web archive named clu.war. By registering the WAR file with the JSP container, all of the resources stored in that file become available for use by the container and, by extension, end users accessing the associated HTTP server.

NOTE The process by which WAR files are registered is currently container-specific. In the case of the Tomcat reference implementation (see appendix A), the container's `server.xml` file must be manually edited to add an application. At the time of this writing, WAR files are relatively new; graphical and/or web-based tools that simplify the installation of applications contained in WAR files will likely be a feature of future versions of this and other JSP containers.

10.1.1 *WAR is XML*

In addition to its web application content, a WAR file also contains a deployment descriptor file—formally referred to as the Web Application Descriptor file—that specifies how that content is used to provide the corresponding application functionality. For example, the descriptor file itemizes the servlets contained in an application, providing any associated initialization parameters or URL mappings. A web application can also contain JSP pages that have already been compiled into servlets, and the descriptor file is where the JSP container looks to find the original URLs for such pages.

TIP By deploying JSP pages as precompiled servlets, you can avoid the run-time overhead of compiling a page the first time it is requested by an end user. It also eliminates the need to include a Java compiler on the production web server, thereby reducing the memory footprint for the server's JVM.

The descriptor file is named `web.xml`, and resides in a special top-level directory of the WAR file named `WEB-INF`. This subdirectory is an analog of the `META-INF` subdirectory found in all JAR files, containing *metainformation* about the archive itself. An archive serves as a repository of information; the data it stores about itself is therefore considered metainformation, in the sense that it is information about information. In a similar vein, the `WEB-INF` subdirectory contains information about how the contents of the repository are deployed via the Web, with the `web.xml` file serving as the central configuration file for the archive.

As its file extension suggests, the markup language for the data in the `web.xml` file is XML. For example, the contents of a basic deployment descriptor file for the `faqtool` application presented in the previous chapter would take the following form:

```
<?xml version="1.0" encoding="ISO-8859-1" ?>
<!DOCTYPE web-app PUBLIC
          "-//Sun Microsystems, Inc.//DTD Web Application 1.2//EN"
          "http://java.sun.com/j2ee/dtds/web-app_1_2.dtd">
<web-app>
  <display-name>FAQ Tool</display-name>
  <servlet>
    <servlet-name>faqs</servlet-name>
    <servlet-class>com.taglib.wdjsp.faqtool.FaqServlet</servlet-class>
  </servlet>
  <servlet>
    <servlet-name>faqtool</servlet-name>
    <servlet-class>com.taglib.wdjsp.faqtool.FaqAdminServlet</servlet-class>
  </servlet>
  <servlet-mapping>
    <url-pattern>/faqs</ url-pattern >
    <servlet-name>faqs</servlet-name>
  </servlet-mapping>
  <servlet-mapping>
    <url-pattern>/faqtool</ url-pattern >
    <servlet-name>faqtool</servlet-name>
  </servlet-mapping>
</web-app>
```

The details of the various entries in a `web.xml` file will be presented later in the chapter. This particular example, however, indicates that the `faqtool` web application contains two servlets, which are mapped to a pair of corresponding URLs.

Note that this deployment descriptor says nothing about the JSP pages used by this application. One might infer that the application does not make use of JSP, but as we saw in chapter 9, this is definitely not the case. Instead, because JSP servlets are generated as needed and are automatically mapped to URLs based on their original file names, there is no need to specify configuration information for them in the `web.xml` file. As a result, the JSP container is able to gather all of the information it typically requires about an application's JSP pages by simply scanning the contents of its WAR file.

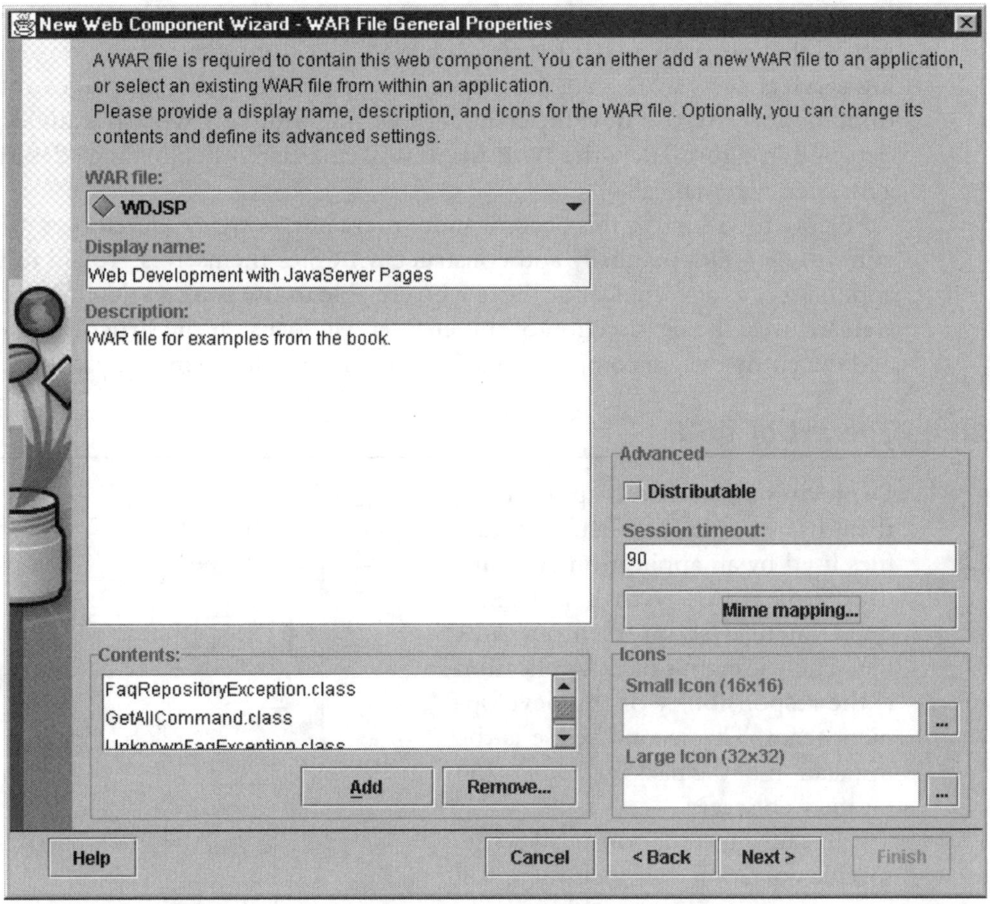

Figure 10.1   The New Web Component wizard of Sun's J2EE `deploytool`

10.1.2 Waging WAR

Like most configuration files, even though it uses a human-readable format, the web.xml is a bit awkward to work with. Manual editing of deployment descriptors, which is currently the preferred method for creating and maintaining web.xml files, is tedious and error-prone. It is therefore anticipated that user-friendly tools tailored for just these tasks will soon be available.

As a preview of what can be expected in such tools, Sun Microsystems has included a prototype application deployment tool, `deploytool`, in its reference implementation of the J2EE platform. This tool includes a New Web Component wizard that provides a GUI for creating WAR files from a set of Java classes (including servlets and JavaBeans), JSP pages, and static files (such as images and HTML documents). As the developer navigates through this wizard's dialog boxes, depicted in figure 10.1, the WAR file and its associated deployment descriptor are generated automatically.

Before tools such as this become more prevalent, however, developers will have to edit web.xml files manually and construct WAR files themselves. To aid in this task, and to serve as a reference for those who are able to use tools to deploy their code as web archives, the next section of this chapter will focus on the structure of WAR files and the entries which comprise an archive's web.xml deployment descriptor.

10.2   *The art of WAR*

Deploying a Java-based application, then, has two phases. First, all of the files used by an application are bundled up, along with a web.xml deployment descriptor, into a WAR file. The packaging of an application is the responsibility of the development team. The second phase is the installation of the package application on the web server.

Because installation is a server-specific operation, our focus here will be on constructing the web archive. WAR files are meant to be portable between JSP containers. As such, their contents and those of the deployment descriptor are well-defined by the servlet and JSP specifications. In the sections to follow we will provide an overview of the WAR file format, and then describe the web.xml entries required to specify an application's servlets and JSP pages.

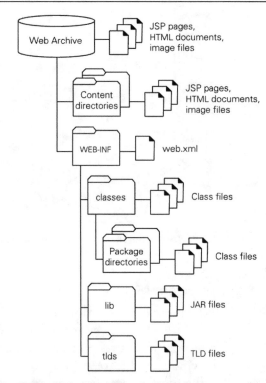

Figure 10.2   Contents of a WAR file for web application deployment

10.2.1 *WAR materiel*

As already described, a WAR file is essentially a JAR file that contains extra information allowing its contents to be deployed in a servlet or JSP container. This extra information is stored in the WAR file's top-level WEB-INF directory, which contains the archive's `web.xml` deployment descriptor, as well as two special subdirectories for storing Java classes. The overall layout of a WAR file is depicted in figure 10.2.

The web-based content for an application can appear at the top-level of a web archive, or in arbitrary content directories and subdirectories. As indicated in figure 10.2, this content typically consists of JSP pages, HTML documents, and image files, but any file type that may be delivered over the web—including sound files, animations, portable documents, and Java applets—can be placed in a WAR file. That file will then be accessible from the web server to which the WAR file is deployed.

Listing 10.1   Contents of an example WAR file, disc.war

```
main.jsp
docs/rules.html
game/catch.jsp
game/deflect.jsp
game/index.jsp
game/ringhit.jsp
game/start.jsp
game/throw.jsp
images/icons/ring.gif
images/players/crom.gif
images/players/flynn.gif
WEB-INF/web.xml
WEB-INF/classes/com/taglib/encom/disc/RingControlServlet.class
WEB-INF/classes/com/taglib/encom/disc/PlayerBean.class
WEB-INF/lib/disc-classes.jar
WEB-INF/lib/discTags_1_0.jar
WEB-INF/tlds/discTags_1_0.tld
```

Content in a Java-based web application is accessed via a URL that begins with the name of the application. Consider, for example, an application named `disc` that is packaged in a web archive named disc.war with the contents indicated in listing 10.1. An end user accessing this application's main.jsp file would use a URL of the form http://server/disc/main.jsp, in which the name of the application, `disc`, provides the top-level directory for all URLs that reference the application's content. Directories and subdirectories are treated similarly. The URL for retrieving the image named crom.gif, for instance, would be http://server/disc/images/players/crom.gif.

On the front

Note from listing 10.1 that the WAR file itself contains no references to a top-level directory named `disc`. This directory name is automatically recognized by the JSP container once the application has been registered with the container. Application names are arbitrary, and are assigned at the time of installation. The name of an application is completely independent of the name of the corresponding WAR file. It is common, but not mandatory for them to be the same. If the local server administrator wished to install the disc.war file as an application named `frisbee`, the JSP container will be happy to translate URLs such as http://server/frisbee/game/start.jsp into the corresponding content from the disc.war archive.

This top-level URL directory, then, is completely under the control of the container. The directory name is mapped to an application, and is removed from the URL behind the scenes when translating it into a file name for retrieving content from the WAR file. Given that the application name is not built into the application, you may be wondering how the pages within an application can refer to one another via URLs. Relative URLs function as expected, but if the first directory in an absolute URL cannot be known until the application is installed, it would appear that absolute URLs must be avoided within an application's documents.

To address this deficiency, JSP containers are required to automatically account for this top-level directory when processing elements that use absolute URLs. Specifically, when a JSP page that is part of an application calls the `include` directive, the `<jsp:include>` action, or the `<jsp:forward>` action with an absolute URL, the container is required to map that URL into the page's application. In effect, the application name is transparently added to the beginning of such absolute URLs so that references within the application are properly maintained. For example, the main.jsp file for the sample application in listing 10.1 might wish to forward control to the start.jsp file in the `game` directory, using an absolute URL as follows:

```
<jsp:forward page="/game/start.jsp" />
```

If the application has been named `disc`, then when the JSP container processes this action it will automatically map the page reference to /disc/game/start.jsp. If `frisbee` was chosen as the application name, it would instead map this absolute URL to /frisbee/game/start.jsp.

References to URLs from standard HTML tags, however, are not automatically mapped. A relative URL appearing in the SRC attribute of an `<IMG>` tag or the HREF attribute of an `<A>` tag would be resolved correctly, but when an absolute URL is more convenient, an alternate approach is warranted. The most direct approach to using absolute URLs is to mandate a specific name under which the application must be installed on the server.

A more flexible approach is to take advantage of HTML's <BASE> tag. When this tag is specified in the <HEAD> section of an HTML document, all relative URLs in the document are resolved relative to the value specified for this tag's HREF attribute. In a JSP page, then, the following construct can be used to set this base URL to that of the application, as in the following page fragment:

```
<HTML>
<HEAD>
<BASE HREF="<%= request.getContextPath() %>/">
...
<HEAD>
<BODY>
...
<A HREF="about/company.jsp"><IMG SRC="images/logo.gif"></A>
...
</BODY>
</HTML>
```

Here, the getContextPath() method of the javax.servlet.http.HttpServletRequest class is used to retrieve the top-level directory of the URL associated with the request, which will correspond to the name assigned to the application on the server. Note that the result returned by this method will start with an initial forward slash character, but will not end with one. The closing directory delimiter is therefore added explicitly by specifying it as static text in the <BASE> tag (i.e., immediately following the JSP expression).

If the application has been assigned the name disc, then the result of calling the getContextPath() method will be "/disc". When the JSP page is processed, the resulting <BASE> tag sent back to the end user's browser will therefore be:

```
<BASE HREF="/disc/">
```

In the example page, the two relative URLs will be resolved by the browser relative to this base URL, resulting in an effective URL of /disc/about/company.jsp for the link and /disc/images/logo.gif for the image. In this way, it becomes possible to reference other resources within the application using URLs that behave very similarly to absolute URLs, without having to know in advance the name (and therefore the top-level URL directory) of the installed application.

The fog of WAR

The translation by the JSP container of URLs into WAR file contents applies to all files and directories in the archive except those appearing within the WEB-INF directory. More specifically, the contents of the WEB-INF directory and its subdirectories cannot be accessed via URLs at all. Instead, these files are reserved for use by the JSP container, and fall into four major categories.

NOTE   The ServletContext object associated with an application, accessible from its JSP pages via the application implicit object, is able to programmatically access the contents of the WAR file's WEB-INF directory, using its getResource() and getResourceAsStream() methods. In this way, developers can use the WEB-INF directory for storing additional application-specific data that can be accessed via Java code, but is not directly exposed to end users via URLs.

The first type of file found in the WEB-INF directory, the web.xml deployment descriptor, has already been mentioned. This file provides configuration information for the JSP container to use when running the application contained in the archive, the details of which are provided later in this chapter.

The second type are compiled Java class files. As illustrated in figure 10.2, Java class files appear in the classes subdirectory of the WEB-INF directory. Classes which are part of the default Java package should be placed directly in the classes directory, while those with explicitly named packages should be placed in subdirectories whose names correspond to the various elements of the package's name. For example, based on their positions in the file hierarchy presented in listing 10.1, it can be presumed that the RingControlServlet and the PlayerBean classes are both in the com.taglib.encom.disc package.

The classes appearing in the WAR file in the WEB-INF/classes directory and its subdirectories are automatically added to the class path used by the JSP container's JVM whenever it is accessing the application associated with the archive. As such, it is intended to provide a convenient location for storing the Java classes used by the application's servlets and JSP pages. The classes implementing the servlets themselves can appear here, as well as any auxiliary classes used by those servlets. JavaBeans and other Java classes referenced by the application's JSP pages can also be stored here.

The third type are JAR files, stored in the lib subdirectory of the WEB-INF directory. Like the individual class files found in the WEB-INF/classes directory, all of the classes found in the JAR files located here are automatically added to the JVM's class path whenever the JSP container is accessing the corresponding application. For the web archive presented in listing 10.1, classes stored in disc-classes.jar would automatically be available when responding to requests for the disc application's servlets and JSP pages.

The fourth type of file often found in the WEB-INF directory are Tag Library Descriptor (TLD) files for custom tag libraries. By convention, these are placed in a subdirectory named tlds. The deployment of custom tag libraries and TLDs will be discussed later in this chapter, but for the complete details see chapters 13 and 14.

In the absence of custom deployment tools, a common means for creating WAR files is Java's standard software package for creating archive files, the jar command-line tool. The jar command can be used both to create archives and to extract their contents. It can also be used to list the contents of an existing JAR file. When creating an archive, jar takes a list of files to be archived, as well as a file name for the archive. To create a WAR file, simply provide the jar command with a list of all of the files to be placed in the archive—web content files as well as those appearing in the WEB-INF directory—and specify a file name with a .war extension as the destination for the new archive.

NOTE When creating an archive, the jar command automatically inserts a top-level directory named META-INF, to which is added a file named MANIFEST.MF. This manifest file contains a listing of the contents of the archive, and may optionally be augmented with additional information about the archive's files. When the jar command is used to create a WAR file, the resulting web archive will also contain a META-INF/MANIFEST.MF file. Like the contents of the archive's WEB-INF directory, the JSP container will not make a manifest file accessible over the web via a URL.

For further details on the use of jar, including descriptions of the various command line options that control its behavior, consult the documentation that accompanies the Java Development Kit (JDK), available from Sun Microsystems.

10.2.2 *Drafting deployment descriptors*

Having looked at the global structure of web archives, we next set our sights on a single file within the archive, the web.xml deployment descriptor. As discussed previously, this file contains entries describing the configuration of the application's Java-based assets. In the sections to follow, we will outline the format of this file and describe the XML directives used in the deployment descriptor to manage an application's servlets and, where appropriate, its JSP pages.

A prelude to WAR

As an XML document, the deployment descriptor must begin with the standard XML header material. Typically, a tag declaring the XML version number and the document's character encoding appear first, followed by a specification of the Document Type Definition (DTD) for the document. As its name implies, it describes the valid tags for a given document type, and may thus be used to validate the syntax of an XML document.

For a Web Application Descriptor file, the DTD is provided by Sun Microsystems, at a published URL associated with the J2EE specification. A typical header for a web.xml file would therefore be as follows:

```
<?xml version="1.0" encoding="ISO-8859-1" ?>
<!DOCTYPE web-app PUBLIC
        "-//Sun Microsystems, Inc.//DTD Web Application 1.2//EN"
        "http://java.sun.com/j2ee/dtds/web-app_1_2.dtd">
```

The root element for deployment descriptors is the <web-app> tag. All of the elements of a web.xml file, except for the header items just described, must appear within the body content of a single <web-app> tag, as in the faqtool example presented earlier in this chapter.

Several subelements of the <web-app> tag are available for specifying properties of the application itself, as illustrated in the following web.xml fragment:

```
<web-app>
   <description>
     Manages a collection of FAQs and displays them in multiple formats.
   </description>
   <display-name>FAQ Tool</display-name>
   <icon>
      <large-icon>/icons/faqtool32x32.gif</large-icon>
      <small-icon>/icons/faqtool16x16.gif</small-icon>
   </icon>
   <welcome-file-list>
      <welcome-file>default.html</welcome-file>
      <welcome-file>index.jsp</welcome-file>
   </welcome-file-list>
   <distributable/>
   ...
</web-app>
```

All of these subelements are optional, and should appear at most once within the parent <web-app> element. The <description> tag is used to document the application, while the <icon> tag and its subelements, <large-icon> and <small-icon>, are provided for use with graphical configuration tools, as is the <display-name> tag.

The `<welcome-file-list>` element is used to specify which file within an application directory should be displayed to the end user when a URL is requested that contains only a directory. Each such file name is specified via the `<welcome-file>` tag, and order is significant. When a directory URL is requested, the JSP container will search the corresponding directory in the application for the files in this list, in the order in which they appear in the deployment descriptor. The first one found generates the response to that request. If none is found, the response will contain an appropriate error message.

The last element in this example is the `<distributable>` tag. Unlike the others, this tag has no body content, but simply signals whether or not the application is distributable by its presence or absence. If this tag is included in the deployment descriptor, it serves as an indicator that the application has been written in such a way as to support distributing the application across multiple JSP containers. If the tag is not present, then it must be assumed that distributed processing is not supported.

DEFINITION A *distributed* web application runs in multiple JSP containers simultaneously, typically on multiple web servers, while sharing some common resources and/or functionality. As discussed in chapter 2, the capacity for a web-based application to be distributed is an important consideration for scalability.

Targeting servlets

A web application's servlets are specified in the deployment descriptor via the `<servlet>` tag and its subelements, as in the following example:

```
<web-app>
   ...
   <servlet>
     <servlet-name>ringControl</servlet-name>
     <servlet-class>
        com.taglib.encom.disc.RingControlServlet
     </servlet-class>
     <description>
        Controls the rings within each player's platform.
     </description>
     <display-name>Ring Controller</display-name>
     <icon>
        <small-icon>/images/icons/ring.gif</small-icon>
     </icon>
     <init-param>
        <param-name>ringCount</param-name>
```

```
        <param-value>7</param-value>
        <description>
          The initial number of rings in each platform.
        </description>
      </init-param>
      <load-on-startup>3</load-on-startup>
    </servlet>
  ...
</web-app>
```

Within the body of the `<servlet>` tag, the `<description>`, `<display-name>`, and `<icon>` tags play an analogous role as when they appear at the top level in the body of the `<web-app>` tag. The functionality of the other tags is specific to servlets. Only the `<servlet-name>` and `<servlet-class>` tags are mandatory.

The `<servlet-name>` tag, as you might expect, provides a name for the servlet. The value provided in the body of this tag can be used to request the servlet via a URL composed of the application name, a subdirectory named `servlet`, and the specified servlet name. For example, if the servlet specified here were part of an application named `disc`, then the URL for accessing this servlet would be http://server/disc/servlet/ringControl.

The `<servlet-class>` tag specifies the Java class that implements the servlet. The JSP container instantiates this class in order to respond to requests handled by the servlet.

After instantiating the servlet class, but before servicing any requests, the container will call the servlet class's `init()` method. Initialization parameters, which are passed to the servlet's `init()` method via an instance of `javax.servlet.ServletConfig`, are specified via the `<init-param>` tag. This tag has three subelements, `<param-name>`, `<param-value>`, and `<description>`, the last of which is optional. There should be one `<init-param>` tag for each initialization parameter to be passed to the `init()` method.

As their names suggest, the body of the `<param-name>` tag corresponds to the parameter name, while the body of the `<param-value>` tag supplies its value. In the example above, an initialization parameter named `ringCount` has been assigned a value of 7. Note that parameter names and values are both passed to the servlet as `String` objects. If the parameter value is intended to represent some other type of data (e.g., a numeric value), then it is up to the servlet's `init()` method to parse the value appropriately. As has been the case elsewhere, the `<description>` tag is provided for documentation purposes.

The remaining `<servlet>` subelement is the `<load-on-startup>` tag. The presence of this tag indicates to the JSP container that this servlet should be loaded into the container's JVM (and initialized via its `init()` method) as during the JSP container's startup process. If this tag is not present, the container is free to wait until a request is received for the servlet before loading it.

The `<load-on-startup>` tag can be specified either as an empty tag (i.e., `<load-on-startup/>`), or with body content specifying an integer value. This tag's body content is used to indicate when the servlet should be loaded, relative to other servlets which are designated as being loaded on startup. If the tag is empty, then the JSP container is free to load the servlet whenever it wishes during startup. If the body content specifies an integer value, then that value is used to order the loading of all servlets that specify integer values for this tag. Lower values are loaded first, followed by servlets specifying higher values. If more than one servlet specifies the same value for `<load-on-startup>`, the ordering of those servlets is arbitrary. The effect is that all servlets which specify a value of 1 for this tag will be loaded first (in an unspecified order), followed by all servlets which specified a value of 2, then all servlets specifying a value of 3, and so on.

Typically, the servlets within one application are not dependent upon those in another application. As long as you specify unique values for the `<load-on-startup>` tags within a single application, you can be assured that the servlets within that application will be loaded in the specified order. Servlets from other applications may also be loaded within that sequence, but you can at least be certain that any order dependencies within that specific application will be maintained.

Mapping the terrain

It is often desirable to specify an alternate URL for a servlet. It is good programming practice to hide the implementation details of a given set of functionality, and URLs that contain the word "servlet" are pretty much a dead giveaway that the underlying implementation of an application is based on servlets. This is not to suggest that you shouldn't be proud of selecting servlets as your implementation technology—indeed, the authors would wholeheartedly endorse that decision—but studies have shown that memorable URLs improve the usability of a web site and, frankly, end users don't care about what's under the hood.

Given that the default URL for an application's servlets, as described in the previous section, includes a subdirectory component named `servlet`, those wishing to follow this advice need a mechanism for specifying alternate URLs. This is accomplished in the `web.xml` file via use of the `<servlet-mapping>` tag, as in the following example:

```
<web-app>
  . . .
  <servlet-mapping>
    <servlet-name>ringControl</servlet-name>
    <url-pattern>/ringMaster</ url-pattern >
  </servlet-mapping>
  . . .
</web-app>
```

Here, the `<servlet-name>` tag identifies the servlet for which the alternate URL is being specified, and should correspond to a servlet defined elsewhere in the deployment descriptor via the `<servlet>` tag. The body of the `<url-pattern>` tag specifies a URL pattern, such that requests whose URLs match the specified pattern will be handled by the indicated servlet. Both of these subelements are required.

Like all URLs associated with an application, any URL specified in this manner must be preceded by the name of the application when it is requested by an end user. For the example shown here then, the alternate URL for the `ringControl` servlet, again assuming `disc` is the name assigned to the application, will be http://server/disc/ringMaster.

Although the URL pattern in the example shown here is just a simple alphabetic string, more involved patterns are also supported. For example, multiple directory levels may be included, as in `/ringMaster/blue/flynn`. An asterisk may take the place of the final element in such a mapping—for example, `/ringMaster/blue/*`—indicating that all URLs that start with this directory pattern (plus the application name, of course), should be mapped to the corresponding servlet. (The additional elements of such URLs will be available to the servlet via the `getPathInfo()` method of `javax.servlet.http.HttpServletRequest`.)

This tag can also be used to map requests for specific file types—based on their file name extensions—to a servlet. In this case the body of the `<servlet-mapping>` tag should take the form of an asterisk followed by a period and the extension to be mapped. For example, a URL pattern of `*.disc` would map all requests within an application that have an extension of .disc to the corresponding servlet.

NOTE   In fact, this is how JSP itself works: all requests for files ending with the .jsp extension are mapped to the page compiler servlet (see chapter 2).

WAR and JSPs

Given that this is a JSP book, you may be wondering why so much space has been devoted here to the configuration of servlets. The first reason, as indicated in chapter 8, is that servlets and JSPs are natural companions in the construction of complex web applications. If you will be deploying an application that uses JSP pages, there's a strong chance the application also includes servlets.

In addition, recall that JSP pages are implemented as servlets. As a result, the deployment descriptor elements provided for configuring an application's servlets are also, in most cases, applicable to the configuration of its JSP pages. As already mentioned in this chapter, it is usually not necessary to mention an application's JSP pages in the web.xml file. When it is necessary, however, the servlet-related tags again come into play.

In the discussion of the `<servlet>` tag earlier in this chapter, it was pointed out that the only required subelements are the `<servlet-name>` and `<servlet-class>` tags. Actually, this is not completely true. When referencing JSP pages, the `<servlet-class>` tag is replaced by, appropriately enough, the `<jsp-file>` tag. In the interest of full disclosure then, the only required subelement of the `<servlet>` tag is the `<servlet-name>` tag. In addition, either the `<servlet-class>` tag or the `<jsp-file>` tag must be present.

In this way, the initialization parameters and startup behavior of the servlet corresponding to a JSP file can be configured using the same techniques described earlier for configuring servlets. The body of the `<jsp-file>` tag is used to specify the full path to the JSP page within the application, as in the following example:

```
<web-app>
   ...
   <servlet>
     <servlet-name>startPage</servlet-name>
     <jsp-file>/game/start.jsp </jsp-file>
     <description>JSP page for starting a new game.</description>
     <init-param>
        <param-name>playerCount</param-name>
        <param-value>2</param-value>
        <description>
           The maximum number of players per game.
        </description>
     </init-param>
     <load-on-startup>4</load-on-startup>
   </servlet>
   ...
</web-app>
```

As with other application-specific paths, the body of the `<jsp-file>` tag does not include the top-level directory named after the application. Note also that when the `<load-on-startup>` tag is specified in the `<servlet>` tag for a JSP page, it is an indication to the JSP container that the page should be compiled as well as loaded during container startup.

Instead of precompiling the JSP servlet during container startup, however, it might be desirable under certain circumstances to deploy the servlet rather than the original JSP page. This can also be accomplished via the `web.xml` deployment descriptor. After writing the JSP file and deploying it in a JSP container, a copy can be made of the compiled JSP servlet constructed by the container. Suppose, for example, that the `/game/throw.jsp` page from our hypothetical `disc` application has been compiled into a servlet class named `_jsp_game_throw_JspImpl`. A copy of the generated class file,`_jsp_game_throw_JspImpl.class`, can be added to the application's WAR file, in place of the original /game/throw.jsp file. Appropriate `<serv-let>` and `<servlet-mapping>` tags must then be added to the deployment descriptor to mimic the original JSP behavior, as in the following `web.xml` fragment:

```
<web-app>
  ...
  <servlet>
    <servlet-name>throwPage</servlet-name>
    <servlet-class>_jsp_game_throw_JspImpl</servlet-class>
  </servlet>
  <servlet-mapping>
    <servlet-name>throwPage</servlet-name>
    <servlet-mapping>/game/throw.jsp</servlet-mapping>
  </servlet-mapping>
  ...
</web-app>
```

As a result of this mapping, the URL associated with the original JSP page is explicitly mapped to the corresponding servlet, rather than relying on the page compiler servlet to make this association automatically. In fact, when responding to requests for a JSP page mapped in this fashion, the page compiler servlet is bypassed altogether, and requests are routed directly to the precompiled page servlet.

WARNING Recall from chapter 3 that the requirement imposed by the JSP specification on servlets generated from JSP pages is that they implement the `jav-ax.servlet.jsp.HttpJspPage` interface. The actual concrete superclass for generated JSP pages is therefore implementation-specific. Keep in mind, then, that if you use the technique described here for deploying JSP pages as precompiled servlets, the resulting WAR file will not be portable. By virtue of its reliance on an implementation-specific servlet class, the WAR file will be compatible only with the JSP container originally used to generate the precompiled servlet.

Mobilizing custom tag libraries

In previous chapters, custom tag libraries have been described as a powerful feature for adding functionality to JSP pages. As indicated in chapter 3, tag libraries are loaded into a JSP page by means of the `taglib` directive, which locates a tag library based on a URL. Until now, however, we haven't been in a position to discuss where this URL comes from.

A custom tag library has two basic components: a set of Java classes implementing the custom action provided by the tag library and a TLD file which provides a mapping between the library's tags and those implementation classes.

A tag library's classes are typically bundled into a JAR file, for storage in an application's `WEB-INF/lib` directory. Alternatively, the individual class files may be placed in the appropriate package-specific subdirectories of the application's `WEB-INF/classes` directory. As already mentioned, TLD files are typically stored in the `WEB-INF/tlds` directory.

The `taglib` directive loads a custom tag library by referencing the library's TLD file in its `uri` attribute. Because the contents of the `WEB-INF` directory are not normally accessible via URLs, it is usually necessary to provide a mapping for the TLD file in the application's deployment descriptor. This is accomplished via the `<taglib>` tag, as in the following `web.xml` fragment:

```
<web-app>
  ...
  <taglib>
    <taglib-uri>/discTags</taglib-uri>
    <taglib-location>/WEB-INF/tlds/discTags_1_0.tld</taglib-location>
  </taglib>
  ...
</web-app>
```

As illustrated in this example, the `<taglib>` tag has two subelements, `<taglib-uri>` and `<taglib-location>`, both of which are required. The `<taglib-uri>` tag is used to specify the URI by which `taglib` directives in the application's JSP pages can access the TLD. The `<taglib-location>` tag specifies the actual location of that TLD within the application's file hierarchy. Multiple `<taglib>` elements may appear in a single `web.xml` file, one for each custom tag library used by the application.

NOTE   When referencing the URI of a TLD in a `taglib` directive, the top-level directory corresponding to the application name should not be specified. To access the TLD in the example presented here, then, the appropriate directive would be of the form `<%@ taglib uri="/discTags" prefix="disc" %>`.

Special forces

In addition to standard web file types, such as HTML and JSP documents and GIF and JPEG images, it is often desirable to provide access to other types of information via a web server. For this reason, whenever the server sends a document to a web browser, it includes a specification of the type of document it is sending, referred to as the document's MIME type. MIME was originally developed for identifying documents sent as electronic mail attachments. It is now used for many applications, including the identification of document types on the World Wide Web.

Most web servers are configured to associate MIME types with specific file name extensions. For instance, file names ending with .html are typically associated with the text/html MIME type, while those whose extension is .doc might be assigned the application/msword MIME type, identifying them as Microsoft Word documents. By examining the MIME type returned by the server for a given request, the browser can determine how to handle the data contained in the response. If the MIME type of the response is text/html, the browser will render that data as an HTML document. If the MIME type is application/msword, the browser might instead attempt to open Microsoft Word in order to view the document contents.

TIP   The official registry of Internet MIME types is managed by the Internet Assigned Numbers Authority (IANA), and is available from their website at http://www.iana.org.

For web applications running in a JSP container, the web server will forward all URLs associated with the application (i.e., all URLs whose top-level directory corresponds to the name of the application) to the application itself for processing. The application is therefore responsible for assigning a MIME type to the generated response. Most JSP containers will automatically recognize the standard extensions for HTML, GIF, and JPEG files, and return the correct MIME type. The default MIME type for responses generated by servlets and JSP files is text/html, but this can be overridden. In a servlet, the setContentType() method of javax.servlet.ServletResponse may be used to set the MIME type of the response. The contentType attribute of the page directive provides the same functionality in a JSP page.

If you are deploying a web application that includes other document types, you must configure the application to recognize the extensions used by those documents and assign the appropriate MIME type. The <mime-mapping> tag is provided for this purpose, as demonstrated in this web.xml fragment:

```
<web-app>
  ...
  <mime-mapping>
    <extension>pdf</extension>
    <mime-type>application/pdf</mime-type>
  </mime-mapping>
  ...
</web-app>
```

The `<mime-mapping>` tag has two subelements, `<extension>` and `<mime-type>`. The `<extension>` element is used to specify the file name extension to be mapped to a particular MIME type, while the `<mime-type>` element identifies the MIME type to which it should be mapped. In the example shown here, the `pdf` extension is mapped to the `application/pdf` MIME type, indicating that file names ending with .pdf are to be identified as being in Adobe's Portable Document Format.

A `web.xml` file can contain an arbitrary number of `<mime-mapping>` elements. While each individual extension should be mapped to only a single MIME type, the reverse is not necessarily the case: multiple extensions can be mapped to the same MIME type. For example, web servers commonly map both the .jpg and .jpeg file extensions to the same `image/jpeg` MIME type.

Controlling the theater of operations

In addition to its capabilities for configuring servlets and JSP pages, the deployment descriptor provides applications with the ability to control certain aspects of the JSP container in which it is running. For example, servlets and JSP pages to which control should be transferred when errors occur can be specified, providing similar functionality to the `errorPage` attribute of the JSP `page` directive. Security restrictions may be specified for controlling access to an application's resources. If the JSP container also happens to be an EJB container, the `web.xml` file can be used to specify means for referencing EJBs.

While space does not permit us to cover these topics in-depth, there are two more deployment descriptor tags we will discuss. First, we will see how the `<session-config>` tag may be used to control the behavior of sessions created by an application. We will then examine the use of the `<context-param>` tag to specify initialization parameters for the application as a whole.

The `<session-config>` tag is used to specify a default timeout value for sessions created by the application's servlets and JSP pages, via its single required subelement, the `<session-timeout>` tag. The body of the `<session-timeout>` tag should be an integral value indicating how many minutes of inactivity are required before a session is considered to have expired, as in the following example:

```
<web-app>
  ...
  <session-config>
    <session-timeout>30</session-timeout>
  </session-config>
  ...
</web-app>
```

In this case, the application's sessions are set to expire, by default, after half an hour of inactivity. This default value can be explicitly overridden for individual sessions by means of the setMaxInactiveInterval() method of the javax.servlet.http.HttpSession interface. At most one <session-config> element may appear in a web.xml application descriptor.

> **NOTE** As the language here suggests, sessions are application-specific. A session object created by one application running in a JSP container cannot be accessed from another application running in that container. As a result, objects stored in that session as attributes cannot be retrieved from the session by code running in another application. The <session-timeout> tag, therefore, only controls the expiration of sessions associated with the application defined in the web.xml file in which that tag appears.

As described earlier, the <init-param> tag specifies values for a servlet's initialization parameters. In a similar manner, the <context-param> tag specifies initialization parameter values for an application or, more specifically, the ServletContext object associated with an application. The <context-param> tag supports the same three subelements as the <init-param> tag, serving analogous roles, as in this web.xml fragment:

```
<web-app>
  ...
  <context-param>
    <param-name>dbUsername</param-name>
    <param-value>dillinger</param-value>
    <description>Username for accessing the score database.</description>
  </context-param>
  <context-param>
    <param-name>dbPassword</param-name>
    <param-value>sarksuser</param-value>
    <description>Password for accessing the score database.</description>
  </context-param>
  ...
</web-app>
```

Here, two application initialization parameters, dbUsername and dbPassword, are specified. Their values can be retrieved from the ServletContext object associated with the application by means of its getInitParameter() method. Within the JSP pages of the application, this ServletContext object is available via the application implicit object. Because this object is accessible from all of an application's servlets and JSP pages, it provides a convenient mechanism for specifying configuration data that is applicable across multiple application resources.

10.3 *Maintaining a WAR footing*

WAR files, then, establish directory conventions for organizing the components of a web application, as well as a standard configuration file for managing its resources. In return, they simplify the deployment of web applications from development to production web servers, and do so in a portable manner. Web applications packaged as WAR files are compatible with all JSP containers that comply with version 1.1 of the JSP specification.

One aspect of WAR files that has not been discussed thus far, however, is the ability of many JSP containers to work with web applications that have been expanded from their WAR files—that is, web archives whose contents have been extracted into the corresponding individual files. Such applications employ the same file hierarchy as WAR files, including the WEB-INF directory, but use actual directories and files instead of consolidating resources into a single archive file. By way of example, the file hierarchy for an expanded application based on the WAR file presented in listing 10.1 is depicted in listing 10.2. Once again, disc has been selected as the application name.

Listing 10.2   File hierarchy for the expanded disc application

```
/disc/main.jsp
/disc/docs/rules.html
/disc/game/catch.jsp
/disc/game/deflect.jsp
/disc/game/index.jsp
/disc/game/ringhit.jsp
/disc/game/start.jsp
/disc/game/throw.jsp
/disc/images/icons/ring.gif
/disc/images/players/crom.gif
/disc/images/players/flynn.gif
/disc/WEB-INF/web.xml
/disc/WEB-INF/classes/com/taglib/encom/disc/RingControlServlet.class
/disc/WEB-INF/classes/com/taglib/encom/disc/PlayerBean.class
```

```
/disc/WEB-INF/lib/disc-classes.jar
/disc/WEB-INF/lib/discTags_1_0.jar
/disc/WEB-INF/tlds/discTags_1_0.tld
```

The advantage of this approach is that modifying the application is simpler. To change a JSP page, you edit the file and save the new version in place of the old. To change the value of an initialization pattern, edit and save the web.xml file (and, typically, restart the JSP container). For applications stored in WAR files, modifications such as these first require you to extract the file to be changed, make the changes, and then update the archive to include the modified file. Clearly, expanded applications are easier to work with when many changes must be made to the application, while WAR files are preferable when it comes time to deploy it.

For this reason, it is good practice to use expanded applications for development, and WAR files for deployment. This allows for rapid turnaround of changes while developing an application and convenient packaging when deploying it. Finally, because both application forms share the same directory structure, it is a simple task to transform the expanded application used for development into a web archive: simply create a JAR file rooted in the top-level directory of the expanded application, containing the latest versions of all of the development application's files. Assign this JAR file an extension of .war, and it's ready to be deployed. *Vive la guerre!*

11

Performing common JSP tasks

In this chapter we will illustrate common tasks associated with web-based applications, and how they may be performed using JSP. For example, the primary means for interacting with end users over the web is via forms. To that end, we include here multiple sections on managing and validating forms. Data associated with end users is often stored in cookies, so JSP techniques for storing and retrieving cookies are also discussed, among other topics. All of the examples presented here take the form of "building blocks" that can serve as basic ingredients in the construction of full-fledged web applications.

11.1 Handling cookies

Cookies are the standard mechanism provided by the HTTP protocol for a web server (or a group of web servers sharing the same Internet domain) to store small amounts of persistent data in a user's web browser for later retrieval. By default, cookies expire as soon as the user exits the browser application. Alternatively, they may be configured to persist across browser sessions until a specified expiration date.

The data stored in a cookie is set by the web server, and therefore can contain only information known to the server. For security reasons, a cookie may be retrieved only by the server that supplied it. Optionally, a cookie can be made accessible to other servers in the same domain as the originating server. A cookie can also be restricted to a specific URL directory hierarchy on the server or servers from which it is accessible. In addition to the data it stores, a cookie is assigned a name; a server can then set multiple cookies and distinguish between them via their names.

11.1.1 Managing cookies

Cookies are set by a web server via HTTP response headers. Whenever a browser requests a URL whose server and directory match those of one or more of its stored cookies, the corresponding cookies are sent back to the server in the form of request headers. If that URL is for a JSP page, the page can access those cookies via the `getCookies()` method of the `request` implicit object (an instance of the `javax.servlet.http.HttpServletRequest` class). In a similar manner, cookies are set by a JSP page via the `addCookie()` method of the `response` implicit object (which is an instance of the `javax.servlet.http.HttpServletResponse` class). These methods are summarized in table 11.1.

For both methods, HTTP cookies are represented as instances of the `javax.servlet.http.Cookie` class. The `getCookies()` method of the `request` object returns an array of `Cookie` instances, while the `addCookie()` method of the `response` object takes an instance of this class as its sole argument.

Table 11.1 **Methods of the JSP implicit objects for managing cookies**

Implicit Object	Method	Description
`request`	`getCookies()`	Returns an array of the cookies accessible from the page.
`response`	`addCookie(cookie)`	Sends a cookie to the browser for storage/modification.

11.1.2 *The Cookie class*

Interacting with cookies in a JSP page, therefore, is accomplished by manipulating instances of the `javax.servlet.http.Cookie` class. A single constructor is provided for creating new instances, which takes two `String` arguments representing the name of the cookie and the corresponding value, as in the following example statement:

```
Cookie cookie = new Cookie("Favorite", "chocolate chip");
```

Here, the first argument represents the name of the cookie (i.e., "`Favorite`") and the second its value (i.e., "`chocolate chip`").

As summarized in table 11.2, accessors are provided for storing and retrieving the properties of a cookie. Note that the text data stored in a cookie value can be modified after its construction using the `setValue()` method, but a cookie's name can only be set using the constructor.

Table 11.2 **Common methods of the `javax.servlet.http.Cookie` class**

Method	Description
`getName()`	Returns the name of the cookie.
`getValue()`	Returns the value stored in the cookie.
`getDomain()`	Returns the server or domain from which the cookie may be accessed.
`getPath()`	Returns the URL path from which the cookie may be accessed.
`getMaxAge()`	Returns the time remaining (in seconds) before the cookie expires.
`getSecure()`	Indicates whether the cookie accompanies HTTP or HTTPS requests.
`setValue()`	Assigns a new value for the cookie.
`setDomain()`	Sets the server or domain from which the cookie may be accessed.
`setPath(name)`	Sets the URL path from which the cookie may be accessed.
`setMaxAge(name)`	Sets the time remaining (in seconds) before the cookie expires.
`setSecure(name)`	Returns the value of a single request header, as an integer.

When using this class, it is important to keep in mind that instances of `javax.servlet.http.Cookie` reside in the JSP container. After constructing a new instance, or modifying an instance retrieved via the `getCookies()` method, it is necessary to use the `addCookie()` method of the `response` object in order to update the cookie data stored in the browser.

TIP   Although it may seem a bit counterintuitive, this approach is also required to delete a cookie. First, call the `setMaxAge()` method of the cookie instance with a value of zero (indicating that the cookie is to be deleted). Then—and here's the unintuitive part—call `addCookie()` to inform the browser that the cookie is to be deleted (i.e., by replacing it with a cookie that has been set to expire immediately).

Cookie data is communicated from the server to the browser via response headers. You may recall from earlier chapters that all headers must be set before any body content is sent to the browser. As such, in order for the `addCookie()` method to succeed in a JSP page, it must be called before the page's output buffer is flushed. This can occur when the buffer becomes full (depending upon the setting of the `autoflush` attribute of the `page` directive). The output buffer is also flushed whenever the `<jsp:include>` action is encountered. The status of output buffering is therefore an important consideration when constructing JSP pages that set cookies.

11.1.3 *Example 1: setting a cookie*

The first step, then, in using a cookie within a JSP page is to set it. This is accomplished by creating an instance of the `javax.servlet.http.Cookie` class and then calling the `addCookie()` method of the `response` implicit object. Listing 11.1 presents a JSP page, /webdev/red-cookie.jsp, which accomplishes these tasks via a scriptlet:

Listing 11.1   Code for a JSP page called /webdev/red-cookie.jsp

```
<html>
<head>
<title>The Red Cookie Page</title>
</head>
<%@ page import="java.util.Date" %>
<%@ page import="java.net.*" %>
<% String cookieName = "RedCookie";
   Date now = new Date();
   String timestamp = now.toString();
   Cookie cookie = new Cookie(cookieName,
```

```
                              URLEncoder.encode(timestamp));
        cookie.setDomain("taglib.com");
        cookie.setPath("/webdev");
        cookie.setMaxAge(7 * 24 * 60 * 60);   // One week
        cookie.setVersion(0);
        cookie.setSecure(false);
        cookie.setComment("Timestamp for red cookie.");
        response.addCookie(cookie);
%>
<body>
<font color="red">
<h1>The Red Cookie Page</h1>
<p>
This is the <i>red</i> cookie page.<br>
The blue cookie page is <a href="blue-cookie.jsp">here</a>.
</p>
</font>
</body>
</html>
```

In this case, the cookie is identified by the string "RedCookie", and is assigned a value containing a string representation of the time at which the request was received by the JSP page. The HTTP protocol imposes certain restrictions on the types of characters that may appear in a cookie's value, so it is generally good practice, as is done here, to URL-encode cookie values via the `java.net.URLEncoder.encode()` static method.

In addition, the domain and path (i.e., base URL directory) are set for the cookie to ensure that it is accessible from related pages on other servers in the host domain. It is set to expire within one week's time. For maximum browser compatibility, it is set to adhere to version 0 of the cookie specification. Secure cookies can only be sent using the HTTPS protocol, which encrypts requests and responses. Here, the argument to the new cookie's `setSecure()` method is `false`, indicating the cookie should be transferred via the standard unencrypted HTTP protocol. After supplying a comment for the cookie, it is marked for transmission back to the browser via the `addCookie()` method.

The response sent to the browser from this JSP page is depicted in figure 11.1. For this particular page, there is no dynamic content in the rendered output. Instead, all of the dynamic content is in the headers, where the request-specific cookie value is supplied.

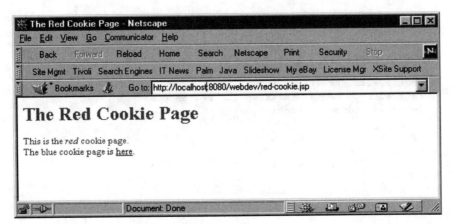

Figure 11.1   Output of JSP page that sets a cookie

11.1.4 *Example 2: retrieving a cookie*

The effect of the JSP page presented in the previous example, then, is to update a time stamp whenever the user visits the page. This time stamp is stored in a cookie, and may be retrieved by other JSP pages which share the domain and path originally assigned to the cookie.

Cookies are retrieved via the getCookies() method of the request implicit object. Here is a sample JSP page, /webdev/blue-cookie.jsp, which attempts to retrieve the cookie set by the page in the previous example:

```
<html>
<head>
<title>The Blue Cookie Page</title>
</head>
<%@ page import="java.net.*" %>
<% String cookieName = "RedCookie";
   Cookie cookies[] = request.getCookies();
   Cookie redCookie = null;
   if (cookies != null) {
     for (int i = 0; i < cookies.length; ++i) {
       if (cookies[i].getName().equals(cookieName)) {
         redCookie = cookies[i];
         break;
       }
     }
   }
%>
<body>
<font color="blue">
```

```
<h1>The Blue Cookie Page</h1>
<p>
This is the <i>blue</i> cookie page.<br>
You last visited the <a href="red-cookie.jsp">red cookie page</a>
<% if (redCookie == null) { %>
    over a week ago.
<% } else { %>
    on <%= URLDecoder.decode(redCookie.getValue()) %>.
<% } %>
</p>
</font>
</body>
</html>
```

The first scriptlet on this page iterates through the array of cookies returned by the `getCookies()` method until it finds one named "RedCookie" (i.e., the same name used in the previous example). The dynamic content displayed by this page is then based on whether or not this cookie was found.

If no such cookie were found, then the conditional scriptlet near the end of the page will cause the page to display the text indicated in figure 11.2. The presumption here is that if the cookie is not found, then it must have expired. Another possibility is that the cookie has not been set in the first place, which would be the case if the user had never visited the page which sets the cookie. The important point here is to note that it is not possible to tell the difference between the expiration of a cookie and its complete absence.

If, on the other hand, the cookie is present, then the iterative search through the array returned by the `getCookies()` method will succeed and the `redCookie` variable will not be `null`. In this case, the second clause of the conditional scriptlet will

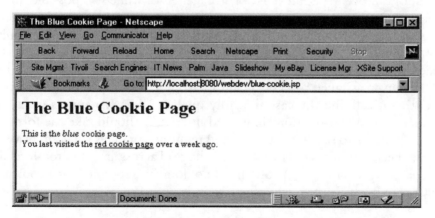

Figure 11.2 Output of JSP page that retrieves a cookie when it has not been set

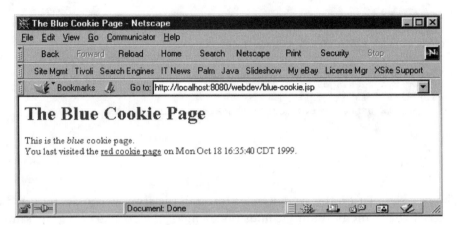

Figure 11.3 Output of JSP page that retrieves a cookie which has been set

be exercised, resulting in the output depicted in figure 11.3. Here, the `java.net.URLDecoder.decode()` static method is used to decode the value stored in the cookie so that it may be displayed in its original form.

WARNING The `java.net.URLDecoder` class was added in Java 2. Earlier versions of the Java specification—i.e., the 1.0 and 1.1 releases—do not include this class. The `java.net.URLEncoder` class, however, is present in those versions.

Finally, when taking advantage of HTTP cookies, a number of restrictions on their use should be kept in mind. First, the data stored in a cookie (i.e., its name and value) can occupy at most 4K of storage. Also, while it is possible for a given server or domain to set multiple cookies, the browser is only required to store up to twenty cookies per domain setting. At the same time, the browser need only store up to 300 cookies. If either limit is exhausted, the browser is expected to delete cookies, beginning with those which have been used least recently.

The domain assigned to a cookie must have at least two periods in its name. This will automatically be the case if a fully qualified server name is used, such as `www.example.com`. If the domain is used instead, it should take the form `.example.com` in order to satisfy the two-period requirement. This rule is in place to prevent the specification of cookies which can be read across an entire top-level domain (i.e., `.com`, `.org`, `.net`, etc.). Note that if no domain is specified for a cookie, it may only be read by the host which originally set it.

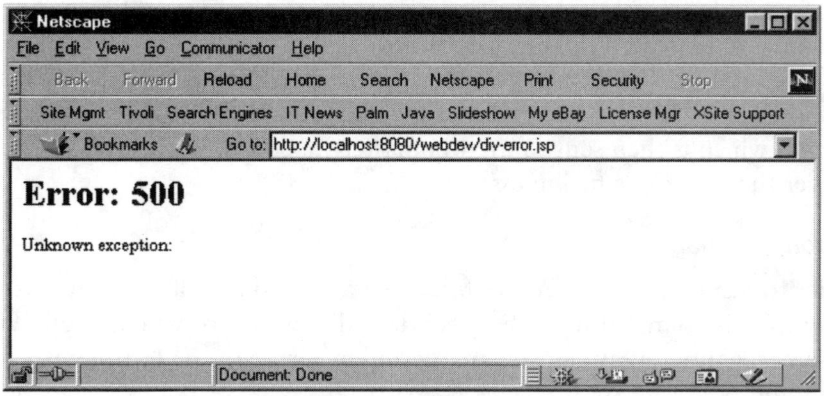

Figure 11.4   Output from a JSP page that generates a run-time error

11.2 Creating error pages

As mentioned in chapter 2, the typical behavior when an error occurs while processing a JSP page is to display an error message—possibly including a stack trace—within or in place of the output from that page. Figure 11.4, for example, displays the results generated by one JSP container when processing a page that attempts to divide a number by zero. The result is not particularly user-friendly, nor does it provide much information that the development team could use to track down the problem.

Fortunately, JavaServer Pages provides a means for addressing both of these issues via the `errorpage` attribute of the `page` directive, introduced in chapter 3. This feature allows you to designate an alternate JSP page to which control will be forwarded whenever the processing of a page causes an error. Furthermore, the exception that is thrown when the error occurs will be accessible from the selected error page via the `exception` implicit object. By taking advantage of this capability, you can ensure the user is clearly informed that a problem has occurred, and reassured that it will be fixed. At the same time, the full circumstances surrounding the error can be captured for use by the developers in resolving it.

Keep in mind that JSP error pages can also be used for handling servlet errors. As mentioned in chapter 8, a JSP error page expects to find the `Throwable` object representing the error in an attribute of the `request` implicit object associated with the name `"javax.servlet.jsp.jspException"`. Servlet code that has the potential of throwing an exception can use a `try/catch` block to catch the exception, store it as a request attribute, then forward it to a JSP error page. The error page is then responsible for displaying an error message to the user and recording the circumstances under which the error occurred.

In this section, an error page will be presented that displays a brief summary (and apology) to the end user, while constructing a detailed error message behind the scenes which is then sent to the webmaster via email. Sun's JavaMail API is used to deliver the electronic mail message.

11.2.1 *An erroneous page*

In order to test this error page, we first need a page that will generate errors. Here, for example, is a small JSP page, /webdev/div-error.jsp, which is guaranteed to throw an exception every time it is requested by virtue of the fact that it attempts to divide a number by zero:

```
<html>
<head>
<%@ page errorPage="error.jsp" session="false" %>
<title>Arithmetic Error</title>
</head>
<body bgcolor="white">
<h1>Arithmetic Error</h1>
<% int x = 5; %>
<P>
In Java, dividing by zero raises an exception:
<tt>25/0 = <%= 25/(5-x) %></tt>
</P>
</body>
</html>
```

Note that, because the compiler recognizes that an explicit divide-by-zero expression is invalid, the local variable x is introduced to make page compilation succeed. When a request is received for this page, however, the arithmetic expression will generate a run-time error when the division by zero is detected.

In the absence of the JSP page directive near the beginning of this file, a request for this page will generate results such as those depicted in figure 11.4. By incorporating this directive, however, more graceful and more thorough handling of the error is possible.

11.2.2 *Data collection methods*

Before examining the error page itself, we will first consider a set of utility methods it will use to collect information about the error. Note that control will be transferred to the error page as if the <jsp:forward> action had been used, meaning that the error page will have access to the request implicit object corresponding to the original page request, as well as an `exception` implicit object representing the error that occurred there.

The first of these utility methods is `makeErrorReport()`, which takes values corresponding to both of these implicit objects as its arguments:

```
public String makeErrorReport (HttpServletRequest req, Throwable e) {
    StringBuffer buffer = new StringBuffer();
    reportException(buffer, e);
    reportRequest(buffer, req);
    reportParameters(buffer, req);
    reportHeaders(buffer, req);
    reportCookies(buffer, req);
    return buffer.toString();
}
```

This method serves as the control routine for collecting information about the request and the resulting error. An instance of `java.lang.StringBuffer` is constructed for storing this information, which is then passed to a series of other methods that store various categories of data into this `StringBuffer`. Once all of the data has been collected, the contents of the buffer are used to generate a full-fledged `String` object.

The first of these methods that add data to the `StringBuffer` is `reportException()`, which collects information about the error itself:

```
public void reportException (StringBuffer buffer, Throwable e) {
    StringWriter writer = new StringWriter();
    e.printStackTrace(new PrintWriter(writer));
    buffer.append(writer.getBuffer());
    buffer.append('\n');
}
```

More specifically, this method wraps a `java.io.PrintWriter` around a `java.io.StringWriter`, into which the exception's stack trace is written. The contents of the `StringWriter` are then added to the `StringBuffer` passed in as an argument to this method.

The stack trace contains all of the information available about the error that occurred, including its type, a brief explanatory message, and the stack of method calls that were in effect when the exception was thrown. As a result, the remaining data collection methods are focused not on the error, but on the context in which the error occurred, as embodied in the request.

Basic information about the request is collected via the `reportRequest()` method. This method reconstructs the URL used to request the original page, as well as information about the user's session (if applicable), and is defined as follows:

```
public void reportRequest (StringBuffer buffer, HttpServletRequest req) {
  buffer.append("Request: ");
  buffer.append(req.getMethod());
  buffer.append(' ');
  buffer.append(HttpUtils.getRequestURL(req));
  String queryString = req.getQueryString();
  if (queryString != null) {
    buffer.append('?');
    buffer.append(queryString);
  }
  buffer.append("\nSession ID: ");
  String sessionId = req.getRequestedSessionId();
  if (sessionId == null) {
    buffer.append("none");
  } else if (req.isRequestedSessionIdValid()) {
    buffer.append(sessionId);
    buffer.append(" (from ");
    if (req.isRequestedSessionIdFromCookie())
      buffer.append("cookie)\n");
    else if (req.isRequestedSessionIdFromURL())
      buffer.append("url)\n");
    else
      buffer.append("unknown)\n");
  } else {
    buffer.append("invalid\n");
  }
}
```

To reconstruct the URL, the HTTP method (e.g., GET, POST, etc.) and query string are retrieved from the `javax.servlet.http.HttpServletRequest` object passed in via the `req` argument. The protocol, host name, and port number are not directly accessible from this object, however; instead one of the utility methods provided by the `javax.servlet.http.HttpUtils` class, `getRequestURL()`, is used to recreate the base URL.

The methods of the `javax.servlet.http.HttpUtils` class are summarized in table 11.3. For further details, see appendix E.

Table 11.3   Methods of the javax.servlet.http.HttpUtils class

Method	Description
getRequestURL(request)	Recreates the URL used by the browser to make the request.
parsePostData(length, stream)	Parses HTML form data submitted via a POST request.
parseQueryString(string)	Parses the query string of a requested URL into a hash table of parameters and values.

The session information reported by this method is likewise retrieved from the request. If session information is present and valid, this information will include the user-specific session identification code, and an indication of how the session information is being transferred between the server and the browser (i.e., via either cookies or URL rewriting). This is accomplished via standard methods provided by the `javax.servlet.http.HttpServletRequest` class, first described in chapter 4.

The next data collection method, `reportParameters()`, lists the request parameters that accompanied the original page request. Note that the `HttpServletRequest` class does not distinguish between parameters supplied in the URL via a query string and those provided in the body of an HTTP POST request. In fact, both may be present in the same request, and will be combined into one overall set of parameters. If values for the same parameter are provided multiple times, all of the values are stored. In such a case, the first value supplied for a parameter takes precedence, and parameter values set in the URL take precedence over those set in the body of the request. The code for this method is as follows:

```
public void reportParameters (StringBuffer buffer, HttpServletRequest req) {
    Enumeration names = req.getParameterNames();
    if (names.hasMoreElements()) {
      buffer.append("Parameters:\n");
      while (names.hasMoreElements()) {
        String name = (String) names.nextElement();
        String[] values = req.getParameterValues(name);
        for (int i = 0; i < values.length; ++i) {
          buffer.append("     ");
          buffer.append(name);
          buffer.append(" = ");
          buffer.append(values[i]);
          buffer.append('\n');
        }
      }
    }
}
```

Here, the `getParameterNames()` method is called to obtain an enumeration of all of the parameters known to the request. If there is at least one parameter present, the next step is to print out the name of each parameter, and its values. Since one parameter may have multiple values, a nested iteration loop is required to iterate over all of the values returned by the `getParameterValues()` method.

After listing out the request parameters, the next step is to list the request headers, using the following `reportHeaders()` method:

```
public void reportHeaders (StringBuffer buffer, HttpServletRequest req) {
    Enumeration names = req.getHeaderNames();
```

```
if (names.hasMoreElements()) {
  buffer.append("Headers:\n");
  while (names.hasMoreElements()) {
    String name = (String) names.nextElement();
    String value = (String) req.getHeader(name);
    buffer.append("    ");
    buffer.append(name);
    buffer.append(": ");
    buffer.append(value);
    buffer.append('\n');
  }
}
}
```

Headers contain information about the browser that made the request, as well as any cookies the browser is submitting with the request. The code for this method is similar to that of reportParameters(). Here, the getHeaderNames() method of the HttpServletRequest instance is called to generate an enumeration of the names of the headers present in the request. We then iterate through this result, adding the name of the header and its corresponding value—retrieved via the getHeader() method of HttpServletRequest—to the StringBuffer object being used to accumulate our error report.

Unfortunately, even though the HTTP protocol allows requests to specify multiple headers with the same name, the HttpServletRequest class only provides methods for fetching one header of a given name. In practice, most headers are only ever specified once, but there are a few which regularly appear multiple times in a single request. In particular, when a request includes multiple cookies, each cookie is generally specified by its own header. For a request containing multiple cookies, only one of the cookie headers will be listed by the reportHeaders() method described previously.

For this reason, the reportCookies() method is provided to ensure that all of the cookies that are relevant to the request are included in the error report. The code for this method is as follows:

```
public void reportCookies (StringBuffer buffer, HttpServletRequest req) {
  Cookie[] cookies = req.getCookies();
  int l = cookies.length;
  if (l > 0) {
    buffer.append("Cookies:\n");
    for (int i = 0; i < l; ++i) {
      Cookie cookie = cookies[i];
      buffer.append("    ");
      buffer.append(cookie.getName());
      buffer.append(" = ");
      buffer.append(cookie.getValue());
```

```
        buffer.append('\n');
    }
  }
}
```

This function relies on several of the cookie-related methods discussed earlier in this chapter in order to iterate through the request's cookies and list their names and values.

11.2.3 *Sending electronic mail*

Given all of these methods for constructing a description of an error and the request that generated it, we next need a mechanism for delivering this text to someone who can fix the underlying problem. For this example, that mechanism will be an electronic mail message. The methods described previously will be used to generate the body of this mail message, which is then sent to one or more recipients by means of the JavaMail API. This specification, provided by Sun Microsystems, defines a set of Java classes for interacting with mail servers, in order to send and receive electronic mail messages.

While a complete description of the JavaMail API is beyond the scope of this book, we will discuss a small subset of this specification in the context of a simple utility method, sendEmail(), which encapsulates all of the JavaMail calls needed to connect to an SMTP server and send a simple text-based mail message. (The full functionality provided by the JavaMail API extends well beyond the straightforward task presented here. For example, JavaMail includes support for retrieving messages from both POP and IMAP servers, as well as for sending messages incorporating styled text and/or attachments.)

For use in a JSP error page, however, sending a plain text message is sufficient. To this end, the sendEmail() method is defined as follows:

```
public void sendEmail (String mailServer, String subject,
                       String to[], String from, String messageText)
    throws AddressException, MessagingException {
    // Create session
    Properties mailProps = new Properties();
    mailProps.put("mail.smtp.host", mailServer);
    Session mailSession = Session.getDefaultInstance(mailProps, null);
    // Construct addresses
    int toCount = to.length;
    InternetAddress[] toAddrs = new InternetAddress[toCount];
    for (int i = 0; i < toCount; ++i) {
       toAddrs[i] = new InternetAddress(to[i]);
    }
    InternetAddress fromAddr = new InternetAddress(from);
```

```
    // Create and initialize message
    Message message = new MimeMessage(mailSession);
    message.setFrom(fromAddr);
    message.setRecipients(Message.RecipientType.TO, toAddrs);
    message.setSubject(subject);
    message.setContent(messageText.toString(), "text/plain");
    // Send message
    Transport.send(message);
}
```

All of the arguments to this method are instances of the Java `String` class, with the exception of the `to` argument, representing the intended recipients, which is an array of strings. The `mailServer` parameter is the name of a network host running an SMTP server that will handle the actual sending of the message. The `subject` argument represents the subject line for the message. The `from` parameter identifies the email address from which the message is being sent. The validity of this return address may or may not be confirmed, depending upon how the SMTP server has been configured. The final argument, `messageText`, should be a string containing the text to be sent as the body of the email message.

A central concept of the JavaMail API is that of a *mail session*, representing a set of interactions with a mail server. Mail sessions are represented by an instance of the `javax.mail.Session` class, which is initialized from an instance of the `java.util.Properties` class. For our purposes here, the only information that needs to be in the property list for this mail session is the identity of the SMTP host, as indicated by a property named `mail.smtp.host`. The next step is to convert the email addresses passed in as `String` values via the `to` and `from` arguments into instances of the `javax.mail.internet.InternetAddress` class. Next, an instance of the `javax.mail.Message` class is constructed. This is an abstract class, however, so the actual object created is an instance of the `javax.mail.internet.MimeMessage` class, whose constructor takes a `MailSession` instance as its sole argument. The properties of this message are then set to identify the sender, subject, recipients, and body. Note that in the call to `setContent()` the MIME type of the message body is set to `"text/plain"`, indicating that the text of the message is standard ASCII text. Finally, the static `send()` method of the `javax.mail.Transport` class is called to actually deliver the message.

Within the body of this method, several of the JavaMail method calls have the potential to throw exceptions. As we will see in the next section, for the current application within a JSP error page it is more convenient to pass these exceptions on to callers of the `sendEmail()` method, rather than attempt to handle them locally. For this reason, `sendEmail()` is declared as throwing two exception classes, `javax.mail.internet.AddressException` and `javax.mail.MessagingException`.

11.2.4 *The error page*

These utility methods for collecting data and sending electronic mail can be combined in a JSP error page that serves both end users and developers. Here is the content of such a page, /webdev/error.jsp, where the method bodies have been removed for brevity's sake:

```
<html>
<head>
<%@ page isErrorPage="true" %>
<%@ page import="java.util.*, java.io.*" %>
<%@ page import="javax.mail.*, javax.mail.internet.*" %>
<title>Oops!</title>
</head>
<body bgcolor="white">
<p>
Sorry, an error has occurred:<br>
<center> <b><%= exception %></b> </center>
</p>
<% try {
   String mailServer = "mail.taglib.com";
   String subject = "JSP Error Notification";
   String [] to = { "webmaster@taglib.com" };
   String from = "JSP Container <webmaster@taglib.com>";
   sendEmail(mailServer, subject, to, from,
             makeErrorReport(request, exception)); %>
<p>Not to worry, though! The guilty parties have been notified.</p>
<% }
   catch (AddressException e) { %>
<p>Invalid e-mail address(es) for error notification.</p>
<% }
   catch (MessagingException e) { %>
<p>Unable to send e-mail for error notification.</p>
<% } %>
</body>
</html>
<%!
  public String makeErrorReport (HttpServletRequest req, Throwable e) {
    ...
  }
  public void reportException (StringBuffer buffer, Throwable e) {
    ...
  }
  public void reportRequest (StringBuffer buffer, HttpServletRequest req) {
    ...
  }
  public void reportParameters (StringBuffer buffer,
                                HttpServletRequest req) {
    ...
```

```
    }
    public void reportHeaders (StringBuffer buffer, HttpServletRequest req) {
      ...
    }
    public void reportCookies (StringBuffer buffer, HttpServletRequest req) {
      ...
    }
    public void sendEmail (String mailServer, String subject,
                         String to[], String from, String messageText)
      throws AddressException, MessagingException {
      ...
    }
%>
```

The first JSP element on this page is the `page` directive, which uses `isErrorPage` to indicate that this page serves as an error page for one or more other JSP pages. As a result, the `exception` implicit object will be available for use by other JSP elements on the page.

The two additional `page` directives which follow are used to import classes from multiple Java packages. These classes are used in the utility methods which appear in a JSP declaration at the end of the page. By using the `import` attribute of the `page` directive in this manner, it is unnecessary to prefix the class names with their corresponding package names when they are referred to in the method bodies.

The `page` directives are followed by a combination of HTML and JSP elements that present the error message to the user, as depicted in Figure 11.5. A JSP expression is used to print out a brief description of the error, by taking advantage of the `toString()` method provided by the `java.lang.Throwable` class. The final line in

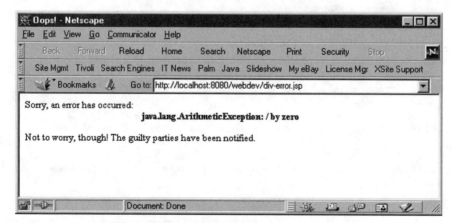

Figure 11.5   Output sent to the browser by the example error page

the browser output is determined by the success (or lack thereof) of the code that submits the error report to the development team.

This last step is accomplished by means of a set of JSP scriptlets implementing a `try`/`catch` block. Within the `try` clause, the first step is to configure the site-specific mail parameters. These parameters are then supplied as arguments to the `sendEmail()` method, along with body text generated via the `makeErrorReport()` method. If any exceptions are thrown by the underlying JavaMail code, then an indication to this effect will appear in the JSP output.

When the configuration parameters are set properly and the mail server is accessible, though, execution of these methods should succeed and no exceptions will be thrown within the error page itself. Under these circumstances, the "guilty parties" message will appear in the JSP output and a report such as the following will be sent to the designated recipients:

```
From: JSP Container <webmaster@taglib.com>
To: webmaster@taglib.com
Subject: JSP Error Notification

java.lang.ArithmeticException: / by zero
    at home.server.user.web-
        dev.div_error_jsp_1._jspService(div_error_jsp_1.java:72)
    at com.sun.jsp.runtime.HttpJspBase.service(HttpJspBase.java:87)
    at javax.servlet.http.HttpServlet.service(HttpServlet.java:840)
    at com.sun.jsp.runtime.JspServlet$JspServletWrapper.service(JspServ-
        let.java:88)
    at com.sun.jsp.runtime.JspServlet.serviceJspFile(JspServlet.java:218)
    at com.sun.jsp.runtime.JspServlet.service(JspServlet.java:294)
    at javax.servlet.http.HttpServlet.service(HttpServlet.java:840)
    at com.sun.web.core.ServletWrapper.handleRequest(ServletWrapper.java:155)
    at com.sun.web.core.Context.handleRequest(Context.java:414)
    at com.sun.web.server.ConnectionHandler.run(ConnectionHandler.java:139)

Request: GET http://localhost:8080/webdev/div-error.jsp
Session ID: To1010mC8608781812051488At (from cookie)
Headers:
    Connection: Keep-Alive
    User-Agent: Mozilla/4.5 [en] (WinNT; U)
    Pragma: no-cache
    Host: localhost:8080
    Accept: image/gif, image/x-xbitmap, image/jpeg, image/pjpeg, image/png, */*
    Accept-Encoding: gzip
    Accept-Language: en
    Accept-Charset: iso-8859-1,*,utf-8
    Cookie: RedCookie=Mon+Oct+18+16%3A35%3A40+CDT+1999;SESSIONID=To1010m…
```

```
Cookies:
    RedCookie = Mon+Oct+18+16%3A35%3A40+CDT+1999
    SESSIONID = To1010mC8608781812051488At
```

This particular request did not include any parameters, but all of the other report elements are present here. The stack trace from the exception appears, and the description of the request indicates that the exception was generated by the /web-dev/div-error.jsp page. The session ID code appears, with an indication that it is being stored in a cookie. This is followed by listings of nine request headers and two cookies.

These headers indicate, among other things, that the request originated from version 4.5 of Netscape's browser (nicknamed Mozilla), running on the Microsoft Windows platform. The cookies correspond to the session ID code and the time stamp cookie associated with the JSP cookie example presented earlier in this chapter. Note that, as mentioned in the earlier discussion of the reportHeaders() method, only one of the two cookie headers appears among the header listings.

11.3 *Mixing JSP and JavaScript*

JSP can work in conjunction with JavaScript (and other client-side technologies) to add server-side processing to operations typically limited to client-side activities. As an example, we'll build a simple form for reporting system problems. As an additional requirement, we've decided that we want to verify the validity of the host name specified by the user before allowing it to submit the problem. We also require that the problem host be identified by its IP address, rather than its host name. The resulting form is shown in figure 11.6.

When the user inputs a host name into the Affected System field of our form, it is changed into the corresponding IP address when they tab over to the next field. (If an actual IP address is supplied, it is not changed.) Furthermore, if the user inputs an invalid host name, an alert window will notify him or her of this fact and he or she will not be allowed to submit the form until the problem is corrected. All of this happens on the client before actually submitting the form, and without the user having to manually reload the page. As a matter of fact, the form page, shown in listing 11.2, is not even a JSP page, it's just standard HTML, with a little JavaScript thrown in. How, then, do we perform this little trick? We cheat.

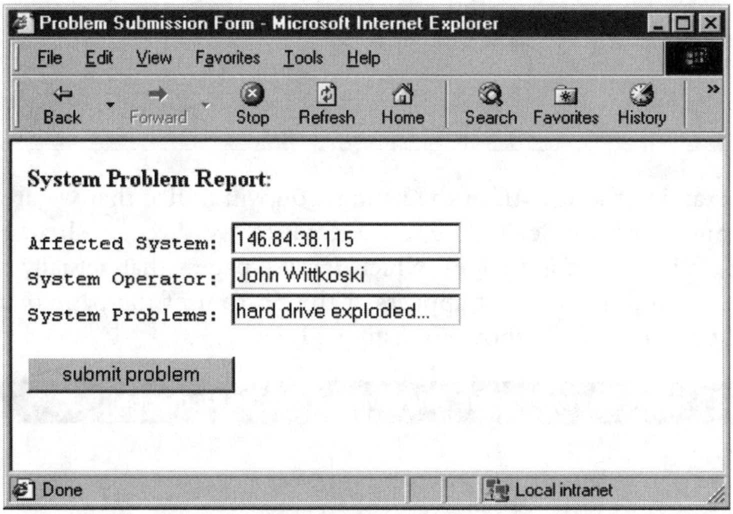

Figure 11.6   Problem submission form

Listing 11.2   HTML source for the JavaScript example form

```
<html>
<head>
<script language="javascript">
resolved=false;

function resolve(element) {
  top.resolver.document.location = "resolver.jsp?host=" + element.value;
}

function isResolved() {
  alert(resolved);
  return resolved;
}
</script>
</head>
<body>
<b>System Problem Report:</b>
<P>
<form name="info" action="/servlet/problem" onSubmit='return isResolved()'>
<TT>
Affected System: <input type="text" name="host" onChange='resolve(this)'> <BR>
System Operator: <input type="text" name="user"> <BR>
System Problems: <input type="text" name="problem"> <BR>
</TT>
```

```
<P>
<input type="submit" value="submit problem">
</form>
</body>
</html>
```

If you closely examine the HTML in the listing, you will notice that we are making references to another frame called `resolver`, which we direct to load the page `resolver.jsp`. It is this second page—which *is* a JSP page—that actually performs the host name resolution for us. It appears at the bottom of the page in a hidden frame, using the frameset code shown in listing 11.3.

Listing 11.3   HTML source for the JavaScript example frameset

```
<html>
<head><title>Problem Submission Form</title></head>
<frameset rows="100%, 0%" border=0 frameborder="no">
<frame src="form.html" name="theform">
<frame name="resolver">
</frameset>
</html>
```

When the user makes a change to the Affected System field, the `onChange()` handler in the field's `<input>` tag calls the `resolve()` function—a client-side JavaScript function—to load our JSP into the hidden frame. This function also appends the value of the field to the request, giving our JSP page the host name it needs to verify. In the JSP page, we attempt to resolve the host name. If we are successful we have two tasks to do. We have to change the value of the Affected System field to the verified IP address, and we have to alert the document that a valid host name has been entered. We do this with cross-frame JavaScript:

```
<script>
top.theform.document.info.host.value="<%= ip %>";
top.theform.resolved=true;
</script>
```

If the host name turns out to be invalid, we alert the user to their evil ways, flip the `resolved` flag to false, and clear the offending value from the form field:

```
<script>
alert("Invalid Hostname: <%= host %>");
top.theform.document.info.host.value="";
top.theform.resolved=false;
```

```
top.theform.document.info.host.focus();
</script>
```

Note that we can embed JSP commands into the midst of our JavaScript code here. This may seem strange at first, but keep in mind how a JSP page is processed. After all the JSP code is handled, what you are left with is the HTML, JavaScript, or other data containing your JSP elements. In this case, we are conditionally inserting blocks of JavaScript into our output. The full source to the resolver.jsp page is presented in listing 11.4.

Listing 11.4 JSP source for the hidden frame

```
<%@ page import="java.net.*" %>
<html>
<body>
<%
String host = request.getParameter("host");
String ip = host;
if (host != null) {
   try {
      ip = java.net.InetAddress.getByName(host).getHostAddress();
%>
<script>
top.theform.document.info.host.value="<%= ip %>";
top.theform.resolved=true;
</script>
<%
   }
   catch (UnknownHostException e) {
%>
<script>
alert("Invalid Hostname: <%= host %>");
top.theform.document.info.host.value="";
top.theform.resolved=false;
top.theform.document.info.host.focus();
</script>
<% }
}
%>
</body>
</html>
```

Note that the `getHostAddress()` method throws an `UnknownHostException` if it is unable to resolve the name correctly. Therefore, we execute it in a `try/catch` block, which has the side effect of determining which block of JavaScript we end up calling.

Autocompleting form fields

This same technique can be used for other client/server cooperative activities. One good example of this is simulating fields with automatic completion through the use of an `onKeyPress()` handler. This JavaScript handler is triggered with each key press, not just when tabbing out of a field or hitting return. With each press, you pass the current value of the field to your hidden JSP, which searches the database for a match, based on what the user has typed so far. So in our example above, as soon as the user typed "John W" into the System Operator field, our JSP could search the user database and automatically fill in the rest of the name.

11.4 Building interactive interfaces

Using JSP we can create web-based applications which look and feel more like traditional desktop programs. Even though we must cope with the transient nature of web requests, it is possible to build interfaces whose elements have a more interactive feel, preserving their state between actions. While Dynamic HTML and JavaScript have begun to allow such behavior for client-side operations, we can also achieve similar results with applications based on server-side operations. To do this, we combine the data collection form and its handler into a single JSP page whose form elements provide an application interface that retains its state across multiple requests.

11.4.1 Sticky widgets

Java developers creating applications or applets with Swing or AWT build their interface around input elements such as text fields, check boxes, and buttons. These elements allow the developer to collect information and direction from the user. When a user clicks a button, the developer uses information from the input elements to perform the corresponding function. When we develop an application using JSP we use HTML form elements in this same role. One important difference, however, is that the stateless nature of HTTP forces us to do more work ourselves in order to maintain the state of the user interface.

When an HTML page containing a form is loaded into the browser the state of its elements is encoded into the HTML. If you fill out a form once and then revisit it, the state and contents of all of the elements on the page are lost and the form reverts to its original condition as specified in the HTML. HTTP requests, unless cookies (which have limited storage capacity) are being used, have no memory. The only way that form elements on a page can appear to maintain state between requests is by dynamically generating the HTML that controls the layout and contents of the form to represent the state you wish to present.

The approach we will follow is to create a JSP page that collects information from its form elements and then targets itself as its own form handler. This HTML interface should emulate the behavior of traditional applications. When the JSP lays out its form on subsequent requests it should reflect the form's most recent state and content. If a user selected a checkbox or radio button before submitting the form, it should be selected again when the form is redisplayed. If a text field had text in it then it should again contain that same text.

While it is easy to combine the form and the results into a single page, creating this interactive interface requires us to understand how each form element can be configured through JSP's dynamic HTML generation capabilities. Each input element's state is preserved through the data in the form submission. For each element of our interface we have a value that represents its state just prior to the pressing of a Submit button. The values of the form elements are then submitted as request parameters, from which they may be extracted when the next form request—initiated by the form submission itself—is processed.

11.4.2 *Utility methods*

To aid in this process of extracting parameter values from requests, we first introduce a set of utility methods that will be used throughout this form-handling example. The first, getParam(), is defined as:

```
public String getParam (HttpServletRequest request, String param) {
  if (request.getParameter(param) == null)
    return "";
  else
    return request.getParameter(param);
}
```

This method retrieves the value of the named parameter from the indicated request. As a convenience, if the parameter is not present in the request, an empty String is returned. (For the request object's own getParameter() method, a null value is returned for parameters that have not been specified.)

For those parameters which may have multiple values assigned to them, a getParamValues() method is provided. Here is the code for this method:

```
public String getParamValues (HttpServletRequest request, String param) {
  String values[] = request.getParameterValues(param);
  if (values == null) return "";
  int count = values.length;
  switch (count) {
    case 1:
        return values[0];
    default:
```

```
        StringBuffer result = new StringBuffer(values[0]);
        int stop = count - 1;
        if (stop > 1) result.append(", ");
        for (int i = 1; i < stop; ++i) {
          result.append(values[i]);
          result.append(", ");
        }
        result.append(" and ");
        result.append(values[stop]);
        return result.toString();
    }
}
```

Like `getParam()`, this method returns an empty `String` when the parameter has not been specified. When one or more values are specified, however, `getParamValues()` will combine them into one `String`, adding comma separators and the word "and" where appropriate.

This next method, `requestContains()` is used to determine whether or not a specific value has been specified for a request parameter, and is defined as follows:

```
public boolean requestContains (HttpServletRequest request,
                                String param, String testValue) {
  String rp[] = request.getParameterValues(param);
  if (rp == null)
    return false;
  for (int i=0; i < rp.length; i++)
    if (rp[i].equals(testValue))
      return true;
  return false;

}
```

In this method, all of the values specified for a parameter are compared to the specified `testValue`. This method only returns `true` if there is a match.

The last two utility methods extend the functionality of the `requestContains()` method to return specific `String` values when a matching value is detected. Here are the definitions for `isChecked()` and `isSelected()`:

```
public String isChecked (HttpServletRequest request,
                         String param, String testValue) {
  return (requestContains(request, param, testValue)) ? "checked" : "";
}
public String isSelected (HttpServletRequest request,
                          String param, String testValue) {
  return (requestContains(request, param, testValue)) ? "checked" : "";
}
```

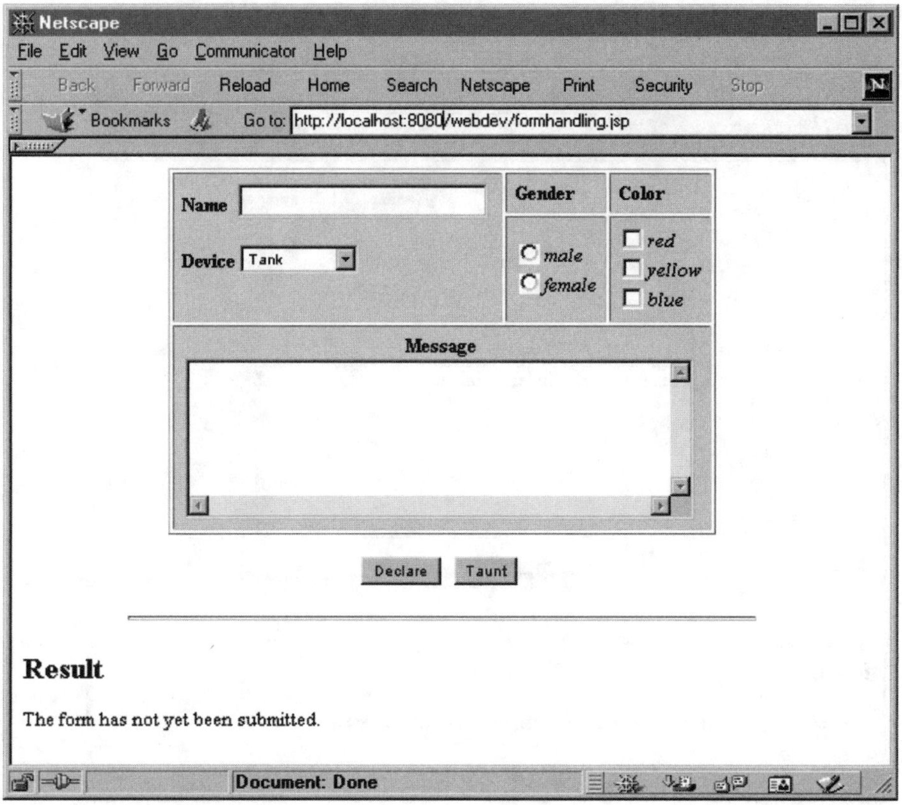

Figure 11.7   The example form, prior to submission

As we will see, these last two methods will be particularly useful in the initialization of radio buttons, check boxes, and select boxes.

11.4.3 *The example form*

The form we will use to motivate this example is depicted in figures 11.7 and 11.8. As illustrated in figure 11.7, various form elements are used to collect input data from the user:

- A text field, for entering a name.
- A select box, for choosing a device.
- A set of check boxes, for selecting one or more colors.
- Radio buttons, for selecting a gender.

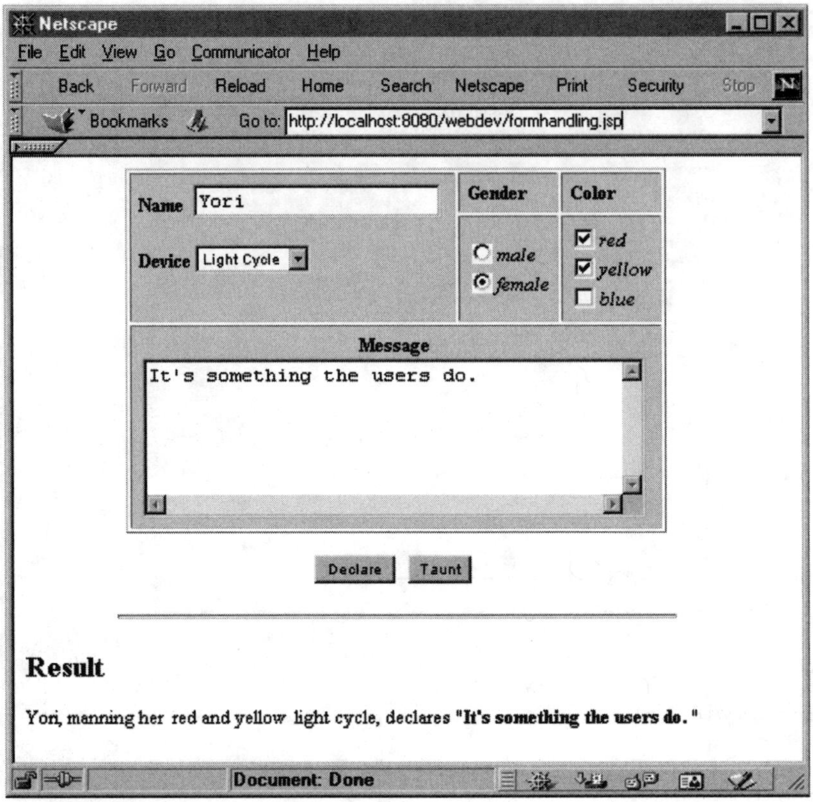

Figure 11.8 The example form, after submission

- A text area, for entering a multiline message.
- Two form submission buttons.

When either one of the form submission buttons is clicked, the form calls itself to process the form data and redisplay the form. The result of processing the form—in this case, a sentence constructed from the values selected for the form elements—is displayed at the bottom of the page (figure 11.8). The form widgets are "sticky": each time the form is displayed, the default values for all of the input fields are based on the final input values from the last time the form was submitted.

Based on this description of the form, then, let's examine how this behavior is implemented as a JSP page.

11.4.4 *Setting up the form*

We can use the following JSP expression to create a form that targets itself no matter what URL it was called from. This will allow us to move our application to any location without having to modify any code.

```
<FORM action="<%= HttpUtils.getRequestURL(request) %>" method="POST">
```

This JSP expression will insert the full URL to the form as its `action` target. Submitting the form, then, will call back to the same URL to handle the form as was used to bring up the form in the first place.

WARNING This technique of querying the request to determine the URL necessary to reach the current page will work only in situations where the JSP was accessed directly. If, for example, the JSP was loaded through a servlet using the `forward()` method of the `RequestDispatcher` class, the path information may be incorrect, since `RequestDispatcher` automatically changes the path information in the `request` object to reflect its new destination address. This can be a problem if your original request was intentionally directed to a servlet, since subsequent requests will likely need to go back through that servlet. In this case, it is possible to obtain a local URL (without the host name, protocol, or port number) for the current page by calling the `getServlet-Path()` method of the `request` object.

11.4.5 *Text and hidden fields*

The initial content of a text field is stored in the `value` attribute of the `<input>` tag defining that field. Hidden fields are initialized in the same manner, but their contents are not displayed and therefore cannot be edited by the end user. To make one of these element types reflect the state of a request parameter, we use a JSP expression containing a call to the `getParam()` method inside the `value` attribute's quotes. In our interface the Name field is specified using a text field. When the form is recreated after processing the request it should retain the original query. We do this as shown below:

```
<input type="text" name="character"
       value="<%= getParam(request, "character") %>">
```

Here, the identifier for the Name input field is specified as `"character"`, using the `name` attribute of the `<input>` tag. If, then, the value submitted for this field was the character string `"Lora"`, when the JSP page is processed as a result of the form submission, it will generate the following output for this tag:

```
<input type="text" name="character" value="Lora">
```

As a result, the default value for this input field—specified via the value attribute—will be "Lora". We have thus rewritten the input tag to contain a default value equal to the last value entered into the form. This is how we maintain the form's state between each request.

WARNING   You must escape any quotes in the string you are using to populate the value attribute of a text field. If you don't, then any quotes in the value will cause a premature end to the value attribute, resulting in invalid HTML.

11.4.6 *Text areas*

In our example form, we provide a text area for entering the message to be included in our output result. Setting the initial contents of the text area from the request data is even more straightforward than initializing a text field: a pair of starting and ending <textarea> tags defines a text area, and the body enclosed by these tags defines its initial contents. The Message field and its initial value can therefore be specified as follows:

```
<textarea cols="40" rows="5" name="message">
<%= getParam(request, "message") %>
</textarea>
```

Again, the getParam() method is used to obtain the value of the request parameter, which in this case is named message. (As with all form elements, the name of the request parameter corresponds to the identifier specified for the form element via the name attribute.)

The text area itself can contain any text whatsoever. HTML tags will not be afforded special treatment—they will come through as plain text. Any HTML entities, such as " or &, will be converted into their character equivalents, the double quote and the ampersand. The only exception to this rule is the text area's closing tag. If the contents of your text area might contain a literal </textarea> tag, you will want to protect the form field from this value by converting its angle braces into their HTML entity equivalents, < and >.

11.4.7 *Radio buttons*

Unlike text fields and text areas whose values are determined by the user, radio buttons have a fixed set of possible values. A user's interaction with these elements does not affect these values, it only determines which of the provided options has been selected. Typically you will have a group of multiple radio buttons with the same name, forming a group. To specify that one of these form elements should be enabled when the page loads you must include the keyword `checked` inside its `<input>` tag. Only one input element in the button group should be marked as checked. In our example form we are using radio buttons to allow the user to select the corresponding gender-specific pronoun for the value supplied in the Name field. When we load the page after servicing a request we want to ensure that the user's choice is reflected in our interface by enabling the radio button that corresponds to the current selection. This involves comparing the value attribute of each radio button with the user's selection, via the `isChecked()` method:

```
<input type="radio" name="gender" value="his"
       <%= isChecked(request, "gender", "his") %>><i>male</i><BR>
<input type="radio" name="gender" value="her"
       <%= isChecked(request, "gender", "her") %>><i>female</i><BR>
```

We use this utility method to compare the value assigned to each radio button with that stored in the request parameter. If there is a match, then this was the selected radio button and we insert the `checked` keyword into the input tag. Otherwise, we insert an empty `String`, which has no effect on the form element.

TIP Note that the values for these radio button form elements—the pronoun strings `"his"` and `"her"`—are different from the labels that appear on the form itself. HTML does not require that the values and labels match. JSP elements, however, only have access to the values of request parameters, and have no knowledge of the labels displayed for the form elements. The third argument to the `isChecked()` method, therefore, must indicate the value to be checked, not the label.

11.4.8 *Select boxes*

While certainly visually different, select boxes are quite similar in many respects to a group of radio buttons. They allow the user to make a selection from an existing set of choices. The initial selection for the group is indicated by the keyword `selected` inside the `<option>` tag defining the selection. We can therefore apply a similar technique to that used for radio buttons:

```
<select name="device">
<option value="tank" <%= isSelected(request, "device", "tank") %>>Tank
<option value="disk" <%= isSelected(request, "device", "disk") %>>Disk
<option value="light cycle"
  <%= isSelected(request, "device", "light cycle") %>>Light Cycle
</select>
```

With respect to the JSP elements, the only difference from the radio button example is the replacement of the request parameter names and values, and the use of the `isSelected()` utility method in place of `isChecked()`. The change in methods merely reflects the change in keywords between radio buttons and select boxes.

11.4.9 Check boxes

Check boxes can be used to select multiple choices from a set of possible values for a request parameter. Whether or not a check box should be enabled is determined by the presence of the `checked` keyword, as was the case for radio buttons. In the case of check boxes, however, it is not a problem if more than one check box is marked as enabled. In the example form, check boxes are used to select one or more colors, and are specified as follows:

```
<input type="checkbox" name="colors" value="red"
    <%= isChecked(request, "colors", "red") %>><i>red</i><BR>
<input type="checkbox" name="colors" value="yellow"
    <%= isChecked(request, "colors", "yellow") %>><i>yellow</i><BR>
<input type="checkbox" name="colors" value="blue"
    <%= isChecked(request, "colors", "blue") %>><i>blue</i><BR>
```

Note that the same identifier, `colors`, is specified for all three check boxes via the `name` attribute of the `<input>` tag. As a result, any and all values selected will be assigned as multiple values to the corresponding request parameter (also named colors).

11.4.10   Form source

The form depicted in figures 11.7 and 11.8 is constructed by combining these form elements into a JSP page. An HTML table is used to control the layout of the form, and a JSP declaration element is used to define the utility methods introduced above. The complete contents of the JSP file are presented in listing 11.5 (although the method definitions have been abbreviated to conserve space).

For the form itself, two Submit buttons have been provided. The JSP code at the bottom of the page, which implements the form handler, can distinguish between these buttons by checking the value of a request parameter named `submittedVia`, which corresponds to the identifier assigned to these two Submit buttons via the `name` attribute of the corresponding `<input>` tags. Furthermore, the form handling code can deduce from the absence of this request parameter that the form has yet to be submitted, as indicated by the scriptlet which checks the result of the `getParam()` call for this parameter to see if it is empty.

Listing 11.5   JSP source code for the example form

```
<html>
<body>
<%!
public String getParam (HttpServletRequest request, String param) { ... }
public String getParamValues (HttpServletRequest request, String param) { ... }
public boolean requestContains (HttpServletRequest request,
                               String param, String testValue) { ... }
public String isChecked (HttpServletRequest request,
                         String param, String testValue) { ... }
public String isSelected (HttpServletRequest request,
                          String param, String testValue) { ... }
%>
<form action="<%= HttpUtils.getRequestURL(request) %>" method="post">
<table bgcolor="lightgrey" align="center" border="1" cellpadding="5">
<tr align="left" valign="top">
<td valign="top" rowspan="2">
<b>Name</b> 
<input type="text" name="character"
       value="<%= getParam(request, "character") %>">
<P>
<b>Select Box</b>
<select name="device">
<option value="tank" <%= isSelected(request, "device", "tank") %>>Tank
<option value="disk" <%= isSelected(request, "device", "disk") %>>Disk
<option value="light cycle"
        <%= isSelected(request, "device", "light cycle") %>>Light Cycle
</select>
</td>
<td><b>Gender</b></td>
<td><b>Color</b></td></tr>
<tr>
<td>
<input type="radio" name="gender" value="his"
       <%= isChecked(request, "gender", "his") %>><i>male</i><BR>
<input type="radio" name="gender" value="her"
       <%= isChecked(request, "gender", "her") %>><i>female</i><BR>
</td>
<td>
<input type="checkbox" name="colors" value="red"
       <%= isChecked(request, "colors", "red") %>><i>red</i><BR>
<input type="checkbox" name="colors" value="yellow"
       <%= isChecked(request, "colors", "yellow") %>><i>yellow</i><BR>
<input type="checkbox" name="colors" value="blue"
       <%= isChecked(request, "colors", "blue") %>><i>blue</i><BR>
</td>
</tr>
<tr>
```

```
<td colspan="3" align="center" valign="center">
<b>Message</b><br>
<textarea cols="40" rows="5" name="message">
<%= getParam(request, "message") %>
</textarea>
</td>
</tr>
</table>
<P>
<center>
<input type="submit" name="submittedVia" value="Declare">
 
<input type="submit" name="submittedVia" value="Taunt">
</center>
</P>
<hr width="75%">
<%-- FORM HANDLING CODE --%>
<h2>Result</h2>
<% String submission = getParam(request, "submittedVia");
   if (submission.equals("")) { %>
       The form has not yet been submitted.
<% } else {
      String verb = (submission.equals("Taunt")) ? "taunts" : "declares";
%>
   <%= getParam(request, "character") %>, manning
   <%= getParam(request, "gender") %>
   <%= getParamValues(request, "colors") %>
   <%= getParam(request, "device") %>,
   <%= verb %> "<b><%= getParam(request, "message") %></b>"
<% } %>
</form>
</body>
</html>
```

Thus, if the form has not yet been submitted, a message to that effect is displayed at the bottom of the page. If it has, then the values of the various request parameters are combined via a set of JSP scriptlets and expressions to generate a sentence based on the user's selections.

11.5 *Validating form data*

When we are collecting information for processing on the server through an HTML input form we often need to validate the data we get from the client browser to make sure it is in the format we expect before passing it off to a JSP or servlet. If we ask for a year, we might want to verify that the user typed in a four-digit year rather than a two-digit one. Indeed we'd want to make sure he/she entered *numbers* in the year field and not letters! Or, we may require that certain fields not be left blank. In any case, there are two choices for how we perform our validation—on the client or the server.

11.5.1 Client- and server-side validation

Client-side input field validation is performed with JavaScript. The general approach is to add an onSubmit handler to our form and use JavaScript methods to check each form field for whatever constraints we wish to enforce on the data. The user is prevented from submitting the form until the data in the input fields meets our requirements. Of course, since it is client-controlled there is nothing to enforce this but the browser—and who said the user is running a browser? The truth is users can submit anything they want by building their own form, creating their own client software, or connecting to the HTTP server directly. If your JSP or servlet isn't prepared to handle illegal or unexpected data you could have a problem. Bottom line: never trust the client to perform important tasks on its own.

Server-side validation on the other hand is completely under your control as the application developer. Server-side validation can be performed in the servlet or JSP which receives the form action and is responsible for processing the information. The server is able to validate the form data only after it has been submitted by the client. At that point it must verify that the data is within limits and either accept it, display an error message, or return the user to the form and give some indication of what needs to be done to correct the problem. This cycle is repeated until the user enters valid data, or gives up and goes home. This is also a good time to massage the data into your preferred form; for example, you want something in all lower

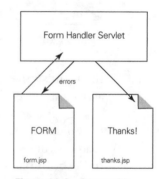

Figure 11.9 Server-side form validation

case or want to strip out dashes and spaces. Once valid data is received, the form handler servlet or JSP can proceed with populating the database, sending email, or whatever it is we had set out to do. This process is illustrated in figure 11.9.

When you send the user back to the form to try again following an error, we don't want him/her to have to fill in all of the fields again, we want to preserve the form data. This is where JSP comes in. If we make our input forms JSP-based, then the servlet can pass the current form field values back to the JSP, which can update

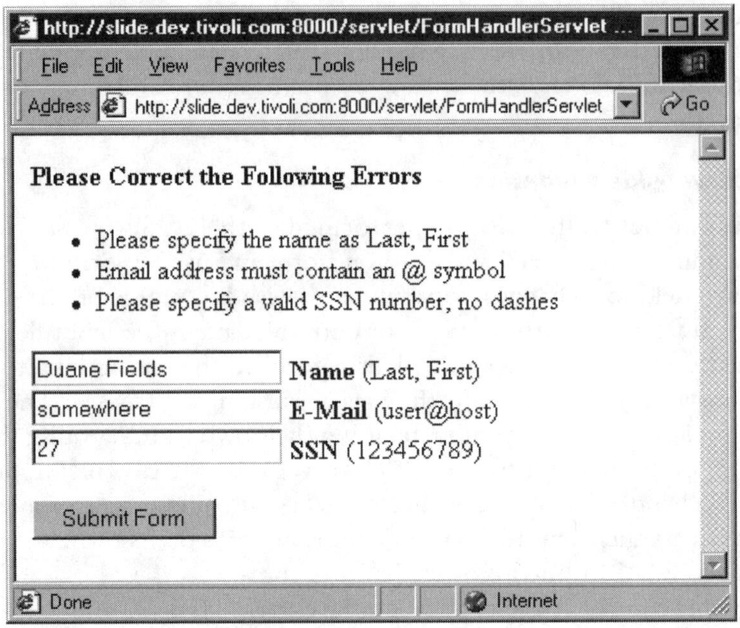

Figure 11.10   Form validation in progress

the form's values. We used a similar technique earlier in this chapter to build inter-active interfaces, but the approach works equally well with plain old forms.

Server-side validation has the downside of the user having to resubmit requests for validation each time. The delay between updates on the client side and the extra load on your server may be unacceptable in some situations. A good compromise is to do both types of validation on the form. Build in client-side validation to catch what you can, but double-check it once the data is submitted to the server. This gives you the performance you would like while preserving the security of server-validated data.

11.5.2 *Example: server-side validation*

In this example we will collect information from a JSP form and validate it through the servlet serving as our form handler. We've got three simple fields in our form: Name, Email, and Social Security number (a unique nine-digit number assigned to U.S. citizens). Since this is only an example, we'll perform extremely simple valida-tion on the data. We want to make sure that the user enters his/her name in the for-mat "Last, First," that the email address appears to really be an email address, and that he/she has entered enough digits for the Social Security number. If an error occurs, we'll send them back to the form to try again, as illustrated in figure 11.10.

We'll build the servlet—which for this example doesn't do anything other than validate the data, the form page, and the results page—where we'll acknowledge our acceptance of the data and redisplay it to show the user what we accepted.

The FormBean

Encapsulating our form data into a JavaBean makes it easy to repopulate the form fields with the user's data following an invalid submission. As you'll see shortly, we can populate the Bean directly from the request parameters and use the Bean tags to update each form field (listing 11.6).

Listing 11.6   Source code for FormBean.java

```java
package com.taglib.wdjsp.commontasks;

public class FormBean {

  private String name;
  private String email;
  private String ssn;

  public FormBean() {
    name = "";
    email = "";
    ssn = "";
  }

  public void setName(String name) {
    this.name = name;
  }

  public String getName() {
    return name;
  }

  public void setEmail(String email) {
    this.email = email;
  }

  public String getEmail() {
    return email;
  }

  public void setSsn(String ssn) {
    this.ssn = ssn;
```

```
    }

    public String getSsn() {
      return ssn;
    }
}
```

The JSP form

The JSP form we use in this example has several jobs. First, it must populate a Form-Bean object using any data present in the request. If there is a problem validating the data following submission, the request will be redirected back to this page, populating the Bean with the data. Each time the page is accessed directly a new FormBean will be created, with its default empty values. Empty Bean or not, we use the <jsp:getProperty> tags to populate the default values of our form fields, giving us sticky form fields. If any errors were detected from a previous submittal attempt, the page must display them above the form data. We'll talk about each of these tasks in detail shortly. The source is shown in listing 11.7.

Listing 11.7   Source code for form.jsp

```jsp
<jsp:useBean id="form" class="com.taglib.wdjsp.commontasks.FormBean">
   <jsp:setProperty name="form" property="*"/>
</jsp:useBean>
<html>
<body bgcolor="white">
<%
   String[] errors = (String[])request.getAttribute("errors");
   if (errors != null && errors.length > 0) {
%>
<b>Please Correct the Following Errors</b>
<ul>
<% for (int i=0; i < errors.length; i++) { %>
<li> <%= errors[i] %>
<% } %>
</ul>
<% } %>

<form action="/servlet/FormHandlerServlet" method="post">
<input type="text" name="name"
value="<jsp:getProperty name="form" property="name"/>">
<b>Name</b> (Last, First)<br>

<input type="text" name="email"
value="<jsp:getProperty name="form" property="email"/>">
<b>E-Mail</b> (user@host)<br>
```

```
<input type="text" name="ssn"
value="<jsp:getProperty name="form" property="ssn"/>">
<b>SSN</b> (123456789)<br>
<p>
<input type="submit" value="Submit Form">
</form>
</body>
</html>
```

The form handler

Before we can talk about the various aspects of the code in the JSP form we must understand how it relates to our servlet. The servlet is responsible in this case for validating the code, performing whatever operation is required by the application, and directing the user to the next page in the process. Take a look at the source in listing 11.8, and then we'll explain the process in detail.

Listing 11.8   Source code for FormHandlerServlet.java

```
import java.io.*;
import javax.servlet.*;
import javax.servlet.http.*;
import java.util.*;

public class FormHandlerServlet extends HttpServlet {

  public void service(HttpServletRequest req,
          HttpServletResponse res)
    throws ServletException, IOException {
    Vector errors = new Vector();

    String name = req.getParameter("name");
    String ssn = req.getParameter("ssn");
    String email = req.getParameter("email");

    if (! isValidName(name))
      errors.add("Please specify the name as Last, First");
    if (! isValidEmail(email))
      errors.add("Email address must contain an @ symbol");
    if (! isValidSSN(ssn))
      errors.add("Please specify a valid SSN number, no dashes");

    String next;
    if (errors.size() == 0) {
      // data is OK, do whatever
      // dispatch to wherever
```

```
        next = "thanks.jsp";
      }
      else {
        // data has errors, try again
        String[] errorArray = (String[])errors.toArray(new String[0]);
        req.setAttribute("errors", errorArray);
        next = "form.jsp";
      }

      String base = "/validate/";
      RequestDispatcher rd;
      rd = getServletContext().getRequestDispatcher(base + next);
      rd.forward(req, res);
    }

    private boolean isValidSSN(String ssn) {
      // check for 9 characters, no dashes
      return (ssn.length() == 9 && ssn.indexOf("-") == -1);
    }

    private boolean isValidEmail(String email) {
      // check an "@" somewhere after the 1st character
      return (email.indexOf("@") > 0);
    }

    private boolean isValidName(String name) {
      // should be Last, First - check for the comma
      return (name.indexOf(",") != -1);
    }
}
```

Handling validation errors

Regardless of what type of data the user enters into the form fields of form.jsp, the data will be sent to the server, as we are not doing any client-side validation in this case. The other thing to keep in mind is that the Bean we created on that page disappears as soon as the page is finished displaying. The form submission is a straight HTTP request, and cannot deliver anything other than name/value pairs to the servlet.

When the request comes in to the servlet, it extracts the three parameters we are interested in from the request and validates them using three very simplistic checks. For each one of these validations that fails, the servlet adds a new message to the errors array, a list of all errors detected during validation. If no errors were found, the servlet dispatches the request to the thank you page, thanks.jsp.

When errors are encountered, they are packaged up as a request attribute before dispatching back to form.jsp, from whence it came. When this request is processed by the JSP, both the original request parameters and the list of error messages are present. The `<jsp:useBean>` tag creates an instance of `FormBean` and uses a wild card to populate it from this new request with the original form data. Just prior to displaying the form, we must check for the presence of the error list, looping through and displaying each one as a bullet in an unordered list:

```
<%
  String[] errors = (String[])request.getAttribute("errors");
  if (errors != null && errors.length > 0) {
%>
<b>Please Correct the Following Errors</b>
<ul>
<% for (int i=0; i < errors.length; i++) { %>
<li> <%= errors[i] %>
<% } %>
</ul>
<% } %>
```

The thank you page

When the form is successfully submitted, we again populate a fresh Bean with data from the successful request. This allows us to display the data to the user, with a message that the form was accurately processed (listing 11.9 and figure 11.11).

Listing 11.9   Source code for thanks.jsp

```
<jsp:useBean id="form" class="validate.FormBean">
  <jsp:setProperty name="form" property="*"/>
</jsp:useBean>
<html>
<body bgcolor="white">
<b>Thanks! Your form as been received</b>
<ul>
<b>Name:</b> <jsp:getProperty name="form" property="name"/><br>
<b>Email:</b> <jsp:getProperty name="form" property="email"/><br>
<b>SSN:</b> <jsp:getProperty name="form" property="ssn"/><br>
</ul>
</body>
</html>
```

11.6   *Miscellaneous tasks*

We conclude this chapter with a set of short examples that quickly demonstrate three additional common tasks. Rather than demonstrate broad principles, however, these examples are focused on implementing very specific functionality. As such, only brief discussions are provided to clarify the accompanying code.

Figure 11.11 Form successfully processed

11.6.1 *Determining the last modification date*

Having a JSP page display its last modification date turns out to be trickier than you might think. We first have to map the page's path to a physical file on disk. We can use the getServletPath() method of the request implicit object to determine its path relative to the application, then use the application implicit object (an instance of ServletContext) to determine the real path to the underlying JSP file. This in turn allows us to create a Date object, based on the last modification time of the JSP file itself:

```
<%@ page import="java.io.*,java.util.*" %>
<% File f =
     new File(application.getRealPath(request.getServletPath()));
%>
<% Date modified = new Date(f.getLastModified()); %>
<HTML>
<BODY>
This page last modified on: <%= modified %>
</BODY>
</HTML>
```

Based on the brevity of this code and its general utility, one might consider packaging up this functionality so that it may be easily reused. One mechanism for doing this is to create a small JSP page that can be incorporated into other JSP pages via the include directive. (Note that the <jsp:include> tag is not an option here, as it would end up computing the last modification date of the included file.)

Alternatively, a custom tag could be created which uses similar code to compute and insert the last modification date.

11.6.2 *Executing system commands*

Just like other Java programs, you can use JSPs to execute external commands. You can even use the Java Native Interface to execute native code stored inside libraries or DLLs. (Remember, of course, that we are talking about code native to the platform of the server, not the client, since JSP pages are executed on the server.) If you are converting your CGI scripts to JSPs and servlets, or building front ends to system administration tasks, the following code example shows how you can display the results of executing a command on the server. This example displays the current uptime and load average for a UNIX server, as reported by the server's /usr/bin/ uptime command.

```
<%@ page import="java.io.*" %>
<%!
public String runCmd(String cmd) {
  try {
    Runtime rt = Runtime.getRuntime();
    Process p = rt.exec(cmd);
    InputStreamReader in = new InputStreamReader(p.getInputStream());
    BufferedReader reader = new BufferedReader(in);
    StringBuffer buf = new StringBuffer();
    String line;
    String newline = "\n";
    while ((line = reader.readLine()) != null) {
      buf.append(line);
      buf.append(newline);
    }
    reader.close();
    p.getInputStream().close();
    p.getOutputStream().close();
    p.getErrorStream().close();
    p.waitFor();
    return buf.toString();
  }
  catch (Exception e) {
    return (e.getMessage());
  }
}
%>
<html>
<body>
The system uptime is currently: <%= runCmd("/usr/bin/uptime") %>
</body>
</html>
```

Note that we are using an instance of `java.io.BufferedReader` in this example, reading output one line at a time. This is the most efficient method—especially for large amounts of data (unlike our example). Additionally, recall that, by default, JSP pages have an 8K buffer. As a result, we won't see the results of long-running commands immediately, but rather in 8K bursts. If your application demands that buffering be turned off, you will need to modify the loop of the `runCmd()` method to grab each character from the input stream, rather than buffered lines, and you'll also need to disable buffering on the page. In this case, replace the initial lines of the example above with the following:

```
<%@ page buffer="none" import="java.io.*" %>
<%!
public String runCmd(String cmd) {
   try {
      Runtime rt = Runtime.getRuntime();
      Process p = rt.exec(cmd);…
         InputStreamReader in = new InputStreamReader(p.getInputStream());
         int c;
         StringBuffer buf = new StringBuffer();
         while ((c = in.read()) != -1) {
            buf.append((char)c);
         }
      ...
```

11.6.3 *Generating XML*

Generating XML data from a JSP page is just as straightforward as generating HTML output: instead of interposing JSP elements for dynamic content generation into a document containing HTML tags, the same JSP elements can be added to a document containing XML tags. The only other major requirement is to use the `page` directive to change the content type for the document, as in the following example:

```
<%@ page contentType="text/xml" %>
<jsp:useBean id="book"
             class="com.taglib.wdjsp.commontasks.BookBean"
             scope="request"/>
<?xml version="1.0" encoding="ISO-8859-1" ?>
<!DOCTYPE book
    PUBLIC "-//Manning Publications Co.//DTD Book Catalog//EN"
    "http://www.manning.com/dtds/catalog.dtd">
<book>
 <title><jsp:getProperty name="book" property="title"/></title>
 <author><jsp:getProperty name="book" property="author"/></author>
 <publisher>
   <jsp:getProperty name="book" property="publisher"/>
 </publisher>
```

```
  <ISBN><jsp:getProperty name="book" property="ISBN"/></ISBN>
</book>
```

Here, the data which populates this XML document is obtained from the properties of a hypothetical `BookBean`. JSP's JavaBeans tags are used to load information about a specific book instance (perhaps it was inserted into the `request` object as the result of a search query) into the corresponding fields of the document's XML tags. If the Bean instance was a reference to the book you're reading now, for example, the output of this JSP page would be as follows:

```
<?xml version="1.0" encoding="ISO-8859-1" ?>
<!DOCTYPE book
    PUBLIC "-//Manning Publications Co.//DTD Book Catalog//EN"
    "http://www.manning.com/dtds/catalog.dtd">
<book>
  <title>Web Development with JavaServer Pages</title>
  <author>Duane K. Fields and Mark A. Kolb</author>
  <publisher>Manning Publications Co.</publisher>
  <ISBN>1884777996</ISBN>
 </book>
```

JSP by example

In this chapter we will present additional examples of JSP programming. While we will highlight important or confusing segments of the code, the main purpose of this chapter is to add context and real world examples to the programming syntax and theory covered earlier in the book. For those of you who learn best by example, this chapter will help tie together the concepts we've been discussing.

12.1 *A rotating banner ad*

Banner ads are now a common fixture on the World Wide Web. Typically, these ads are comprised of graphical images conforming to a fixed size requirement, to be displayed across the top of a page or some other standard location. A site will often be presenting multiple banner ads on its pages at the same time, alternating which banner is displayed as the user moves from page to page. For this reason, an automated mechanism for selecting a banner from those available and displaying it on a page is highly desirable.

This example, because it will be used from multiple pages, utilizes JSP's Java-Beans tags to promote reusability. The first requirement, then, is a working Bean that provides the required functionality.

12.1.1 *The BannerBean*

For the purposes of this example, it is assumed that the banners take the form of image files accessible via URLs. The primary role of this Bean, then, is to select one entry from a set of such URLs to serve as the value for the `src` attribute of an HTML `img` tag in order to display the banner.

This is accomplished by means of a `bannerURL` property, provided by the Bean's `getBannerURL()` method. In addition, the Bean must keep track of all of the available banner images, and rotate among them each time the `bannerURL` property is retrieved. The complete source code for this Bean is shown in listing 12.1:

Listing 12.1 Source code for BannerBean

```
package com.taglib.wdjsp.byexample;
import java.util.Random;

public class BannerBean {
    private int index, count;
    static private String[] BANNER_URLS = {
      "/webdev/images/PlainBanner.gif",
      "/webdev/images/StripedBanner.gif",
      "/webdev/images/SpottedBanner.gif" };
    public BannerBean () {
```

```
        count = BANNER_URLS.length;
        Random r = new Random();
        index = r.nextInt(count);
    }
    public String getBannerURL () {
        return BANNER_URLS[nextIndex()];
    }
    private int nextIndex () {
        if (++index == count) index = 0;
        return index;
    }
}
```

As you may recall from the discussion in chapter 6, the aspects of this class definition that qualify it as a Bean are its constructor, which takes no arguments, and the
`getBannerURL()` method, which provides an abstract interface for accessing the
Bean's sole property, `bannerURL`.

For simplicity's sake, the URLs of the available banners are stored in a `String`
array, which is referenced by the static variable `BANNER_URLS`. Similarly, although a
variety of schemes might be imagined for determining the selection and/or order in
which the banners should be displayed—for example, based on which pages have
already been viewed, or on demographic information tied to a specific user—a simple iterative approach is taken here. An integer instance variable, `index`, indicates
which of the banners to display. A random value is used to initialize this variable,
which is incremented each time the `bannerURL` property is accessed via the `getBan-
nerURL()` method. Incrementing is performed via the `nextIndex()` method, which
resets the counter to zero if the number of available URLs is exceeded.

12.1.2 *Using the Bean*

By storing an instance of this Bean in the user's session, the user is guaranteed of
seeing a new banner on each page which uses it. This is because each request for the
`bannerURL` property increments the instance's `index` variable. When the Bean is
stored in the session, it will not be necessary to create a Bean each time a page
which uses the Bean is encountered. Instead, the Bean will be retrieved from the
session and reused. Here is the source code for a sample JSP page, /webdev/ban-
ner.jsp, that implements this approach:

```
<%@page import="com.taglib.wdjsp.byexample.*"%>
<html>
<head>
<title>Banner Page</title>
</head>
```

```
<body>
<center>
<jsp:useBean id="banner" scope="session" class="BannerBean"/>
<img src="<jsp:getProperty name="banner" property="bannerURL"/>">
</center>
<P>Click <a href="banner.jsp">here</a> to see the next banner.</P>
</body>
</html>
```

Note that only two JSP elements are needed to access the banner rotation functionality, a `<jsp:useBean>` tag and a `<jsp:getProperty>` tag. To enhance the reusability of this code even further, the two lines containing these JSP elements could be placed in a separate JSP file for inclusion by multiple pages using either the `include` directive or the `<jsp:include>` action. Alternatively, the `BannerBean` could provide the basis for a custom tag.

The output for this JSP page is depicted in figure 12.1. Here, the URL selected for the banner was the third value in the `BANNER_URLS` array, `/webdev/images/SpottedBanner.gif`. If the page's link were followed, the browser would redisplay the same page, since the link points back to `/webdev/banner.jsp`. Because this would correspond to a new request for that page, however, the JSP container would be required to process the page again. In doing so, `<jsp:useBean>` tag would cause the original `BannerBean` instance to be retrieved from the session, after which the `<jsp:getProperty>` tag would result in a new call to the Bean's `getBannerURL()` method. This would cause the next image in the rotation to be displayed. In this case, since the `BANNER_URLS` array only has three elements, the `index` variable would

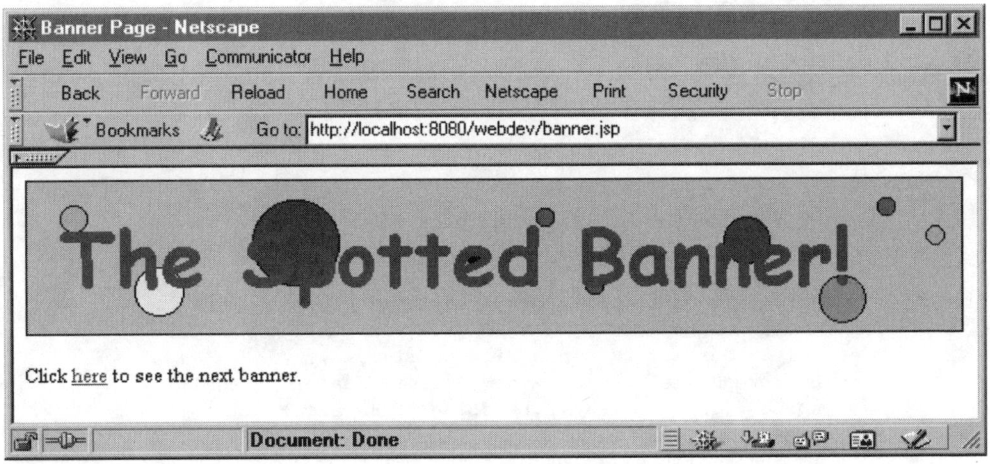

Figure 12.1 Output sent to the browser by the banner page

loop back around to the beginning, so that the next image to be displayed would be
/webdev/images/PlainBanner.gif.

12.2 A random quote generator

In this example, which builds on the preceding banner rotation example, we select a
random quote for the user from a list read in from disk at run time. Here we'll see
how to bring in our quotes from a file and select a random element for inclusion.
The resulting Bean provides a great way to add dynamic hints and tips or fortune
cookie quotes to your pages.

12.2.1 The QuoteBean

The QuoteBean class will store all of our quotes, which are loaded in from disk
using a file name supplied through the quoteFile property. Changing the quote-
File property will cause the Bean to reload its quote selections from disk. This
means that we will want the Bean to stick around since it's a relatively expensive
operation to go to disk each time. The solution here is to stick the Bean in the
application scope and reuse it for all users visiting our site.

The source for QuoteBean: is shown in listing 12.2:

Listing 12.2   Source code for QuoteBean

```
import java.io.*;
import java.util.*;

public class QuoteBean {
  private String[] quotes = {"No quotes today!"};
  private Random rand;

  public QuoteBean() {
    rand = new Random();
  }

  public void setQuoteFile(String path) {
    try {
      File file = new File(path);
      ArrayList quoteList = new ArrayList();
      String quote;
      FileReader stream = new FileReader(file);
      BufferedReader reader = new BufferedReader(stream);
      while ((quote = reader.readLine()) != null)
        quoteList.add(quote);
      if (quoteList.size() > 0)
        quotes = (String[])quoteList.toArray(quotes);
```

```
    }
    catch (IOException e) {
        System.err.println("Error: " + e.getMessage());};
    }

  public String getQuote() {
    return quotes[rand.nextInt(quotes.length)];
  }
}
```

In our constructor we just need to create an instance of the `java.util.Random` class, which provides a set of easy-to-use pseudorandom number generation methods, and stores it in an instance variable. All of the quotes will be stored in a simple `String` array called `quotes`. Notice that we make sure that the array always has something in it by initializing it to a default value, and not modifying it directly until we've read in our file completely. We could also elect to load in a default file of quotes in the constructor, but we chose to keep the implementation simple for this example.

We use a `BufferedReader` to read each quote, one quote per line, from the file specified through the argument to the `quoteFile` property. Note that this file's path is not assumed to be relative to your web server's document root directory—it can be anywhere on your system. The initial working directory location will be determined by the process that starts your JVM, but in practice this can be difficult to determine and you will likely find it easiest to stick to absolute paths.

Each time you access the `quote` property of this Bean, a new quote is selected by choosing a random array index value, and returning the corresponding `String`. Because we process the entire file in the `setQuoteFile()` method, we don't have to go back to the disk for a new quote each time—only when we change the quote file from which we are selecting.

12.2.2 *Using the Bean*

As we mentioned, this Bean was designed to be reused between requests, and would typically be placed into application scope, as shown here. We use the body of the `<jsp:useBean>` tag to initialize the Bean by setting the path to our quote file.

```
<%@page import="com.taglib.wdjsp.byexample.*" %>
<jsp:useBean id="quotes" class="QuoteBean" scope="application">
<jsp:setProperty name="quotes" property="quoteFile"
 value="/games/fortunes.txt"/>
</jsp:useBean>
<html>
<body>
```

```
Tip of the day: <jsp:getProperty name="quotes" property="quote"/>
</body>
</html>
```

Another way you could use this Bean is at the session scope level, with the selection of quote file based on other parameters such as the user's native language, status, or other dynamic attributes which you can determine at run time. Here's an example of selecting the quote file dynamically on a per-user basis, based on the authenticated username—we'll assume that we've created a quote file based on each user's name, in the /quotes/ directory. So for example, user cwalton would correspond to /quotes/cwalton.txt.

```
<%@page import="com.taglib.wdjsp.byexample.*" %>
<jsp:useBean id="quotes" class="QuoteBean" scope="session">
<jsp:setProperty name="quotes" property="quoteFile"
  value="<%= "/quotes/" + request.getRemoteUser() + ".txt" %>"/>
</jsp:useBean>
<html>
<body>
Greetings <%= request.getRemoteUser() %>, our advice to you is:
<jsp:getProperty name="quotes" property="quote"/>
</body>
</html>
```

12.3 *The Tell a Friend! sticker*

In this example we'll build a JSP component that will provide the capability of mailing the current page to a friend or colleague. This feature is found on many of the popular news sites because it is an easy way to get your users to promote your site and attract new users. We'll create a Tell a Friend! module that can easily be added to any page on the site to provide this new capability. The module adds a sticker (so called because it's a reusable element that we can stick onto any page) to the page from which it is called (figure 12.2). Clicking the sticker activates the module, asking the user for the friend's email address before sending the mail and returning the user to the original page.

There are several parts to this example. There's the sticker itself, a page that gets the information required to send the email, and the page or servlet that actually sends the email. The flow between them is illustrated in figure 12.3. The sticker may be included on any page. Clicking the sticker activates this process, directing the user to a page that asks for the information required to send the mail, such as the intended recipient's email address. This form then submits its information to

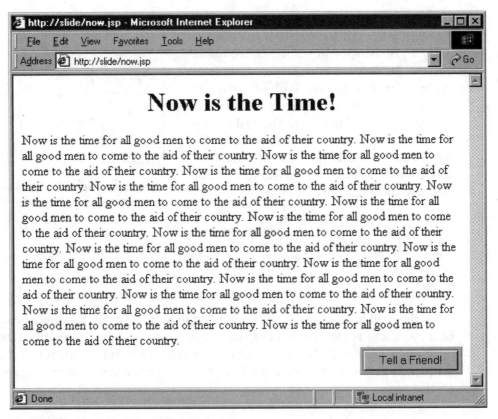

Figure 12.2   The Tell a Friend! sticker in action

another page (or a servlet) to actually send the mail, and the user is redirected back to the original page. It's all simpler than it looks, surprisingly.

You could apply this same principal in other ways, skipping the second step if you didn't need any additional information from the user before sending the mail.

12.3.1 *The sticker*

The sticker is the little icon, table, form, or link that we want to appear on pages throughout our site. Clicking it is what initiates the mailing process. We'll use a little form button in this example, but an image link would work just as well. The beauty of this approach is that the design of the sticker itself is completely independent of its usage and its HTML source code is isolated to its own file. Because the sticker will be added to each page at run time, you are free to alter its look at any time and it will be instantly updated throughout the site.

The Tell a Friend! sticker

The Tell a Friend! sticker itself isn't necessarily a JSP. Its specific contents are unim-
portant. Its only job is to create a link from
the current page to our MailForm page so
we can get the information we need to send
the electronic mail message. The real work is
done once we get to the MailForm page.
Here's a simple example sticker which creates a small tan table with a Submit button
to create the linkage we need:

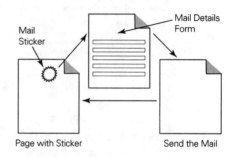

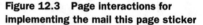

**Figure 12.3   Page interactions for
implementing the mail this page sticker**

```
<table bgcolor="tan" border="1">
<form action="MailForm.jsp" method="post">
<tr><td align="Center">
<input type="Submit" value="Tell a Friend!">
</td></tr>
</form>
</table>
```

Since the Mail Sticker page will be included in another page, we don't need this to
be a complete HTML document (in fact it should not be). Therefore we don't
need <HTML> or <BODY> tags here. Here's another example sticker that uses an
image and an anchor to create the link. Note that it's not necessary to have a form
on this page.

```
<a href="MailDetails.jsp">
<img src="/images/mailsticker.gif">
</a>
```

Again, the reason we have a separate page is to componentize our sticker, so that its
look and feel can be managed separately from that of the pages on which it will
appear. You could even create several different stickers for different areas of the site.

Using the sticker

Using the sticker is very easy; we just include it into the page with the include action:

```
<html>
<body>
Now is the time!
<div align="right">
<jsp:include page="MailSticker.jsp" />
</div>
</body>
</html>
```

Nothing to it! The contents will be added to the page at run time, and will automatically pick up any changes to the MailSticker.jsp page.

12.3.2 *The MailForm page*

This is where most of the action takes place, but as you'll see it's still easy to understand. What we have to do here is to grab the contents of the REFERER header, a hidden bit of information enclosed in the HTTP request from the user's browser that tells us the URL of the page from which the request originated, which in our case should be the page the sticker was on (figure 12.4).

Note that it is not the URL of the sticker itself: recall that we included its contents directly into our page. This is the URL that we mail to the address specified by the user, and is the URL that we will send the user back to when we are finished with the whole process. We need to pass the referrer information, along with some mail-related details, to our servlet or JSP page that will handle the actual sending of the mail. The contents of the MailForm.jsp page are shown in listing 12.3.

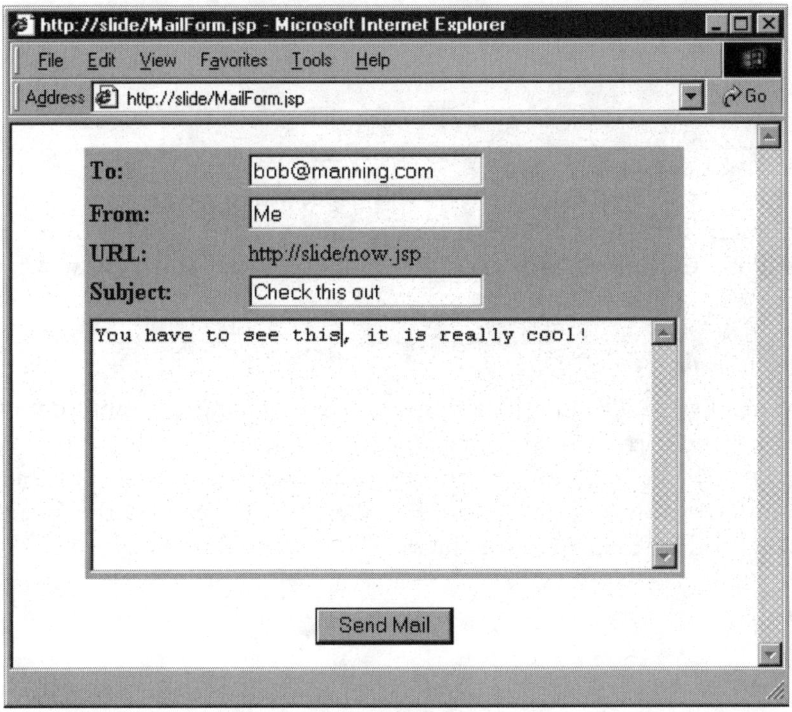

Figure 12.4   Passing along the referrer information via email

Listing 12.3   Contents of the MailForm.jsp page

```
<html>
<body>
<form action="SendMail.jsp" method="post">
<table border="0" align="center" bgcolor="tan">
<tr><td><b>To:</b></td><td>
<input type="TEXT" name="to"></td></tr>
<tr><td><b>From:</b></td><td>
<input type="TEXT" name="from"></td></tr>
<tr><td><b>URL:</b></td><td>
<%= request.getHeader("REFERER") %></td></tr>
<tr><td><b>Subject:</b></td><td>
<input type="TEXT" name="subject" value="Check this out"></td></tr>
<tr><td colspan="2"><textarea name="body" rows=10 cols=45>
Check out this site, it is really cool!
</textarea>
</td></tr>
</table>
<p>
<input type="HIDDEN" name="destination"
value="<%= request.getHeader("referer") %>">
<center><input type="SUBMIT" value="Send Mail"></center>
</form>
</body>
</html>
```

There is only one actual JSP element on this page, which we use to grab the value of the referrer and store it in a hidden form element called destination. The form handler will use this information, and the to and from fields, to know what to send and where to send it.

12.3.3 *Sending the mail*

The form handler SendMail.jsp is responsible for taking the input data from the form, sending the corresponding email message, and then returning the user to the original page. The code for our example is shown in listing 12.4, but there are, of course, a number of ways to process the request. We've omitted the JavaMail code that actually sends the email, as it's the same as discussed in chapter 11.

Listing 12.4   Code for sending email and returning user to the page

```
<html>
<%@ page import="javax.mail.*, javax.mail.internet.*" %>
<%
  try {
    String mailServer = "devmail.dev.tivoli.com";
    String subject = request.getParameter("subject");
    String[] to = { request.getParameter("to" };
    String from = request.getParameter("from");
    String body = request.getParameter("destination") +
      "\n\n" + request.getParameter("body");
    sendEmail(mailServer, subject, to, from, body);
 %>
<body>
<P> Mail has been sent! </P>
<% }
  catch (AddressException e) { %>
<P>Invalid e-mail address(es) for forwarding</P>
<% }
  catch (MessagingException e) { %>
<P>Unable to send e-mail notification</P>
<% } %>
Return to
<a href="<%= request.getParameter("destination") %>">
Original Page</a>
</body>
</html>
```

This JSP page uses a scriptlet and a pair of method declarations to implement the form handler. The `getParameter()` method of the request object is used to retrieve the form inputs, which are then used with the `sendEmail()` method, introduced in chapter 11, to deliver the electronic mail message.

Instead of simply mailing the interesting URL to the user we could have directed the request to a servlet which would read in the contents of the URL (perhaps even converting it to plain text) and then send the whole thing off to the indicated user as an email attachment.

Also, rather than redirecting the user back to the original page, we could have the sticker create a separate pop-up window, which would ask for the mail details. This would keep the user's main browser on the same page the entire time. When complete, we could simply close the pop-up window.

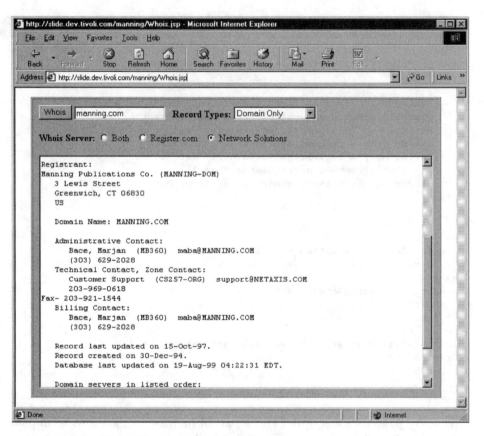

Figure 12.5   User interface for the JSP-based Whois client

12.4   A JSP Whois client

The *Whois* database is an Internet directory service that stores contact information for Internet domains and the administrators responsible for running them. A Whois client can search the contents of this database to find out the owner of a particular domain name, the contact information, and when the name was registered. In this example we will use JSP to design a Whois client with a web interface (figure 12.5).

12.4.1 The Whois protocol

In order to build this application we must understand a little bit about the Whois protocol, which is defined by RFC954, and decide what features we will support.

The Whois protocol is a simple query/response service that is hosted by the companies authorized by the Internet Corporation for Assigned Names and Numbers (ICANN) to handle Internet domain name registration. Searching the Whois database with a client application involves:

1 Establishing a socket connection to port 43 of a Whois server

2 Sending a search query terminated with a linefeed

3 Retrieving results from the Whois server, which will then close the connection

The format of a Whois search query is fairly basic: simply pass the name of the person or domain in which you are interested. If you do not specify any search keywords, the default action is to conduct a very broad search, looking for matches to your query in any field of any type of record in the database. You can prefix your query with a special set of keywords, which can be used to restrict the search to particular record types or fields. While there are many keywords and search control parameters supported by the Whois service, the most useful ones are summarized in table 12.1.

Table 12.1   Common search keywords for the Whois protocol

Keyword	Function
DO	Restrict searches to Domain records only
HO	Restrict searches to Host records only
GA	Restrict searches to Gateway records only
Full	Gives a long display for each record
SUM	Return only summaries

Prior to the explosive growth of the Internet, a single company was responsible for registering top-level Internet domain names. This meant that by searching a single Whois server you could retrieve information about any .com, .net, or .org site on the Internet. In October 1998, the U.S. government developed a Shared Registration System that permits multiple registrars to provide registration services for the Internet, and appointed ICANN to oversee this system. At the time of this writing, several new registrars have been approved, and more are planned. This makes searching for registration information a somewhat more challenging task because records for new domain name registrations are now spread across a growing number of individual Whois databases. It is uncertain whether or not anyone plans to consolidate information from each of the registrars into a single database.

> **NOTE**   Information on the implementation of NSI's Shared Registration System is available at http://www.nsiregistry.com, while information about ICANN's registrar accreditation process is available at http://www.icann.org.

12.4.2 *Requirements and design considerations*

What we are building is a Whois client that can be accessed through a web browser, making it accessible to anyone on our network, no matter what type of computer he/she happens to have. While the primary interface will be designed in HTML, this project involves remote network connections, so some server-side code will be required.

Unlike the Whois clients that are built into UNIX or bundled with most networking packages, our client will need to be able to search multiple Whois databases simultaneously, so that we can locate records regardless of which registrar's database they happen to be on. We should also expect that new registrars will be approved in the future, and be prepared to handle these new servers as they become available.

Our client should also include options that allow the user to restrict searches to certain sets of records or fields. While we could simply require the user to encode the query with the appropriate keywords and modifiers, it is preferable to assume that not all of our users are quite so familiar with the Whois protocol.

From an architectural perspective it makes sense to divide our development tasks into two parts: a front-end user interface and a back-end network service. The capability to look up records in a Whois server will be encapsulated into a JavaBean running on the server. We can develop this component independently from our front-end interface, which might change over time.

12.4.3 *The WhoisBean*

All of the code required to perform searches against a Whois database will be encapsulated into our server-side component for this application, the WhoisBean. The WhoisBean can provide Whois lookup services to any application capable of accessing its properties. In this case we are building an HTML interface through JSP, but a servlet, applet, or Java application could just as easily use the Bean's services. By packaging our service into a JavaBean like this, we don't have to worry about how or when it will be used, and we won't need to rewrite it for every project or new user interface that comes up.

To actually perform the lookup, we first create a socket connection to port 43 of the server. Once connected, we issue our query to the socket's OutputStream and read the results from its `InputStream`. The following code will establish a connection to the Whois server at Networks Solutions, Inc. (whois.internic.net), which will search for the domain manning.com and print the response to the screen.

```
Socket connection = new Socket("whois.internic.net", 43);
out = new PrintStream(connection.getOutputStream());
in = new BufferedReader(new InputStreamReader(connection.getInputStream()));
out.println("DO manning.com");
while ((line = reader.readLine()) != null)
  System.out.println(line + "\n");
```

Code like this will form the core of our `WhoisBean` class, as it performs the primary service we are interested in delivering. The rest of the code for this class will be concerned with supporting our Bean's properties, which will form the interface required to access the Bean through JSP.

Bean properties

The first step in designing our Bean is to determine what properties it will support. We know that at minimum the front-end interface will need to set a query and view the results of the search, so there are two properties right there: `query` and `results`. How should we handle the search keywords and options? One choice would be to implement properties and corresponding access methods for each search option supported by the Whois protocol. While this might seem to be the most exacting approach, it would create a needlessly complex interface that could be eliminated by simply accepting all search modifiers through a single property, `options`. We'll make the `query` and `options` properties read/write, since the front-end code might need to view their state as well as modify it. The `results` property however, will be read-only because instead of reflecting the state of an instance variable it will actually be used to return the response from the Whois server. Since the value of the `results` property will be computed dynamically each time it is requested, it requires only a getter method, not a setter.

It would also be a good idea to allow the front-end code to specify which Whois servers we wish to search. Given the fact that the growth of the Internet is creating the need for additional registrars and Whois databases, we can expect that we will need to update our code to include support for additional Whois server addresses in the future. That being said, we should try to isolate that portion of the code to the front-end, which is easier to revise. It also gives us a more flexible solution. The front-end code can decide what servers are searched and give the user as many or as few options as desired. Otherwise, we would be restricted to a rigid, Bean-enforced selection of servers each time, or end up with an overly complex interface between the Bean and the front-end code. We've therefore added an indexed property, servers, which holds the names of the Whois servers we wish to search. We've also included a convenience property that allows the JSP page to treat the `servers` property as a single String value by separating each server name with a comma. In the absence of custom JSP tags for handling indexed properties, this will make the front-end JSP code much cleaner.

The property sheet for this Bean is presented in table 12.2.

Table 12.2 Property sheet for `com.taglib.wdjsp.byexample.WhoisBean`

Name	Access	Java Type	Use
`query`	read/write	`java.lang.String`	Specify the query data
`options`	read/write	`java.lang.String`	Search keywords and modifiers
`results`	read only	`java.lang.String`	Results from whois
`servers`	read/write	`java.lang.String[]`	Whois servers to search through
`serverList`	read/write	`java.lang.String`	Convenience property for setting servers, accepts a comma separated list of servers

Instance variables and constructor

In order to maintain its state our `WhoisBean` class will need instance variables for the query, the search options, and the list of servers.

```
public class WhoisBean {
  private String query;
  private String options;
  private String[] servers;
}
```

In the constructor we will initialize our state variables with empty data.

```
public WhoisBean() {
  query = "";
  options = "";
  servers = new String[0];
}
```

Access Methods

The access methods for our `query` and `options` properties are relatively straightforward. Each can map directly to an instance variable, with getters and setters that access these instance variables to manage the Bean's state.

```
public String getQuery() {
  return query;
}
public void setQuery(String query) {
```

```
      this.query = query;
   }
   public String getOptions() {
      return options;
   }
   public void setOptions(String options) {
      this.options = options;
   }
```

Designing the access methods for the `servers` and `serverList` properties is a little more complex. Internally, we can store our list of Whois servers as an array of `String` objects. This will let us easily loop through the list of servers to perform our searches. In order to better support JSP access to this Bean, we decided that our list of servers could be modified by the user through two different properties, `servers` and `serverList`. This means that we need to create methods to read and write the array through both properties. `Servers` is an indexed property that deals with arrays directly, and its access methods are fairly straightforward. Don't forget however, that while not entirely necessary, it's a good idea to go ahead and add additional access methods that can be used to access the entire contents of the list at once as an array:

```
   public String getServers(int index) {
      return servers[index];
   }
   public void setServers(String server, int index) {
      servers[index] = server;
   }
   public String[] getServers() {
      return servers;
   }
   public void setServers(String[] servers) {
      this.servers = servers;
   }
```

Writing the `serverList` property access methods requires us to do a little more work. We must convert the `servers` array to and from a comma-delimited list. It is important to preserve the ordering of the list of servers so that the front-end code will get consistent results back from the property. We have used the `java.util.Vector` class to assure that we preserve the order of the elements in the list.

```
   public void setServerList(String values) {
      Vector v = new Vector();
      StringTokenizer tok = new StringTokenizer(values, ", ");
      while (tok.hasMoreTokens())
         v.addElement(tok.nextToken());
      servers = new String[v.size()];
```

```
  for (int i=0; i < servers.length; i++)
    servers[i] = (String)v.elementAt(i);
}

public String getServerList() {
  String values = "";
  for (int i=0; i < servers.length; i++) {
    values += servers[i];
    if (i < (servers.length - 1))
      values += ", ";
  }
  return values;
}
```

The `results` property access method will be read-only, so we only need to create the method `getResults()`. As indicated, this getter method will actually perform the specified query. The first step is to create the query string that we will send to each Whois server. As you may remember from our discussion of the Whois protocol, we build our query string by simply prepending our search options to the string for which we wish to search. We'll also need to test for the possibility that there aren't any options, in which case we will use the query property as the search string, as follows:

```
String queryString;
if (options.length() > 0)
  queryString = options + " " + query;
else
  queryString = query;
```

We'll use the networking code we looked at earlier as the core of this method. To simplify the implementation, we'll collect the search results from all of the servers we're interested in by looping through the array of servers, conducting a search against each one, and appending the results of each search to a `String` variable that will by returned by the `getResults()` method.

```
String output = "";
for (int i=0; (i < servers.length) && (query.length() > 0); i++) {
  try {
    String line = "";
    Socket connection = new Socket(servers[i], 43);
    InputStream sock = connection.getInputStream();
    PrintStream out = new PrintStream(connection.getOutputStream());
    BufferedReader in = new BufferedReader(
      new InputStreamReader(sock));
    output += "Results from " + servers[i] + " for \"" +
      query + "\"\n\n";
    out.println(query);
```

```
      while ((line = in.readLine()) != null)
        output += line + "\n";
    }
    catch(Exception e) {
      output += "Could not contact Whois server on "+servers[i]+ "\n";
    }
    output += "\n\n\n";
  }
  return output;
```

As far as handling error conditions, we've decided here to keep things simple. Attempting to access the `results` property without properly setting the query or servers properties is an error condition, but rather then throw an exception we will simply return an empty string from `getResults()`. This approach will keep the front-end code simple and will allow it to display the `results` property, which evaluates to an empty `String` in such cases, without having to test for error states or valid properties. Likewise, if we encounter an error contacting or reading data from the Whois server we will simply include the error message in our results. If one particular server did not respond, we would still like to receive results from the others in the list. This seems reasonable for this particular Bean: if you haven't set the `query` or `servers` properties, the `results` property will be empty. Other Beans might require more sophisticated error-handling capabilities.

The complete source for the `WhoisBean` class is provided in listing 12.5.

Listing 12.5   Source code for the com.taglib.wdjsp.byexample.WhoisBean class

```
package com.taglib.wdjsp.byexample;

import java.io.*;
import java.net.*;
import java.util.*;

public class WhoisBean {
  private String query;
  private String options;
  private String[] servers;
  private String serverList;


  public WhoisBean() {
    this.query = "";
    this.options = "";
    this.servers = new String[0];
  }

  public void setOptions(String options) {
```

```
    this.options = options;
  }

  public String getOptions() {
    return this.options;
  }

  public String getQuery() {
    return query;
  }

  public void setQuery(String query) {
    this.query = query;
  }

  public String getServers(int index) {
    return servers[index];
  }

  public String[] getServers() {
    return servers;
  }

  public void setServers(String server, int index) {
    servers[index] = server;
  }

  public void setServers(String[] servers) {
    this.servers = servers;
  }

  public void setServerList(String values) {
    Vector v = new Vector();
    StringTokenizer tok = new StringTokenizer(values, ",");
    while (tok.hasMoreTokens())
      v.addElement(tok.nextToken());
    servers = new String[v.size()];
    for (int i=0; i < servers.length; i++)
      servers[i] = (String)v.elementAt(i);
  }

  public String getServerList() {
    String values = "";
    for (int i=0; i < servers.length; i++) {
      values += servers[i];
      if (i < (servers.length - 1))
        values += ",";
    }
    return values;
  }
```

```
public String getResults() {
  String queryString;
  if (options.length() > 0)
    queryString = options + " " + query;
  else
    queryString = query;
  String output = "";
  for (int i=0; (i< servers.length) && (query.length()>0); i++) {
    try {
      String line = "";
      Socket connection = new Socket(servers[i], 43);
      InputStream sock = connection.getInputStream();
      PrintStream out =
        new PrintStream(connection.getOutputStream());
      BufferedReader in =
        new BufferedReader(new InputStreamReader(sock));
      output += "Results from " + servers[i] +
        " for \"" + queryString + "\"\n\n";
      out.println(queryString);
      while ((line = in.readLine()) != null)
        output += line + "\n";
    }
    catch(Exception e) {
      output += "Could not contact Whois server at " +
        servers[i] + "\n";
    }
    output += "\n\n\n";
  }
  return output;
}

public static void main(String[] args) {
  WhoisBean bean = new WhoisBean();
  bean.setServerList("whois.internic.net");
  bean.setQuery("manning.com");
  System.out.println(bean.getResults());
  bean.setQuery("metafirm.com");
  System.out.println(bean.getResults());
}
}
```

Improving the design of the Bean

If instances of this Bean were handling lots of requests or performing a critical service, we might want to make a few minor improvements to the design of the Bean. We could, for example, only perform a new Whois lookup when one of the input parameters—i.e., the contents of the query and options properties—has changed.

To do this we would create an internal boolean cache variable that would be flipped to `true` in the `getResults()` method, and back to `false` in any of the setter methods for our properties. Of course when we use this Bean in conjunction with JSP, such a change would provide no benefits unless the Bean instances were reused across multiple request. To do so, the JSP developer would need to place user-specific instances of the `WhoisBean` into the session scope.

Another minor improvement we could introduce would be better handling of the error conditions that might arise. We could, for example, remove Whois servers that aren't responding from our server list, throw more meaningful exceptions, and/or validate property values in our setter methods.

12.4.4 *Building the front end*

Now that we have completed the `WhoisBean` implementation, we need to design the JSP page that will form the user interface of our application. Various approaches are possible from implementing the front end. The traditional approach to web applications such as this is to implement a form in HTML, which then calls a CGI program to perform the specified query. In light of the form-handling example presented in chapter 11, however, a form that incorporates sticky widgets via JSP elements would seem to provide a more user-friendly interface. When coupled with the functionality available in the `WhoisBean`, however, the JSP approach is a natural fit, the results of which are presented in figure 12.5.

Coupling the use of a Bean with the sticky widgets approach provides two additional benefits. First, initialization of the Bean properties is greatly simplified by supplying identifiers for the form elements that map directly to those properties. This allows us to use the wild card setting for the `property` attribute (i.e., `property="*"`) of the `<jsp:setProperty>` tag. As a result, we can create and initialize our Bean with just two tags:

```
<% @page import="com.taglib.wdjsp.byexample" %>
<jsp:useBean id="whois" class="WhoisBean" scope="request"/>
<jsp:setProperty name="whois" property="*"/>
```

Recall that the input values from the form elements are translated into request parameters when the form is submitted. The effect of the wild card value in the `<jsp:setProperty>` tag is to create a mapping from request parameters to Bean properties, meaning that we can now access all of the data from the form inputs via the Bean instance.

NOTE In the actual JSP code for this form, as presented in listing 12.6, we use four tags to create and initialize the `WhoisBean` instance. Two additional tags are required to add a body to the `<useBean>` tag in which we provide a default value for the Bean's `serverList` property.

This in turn means that, rather than embedding scripting elements into our page for interacting with request parameters, we can instead use JSP's built-in JavaBeans tags to manipulate these request parameters via the corresponding Bean properties. For example, the text field corresponding to the Whois query can be initialized via the `<jsp:getProperty>` tag, rather than via a JSP expression as in the earlier example, as follows:

```
<INPUT type="text" name="query" SIZE="20"
 value="<jsp:getProperty name="whois" property="query"/>">
```

Note that the identifier specified for the `<input>` tag, `query`, has the same name as the Bean property. This ability to replace scripting elements with Bean tags is the second added benefit implementing form-handling with JavaBeans: eliminating Java code from the JSP page in order to promote greater separation of presentation and implementation.

Rather than relying extensively on scripting elements containing raw Java code to initialize form fields and handle requests, the Whois client has little Java code in the page itself. What Java code remains in the page is focused entirely on the presentation: setting the `action` attribute for the `<form>` tag, and determining which of the select box options and radio buttons should be enabled. All of the application-specific code (i.e., contacting the Whois servers and collecting the results) resides in the implementation of the `WhoisBean` class.

Another noteworthy aspect of this example is the use of a text area for displaying the results of the Whois lookup. In this case, the text area form element is used for output rather than input. This was done primarily for stylistic reasons, so that the form as a whole resembles a self-contained window from a conventional desktop application. By presenting the query results in a text area with a fixed size and its own scroll bar, the form itself maintains a fixed size that is more consistent with the behavior of desktop application windows (listing 12.6).

Listing 12.6   Source code for the JSP Whois form

```
<%@page import="com.taglib.wdjsp.byexample.*" %>
<jsp:useBean id="whois" class="WhoisBean" scope="session">
  <jsp:setProperty name="whois" property="serverList"
```

```
      value="whois.internic.net,whois.register.com"/>
</jsp:useBean>
<jsp:setProperty name="whois" property="*"/>
<HTML>
<HEAD><TITLE>Whois Client</TITLE></HEAD>
<BODY BGCOLOR="white">
<TABLE bgcolor="tan" align="center" border="1" cellpadding="10">
<FORM action="<%= HttpUtils.getRequestURL(request) %>" method="GET">
<TR><TD>
<INPUT type="submit" value="Whois">
<INPUT type="text" name="query" SIZE="20"
 value="<jsp:getProperty name="whois" property="query"/>">
 
<B>Record Types:</B>
<SELECT name="options" SIZE="1">
<OPTION <%= whois.getOptions().equals("")?"selected":"" %>
  VALUE="">All
<OPTION <%= whois.getOptions().equals("Do")?"selected":"" %>
VALUE="Do">Domain Only
<OPTION <%= whois.getOptions().equals("Person")?"selected":"" %>
VALUE="Person">People Only
<OPTION <%= whois.getOptions().equals("Organization")?"selected":"" %>
 VALUE="Organization">Organizations Only
</SELECT>
<P></P>
<B>Whois Server:</B>
<INPUT TYPE="RADIO" NAME="serverList"
<%= whois.getServerList().equals("whois.internic.net,whois.register.com")
    ?"checked":"" %> VALUE="whois.internic.net,whois.register.com">
Both  
<INPUT TYPE="RADIO" NAME="serverList"
<%= whois.getServerList().equals("whois.register.com")
    ?"checked":"" %>
VALUE="whois.register.com">
Register.com  
<INPUT TYPE="RADIO" NAME="serverList"
<%= whois.getServerList().equals("whois.internic.net")?"checked":"" %>
VALUE="whois.internic.net">
Network Solutions
<P></P>
<TEXTAREA rows="24" cols="80">
<jsp:getProperty name="whois" property="results"/>
</TEXTAREA>
</TD></TR>
</TABLE>
</FORM>
</BODY>
</HTML>
```

12.5 *An index generator*

In this example we'll build a JSP page which generates an index of the files in its directory. It is typical for a web server to look for a welcome file, a default filename to display if a browser requests a directory, rather than a specific file. Typically this file is called index.html, but JSP web servers can of course be configured to look for the presence of an index.jsp file, and load that instead. Most web servers have some built-in mechanism to generate a file listing for directories that do not have an appropriate welcome file. Typically, these look like a raw directory listing, with anchors to each file, allowing you to browse the file tree without having to create your own index pages.

In this example, we'll create our own index.jsp page which can be used as a replacement to your web server's built-in directory listing mechanism. We'll add a number of new features over the average web server, including icons that are sensitive to the type of items in the directory, and alphabetical sorting. Now even if you're happy with the directory listings created by your web server, there are a number of advantages to rolling your own. First, you have complete control of the look and feel of your page—you can make it look as fancy as you'd like. You can also add your own security, filtering, or other options to your index page. An example of the page we created is shown in figure 12.6.

12.5.1 *A basic implementation*

First, let's create a very basic index which provides an equivalent bare-bones implementation like that provided by most web servers by default. This will help us understand the concepts without being overburdened by the decorative details for now.

Directory independence

One of the initially tricky things about this example is achieving directory independence. We didn't want to have to hard code the directory path, the document root, or other directory location dependent information into the page, modifying them for each directory we wanted to enable with our index generator. Ideally, we can have one copy of the index page, shared by all of our directories.

To use our autoindexing JSP page, we'll configure the web server to look for index.jsp (or whatever we would like to call this welcome page). We'll store the index page in a shared directory as `/utils/index.jsp`. We will then create a link or copy of the page called index.jsp pointing to this index file from every directory we want to use it. Some web servers will let you specify an absolute path to your

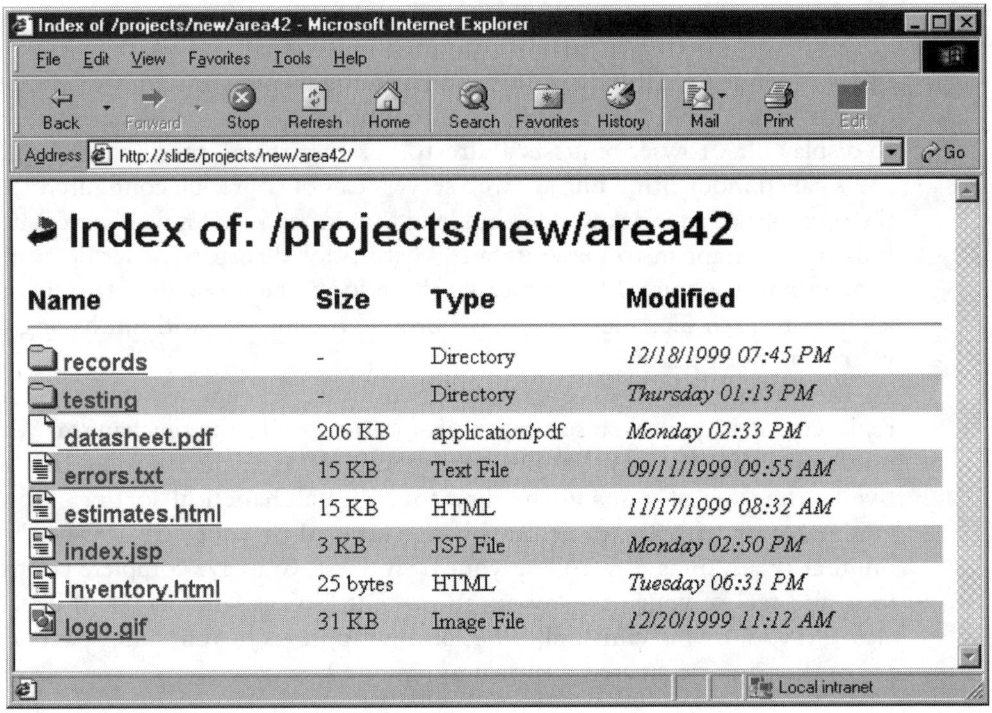

Figure 12.6 Our new and improved index in action

welcome file, allowing you to use the same file for all directories, eliminating the need for the link.

We therefore have to make the page itself determine both the logical path that the user sees, as well as the physical path to the directory in order to access details about its files. The first thing then, is to determine the logical path to the current directory. This can be done by examining the request:

```
String cd = new File(request.getRequestURI()).getParent();
```

The request will return something like `/projects/stuff/index.jsp`. We'll temporarily convert this string into a `File` object, so we can utilize its `getParent()` method, which chops of the last bit of the path to yield `/projects/stuff`. (The `File` object's constructor doesn't care if the file exists or not, it can still manipulate the filenames in a platform independent manner). We then use the `getRealPath()` method of the `application` object to locate the physical directory beneath the server's document root.

```
File realPath = new File(application.getRealPath(cd));
```

Now we're home free. We use the `listFiles()` method of the `File` object (a method new to Java 2) to retrieve an array of `File` objects corresponding to each file in that directory. We can then loop through this list, and interrogate each file for its information, displaying them in a table.

```
File[] files = realPath.listFiles();
for (int i=0; i < files.length; i++) {
  // display file info
}
```

The complete source code for this simple indexer is shown in listing 12.7 and a screen shot in figure 12.7.

Listing 12.7   Source code for simpleindex.jsp

```
<%@ page import="java.io.*,java.util.*" %>
<%
  String cd = new File(request.getRequestURI()).getParent();
  File realPath = new File(application.getRealPath(cd));
%>
<html>
<body>
Index of: <%= cd %><p>
<table border="0" cellpadding="0" cellspacing="0" width="100%">
<tr><td>Name</td><td>Size</td><td>Modified</td></tr>
<tr><td colspan="3"><hr></td></tr>
<%
  File[] files = realPath.listFiles();
  for (int i=0; i < files.length; i++) {
%>
<tr>
<td><a href="<%= files[i].getName() %>">
<%= files[i].getName() %></a></td>
<td><%= files[i].length() %></td>
<td><i><%= new Date(files[i].lastModified()) %></i></td>
</tr>
<% } %>
</table>
</body>
</html>
```

As you can see, implementing the basic functionality was easy. Now we'll get fancy and add improvements over most built-in indexes.

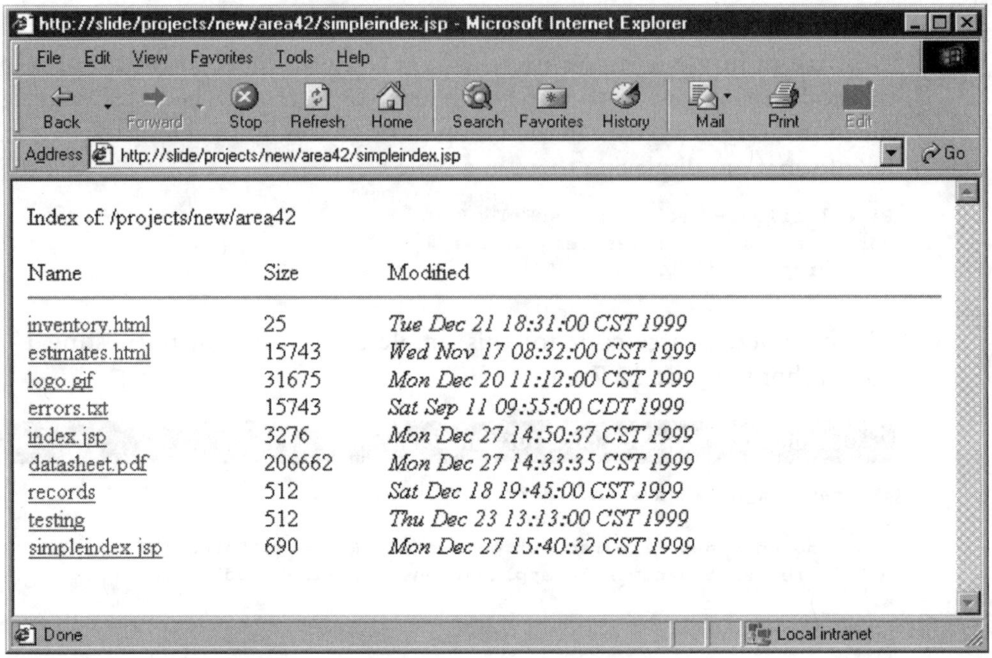

Figure 12.7   A simple index

12.5.2 *An improved version*

The source code for the final page is shown in listing 12.8; the screen shot in figure 12.6 was generated from this source, which is greatly enhanced over the simple example in listing 12.7. Other than basic HTML formatting, most of the work to make our index more useful comes from better interpreting information about each file. The raw dates, file sizes, and ordering returned from the underlying operating system are not necessarily the most convenient way to display that data. Therefore, as you see, we've created a number of utility methods.

Listing 12.8   Source code for autoindex.jsp

```
<%@ page import="java.io.*,java.util.*,java.text.*" %>
<%
  String cd = new File(request.getRequestURI()).getParent();
  File realPath = new File(application.getRealPath(cd));
%>
<html>
<head><title>Index of <%= cd %></title></head>
```

```
<body bgcolor="White">
<% if (! cd.equals("/")) { %>
<a href=".."><img src="/icons/back.gif" border="0"></a> 
<% } %>
<font face="arial" size="+3"><b>Index of: <%= cd %></b></font><p>

<table border="0" cellpadding="0" cellspacing="0" width="100%">
<tr>
<td><font size="+1" face="arial"><b>Name</b></font></td>
<td><font size="+1" face="arial"><b>Size</b></font></td>
<td><font size="+1" face="arial"><b>Type</b></font></td>
<td><font size="+1" face="arial"><b>Modified</b></font></td>
</tr>
<tr><td colspan="4"><hr></td></tr>
<%
  File[] files = sort(realPath.listFiles());
  String[] colors = { "white", "#cccccc" };
  for (int i=0; i < files.length; i++) {
%>
<tr bgcolor="<%= colors[i % 2] %>"><td>
<a href="<%= getName(files[i]) %>">
<img src="<%= getIcon(files[i]) %>" border="0">
<font face="arial"><b><%= getName(files[i]) %></b></font></a></td>
<td><%= getSize(files[i]) %></td>
<td><%= getType(files[i]) %></td>
<td><i><%= getDate(files[i]) %></i></td>
</tr>
<% } %>
</table>

</body>
</html>

<%!

private File[] sort(File[] files) {
  Arrays.sort(files);
  List dirs  = new ArrayList(files.length);
  List other = new ArrayList(files.length);
  for (int i=0; i < files.length; i++) {
    if (files[i].isDirectory())
      dirs.add(files[i]);
    else
      other.add(files[i]);
  }
  dirs.addAll(other);
  return (File[])dirs.toArray(files);
}

private String getName(File file) {
```

```
        return file.getName();
    }

    private String getIcon(File file) {
      if (file.isDirectory()) return "/icons/folder.gif";
      if (file.toString().endsWith(".jsp")) return "/icons/html.gif";
      String type = getServletContext().getMimeType(file.toString());
      if (type == null) return "/icons/unknown.gif";
      if (type.equals("text/html")) return "/icons/html.gif";
      if (type.startsWith("text/")) return "/icons/text.gif";
      if (type.startsWith("image/")) return "/icons/image2.gif";
      return "/icons/generic.gif";
    }

    private String getType(File file) {
      if (file.isDirectory()) return "Directory";
      if (file.toString().endsWith(".jsp")) return "JSP File";
      String type = getServletContext().getMimeType(file.toString());
      if (type == null) return "Unknown";
      if (type.equals("text/html")) return "HTML";
      if (type.startsWith("text/")) return "Text File";
      if (type.startsWith("image/")) return "Image File";
      return type;
    }

    private String getSize(File file) {
      if (file.isDirectory()) return ("-");
      long size = file.length();
      if (size > 1000)
        return ((size / 1000) + " KB");
      return size + " bytes";
    }

    private String getDate(File file) {
      String pattern = "";
      Calendar now = Calendar.getInstance();
      now.roll(Calendar.DATE, true);
      now.add(Calendar.DATE, -7);
      Date fileDate = new Date(file.lastModified());
      if (fileDate.before(now.getTime()))
        pattern = "MM/dd/yyyy hh:mm a";
      else
        pattern = "EEEE hh:mm a";
      SimpleDateFormat formatter;
      formatter = new SimpleDateFormat(pattern);
      return formatter.format(fileDate);
    }
%>
```

Creating color bars

We made each row easier to see by alternating the background color of our table rows with each time through the loop. This is a useful technique that can be applied to any iterative situation. We do this by selecting one color for the odd rows, and another for the even rows. We first create a two-element array, the first color will be used on even numbered rows (those divisible by 2) and the second will be used by odd numbered rows. Since we'll be using these values inside HTML, any valid HTML color value can be used, for example, to get white and gray bars we would use this:

```
String[] colors = { "white", "#cccccc" };
```

To display a color, we simply take the remainder (using the modulo operator) of the index counter divided by 2. Even numbered rows will have a remainder of 0, corresponding to the first element of our `colors` array while the odd numbered ones will have a remainder of 1.

```
<tr bgcolor="<%= colors[i % 2] %>"><td>
```

Sorting the files

One annoying aspect about our first implementation of this application is that all of the directories and files are displayed in a jumbled order. We'll fix that by sorting the files by name, with directories listed first. This operation is performed in the `sort()` method. We simply sort the entire array of files first, then extract directories and files to separate arrays. This gives us a sorted set of files, and a sorted set of directories; we simply put the two arrays together, directories first.

Determining the file type and selecting an icon

We can use the `application.getMimeType()` method to determine the type of file with which we are dealing. This method relies on the file's extension and the server's configuration to assign a MIME type. In the `getType()` method, we determine the MIME type directly, and in the `getIcon()` method we choose an appropriate icon. If we wanted to get fancy, we could easily group like files together in the listing by sorting on their respective types.

WARNING From scriptlets in the page we can use the `application` implicit object to gain reference to the current servlet context. However, inside a page's declared methods (such as our `getType()` method in this example) the implicit objects are not defined, and we can only use the methods provided by the Servlet and JSP APIs. The current `PageContext` instance, obtainable through the `getPageContext()` method, can be used to access any of the implicit objects available to the page.

A more flexible modification date

To make our dates a little more relevant, we decided that any date younger than a week would be shown simply as being modified on the day of the week, rather than the full date. Therefore, something modified on Monday of this week at 4:00 says "Mon 4:00pm" instead of "Monday, January 10, 2000 4:00:00 pm."

Cleaning up file size

We also wanted to convert file size information from a confusing byte format, to terms of kilobytes and megabytes. We simply divide by the appropriate numbers to convert bytes to the appropriate format. This is done in the `getSize()` method.

12.5.3 Going further

There are a number of ways to expand on this example. Instead of creating a generic index, you could create a more topical one, using the JSP to automatically generate a table of contents for a particular directory to save you the hassle of updating it, for example. You could also add more features to the listing, such as the ability to view, delete, or edit the files in the listing. You could use native methods to retrieve ownership information (if supported by your OS) and other details.

12.6 A button to view JSP source

One thing about JSP development that can be a bit confusing at first is that if you attempt to use the browser's view source feature to look at the HTML behind the JSP page you are visiting you will see the rendered HTML, rather than the JSP code you might first expect. This, of course, is because the JSP code is processed by the server into HTML—the browser never sees the original JSP code. In this example, we'll build a button and a bookmark that allow you to view the original JSP source that lies behind the current HTML page. This restores our ability to look at source code on the fly, without having to have direct access to the web server. Figure 12.8 shows our source code viewer in action.

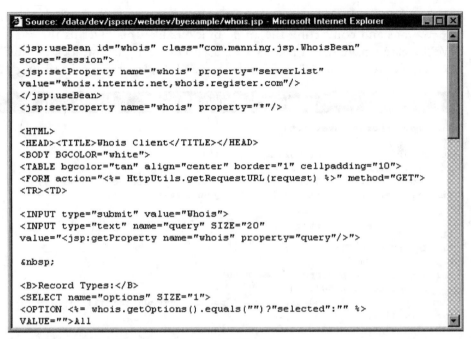

Figure 12.8   Viewing JSP source from a browser

12.6.1 Displaying the source

This isn't, as it turns out, very complicated—but unfortunately it's more complicated than it should be. All we have to do in theory is calculate the URL of the page we are looking at, and then use the `application.getRealPath()` method to determine the path to the actual file on the server. Knowing the location of the original JSP page, we simply load the contents of the file, set the `contentType` attribute of the page to a value of `text/plain` (so that the page doesn't render HTML tags), and display the contents of the file to the screen. However, some browsers blatantly ignore the server-specified content type of the page, instead attempting to guess the format. The presence of any HTML tags in the contents of the page will cause such browsers to go ahead and render it as HTML, regardless of the server's insistence that it should be shown as text.

So we have to eliminate the HTML tags from the file, but, of course, deleting them would defeat the purpose of this project, so that won't work. What we do then is bend to the browser and display everything in HTML, but convert the angle brackets of HTML tags (and the ampersands of existing entity tags) into their

HTML entity forms: <, >, and &. Wrapping the file contents between
<pre> tags and converting the angle brackets like this gives us the source code.
We'll create a page which takes a URL as a request argument, locates the file, con-
verts its contents into HTML friendly text, and displays the results (listing 12.9).

Listing 12.9 Source code for viewsource.jsp

```jsp
<%@ page import="java.io.*" %>
<%
String url = request.getParameter("url");
if (url.indexOf("..") > -1)
  throw new java.io.IOException("Relative paths are not allowed");
File realPath = new File(application.getRealPath(url));
%>
<html><head><title>Source: <%= url %></title></head><body><pre>
<%
FileInputStream fis = null;
try {
  fis = new FileInputStream(realPath);
  BufferedReader reader;
  reader = new BufferedReader(new InputStreamReader(fis));
  String line;
  while ((line = reader.readLine()) != null) {
    line = replace(line, "&", "&amp;");
    line = replace(line, "<", "&lt;");
    line = replace(line, ">", "&gt;");
    out.println(line);
  }
}
catch (IOException e) {
  out.println("IOException: " + e.getMessage());
}
finally { if (fis != null) fis.close(); }
%>
</pre></body></html>
<%!
public String replace(String s, String old, String replacement) {
    int i = s.indexOf(old);
    StringBuffer r = new StringBuffer();
    if (i == -1) return s;
    r.append(s.substring(0,i) + replacement);
    if (i + old.length() < s.length())
      r.append(replace(s.substring(i + old.length(), s.length()),
        old, replacement));
    return r.toString();
}
%>
```

12.6.2 *Limitations of the view source program*

There are limitations to this approach however. Since we are relying on the application object's ability to determine the actual path to our JSP file, the application will only be able to handle JSP pages on the same server as itself. In fact, it will only be able to handle JSPs in the same application as itself. If you are using multiple servers or your server has multiple JSP applications installed, you will have to have multiple copies of the JSP page.

12.6.3 *Adding a view source button to a page*

As you can see, this code must be passed to the URL of the page for which we are interested in seeing the source, through the `url` request parameter. To make it as easy as possible, we'll create another JSP page, vsbutton.jsp, which contains the necessary form elements and JSP code to add an HTML form button to the page (listing 12.10).

Listing 12.10   Source code for vsbutton.jsp

```
<%@ page import="java.io.*,java.util.*,java.text.*" %>
<% String me = request.getRequestURI(); %>
<script language="JavaScript">
function show(url) {
  opts="height=400,width=600,scrollbars=yes,resizable=yes"
  window.open("viewsource.jsp?url=" + escape(url), "src", opts);
}
</script>
<form><div align="right">
<input type="button" value="View Source"
onClick="show('<%= me %>')"></div>
</form>
```

We can then include this page into any other page to which we wish to add the button. It will appear wherever we like on the page, and clicking it will display the source code for the page in its own little window, thanks to JavaScript.

```
<jsp:include page="vsbutton.jsp" flush="true"/>
```

This is cool, but it requires us to add a line of code to each and every page for which we would like to view source. That's not real handy, and we can do better.

12.6.4 *Viewing source through a bookmark*

To avoid adding code to each page, we can encapsulate our request into a JavaScript URL which we can add to our browser's bookmark list. Clicking the bookmark will pop up a window displaying the source code of the current page, just as our button did. This works because a JavaScript URL in a bookmark is executed in the context of the current document, meaning it can determine the document location, which it passes to the original viewsource.jsp page through the url parameter (listing 12.11).

Listing 12.11   Source code for jsvvs.html

```
<html>
<body>Right Click and add to Boomarks/Favorites:
<a href="javascript:void
window.open('/utils/viewsource.jsp?url='+escape(location.pathname),
'src','height=400,width=600,scrollbars=yes,resizable=yes');">
View JSP Source</a>
</body>
</html>
```

Creating custom tags

## 13

This chapter covers

- How custom tags work
- Constructing tag libraries and tag library descriptors
- Java classes for implementing custom tags
- Custom tag examples for content substitution and content translation

Custom tags are among the most recent features added to JSP. While the `taglib` directive was introduced in version 1.0 of the JSP specification, the Java classes that could be used to implement custom tags in a portable fashion were not added until version 1.1. In this chapter, we discuss both the use and implementation of custom tags for JSP. We start by examining their role and capabilities, and provide an overview of how they work. We next take a look at the set of Java classes and interfaces provided by JSP for developing custom tags, and then demonstrate their features by applying them to the implementation of basic custom tags. These, in combination with the advanced custom tags to be presented in chapter 14, will form the basis of a small library for demonstrating their use in a series of example pages.

13.1 *Role of custom tags*

As discussed in chapter 1, a key advantage of JSP over many of the other commonly used dynamic content systems is its ability to separate presentation from implementation through the use of HTML-like tags. By avoiding the use of JSP elements that embed scripting language code in the page, maintenance of JSP pages is greatly simplified, and the opportunity to reuse the Java code that provides the underlying functionality is preserved.

Unfortunately, JSP provides only three built-in actions for interacting with Java-Beans objects: `<jsp:useBean>`, `<jsp:getProperty>`, and `<jsp:setProperty>`. With the exception of these three Bean tags, the only standard means provided by JSP for accessing arbitrary Java code are the scripting elements (i.e., scriptlets and expressions). If the needs of your application cannot be met via the standard Bean tags, it would appear that the need to embed Java code in the page is unavoidable.

Fortunately, JSP provides custom tags as an extension mechanism for adding new action tags. As such, custom tag libraries can be written to provide added functionality for a JSP application without having to resort to the use of Java code within your JSP pages.

Similarly, as pointed out in chapter 1, it is undesirable to implement dynamic HTML generation via JavaBeans properties, because Beans are intended to be stand-alone components that are independent of the type of application within which they are used. Dynamic HTML generation is a fairly uncommon requirement outside of the context of JSP, suggesting that Beans which generate HTML may be too closely tied to a specific application.

On the other hand, custom tags are explicitly designed to add functionality to JSP pages, including the dynamic generation of page content such as HTML. If you need to generate HTML content programmatically via Java, custom tags are an ideal implementation technique. Custom tags can be used to insert text into the page, and also to implement flow of control. Attributes can be specified for custom tags, as parameters that influence their behavior. Custom tags can be empty or have bodies, which contain either nested JSP elements (including other custom tags) or tag-specific content to be processed by the tag itself. Custom tags can also interact with each other, either by requesting information through the hierarchy of nested tags, or by introducing new scripting variables which may be accessed by subsequent custom tags, as well as by the standard JSP scripting elements.

As with all other JSP features, custom tags are implemented via Java objects. Developers who are creating their own custom tags do so by creating Java classes that produce the desired functionality. As such, custom tags can access the full range of Java APIs. For example, custom tags can employ the JDBC classes to make database calls, or use the JavaMail API to send or receive electronic mail.

Of course, embedding too much functionality into custom tags has its disadvantages. In particular, since custom tags are only meant to be accessed from JSP pages, any operations built into the implementation of these tags can be used only from JSP. To promote reusability, it is preferable to implement the generic functionality via JavaBeans, and use custom tags for controlling presentation and translating between Bean properties and methods and the page markup language.

The implication, then, is that there are no limits on the types of behavior that can be implemented via custom tags. If you have need for a specific computational task to be accomplished on a JSP page, an implementation based on a combination of custom tags and JavaBeans can be developed which maintains a strong separation between presentation and implementation.

13.2 *How tag libraries work*

As described in chapter 3, a JSP page that uses custom tags must first load the libraries containing those custom tags by means of the `taglib` directive. Two attributes must be specified with this directive, a URL indicating the location of the TLD file for the library, described below, and a string specifying a page-specific XML namespace for the library's tags.

When the JSP container is compiling a page that uses a custom tag library, its first response to the `taglib` directive is to determine whether or not it needs to load the corresponding TLD (figure 13.1). If this is the first time the specified library has been requested by a page, the JSP container will read the TLD from the indicated URI. If, however, the specified library has been encountered before, such as during

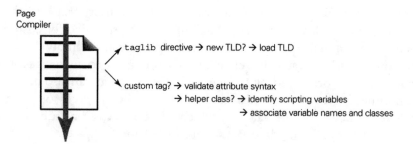

Page
Compiler

taglib directive → new TLD? → load TLD

custom tag? → validate attribute syntax
          → helper class? → identify scripting variables
                        → associate variable names and classes

Figure 13.1   Page compilation steps for custom tags

compilation of another page that uses the same library, the TLD will not be loaded a second time.

A tag library is typically packaged as a JAR file, which in turn contains the class files that implement the library's tags. If you are familiar with the JAR format, then you know that, in addition to Java class files, a JAR file includes a top-level directory named META-INF that stores information about the archive itself. For example, standard JAR files include a file named MANIFEST.MF in this META-INF directory that contains a listing of all of the files in the archive, along with authentication data that may be used to verify the archive's integrity. JAR files representing JSP tag libraries must also include a file named taglib.tld in

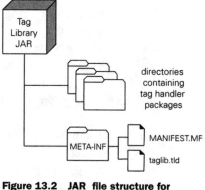

Figure 13.2   JAR file structure for custom tag libraries

this directory, which holds a copy of the library's TLD (figure 13.2). The TLD is an XML document that identifies and describes the custom tags provided by the library.

You may recall from chapter 10 that a copy of the TLD also resides in the WEB-INF/tlds directory associated with the application making use of the tag library. The name used for this copy is arbitrary. The application's web.xml deployment descriptor is used to designate a URI for this copy of the TLD, and it is this URI that is referenced in the uri attribute of the taglib directive within the application's JSP pages.

NOTE   When naming the TLD stored in the `WEB-INF/tlds` subdirectory, the convention is to use the name of the library, the current version number, and the same .tld extension as the copy in the library's JAR file. For version 1.7 of a library named `EncomTags`, for example, this TLD would typically be named EncomTags_1_7.tld.

While compiling a page, the JSP container need only examine the TLD in order to validate most of the page's custom tags. This is because the TLD fully specifies each tag's attributes, including which are required and which are optional, as well as whether or not the tag supports body content (and what the body may contain). Each custom tag encountered while the page is being compiled can be compared against the corresponding specification in the TLD to make sure that the syntax of the tag call is correct. Thus, there is no need to unpack and load the implementation class for the tag in order to check its syntax.

If a custom tag is used to introduce new scripting variables, however, some additional work must be done. In this case, the TLD specifies a helper class that can be loaded by the JSP container to identify the names and types of the scripting variables introduced by a specific occurrence of the custom tag. This helper class can also be used to perform additional validation of the custom tag, beyond the simple syntax checks described earlier. For example, if the attributes of a custom tag have mutual dependencies between them, the helper class can be used to check the values specified for those attributes to ensure those dependencies are satisfied.

These helper classes, because they have limited functionality, are often much smaller than the tag implementation classes with which they are associated. In fact, their small size—and the resulting efficiency in their use—is their primary reason for existence. Since the page compilation servlet can get all of the information it needs about a page's custom tags from a combination of the TLD and the helper classes identified by the TLD, it can compile a page much more efficiently than if it had to load the classes which actually implement the custom tags.

Thus, by using the result of the TLD syntax validation, along with the information provided by any helper classes associated with a page's custom tags, the JSP container is able to compile the page into a servlet. As with other JSP pages, this servlet is then run whenever a request is received for the corresponding JSP page. It is when the servlet is actually run, as depicted in figure 13.3, that the tag implementation classes—commonly referred to as *tag handlers*—are unpacked from their library's JAR file, loaded into the container's JVM, and executed.

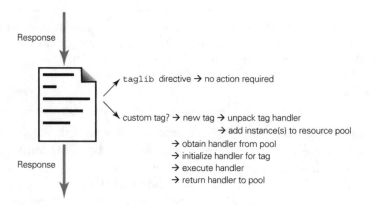

Response

taglib directive → no action required

custom tag? → new tag → unpack tag handler
→ add instance(s) to resource pool
→ obtain handler from pool
→ initialize handler for tag
→ execute handler
→ return handler to pool

Response

Figure 13.3   Request-time processing of custom tags

As another concession to run-time efficiency, custom tag handlers are stored in a shared resource pool. As a result, instances of the tag handler classes are reused by the JSP container as it processes pages, rather than creating an instance each time the corresponding tag is encountered on a page. Because object instantiation is one of the most expensive operations performed by the JVM, the reuse of tag handlers afforded by using such a resource pool can result in significant run time efficiency when processing pages that make heavy use of custom tags.

Implementing a custom JSP tag, then, requires two major components: the class that implements its handler, and a corresponding entry for the TLD of the library that includes the tag. In the case of tags that define new scripting variables, or which need additional validation beyond the standard syntax checking, a helper class must also be defined. The various classes, along with the completed TLD are then packaged into a JAR file for deployment to JSP containers.

13.3   *Tag library descriptors*

The TLD is an XML document, and, as such, it must include the standard XML header information, including specification of its DTD. The appropriate header for a JSP tag library descriptor is as follows:

```
<?xml version="1.0" encoding="ISO-8859-1" ?>
<!DOCTYPE taglib PUBLIC
 "-//Sun Microsystems, Inc.//DTD JSP Tag Library 1.1//EN"
 "http://java.sun.com/j2ee/dtds/web-jsptaglib_1_1.dtd">
```

As you can see from its URL, the standard DTD for TLD files is maintained by Sun Microsystems and stored with the other J2EE DTDs on the `java.sun.com` web-server.

The root element for a TLD is the `<taglib>` element, which supports several subelements. One of these, the `<tag>` element, supports it own subelements and is used to specify the library's tags. The other subelements specify properties of the library itself.

13.3.1 *Library elements*

Five `<taglib>` subelements are provided for describing the library, as in the following TLD fragment:

```
<taglib>
    <tlibversion>1.0</tlibversion>
    <jspversion>1.1</jspversion>
    <shortname>mut</shortname>
    <info>Utility tags for JSP.</info>
    <uri>http://www.taglib.com/wdjsp/tlds/mut_1_0.tld</uri>
    ...
</taglib>
```

None of these elements has attributes. Their values are specified only through the element bodies. Of these five, only the `<tlibversion>` and `<shortname>` elements are required.

The `<tlibversion>` element is used to provide a version number for the tag library. As new versions of a tag library are released, the version number should be increased so that pages and tools which interact with the tag library can be aware of version information and any related compatibility issues. The full format for version numbers is *N.N.N.N*, where each *N* is a single-digit integer. In the case where *N*=0 and all subsequent *N*s are zero, they may be omitted, but under no circumstances may the major version number (i.e., the *N* preceding the first period) be omitted.

The `<jspversion>` element indicates the version of the JSP specification with which the tag library is compatible. The default value is `1.1`, the first version of the specification that fully supports custom tag libraries.

The `<shortname>` tag is used to specify an abbreviated name for the tag library. Because it will be made available to the JSP container and JSP development tools for the creation of variable names, it is required to begin with an alphabetic character and contain no white space characters. It may also serve as the default namespace prefix for the tag library when used by JSP development tools in the authoring of pages.

The `<info>` element is used to supply a documentation string for the custom tag library. The default value is the empty string.

The optional `<uri>` element is provided as an additional source of documentation for tag libraries. The body of this tag is used to specify a URL pointing to a publicly available copy of the TLD for the current version of the library, against which other copies may be verified. This feature is particularly useful for JSP developers who make their custom tag libraries available over the Internet for use by others. Page authors who make use of such third-party libraries can then consult this element of the TLD whenever they need to refer back to the software's original source.

13.3.2 *Tag elements*

The `<taglib>` element of a TLD is also required to specify one or more `<tag>` subelements. There will be one `<tag>` specification for each custom tag defined in the library. The `<tag>` element itself supports five subelements for specifying the properties of the tag, as well as a sixth for specifying the tag's attributes, if any. The tag property subelements are demonstrated in the following TLD fragment:

```
<tag>
    <name>forProperty</name>
    <tagclass>com.taglib.wdjsp.mut.ForPropertyTag</tagclass>
    <teiclass>com.taglib.wdjsp.mut.ForPropertyTEI</teiclass>
    <bodycontent>JSP</bodycontent>
    <info>
      Loop through an indexed property.
    </info>
    ...
</tag>
```

Of these five subelements, only the `<name>` and `<tagclass>` elements are required.

The `<name>` element is used to specify an identifier for the tag, which will be used in combination with the library's namespace prefix to name the tag when it is used on a JSP page. For the example shown here, then, a JSP page using this tag's library with a prefix of mut would call this tag using the name `<mut:forProperty>`.

The `<tagclass>` element is used to specify the class that implements the handler for this tag, fully qualified with its package name. The `<teiclass>` element is used to specify the helper class for this tag, if any. The name of this element is derived from the `javax.servlet.jsp.tagext.TagExtraInfo` class, which is the base class that all tag handler helper classes must extend.

The next `<tag>` subelement, `<bodycontent>`, is used to indicate the type of body content that may appear between opening and closing tags of the current type. The three valid values for this element are empty, JSP, and tagdependent. The empty value indicates that no body content is supported by the tag, while the JSP value indicates that additional JSP elements (including other custom tags) may appear within the body of the tag. In both cases, the JSP container will perform syntax validation on the body of the tag when it is encountered during normal page compilation.

If the value of the `<bodycontent>` element is `tagdependent`, the body of the tag is expected to be interpreted by the tag itself. For example, a custom tag for executing database queries might specify the query as its body content, as follows:

```
<db:query connection=conn>
   SELECT ID, SALARY FROM EMPLOYEES WHERE SALARY > 50000
</db:query>
```

As formulated here, the body of this tag is an SQL statement. Since the query is to be interpreted by the tag (presumably by means of JDBC), the TLD specification for this tag should specify a value of `tagdependent` for its `<bodycontent>` element.

The fifth `<tag>` subelement for specifying tag properties is `<info>`. This element is used to specify a documentation string for the tag.

13.3.3 *Attribute elements*

If a custom tag takes attributes, these are specified using the `<attribute>` element, which is the sixth subelement supported by the `<tag>` element. The `<attribute>` element itself has three subelements, as in the following TLD fragment:

```
<tag>
   ...
   <attribute>
      <name>id</name>
      <required>true</required>
      <rtexprvalue>false</rtexprvalue>
   </attribute>
   ...
</tag>
```

There will be one `<attribute>` element for each of the tag's attributes. Only the `<name>` subelement is required, the other two are optional.

The `<name>` element, used to identify the attribute, represents the string that will be used to name the attribute when it appears in a tag. For the example shown here, if it were associated with the example tag presented in the previous section, the attribute and its value would be specified as:

```
<mut:forProperty id="loopVar">
```

Because it will be used in this manner, the attribute name should begin with an alphabetic character, and should not contain any white space characters.

The `<required>` element indicates whether the attribute is required or optional. Required attributes must be explicitly specified whenever the associated tag appears. The permitted values for this element are `true` and `false`. The default value is `false`, indicating that the attribute is optional.

The `<rtexprvalue>` element indicates whether or not a request-time attribute value may be used to specify the attribute's value when it appears in the tag. As with the `<required>` element, the permitted values for this element are `true` and `false`. When this element is set to `false` (the default), only fixed, static values may be specified for the attribute, as for the `id` attribute in the previous example. When this element is set to `true`, a JSP expression may be used to specify the value to be assigned to the attribute, as in the following example tag:

```
<mut:item text="<%= cookies[i].getName() %>"/>
```

13.4 API overview

All of the classes and interfaces provided by JSP for implementing tag handlers and helper classes are in the `javax.servlet.jsp.tagext` package. This package also includes three auxiliary classes used by the JSP container in interpreting the contents of a TLD.

13.4.1 Tag handlers

Tag handlers are the Java objects that perform the action associated with a custom tag. When a request is received by the JSP container for a page containing custom tags, each time a custom tag is encountered, an instance of the corresponding tag handler is obtained. The tag handler is initialized according to any attribute values explicitly set by the tag on the page, and then various methods of the tag handler are called to perform the corresponding action. Once the action has been performed, the tag handler is returned to a resource pool for reuse.

The methods that the tag handler must support in order to perform the custom action are proscribed by the `javax.servlet.jsp.tagext.Tag` and `javax.servlet.jsp.tagext.BodyTag` interfaces. By specifying tag handlers in terms of interfaces, JSP allows developers to turn existing classes, which may already have a well-defined inheritance hierarchy, into tag handlers. If you will be developing tag handlers from scratch, however, your task will be simplified by using one of the two tag handler base classes also available in the `javax.servlet.jsp.tagext` package, named `TagSupport` and `BodyTagSupport`. These classes provide default implementations for all of the methods in the corresponding interfaces, so that you will only have to redefine those methods that require custom behavior in order to implement the desired action.

At this point, you may be wondering why there are two different tag handler interfaces. The reason is that, in practice, tags which manipulate their body content tend to be more complicated than tags which are either empty or just pass the contents of the tag body straight through to the page. In recognition of this, the `BodyTag` interface and the corresponding `BodyTagSupport` class are geared toward the implementation of tags that need to process their body content in some manner, while the `Tag` interface and the `TagSupport` class are geared toward the simpler case. There are thus fewer methods required by the `Tag` interface. Of course, both types of tag handlers must provide the same base functionality. As a result of this underlying commonality, `BodyTag` is implemented as an extension of the `Tag` interface. The `BodyTagSupport` class is likewise a subclass of `TagSupport`.

The life cycle of a tag handler implementing the `Tag` interface is depicted in figure 13.4. The first step is to obtain an

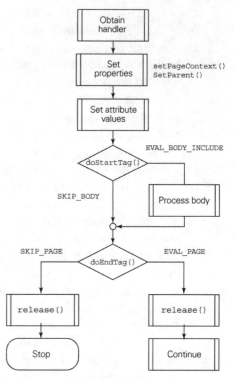

Figure 13.4   Life cycle of handlers implementing the Tag interface

instance of the appropriate class, either from the tag handler resource pool or, if no instances are currently available, by creating one. Next, various tag handler properties are set. First, the handler's `setPageContext()` method is called by the JSP container to assign it the appropriate `PageContext` object (see chapter 3 for a description of the `PageContext` class). Next, the handler's `setParent()` method is called. This provides access to the tag handler instance, if any, within whose body the current handler appears.

After these properties have been set, the attribute values specified by the tag, if any, are set. Tag attributes are handled like JavaBeans properties, via accessor methods defined by the tag handler class. A custom tag attribute named `id`, for instance, should have corresponding getter and setter methods: `getId()` and `setId()`, or equivalents specified via an associated `BeanInfo` class. These setter methods are called by the JSP container to assign the attribute values specified in the tag to the corresponding tag handler instance.

The JSP container next calls the tag handler's `doStartTag()` method. At this point, all of the contextual information needed to execute the tag handler will have been provided by the JSP container (i.e., the tag handler properties and attribute values), so the `doStartTag()` method can begin performing the action associated with its custom tag. This method should return one of two integer values indicating how processing is to proceed. These two possible values are represented by the class variables `Tag.SKIP_BODY` and `Tag.EVAL_BODY_INCLUDE`. `Tag.SKIP_BODY` indicates that the body contents of the tag, if any, should be ignored. `Tag.EVAL_BODY_INCLUDE` indicates that the body contents should be processed normally.

In either case, the next step is to call the handler's `doEndTag()` method. As with the `doStartTag()` method, the actions performed here are tag-specific. Once again, the method is expected to return one of two integer values indicating how processing is to proceed, either `Tag.SKIP_PAGE` or `Tag.EVAL_PAGE`. A return value of `Tag.SKIP_PAGE` from the `doEndTag()` method indicates to the JSP container that processing of the page should be halted immediately. Any further content on the page, both JSP elements and static text, should be ignored and any output generated thus far should be returned to the user's browser. A return value of `Tag.EVAL_PAGE` indicates that page processing should continue normally.

Regardless of the result returned by `doEndTag()`, the final step in the processing of a tag handler is for the JSP container to call the handler's `release()` method. This method gives the tag handler the opportunity to perform cleanup operations—such as resetting its state and releasing any resources it created or obtained while processing the tag—before it is sent to the shared resource pool for subsequent reuse.

As indicated in figure 13.5, the life cycle for tag handlers implementing the `BodyTag` interface has the same general outline, but adds steps for accessing and manipulating the tag's body content.

The process is identical to that shown in figure 13.4, up to the point at which the result of the `doStartTag()` method is returned. For tag handlers implementing the `BodyTag` interface, however, the permitted `doStartTag()` return values are `Tag.SKIP_BODY` and `BodyTag.EVAL_BODY_TAG`. As before, the `Tag.SKIP_BODY` return value indicates that the body content of the tag should be ignored. A return value of `BodyTag.EVAL_BODY_TAG`, however, indicates to the JSP container that, not only should the body content be processed, but that the results of processing it should be stored for further manipulation by the tag handler.

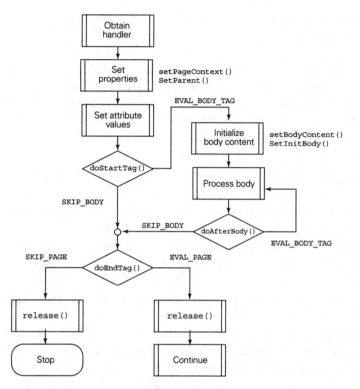

Figure 13.5 Life cycle of handlers implementing the BodyTag interface

The results of processing the body content are stored by means of the Body-Content class. BodyContent is a subclass of JspWriter, an instance of which is used to represent the output stream for the content generated by a JSP page (see chapter 3 for details). Rather than buffer its output for eventual submission to the user's browser, as is the case with JspWriter, the BodyContent class stores its output for use by the tag handler. It is then up to the tag handler to decide whether that output should be discarded or sent to the browser in either its current or some modified form.

In order to process the body content, then, the first step is to create (or obtain from a resource pool) an instance of the BodyContent class. This is assigned to the tag handler by means of its setBodyContent() method. The JSP container then calls the tag handler's doInitBody() method, in order to give the tag handler an opportunity to perform additional initialization steps after the BodyContent instance has been assigned. The body is then processed, with all of its output going to the BodyContent instance.

> **WARNING** While processing the body content of a custom tag which implements the BodyTag interface, the out implicit object, accessible as a scripting variable via the JSP scripting elements, will reference the tag handler's BodyContent instance. After processing of the custom tag is completed, the out implicit object will reference its previous value.

After processing of the body content, the JSP container calls the tag handler's doAfterBody() method. The action performed by this method is typically tag-dependent, and often includes interactions with the tag's BodyContent instance. Like doStartTag(), this method is expected to return either Tag.SKIP_BODY or BodyTag.EVAL_BODY_TAG. If the latter value is returned, then the tag's body content will be processed a second time, after which doAfterBody() will be called once again. Repeated processing of the body content will continue until the doAfterBody() method returns Tag.SKIP_BODY. In this way, custom tags which process their body content iteratively may be implemented.

Once processing of the body content has been skipped (either by doStartTag() or doAfterBody()), control is passed to the tag handler's doEndTag() method. From this point, processing is identical to that of a tag handler implementing the Tag interface.

13.4.2 *Helper classes*

As mentioned earlier, all tag handler helper classes are subclasses of the javax.servlet.jsp.tagext.TagExtraInfo class. When the JSP container is compiling a page that includes a custom tag whose TLD specification includes a <teiclass> entry, the container will create (or obtain from a resource pool) an instance of the indicated helper class. The role of this helper class is two-fold: to provide information about any scripting variables introduced by the tag and/or to perform additional tag validation beyond the automatic syntax validation performed by the page compiler.

To accomplish this, the TagExtraInfo base class specifies two methods that subclasses are expected to override as necessary. The getVariableInfo() method is called to obtain information about scripting variables, while the isValid() method is called to allow the subclass to perform tag-specific validation.

Both of these methods take a single argument, which is an instance of the Tag-Data class. This instance will contain a representation of all of the attribute/value pairs specified in the custom tag being examined. Consider, for example, the following custom tag:

```
<mut:forProperty name="repository" property="faqs"
                id="faq" class="com.taglib.wdjsp.faqtool.FaqBean"/>
```

When calling the helper class associated with this tag (assuming one exists), the `TagData` object would have entries for each of the four specified attributes. The methods defined by the `TagData` class allow the developer to obtain the value associated with a given attribute name. In the particular case of an attribute whose value is specified via a request-time attribute value, these methods will return `TagData.REQUEST_TIME_VALUE` to indicate that no static value is available for use during page compilation. In this way, the `getVariableInfo()` and `isValid()` methods can obtain information about tag attributes in order to perform their required tasks.

The contract of the `isValid()` method is quite straightforward. Given access to the data stored in the supplied `TagData` object, if the custom tag is considered valid, the method should return `true`. Otherwise, the method should return `false`. The default implementation of this method in the `TagExtraInfo` base class simply returns `true`.

This method allows the developer to perform additional checks on the attributes and their values beyond those performed by the page compiler based on the information in the TLD. For example, the TLD can only indicate whether an individual attribute is optional or required. Your tag, however, might have an attribute that is normally optional, but must always appear whenever some other attribute is specified. The TLD does not provide a mechanism for specifying relationships between attributes, so dependencies such as this can only be verified by means of the `isValid()` method.

The `getVariableInfo()` method is a bit more involved. Its task is to return an array of `VariableInfo` instances that specify the scripting variables to be introduced by the corresponding tag. There should be one element in this array for each scripting variable. The default implementation of the `getVariableInfo()` method returns an empty array, indicating that no scripting variables are being introduced.

Four pieces of information are required for each scripting variable, all of which must be specified as arguments to the `VariableInfo` constructor. First, the name of the scripting variable must be specified, as well as the object class for the variable's value. This information is used by the page compiler to resolve variable references appearing later on the page. The variable name is also used by the JSP container when processing requests to find the value of the scripting variable at run time. Values of scripting variables are expected to be stored as attributes of the `PageContext` object associated with the page. The tag handler should set this attribute, from which the JSP container will extract the value of the scripting variable. The container can then make the appropriate assignment and continue processing the request, resolving references to the variable name with the retrieved value.

The next argument to the `VariableInfo` constructor is a boolean flag—referred to as the *declare flag*—that indicates whether the tag is introducing a new variable, or simply assigning a new value to an existing variable. (This is used to determine whether or not the scripting language needs to specify a declaration for the variable.) The fourth and final argument specifies the scope of the scripting variable. In the context of custom tag scripting variables, scope—also referred to as *visibility*—indicates the range of page content over which the variable remains valid, and is specified relative to the locations of the custom tag's start and end tags within the page. Three static variables are provided for specifying scripting variable scope, as follows:

- `VariableInfo.AT_BEGIN`—Indicates that the scripting variable is in scope immediately after the start tag.

- `VariableInfo.AT_END`—Indicates that the scripting variable is not in scope until after the end tag.

- `VariableInfo.NESTED`—Indicates that the scripting variable is in scope only between the start and end tags (i.e., within the body of the tag).

For the `<mut:forProperty>` example tag presented previously, then, the corresponding call to the `VariableInfo` constructor for the indicated attribute values might take the following form:

```
new VariableInfo("faq", "com.taglib.wdjsp.faqtool.FaqBean",
                 true, VariableInfo.NESTED);
```

The resulting `VariableInfo` instance thus specifies a scripting variable named `faq`, whose value will be an instance of the `com.taglib.wdjsp.faqtool.FaqBean` class. The declare flag is set to `true`, indicating that this will be a new variable. Finally, its scope is set to `VariableInfo.NESTED`, indicating that the `faq` scripting variable will only be available between the associated `<mut:forProperty>` start tag and the corresponding `</mut:forProperty>` end tag.

13.4.3 *Auxiliary classes*

There are three auxiliary classes provided by the `javax.servlet.jsp.tagext` package for use by the JSP container to represent the contents of a TLD file. These are `TagLibraryInfo`, `TagInfo`, and `TagAttributeInfo`. Because these classes are intended for use by the JSP container, however, their use by web developers and library implementers is rare.

The `TagLibraryInfo` class stores information on the library as a whole, and provides accessors for retrieving its properties. Among them is a listing of the tags provided by the library, which are represented by instances of the `TagInfo` class. These instances in turn store the set of attributes supported by each tag, which are represented by instances of the `TagAttributeInfo` class. For further details, see appendix E.

13.5   *Example tag library*

To take this discussion of custom tags from the abstract to the concrete, the remainder of this chapter will focus on examples, as will chapter 14. We will examine in detail the implementation of several custom tags, and demonstrate their use within corresponding JSP pages. As discussed earlier in this chapter, use of custom tags within a JSP page first requires the construction of a tag library containing the tag handler classes and the associated TLD. To this end, we will also be packaging up our example tags into a custom tag library.

A well-designed custom tag library will typically contain a focused set of interrelated tags that provide common or integrated functionality. For example, one library might contain a set of debugging tags for use during page development, while another might provide extensions to the standard JSP Bean tags for improved flow control. Alternatively, a set of application-specific tags—for example, custom tags for interacting with the FAQ tool presented in chapter 9—would be a good candidate for a stand-alone tag library.

In order to give the reader exposure to a variety of custom tag examples, the library we will be constructing here will not be quite so unified in purpose. While this library will focus on general-purpose rather than application-specific tags, its tags cover a broad range of functionality, such as debugging, flow control, and extended HTML support. Any one of these areas would be an appropriate domain for a tag library of its own. Combining a few tags from each into a single library is less than ideal, but hopefully acceptable in a pedagogical context such as this. In recognition of the rather mongrel nature of the tag library presented here, it will henceforth be referred to as the Manning Utility Tags library, fittingly abbreviated by the namespace prefix `mut`.

The `TLD for this library is outlined in listing 13.1. The TLD entries for the tags will follow and must be inserted into the TLD in the indicated location in order to provide a complete specification of the tag library.

Listing 13.1   Skeleton TLD for the custom tag library

```
<?xml version="1.0" encoding="ISO-8859-1" ?>
<!DOCTYPE taglib PUBLIC
"-//Sun Microsystems, Inc.//DTD JSP Tag Library 1.1//EN"
"http://java.sun.com/j2ee/dtds/web-jsptaglib_1_1.dtd">
<taglib>
    <tlibversion>1.0</tlibversion>
    <jspversion>1.1</jspversion>
    <shortname>mut</shortname>
    <info>
      Manning Utility Tags from
      Web Development with JavaServer Pages.
    </info>

  <tag></tag> entries go here

</taglib>
```

13.6   Content substitution

The most basic type of custom JSP action simply substitutes some text—often dynamically generated—in place of the custom tag. The first example tag for our library is of this sort, and is a debugging tag for displaying the status of a page's output buffer. This tag will be named `debugBuffer`, and will take no attributes, so the TLD entry for this tag is fairly straightforward:

```
<tag>
    <name>debugBuffer</name>
    <tagclass>com.taglib.wdjsp.mut.DebugBufferTag</tagclass>
    <bodycontent>empty</bodycontent>
    <info>Report the current status of output buffering.</info>
</tag>
```

As indicated in this TLD fragment, the class name for `debugBuffer`'s tag handler is `com.taglib.wdjsp.mut.DebugBufferTag`. A documentation string is provided via the `<info>` element, which will be available for use by JSP page development tools that wish to use this library. In addition, this tag's `<bodycontent>` entry indicates that there is no body content associated with this tag. If the page compiler encounters usage of this custom tag with associated body content, a compilation error will occur.

NOTE   It is standard practice to name the tag handler class after the tag, with an added `Tag` suffix. This class, as with all of the tag handler classes in the `mut` library, is defined in the `com.taglib.wdjsp.mut` package.

Because there is no body content associated with this tag, it needs only to implement the `Tag` interface, rather than the more complicated `BodyTag` interface. Furthermore, since we will be developing this custom tag from scratch, we can take advantage of the `TagSupport` class to simplify the implementation. As a result, the only method that needs to be implemented by the `DebugBufferTag` class is `doStartTag()`. The full source code for the tag handler appears in listing 13.2.

Listing 13.2 Source code for the DebugBufferTag tag handler

```
package com.taglib.wdjsp.mut;

import java.io.IOException;
import java.io.PrintStream;
import java.text.NumberFormat;
import javax.servlet.jsp.JspWriter;
import javax.servlet.jsp.PageContext;
import javax.servlet.jsp.tagext.Tag;
import javax.servlet.jsp.tagext.TagSupport;

public class DebugBufferTag extends TagSupport {
   public int doStartTag () throws JspException {
      JspWriter out = pageContext.getOut();
      int total = out.getBufferSize();
      int available = out.getRemaining();
      int used = total - available;
      try {
         out.print("Buffer Status: ");
         out.print(Integer.toString(used));
         out.print('/');
         out.print(Integer.toString(total));
         out.print(" = ");
         NumberFormat percentFmt = NumberFormat.getInstance();
         percentFmt.setMinimumFractionDigits(1);
         percentFmt.setMaximumFractionDigits(3);
         out.print(percentFmt.format((110D * used)/total));
         out.println("%");
      }
      catch(IOException e) {
         throw new JspTagException("I/O exception "
                     + e.getMessage());
      }
      return SKIP_BODY;
   }
}
```

The first tag handler property set by the JSP container when applying a tag handler is its `PageContext` object. As indicated in chapter 3, the methods of the `Page-Context` class provide programmatic access to all of the implicit objects available to the JSP scripting elements (table 4.16), as well as to all of the standard attribute scopes (table 4.19). Because tag handlers are passed a reference to the local `Page-Context` instance during their initialization, they in turn will have access to all of these objects and attributes through that instance. Indeed, the `PageContext` object is the tag handler's primary window into the workings of the JSP container.

For tag handler classes that extend either `TagSupport` or `BodyTagSupport`, the local `PageContext` instance will be available through an instance variable named `pageContext`. This instance variable is set when the JSP container calls the handler's `setPageContext()` method which, as indicated in figures 13.4 and 13.5, is one of the first steps in the tag handler life cycle. The `DebugBufferTag` class takes advantage of this instance variable in the very first line of its `doStartTag()` method, in order to retrieve the page's `JspWriter` instance. It then calls various methods defined by the `JspWriter` class in order to determine the current status of the output buffer, which are then displayed on the page by calling the same object's output methods, with help from the `java.text.NumberFormat` class to control the display of the numerical results.

With respect to error handling, all of the tag handler life cycle methods are specified as potentially throwing instances of the `JspException` class. By convention, however, when an error is actually thrown by a tag handler method it takes the form of a `JspTagException` instance, to signal that the error originated in a tag handler rather than some other JSP entity. All of the tag handler methods presented here and in chapter 14 follow this practice. As you might expect, `JspTagException` is a subclass of `JspException`, so the fact that the `throws` clause in the method signature only mentions `JspException` is not an issue.

Finally, the default behavior of the `doEndTag()` method, inherited by the `Debug-BufferTag` class from `TagSupport`, is to simply return `Tag.EVAL_PAGE`, indicating that normal processing of the remainder of the page should continue.

An example page which uses this tag, as well as the resulting output, are presented in the next section of this chapter.

13.7 *Tag attributes*

Now we look take a closer look at how tag handlers manage the attributes of a custom tag. For this example, we will consider a second debugging tag that allows the developer to display the cookies available on the current page. The TLD entry for this tag is:

```
<tag>
 <name>debugCookies</name>
 <tagclass>com.taglib.wdjsp.mut.DebugCookiesTag</tagclass>
 <attribute><name>style</name></attribute>
 <bodycontent>empty</bodycontent>
 <info>List the cookies accessible from this page.</info>
</tag>
```

This tag is named `debugCookies`, and is implemented via the `DebugCookiesTag` class. As with the `debugBuffer` tag, it has no body content, but unlike the `debug-Buffer` tag, this tag supports a single attribute named `style`.

Note that the `<attribute>` entry does not specify either the `<required>` or the `<rtexprvalue>` subelement. As a result, the default values for those subelements apply, implying that this is an optional attribute that may not be specified via a request-time attribute value.

The `style` attribute will be used to control how the cookie information reported by the tag is to be displayed. Since the tag needs to be able to display multiple cookies, the tag can present either a plain text version (as was the case with the `debugBuffer` tag), or an HTML list. As such, the style attribute will accept two different string values, either `text` or `HTML`, depending upon how the results are to be displayed.

As mentioned earlier in the chapter, tag attributes are represented in the tag handler class as JavaBeans properties. For the `style` attribute, then, the `Debug-CookiesTag` class must define the appropriate instance variables and methods, as in the following:

```
public class DebugCookiesTag extends TagSupport {
    private String style = text;

    public void setStyle (String style) {
     this.style = style;
    }
    public String getStyle () {
     return style;
    }
 ...
}
```

When the JSP container is processing a page request and encounters the `debug-Cookies` tag, the value specified for the `style` attribute will be passed to the corresponding `DebugCookiesTag` instance via its `setStyle()` method. The default value for this optional tag attribute is `text`.

For the `DebugCookiesTag` class, two of the tag handler life cycle methods must be implemented: `doStartTag()` and `release()`. The default implementation of the doEndTag() method can be used as is. The code for this class's doStartTag() method is as follows:

```
public int doStartTag () throws JspException {
    JspWriter out = pageContext.getOut();
    javax.servlet.ServletRequest req = pageContext.getRequest();
    if (req instanceof HttpServletRequest) {
        HttpServletRequest httpReq = (HttpServletRequest)req;
        Cookie[] cookies = httpReq.getCookies();
        int l = cookies.length;
        try {
            boolean doHTML = style.equalsIgnoreCase("HTML");
            if (doHTML) out.println("<ul>");
            for (int i = 0; i < l; i++) {
                Cookie cookie = cookies[i];
                if (doHTML) out.println("<li><b>");
                out.println(cookie.getName());
                if (doHTML) out.println("</b>");
                out.println(" = ");
                out.println(cookie.getValue());
                out.println('\n');
            }
            if (doHTML) out.println("</ul>");
        }
        catch(IOException e) {
            throw new JspTagException("I/O exception "
                + e.getMessage());
        }
    }
    return SKIP_BODY;
}
```

Here, the pageContext instance variable is used to fetch both the output stream and the request object for the page on which the tag appears. The request object must first be cast to the appropriate HTTP-specific class in order to retrieve its array of Cookie instances, after which the cookie's names and values are written to the output stream in accordance with the selected style. If the value of the style instance variable is HTML, then the HTML markup for displaying an unordered list is produced, along with some gratuitous boldfacing. Otherwise, the cookie data is output as multiple lines of text, one per cookie.

This class must also provide its own implementation of the release() method. Recall that the purpose of this method is to restore the tag handler instance to its original state before returning it to the shared resource pool, so that it may be reused during subsequent JSP requests. For this particular tag, then, it is necessary to reset the value of its style instance variable to text, as follows:

```
public void release () {
 super.release();
 style = "text";
}
```

This is done in order to ensure that the tag handler will use its proper default value for the corresponding `style` attribute in the event that the next tag this handler is applied to does not explicitly specify a value for that attribute. If this instance variable is not reset, then any tag which does not explicitly set that attribute will simply reuse the `style` value from the tag to which the handler was last applied, which may or may not be the correct default value.

TIP Note the call to `super.release()` as the first operation in the tag handler's own `release()` method. It is an essential practice when resource management is a concern to make certain that all of the classes in the inheritance hierarchy are accounted for.

The final source code for the tag handler is presented in abbreviated form in listing 13.3.

Listing 13.3 Source code for the DebugCookiesTag tag handler

```
package com.taglib.wdjsp.mut;

import java.io.IOException;
import javax.servlet.http.Cookie;
import javax.servlet.http.HttpServletRequest;
import javax.servlet.jsp.JspWriter;
import javax.servlet.jsp.tagext.TagSupport;

public class DebugCookiesTag extends TagSupport {
    private String style = text;

    public void setStyle (String style) {
     this.style = style;
    }
    public String getStyle () {
     return style;
    }
    public int doStartTag () { ... }
    public void release () { ... }
}
```

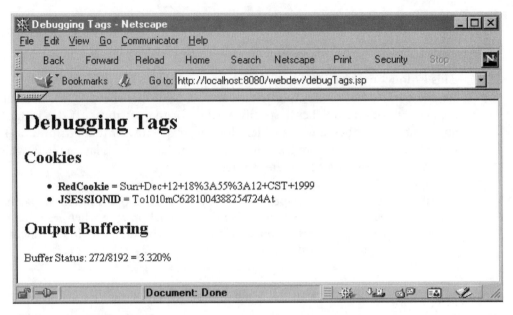

Figure 13.6   Output generated by the example debugging tags

To see this tag handler in action, along with DebugBufferTag, the following example JSP page is presented:

```
<%@ taglib uri="/mutlib" prefix="mut" %>
<html>
<head>
<title>Debugging Tags</title>
</head>
<body>
<h1>Debugging Tags</h1>

<h2>Cookies</h2>
<mut:debugCookies style="html"/>

<h2>Output Buffering</h2>
<mut:debugBuffer/>

</body>
</html>
```

This page simply loads the tag library via the taglib directive and calls the two custom tags just as it might call any other JSP tags. The resulting output is presented in figure 13.6.

13.8 *Content translation*

As we continue to add complexity to our tag handler implementation classes, the next step is to demonstrate tags that interact with their body content. To that end, we introduce two tags named `url` and `encodeHTML`, which perform request-time translation on the body content enclosed by their start and end tags. The `url` tag performs automatic URL rewriting, in support of the session management features in the servlet and JSP APIs. The `encodeHTML` tag is a more general-purpose variant of HTML's built-in `<pre>` tag: it translates any characters in its body which are special to HTML into their equivalent entities, in order to display that content literally, rather than having it be interpreted by the browser.

The TLD entries for these two tags are as follows:

```
<tag>
 <name>url</name>
 <tagclass>com.taglib.wdjsp.mut.UrlTag</tagclass>
 <bodycontent>tagdependent</bodycontent>
 <info>Perform URL rewriting if required.</info>
</tag>
<tag>
 <name>encodeHTML</name>
 <tagclass>com.taglib.wdjsp.mut.EncodeHtmlTag</tagclass>
 <bodycontent>tagdependent</bodycontent>
 <info>Perform HTML encoding of enclosed text.</info>
</tag>
```

The only new feature in these two entries is the use of the `tagdependent` value in the `<bodycontent>` elements. This indicates that the content delimited by the start and end tags for these custom actions should not be interpreted by the JSP container, but should instead be stored and passed to their respective tag handlers for further processing.

13.8.1 *URL rewriting*

As described in chapter 2, JSP employs two different techniques for managing user sessions: cookies and URL rewriting. Using cookies means that no changes need to be made to your site's pages in order to support session management, since the HTTP protocol supports cookies transparently and the JSP API handles session management cookies behind the scenes. Unfortunately, many users disable cookie support in their browsers due to security concerns. If you cannot mandate that your users enable cookie support, then URL rewriting is your only alternative for foolproof session management. Unfortunately, URL rewriting has a major drawback:

every URL on every page must be rewritten dynamically in order to embed the user's session ID in every request.

Using only the tags built into JSP, URL rewriting can only be accomplished via scripting. To alleviate this burden, the `url` tag described here can be used to cause any URL delimited by this tag to be rewritten each time the page it appears on is requested, as in the following JSP page fragment:

```
<ul>
<li> <a href="<mut:url>bin/programs.jsp</mut:url>">Programs</a>
<li> <a href="<mut:url>employees/users.jsp</mut:url>">Users</a>
<li> <a href="<mut:url>sbin/mcp.jsp</mut:url>">Master Control</a>
</ul>
```

The presence of the custom `url` tags here ensures that each of the URLs associated with these three links will be rewritten. Furthermore, the rewriting is applied intelligently: URLs are only rewritten if the user has disabled cookie support. If cookies are enabled, the underlying code will recognize this and refrain from adding the session ID to the URL. And while this markup code may appear a bit crowded, it is arguably much cleaner than using three JSP expressions containing scripting code to perform the URL rewriting.

Because the action implemented by this tag requires access to its body content, this tag must implement the `BodyTag` interface, rather than the simpler `Tag` interface. For this tag, however, all of the work takes place in its `doAfterBody()` method. By extending the `BodyTagSupport` class and taking advantage of its default method implementations, this tag handler can be implemented with just a single method definition, as indicated in listing 13.4.

Listing 13.4 Source code for the UrlTag tag handler

```
package com.taglib.wdjsp.mut;

import javax.servlet.http.HttpServletResponse;
import javax.servlet.jsp.tagext.*;
import javax.servlet.jsp.*;
import java.io.IOException;

public class UrlTag extends BodyTagSupport {
  public int doAfterBody () throws JspException {
    BodyContent body = getBodyContent();
    String baseURL = body.getString();
    body.clearBody();
    try {
      HttpServletResponse response =
        (HttpServletResponse) pageContext.getResponse();
```

```
        String encodedURL = response.encodeURL(baseURL);
        getPreviousOut().print(encodedURL);
      }
    catch (IOException e) {
      throw new JspTagException("I/O exception "
        + e.getMessage());
    }
    return SKIP_BODY;
  }
}
```

The first step in this handler's doAfterBody() method is to obtain the BodyContent instance associated with processing the tag's body content. Since this is the doAfterBody() method, the body content will already have been processed by the time it is called, so the next step is to retrieve the body content as a String instance—to be stored in a local variable named baseURL—via the getString() method of the BodyContent class. Because the <bodycontent> element of the TLD entry for this tag was specified as tagdependent, this String will contain the original, unmodified contents of the tag's body. The clearBody() method is then called to clear out the contents of the BodyContent instance, allowing it to be safely reused by the JSP container after this method returns.

The next step is to encode the URL extracted from the tag's body content. This is most easily accomplished by taking advantage of the encodeURL() method defined by the HttpServletResponse class. The response object is obtained from the tag handler's pageContext instance variable and cast to the appropriate class. The encodeURL() method, which implements all of the logic required to determine whether or not a session ID is required and whether the user's session is being managed via cookies or URL rewriting, is then called to actually encode the URL as necessary.

The next step is to obtain an output stream for printing the transformed URL. This is accomplished by calling the getPreviousOut() method, provided by the BodyTagSupport base class. This method returns the JspWriter instance for the content immediately surrounding the custom tag being processed, which is then used to print the encoded URL. The doAfterBody() method concludes by returning Tag.SKIP_BODY, since no iterative processing of the body content is required.

TIP   At this point, you may be wondering why `getPreviousOut()` is being called to obtain the `JspWriter` instance, rather than fetching it from the `pageContext` instance variable, or from the response object. This is done in order to account for custom tags which are nested inside one another. When custom tags are nested, the output from the inner custom tag may require further processing by the outer tag. If this is the case, then we need to make sure that the output from the inner tag is written to the `BodyContent` object associated with the outer tag, rather than to the outermost `JspWriter` associated with the page. (Recall that `BodyContent` is a subclass of `JspWriter`.) The `getPreviousOut()` method returns the next `BodyContent` or `JspWriter` instance currently associated with the processing of the page's output, and is thus the recommended method for obtaining an output stream for tag handlers which implement the `BodyTag` interface.

The use of this tag is demonstrated in the following example page, which uses the `url` tag to rewrite the URL of a linked page. In addition, the page also prints out the user's session ID.

```
<%@ page session="true" %>
<%@ taglib uri="/mutlib" prefix="mut" %>
<html>
<head>
<title>URL Tag</title>
</head>
<body>
<h1>URL Tag</h1>
<p>
<a href="<mut:url>urlDest.jsp</mut:url>">Here</a> is a link to another page.
</p>
<p>
Your session ID is <%= session.getId() %>.
</p>
</body>
</html>
```

If this page is the first page requested from the server, then output such as that depicted in figure 13.7 will result. In particular, note that the link destination displayed at the bottom of the browser includes a request parameter specifying the session ID. If cookie support is enabled in the browser, then subsequent requests for the page will generate output such as that in figure 13.8, in which the session ID no longer appears in the link destination display. If cookie support is not enabled, then all requests for the page will produce the results displayed in figure 13.7.

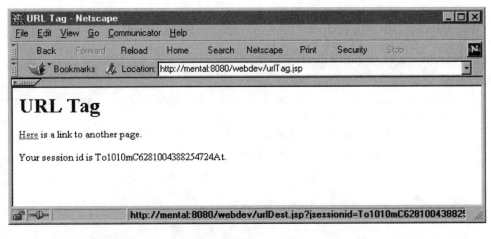

Figure 13.7 Output of URL rewriting tag for the first request, and all requests when cookie support is disabled

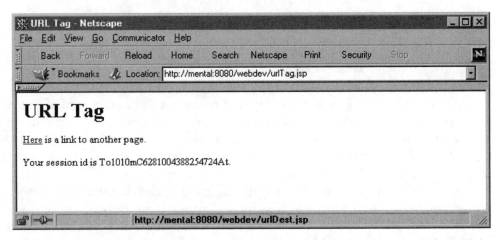

Figure 13.8 Output of URL rewriting tag for subsequent requests when cookie support is enabled

13.8.2 *HTML encoding*

Browsers interpret HTML content by applying special interpretations to certain characters, such as the < and > characters which delimit HTML tags. In order to cause these special characters to appear in the browsers, it is necessary to replace them with other special HTML constructs, referred to as *entities*. For example, the HTML entity for the < character is < and the HTML entity for the > character is

>. As you might infer from these two examples, the & character also has special meaning in HTML. In order to display an ampersand in the browser, the HTML entity & must be used.

When developing web content, it is occasionally desirable to apply these translations to a large block of text. It is the role of the encodeHTML custom tag to perform such translations automatically, so that the developer can avoid having to apply these translations manually.

The first requirement, then, is code for translating characters into their equivalent HTML entities, such as the following:

```
static private Hashtable translations = makeTranslationTable();
static private Hashtable makeTranslationTable () {
 Hashtable table = new Hashtable();
 table.put(new Character('<'), "&lt;");
 table.put(new Character('>'), "&gt;");
 table.put(new Character('&'), "&amp;");
 table.put(new Character(''), "&quot;");
 table.put(new Character('\n'), "<BR>");
 table.put(new Character('\t'), "  ");
 return table;
}
static public String getTranslation (char c) {
 return (String) translations.get(new Character(c));
}
```

Here, a Hashtable is used to store the characters to be translated and their corresponding HTML entities. (Only a representative sampling of the available HTML entities is presented here.) Also, because the translation table need only be constructed once and can be shared by all tag handler instances, static variables and methods are used to implement the translation routine.

As was the case with UrlTag, the tag handler class for the encodeHTML tag, by taking advantage of the BodyTagSupport base class, needs only to override the definition of the doAfterBody() method in order to implement the desired functionality. The definition of this method for the com.taglib.wdjsp.mut.EncodeHtmlTag tag handler class follows:

```
public int doAfterBody () throws JspException {
    BodyContent body = getBodyContent();
    String orig = body.getString();
    body.clearBody();
    int length = orig.length();
    StringBuffer result =
        new StringBuffer(Math.round(length * 1.1f));
    for (int i = 0; i < length; ++i) {
        char c = orig.charAt(i);
```

```
        String translation = getTranslation(c);
        if (translation == null) {
         result.append(c);
        } else {
         result.append(translation);
        }
   }
   try {
        getPreviousOut().print(result.toString());
   }
   catch (IOException e) {
        throw new JspTagException("unexpected IO error");
   }
   return SKIP_BODY;
}
```

This method follows the same general outline as the doAfterBody() method of the UrlTag class, obtaining the tag's body contents in the form of a String, performing a translation operation on that String, and then printing out the translation results. In this case, however, the translation is carried out on a character-by-character basis using the static getTranslation() method. For efficiency reasons, the translation results are accumulated into an instance of StringBuffer, which is later transformed into a String for output.

The full source code for the EncodeHtmlTag class is presented in abbreviated form in listing 13.5. An example JSP page that makes use of the encodeHTML tag appears in listing 13.6. Note that, in order to prevent excessive translation of carriage return characters into <BR> tags, the <mut:encodeHTML> tags in this sample page appear on the same line as the content being encoded. The results of processing this example page are depicted in figure 13.9.

Listing 13.5 Source code for the UrlTag tag handler

```
package com.taglib.wdjsp.mut;

import javax.servlet.jsp.PageContext;
import javax.servlet.jsp.tagext.*;
import javax.servlet.jsp.*;
import java.io.IOException;
import java.util.Hashtable;

public class EncodeHtmlTag extends BodyTagSupport {
    public int doAfterBody () throws JspException { ... }
    static private Hashtable translations = makeTranslationTable();
    static private Hashtable makeTranslationTable () { ... }
    static public String getTranslation (char c) { ... }
}
```

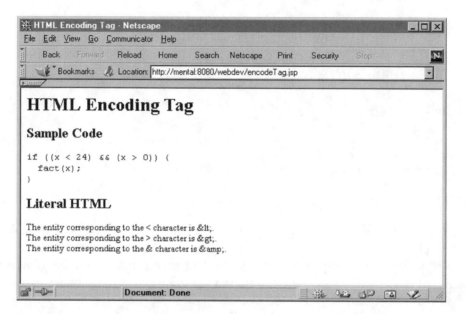

Figure 13.9   Output of the HTML encoding tag

Listing 13.6   Sample page employing the encodeHTML custom tag

```
<%@ taglib uri="/mutlib" prefix="mut" %>
<html>
<head>
<title>HTML Encoding Tag</title>
</head>
<body>
<h1>HTML Encoding Tag</h1>

<h2>Sample Code</h2>
<tt><mut:encodeHTML>if ((x < 24) && (x > 0)) {
   fact(x);
}</mut:encodeHTML></tt>

<h2>Literal HTML</h2>
<mut:encodeHTML>The entity corresponding to the < character is &lt;.
The entity corresponding to the > character is &gt;.
The entity corresponding to the & character is &amp;.
</mut:encodeHTML>

</body>
</html>
```

13.9 *To be continued*

In this chapter, we have looked at how custom tags are compiled and executed by a JSP container, and how their operation is reflected in the underlying `javax.serv-let.jsp.tagext` class hierarchy. We have also described the use of TLD files and the packaging of tag libraries into JAR files, and examined a number of example tags. The examples presented thus far have focused on key custom tag functionality such as content generation and translation. In the next chapter, we will consider tags that take advantage of more advanced features of JSP and Java, in order to implement paired tags that interact with one another within a single JSP page, as well as tags that interface with JavaBeans components. At the end of chapter 14 we will briefly revisit the topic of packaging tag libraries, to complete our presentation of the `mut` tag library.

14

Implementing advanced custom tags

This chapter covers

- Creating families of interacting tags
- Custom tags for flow of control
- Using introspection and reflection to access JavaBeans properties
- Packaging the example custom tag library

In chapter 13, we introduced the classes used to create JSP custom tags, and described how those classes interact with the JSP container to perform custom actions within a page. Example tags and their implementations were presented, as was the use of JAR files and TLDs to package tags into a library. In this chapter we build upon that foundation to develop additional tags that leverage advanced JSP and Java APIs to provide enhanced capabilities.

First, we will describe how data can be transferred between the tags on a page in order to spread functionality across two or more interacting custom actions. Such behavior will be demonstrated via a pair of tags that implement hierarchical numbering of content items, in the form of outlines. We will then create a pair of custom actions that provide tag-based flow of control for JSP pages. In addition, these tags will take advantage of Java's introspection and reflection facilities to access JavaBeans properties, in much the same manner as the built-in `<jsp:getProperty>` and `<jsp:setProperty>` tags. Finally, these new tags will be combined with those from chapter 13 to construct a JAR file for the completed mut custom tag library.

14.1   Interacting tags

HTML contains a number of tags whose behavior is dependent upon the context in which they appear. For example, the `<LI>` tag for designating the items in a list produces bulleted content when enclosed in a `<UL>` tag, and numbered content when it appears within the `<OL>` tag. The `<TD>` tag is only meaningful within the body of a `<TR>` tag, which itself must appear within the body of a `<TABLE>` tag.

The built-in JSP tags also include such interdependencies, for example, the relationship among the `<jsp:getProperty>`, `<jsp:setProperty>`, and `<jsp:useBean>` tags. The `page` directive, with its ability to set global properties such as imported packages, the scripting language, and participation in session management, has the potential to influence almost every JSP element that appears in a page.

14.1.1 Interaction mechanisms

As you can see, the ability for tags to interact can add powerful capabilities to a markup language. In recognition of their potency, support for interacting tags is an important part of the JSP custom tag API. JSP provides two different mechanisms, in addition to the general techniques supported by the Java programming language, for enabling data transfer between tag handlers.

Attributes

The simplest mechanism for tags to interact is the use of attributes. Through their access to the local `PageContext` instance, as described in chapter 13, a tag handler can gain access to all four of the standard page objects which are capable of storing attributes: the application object, the session object, the request object, and the `PageContext` instance itself. If the data to be stored in an attribute by a custom tag really does have the scope associated with the corresponding object, then this is a reasonable way of transmitting data from one tag to another. It is somewhat unreliable, however, because there is no way to prevent others from using the same attribute name and corrupting the data stored there. Since a given page may include any number of arbitrary scriptlets, `<jsp:useBean>` tags, and custom tags from other libraries—all of which can get and set any of the attributes accessible from that page—there is always the chance, however slim, that another developer has chosen to use the same attribute name as you.

If the visibility of the shared data does not match that of any of the standard scopes, an alternate approach should be taken. This will be true, for example, if the data to be shared should only be accessible within the body of an enclosing tag. In cases such as this, a more direct transfer of data between tag handlers is required. In fact, unless the data has application or session scope (which can only be stored by means of attributes), the approach we describe next is preferable to setting attributes with page or request scope because it does not introduce the possibility of namespace collisions.

The custom tag hierarchy

From the discussion of how tag handlers work in the previous chapter (figures 13.4 and 13.5), recall that one of the first methods called when a tag handler is invoked is setParent(). The JSP container uses this method to keep track of the context in which a tag appears by means of a parent/child hierarchy. If one custom tag is called within the body of another, the outer tag is designated as the parent of the inner. After the JSP container has assigned a tag's parent—in the form of a tag handler instance—via setParent(), that handler can later be retrieved by its child using the corresponding getParent() method.

NOTE While any tag handler can access its parent handler by means of the getParent() method, the custom tag API provides no methods for determining a tag handler's children. As a result, the parent/child hierarchy can only be traversed in a bottom-up manner.

By calling its `getParent()` method, then, a tag can obtain a reference to its parent tag, and thereby retrieve data by calling its parent's methods. Because nesting of tags is arbitrary, though, never make assumptions about the parenthood of a given tag. Even if your tag library defines two tag handlers named `myParentTag` and `myChildTag`, with an implied relationship between the two, there is no way to guarantee that every instance of `myChildTag` will have an instance of `myParentTag` as its immediate parent. Perhaps the page author is also using the `mut` library, and has wrapped a call to the `<mut:encodeHTML>` tag between your two tags in order to encode the output of your `myChildTag` handler. While the `myChildTag` instance may still be descended from an instance of your `myParentTag` handler within the page's parent/child hierarchy, the result of calling `getParent()` from your `myChildTag` handler will yield an instance of `EncodeHtmlTag`, rather than an instance of `myParentTag`.

Coping with this inevitability is the role of `findAncestorWithClass()`, a static method defined by the `TagSupport` class. As its name suggests, this method is used to search up the parent/child hierarchy for the first ancestor of a tag that is an instance of a particular class. The signature for this method is:

```
static Tag TagSupport.findAncestorWithClass(Tag from, Class class)
```

The first argument, `from`, identifies the child tag from which the search is initiated. The second argument, `class`, specifies the tag handler class (or interface) for which an instance is sought. Starting from the handler identified by `from`, then, its parent handler is checked to see if it is an instance of `class`. If so, the parent handler is returned. If not, the parent's parent is checked. This process continues recursively until an instance of `class` is found, or a tag handler with no parent is reached, in which case the method returns `null`. In this way, a handler searching for an enclosing tag of a certain type can locate it by means of its class.

NOTE   The base requirement for custom tag handlers is that they implement the `Tag` interface. The `findAncestorWithClass()` method is provided by the `Tag-Support` class so that a full implementation can be provided, since interfaces can only specify abstract methods. Because it is a static method, however, it can readily be called by tag handlers based on the `Tag` or `BodyTag` interfaces, as well as those extending the `TagSupport` and `BodyTagSupport` classes.

14.1.2 Outlining tags

To demonstrate the use of `findAncestorWithClass()`, we will implement a pair of tags for rendering outlines. While the standard ordered list tags provided by HTML

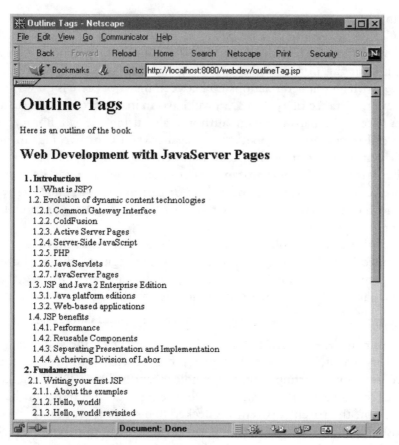

Figure 14.1   Output of the outlining tags

(i.e., `<OL>` and `<LI>`) can be used to create enumerated lists, and even to nest them, the tags implemented here will enable the display of enumerated lists that propagate item numbering into nested lists (figure 14.1). The transfer of item numbers from parent to child is accomplished via `findAncestorWithClass()`.

Descriptors

In much the same way as HTML uses two tags to create enumerated lists, two custom tags will be introduced to support outlining. These two tags are named `outline` and `item`, and their TLD entries are as follows:

```
<tag>
    <name>outline</name>
    <tagclass>com.taglib.wdjsp.mut.OutlineTag</tagclass>
    <bodycontent>JSP</bodycontent>
    <info>
        Delimits a set of items comprising a nested outline.
    </info>
</tag>
<tag>
    <name>item</name>
    <tagclass>com.taglib.wdjsp.mut.OutlineItemTag</tagclass>
    <bodycontent>JSP</bodycontent>
    <info>
        Delineates an item, possibly including subitems,
        within a nested outline.
    </info>
    <attribute>
        <name>text</name>
        <required>true</required>
        <rtexprvalue>true</rtexprvalue>
    </attribute>
</tag>
```

The `outline` tag is implemented via a tag handler class named `OutlineTag`, while the `item` tag takes a single required attribute named `text`, and is implemented via a class named `OutlineItemTag`. Both tags can contain nested JSP content.

Syntax

With respect to syntax, the `outline` tag simply serves as a delimiter for a set of `item` tags, just as HTML's `<OL>` tag delimits a set of `<LI>` tags. The `item` tag, however, operates somewhat differently from the `<LI>` tag. Whereas the body content of an `<LI>` tag serves as the text of the corresponding enumerated item, the body of the `item` tag contains nested `item` tags, representing the next level of items within the outline. Since the body of an `item` tag serves as a container for more `item` tags, the text to be associated with a given item in the outline is instead specified via the corresponding `item` tag's `text` attribute.

As indicated in listing 14.1, which contains the abbreviated source for the JSP page depicted in figure 14.1, an outline is therefore constructed using a pair of matching `outline` tags, delimiting a set of nested `item` tags. Outline topics that contain nested topics, such as the top-level item marked "Introduction" and the second-level item marked "Evolution of dynamic content technologies," are represented via `item` tags with body content consisting of additional `item` tags for the nested entries. Outline topics that contain no subtopics are represented by empty `item` tags, such as the top-level item marked "What is JSP?"

In order to keep the implementation simple, no alternate numbering styles are supported, and all items are displayed in whatever font, face, and size happen to be current on the page. Additional presentation features could readily be added to the basic functionality presented here.

Listing 14.1   Sample page employing the outlining custom tags

```
<%@ taglib uri="/mutlib" prefix="mut" %>
<html>
<head>
<title>Outline Tags</title>
</head>
<body>
<h1>Outline Tags</h1>
<p>
Here is an outline of the book.
</p>
<h2>Web Development with JavaServer Pages</h2>
<mut:outline>
  <b><mut:item text="Introduction"></b>
  <mut:item text="What is JSP?"/>
  <mut:item text="Evolution of dynamic content technologies">
      <mut:item text="Common Gateway Interface"/>
      <mut:item text="ColdFusion"/>
      <mut:item text="Active Server Pages"/>
      <mut:item text="Server-Side JavaScript"/>
      <mut:item text="PHP"/>
      <mut:item text="Java Servlets"/>
      <mut:item text="JavaServer Pages"/>
  </mut:item>
  <mut:item text="JSP and Java 2 Enterprise Edition">
      <mut:item text="Java platform editions"/>
      <mut:item text="Web-based applications"/>
  </mut:item>
  <mut:item text="JSP benefits">
      <mut:item text="Performance"/>
      <mut:item text="Reusable components"/>
      <mut:item
          text="Separating presentation and implementation"/>
      <mut:item text="Acheiving division of labor"/>
  </mut:item>
  </mut:item>
    ...
</mut:outline>
</body>
</html>
```

Tag handler base class

The primary function of the item tag, then, is to display the numeric and textual labels for the corresponding entry in the outline. The outline tag simply marks the beginning and end of an outline, making it possible for a page to include more than one outline. An alternate way of viewing the outline tag is to think of it as a degenerate version of the item tag: both contain nested item tags. With respect to displaying itself, however, both the number and text fields for an outline tag are empty.

The recursive nature of the nested outline structure, in combination with this view of the outline tag as a special case of the item tag, suggests that the aspects common to both could be put into a shared base class. A shared base class would also make it easier to identify the parent handler for any tag within an outline, since findAncestorWithClass() could be used to search for the common base class, rather than first searching the tag's parents for an instance of OutlineItemTag, and then searching for an instance of OutlineTag.

To that end, we will first define a tag handler base class named OutlineBase, which will be inherited by both OutlineTag and OutlineItemTag. First however, we need to more thoroughly identify the common behavior of these tags.

Neither tag does any special processing of its body content, so it is only necessary for them to support the Tag interface, rather than the BodyTag interface. This is most easily accomplished by having OutlineBase itself be a subclass of TagSupport. As indicated, the primary function of the outline tags is to display their numeric and textual labels. The text label is local to the individual item tags, but the numeric label is a function of the item's position within the outline. In particular, it is dependent upon the numeric label of the item's parent, as well as how many of the parent's children precede the current item.

This suggests that both item and outline tags need to keep track of their parents (i.e., where they are in the hierarchy), their own item numbers (for generating their numeric label), and how many children they have (to assign item numbers to them.). The instance variables of the OutlineBase class, then, should be:

```
public class OutlineBase extends TagSupport {
  private OutlineBase outlineParent = null;
  int count = 0;
  int childCount = 0;
  ...
  public void release () {
    super.release();
    outlineParent = null;
    count = 0;
    childCount = 0;
  }
}
```

Note that a `release()` method is provided which resets these instance variables in order to enable reuse of tag handler instances. Note also that the `outlineParent` instance variable is itself an instance of the `OutlineBase` class. We will have to successfully implement all of the recursive functionality of the outline hierarchy in this base class if we are to avoid having to cast this instance variable to one of its two subclasses (`OutlineTag` and `OutlineItemTag`) elsewhere in the implementation.

To manage the `outlineParent` instance variable, we will need two methods. The getter is defined as:

```
public OutlineBase getOutlineParent () {
  return outlineParent;
}
```

The instance variable is assigned by means of the `fetchOutlineParent()` method, which is defined as:

```
public OutlineBase fetchOutlineParent () {
  outlineParent =
    (OutlineBase) findAncestorWithClass(this, OutlineBase.class);
  return outlineParent;
}
```

As you might have anticipated, this is simply a wrapper around the `findAncestor-WithClass()` method, supplying the `OutlineBase` class as its second argument. It likewise casts its result to that same class.

NOTE Although the `fetchOutlineParent()` method is available to all instances of the `OutlineBase` class, it will only be called by instances of `Outline-ItemTag`. This is because instances of `OutlineTag`, in their role as outline delimiters, do not need to identify their parents.

For this reason, one could argue that this method should be defined by the `OutlineItemTag` class, rather than `OutlineBase`. Our motivation for retaining it as a method of `OutlineBase` is simply one of flexibility: we may ultimately decide to expand our set of outlining tags with new subclasses of `OutlineBase`, that would then be able to reuse this method if it is kept with the base class.

Three methods for managing the `count` and `childCount` instance variables are required. The first two are typical property accessors for the `count` instance variable:

```
public int getCount () {
  return count;
}
public void setCount (int count) {
  this.count = count;
}
```

An alternate approach is taken for managing `childCount`, as embodied in the `addChild()` method:

```
public void addChild (OutlineBase child) {
  child.setCount(++childCount);
}
```

This is intended to be called by an `item` tag once it has fetched its parent. The tag supplies itself as the argument to the method, causing the parent to increment its `childCount` instance variable, and then send that result back to the original tag to serve as the newly added child's own item number.

The final method of the `OutlineBase` class is `getNumericLabel()`, which calculates the numeric label for an entry in the outline. This method takes full advantage of the recursive nature of an outline's parent/child hierarchy to construct the label:

```
public String getNumericLabel () {
  if (outlineParent == null) {
    return "";
  } else {
    return "  "
      + outlineParent.getNumericLabel()
      + Integer.toString(count) + ".";
  }
}
```

As we will see in the handler implementations to follow, `fetchOutlineParent()` is called only by the `OutlineItemTag` handler. It is not called by instances of `OutlineTag`. As a result, the `outlineParent` instance variable will be `null` for tag handlers representing the `outline` tag, and non-null for tag handlers representing the `item` tag. The numeric label for `outline` tags will therefore be the empty string. For item tags, the numeric label is constructed by adding text to its parent's numeric label. Indentation is added to the beginning of the parent's label in the form of HTML nonbreaking space entities, and the current entry's item number is added to the end. For the first-level items in an outline, the parent's label will be the empty string, so only one level of indentation and one item number will appear. For second-level items, there will be an additional pass through the `else` clause: the final result will be two levels of indentation and a pair of item numbers, delimited by periods, as depicted in figure 14.1.

The combined source code for the `OutlineBase` class is presented in abbreviated form in listing 14.2.

Listing 14.2   Source code for the OutlineBase tag handler base class

```
package com.taglib.wdjsp.mut;

import javax.servlet.jsp.tagext.TagSupport;

public class OutlineBase extends TagSupport {
    private OutlineBase outlineParent = null;
    int count = 0;
    int childCount = 0;

    public OutlineBase getOutlineParent () { ... }
    public OutlineBase fetchOutlineParent () { ... }
    public int getCount () { ... }
    public void setCount (int count) { ... }
    public void addChild (OutlineBase child) { ... }
    public String getNumericLabel () { ... }
    public void release () { ... }
}
```

Item tag handler

As you can see, most of the hard work required to display an item in an outline is accomplished via the methods defined in `OutlineBase`. Compared to generating the numeric label, managing the text label is easy. As indicated in listing 14.3, the `OutlineItemTag` class is a subclass of `OutlineBase`, and defines only one additional instance variable named `text`, corresponding to the `text` attribute of the associated custom tag.

Getter and setter methods are provided for this instance variable, as is a `release()` method for resetting the tag handler to its original state. This method in turn calls the `release()` method of its superclass, to make certain that all classes in the inheritance hierarchy are properly reset.

Listing 14.3   Source code for the OutlineItemTag tag handler

```
package com.taglib.wdjsp.mut;

import java.io.IOException;
import javax.servlet.jsp.JspWriter;

public class OutlineItemTag extends OutlineBase {
  private String text = null;
```

```
  public void setText (String text) {
    this.text = text;
  }
  public String getText () {
    return text;
  }
  public int doStartTag () throws JspException {
    fetchOutlineParent().addChild(this);
    JspWriter out = pageContext.getOut();
    try {
      out.print(getNumericLabel());
      out.print(' ');
      out.print(text);
      out.println("<BR>");
      return EVAL_BODY_INCLUDE;
    }
    catch (IOException e) {
      throw new JspTagException("I/O exception " + e.getMessage());
    }
  }
  public void release () {
    super.release();
    text = null;
  }
}
```

The only complicated element of this tag handler class is its `doStartTag()` method, which is actually responsible for printing out the item's numeric and textual labels. Given that an `OutlineItemTag` instance may serve as the tag handler for multiple `item` tags on multiple pages, the call to `fetchOutlineParent()` cannot be made in a constructor. The constructor would only be called the first time this handler was applied to a tag, rather than every time it is applied to a new tag. The call to `fetchOutlineParent()` must instead be made via one of the life cycle methods called by the JSP container when it is processing an individual custom tag.

Of these life cycle methods (figure 13.4), `setParent()` seems to be the most appropriate because it is already performing a related task. We could override the implementation provided by `TagSupport` (inherited through `OutlineBase`) to produce the desired result:

```
public void setParent (Tag tag) {
  super.setParent(tag);
  fetchOutlineParent();
}
```

Note that the superclass implementation must be called first, so that the parent reference privately maintained by TagSupport is in place before fetchOutlineParent() attempts to call Tag.findParentWithClass().

This is a perfectly acceptable approach. In order to save an additional method definition, however, we have elected to add the call to fetchOutlineParent() to the beginning of the doStartTag() method, since we have no choice but to provide a local definition for it. This is immediately followed by a call to the addChild() method, also provided by the OutlineBase superclass. Recall that these two methods have the effect of storing a reference to the containing Outline-Base tag handler, incrementing its childCount instance variable, and setting the current item's count instance variable.

Once these steps are accomplished, the remaining steps of the *doStartTag()* method should be fairly familiar. An output writer is obtained from the handler's *pageContext* instance variable, onto which the content generated by the custom tag—the item's numeric label, a space character, and the item's text label—is written. Finally, the method returns *Tag.EVAL_BODY_INCLUDE* to signal that processing of the tag's body content should proceed as usual.

Outline tag handler

As indicated in listing 14.4, the OutlineTag class relies almost entirely on the methods provided by OutlineBase. The only addition is its implementation of the doStartTag() method, which returns Tag.EVAL_BODY_INCLUDE to continue processing the tag's body content. Note that none of the methods of OutlineTag—including those inherited from OutlineBase—call fetchOutlineParent(). Its outlineParent instance variable will remain set to null, ensuring the correct behavior from the getNumericLabel() method.

Listing 14.4   Source code for the OutlineItemTag tag handler

```
package com.taglib.wdjsp.mut;

public class OutlineTag extends OutlineBase {
  public int doStartTag () {
    return EVAL_BODY_INCLUDE;
  }
}
```

14.2 *Flow of control*

As discussed in chapter 3, the only mechanism provided by JSP for implementing conditional or iterative presentation logic is the scriptlet. If you wish to reduce the use of scripting language code in your JSP pages, but still need to apply such constructs, custom tags are your only alternative.

To that end, we present here a pair of custom tags for implementing flow of control. These tags are modeled after JSP's built-in Bean tags, keying off of Bean properties to control conditional content and iteration. The TLD entries for these two tags, named ifProperty and forProperty, appear in listing 14.5.

> **Listing 14.5 Tag library descriptor entries for the flow of control custom tags**

```
<tag>
  <name>ifProperty</name>
  <tagclass>com.taglib.wdjsp.mut.IfPropertyTag</tagclass>
  <bodycontent>JSP</bodycontent>
  <info>
    Conditionally include or exclude page content
    based on a bean property.
  </info>
  <attribute>
    <name>name</name><required>true</required>
  </attribute>
  <attribute>
    <name>property</name><required>true</required>
  </attribute>
  <attribute><name>action</name></attribute>
</tag>
<tag>
  <name>forProperty</name>
  <tagclass>com.taglib.wdjsp.mut.ForPropertyTag</tagclass>
  <teiclass>com.taglib.wdjsp.mut.ForPropertyTEI</teiclass>
  <bodycontent>JSP</bodycontent>
  <info>
    Loop through an indexed property.
  </info>
  <attribute>
    <name>name</name><required>true</required>
  </attribute>
  <attribute>
    <name>property</name><required>true</required>
  </attribute>
  <attribute>
    <name>id</name><required>true</required>
  </attribute>
  <attribute>
```

```
   <name>class</name><required>true</required>
 </attribute>
</tag>
```

The only feature in these TLD entries that is not present in the earlier examples in this book is the specification of a `<teiclass>` entry for the `forProperty` tag. This is necessary because the `forProperty` tag introduces a scripting variable to represent the current iteration element of an indexed property. As such, a helper class is necessary to transmit information about the scripting variable to the JSP container during page compilation.

14.2.1 *Conditionalization*

As indicated in the TLD, the `ifProperty` tag supports three attributes, two of which are required. Since this is the first custom tag presented in this book that has more than one attribute, a good place to start is its syntax. The basic syntax for the `ifProperty` tag is:

```
<mut:ifProperty name="bean" property="property" action="action">
  bodyContent
</mut:ifProperty>
```

The `name` and `property` attributes have the same meaning as in the standard `<jsp:getProperty>` and `<jsp:setProperty>` tags: the `name` attribute identifies a JavaBean introduced earlier via `<jsp:useBean>`, and the `property` attribute names one of that Bean's properties. In this case, however, it is expected that the Bean property thus specified has a boolean value.

The `action` attribute specifies what to do with the tag's body content when the value of that boolean property is `true`. If the `action` attribute is set to `"include"`, the body content will become part of the displayed page. If the `action` attribute is set to `"exclude"`, the body content will be ignored. Furthermore, if the value of the specified Bean property is `false`, the opposite action will be taken. As indicated in the TLD entry for this tag, the `name` and `property` attributes are required, while the `action` attribute is optional. The default value for `action` is `"include"`.

The `ifProperty` tag is implemented via a tag handler class named `IfPropertyTag`. The tag's attributes, as was the case for the `DebugCookiesTag` class in the previous chapter, are implemented as Bean properties, the code for which is in listing 14.6. Each attribute is represented by an instance variable of class `String`, with a corresponding getter and setter method.

Although this tag has an effect on its body content, it does not need to interact with it directly, as was the case with the content translation tags. Because it is simply controlling whether or not the body content is processed, this tag can be implemented using only the `Tag` interface, rather than `BodyTag`. More specifically, by extending the `TagSupport` base class, the only tag handler life cycle methods that need to be overridden are `doStartTag()` and `release()`, the first of which is defined as:

```
public int doStartTag () throws JspException {
    try {
        boolean propertyValue = evalPropertyValue();
        boolean exclude = action.equalsIgnoreCase("exclude");
        if (exclude) propertyValue = (! PropertyValue);
        return propertyValue ? EVAL_BODY_INCLUDE : SKIP_BODY;
    }
    catch (IntrospectionException e) {
        throw new JspTagException(e.getMessage());
    }
}
```

The first thing this method does is retrieve the value of the Bean property specified by the tag's `name` and `property` attributes, via a call to the auxiliary method `eval-PropertyValue()`. If the tag's `action` attribute is set to `"exclude"`, then the sense of this boolean value is reversed, given that content exclusion is the opposite effect to content inclusion. Finally, based on the resulting value for the retrieved property, the method returns either `Tag.EVAL_BODY_INCLUDE` or `Tag.SKIP_BODY`, in order to control whether or not the tag's body content is processed.

So far, so good. Up to this point, the implementation is fairly straightforward. It's clear, though, that most of the real work is hidden in the `evalProperty-Value()` method, since it is responsible for turning a pair of strings describing a Bean property into the actual value represented by those strings.

There are three major steps by means of which this magical transformation takes place, as outlined in the source code of the method itself:

```
private boolean evalPropertyValue ()
  throws IntrospectionException {
    Object bean = pageContext.getAttribute(name);
    if (bean != null) {
        Method reader = getPropertyReader(bean);
        return readProperty(bean, reader);
    }
    throw new IntrospectionException(
        "Bean \"" + name +"\" not found for <ifProperty> tag.");
}
```

The first step, then, is obtaining the Bean instance from its name, and this is performed via the `pageContext` object. All Beans introduced via the `<jsp:useBean>`

tag, in the course of being made available for use in scripting elements, are stored as attributes of the page. As a result, they can be retrieved by means of the pageContext object's getAttribute() method.

After retrieving the Bean, the next step is to obtain a reference to the getter method for accessing the desired property. This computation is encapsulated in the call to the getProperty() method, which takes advantage of Java's *introspection* API. The final step, represented by the call to the readProperty() method, is to call the getter method in order to obtain the actual property value. This process is accomplished via the Java *reflection* API.

Introspection

In the getPropertyReader() method, the java.beans.Introspector class obtains information about the class of the Bean being accessed by the tag. In particular, the Introspector class provides access to the BeanInfo object that describes the Bean class and its properties. For classes that conform with the standard Bean naming conventions, the corresponding BeanInfo object can be constructed automatically. As pointed out in chapter 6, however, Bean developers can also provide their own implementations of the BeanInfo interface for classes that do not strictly adhere to the Bean conventions.

In either case, the Introspector class provides a static method named get-BeanInfo() for obtaining the BeanInfo instance corresponding to a given class. Calling this method is one of the first steps performed by the getProperty-Reader() method:

```
private Method getPropertyReader (Object bean)
    throws IntrospectionException {
    Class beanClass = bean.getClass();
    BeanInfo beanInfo = Introspector.getBeanInfo(beanClass);
    PropertyDescriptor[] descriptors =
        beanInfo.getPropertyDescriptors();
    int stop = descriptors.length;
    for (int i = 0; i < stop; ++i) {
        PropertyDescriptor descriptor = descriptors[i];
        if (descriptor.getName().equals(property)
            && (descriptor.getPropertyType() == boolean.class)) {
            return descriptor.getReadMethod();
        }
    }
    throw new IntrospectionException(
        "Bean \"" + name + "\" has no boolean property named \""
        + property + "\" for <ifProperty> tag.");
}
```

Once the appropriate `BeanInfo` instance has been obtained, the next step is to query its properties. This is accomplished by calling its `getPropertyDescriptors()` method, which returns an array of instances of the class `java.beans.PropertyDescriptor`. Each `PropertyDescriptor` instance contains information about the name and type of the corresponding Bean property, and provides accessors for retrieving the property's getter and setter methods. The `getPropertyReader()` method iterates through this array of `PropertyDescriptor` instances looking for a property whose value is a boolean and whose name matches the string value supplied for the tag's property attribute. If an appropriate descriptor is found, its `getReadMethod()` method is called to retrieve the corresponding getter method. Otherwise, an error is signaled.

Reflection

Assuming the desired method is found, it is the role of the tag handler's `readProperty()` method to call this method in order to obtain the Bean property's current value. This is accomplished via the Java reflection API, the classes of which are found in the `java.lang.reflect` package. In this case, we are interested in the `java.lang.reflect.Method` class, an instance of which should have been returned by the tag handler's `getPropertyReader()` method. The method represented by this `Method` instance is called by means of the instance's `invoke()` method:

```
private boolean readProperty (Object bean, Method reader)
    throws IntrospectionException {
    try {
        Object result = reader.invoke(bean, null);
        return ((Boolean) result).booleanValue();
    }
    catch (InvocationTargetException e) {
        throw new IntrospectionException(
          "Unable to access property \"" + property
        + "\" of bean \"" + name
        + "\" for <ifProperty> tag.");
    }
    catch (IllegalAccessException e) {
        throw new IntrospectionException(
          "Unable to access  property \"" + property
        + "\" of bean \"" + name
        + "\" for <ifProperty> tag.");
    }
}
```

The `invoke()` method takes two arguments: the instance for which the `Method` instance's method should be invoked, and an array of objects representing the arguments with which that method should be invoked. Since the method to be invoked is the property's getter method, the object for which it should be invoked is the Bean. Since the getter method takes no arguments, the `null` value is provided as the second argument to `invoke()`.

JARGON If this is your first exposure to introspection and reflection, you have probably come to the conclusion that they are very powerful features, but an explanation of their use makes for very convoluted sentences. Bear with us: we're almost out of the woods, at least as far as the `ifProperty` tag is concerned.

In order to support the most general case, the result returned by the `invoke()` method takes the form of an instance of Java's `Object` class. Because the property's getter method returns a boolean value, it will be packaged by the `invoke()` method as an instance of the `java.lang.Boolean` class. The `Object` returned by `invoke()` must therefore first be cast to a `Boolean`, after which its `booleanValue()` method can be called to retrieve the actual value.

Of course, calling `invoke()` can be a fairly dangerous operation, since there's no guarantee that the method being invoked, the instance on which it is being invoked, and the arguments supplied for invoking it are mutually compatible. For that reason numerous exceptions can be raised if such incompatibilities arise, as indicated by the `catch` clauses in the `readProperty()` method. For convenience, if any of these exceptions are thrown, they are transformed into instances of the `java.beans.IntrospectionException` class, which is caught by our original `doStartTag()` method.

Cleanup

The final step is the implementation of its `release()` method, which is defined as:

```
public void release () {
  super.release();
  name = null; property = null;
  action="include";
}
```

As with the `release()` methods presented earlier in this book, the first step is to call the `release()` method of the superclass. The next step is to reset all of the instance variables to their original values. As before, this allows the values used while processing the current tag to be garbage collected, and ensures that the appropriate default values are in place for the next tag.

The full source code for the tag handler is presented in abbreviated form in listing 14.6.

Listing 14.6   Source code for the IfPropertyTag tag handler

```
package com.taglib.wdjsp.mut;

import javax.servlet.jsp.PageContext;
import javax.servlet.jsp.tagext.TagSupport;
import javax.servlet.jsp.JspException;
import javax.servlet.jsp.JspTagException;
import java.lang.reflect.*;
import java.beans.*;

public class IfPropertyTag extends TagSupport {
    private String name, property;
    private String action="include";

    public void setName (String name) {
        this.name = name;
    }
    public String getName () {
        return name;
    }
    public void setProperty (String property) {
        this.property = property;
    }
    public String getProperty () {
        return property;
    }
    public void setAction (String action) {
        this.action = action;
    }
    public String getAction () {
        return action;
    }
    public int doStartTag () throws JspException { … }
    private boolean evalPropertyValue ()
        throws IntrospectionException { … }
    private Method getPropertyReader (Object bean)
        throws IntrospectionException { … }
    private boolean readProperty (Object bean, Method reader)
        throws IntrospectionException { … }
    public void release () { … }
}
```

Application

Before we can see the tag in action, we first need a Bean on which it will operate. To this end, the source code for the com.taglib.wdjsp.advtags.TimeOfDayBean class is presented in listing 14.7. As you can see, this Bean implements getters for three boolean properties named morning, afternoon, and daytime. The morning property is true between 6 a.m. and noon, while the afternoon property is true from noon to 6 p.m. The daytime property is true whenever either of the other two properties is true. An accessor for an integer property named hour is also available for accessing the current time of day directly.

Listing 14.7 Source code for the TimeOfDayBean class

```
package com.taglib.wdjsp.advtags;
import java.util.Date;
public class TimeOfDayBean {
  public int getHour () {
    Date now = new Date();
    return now.getHours();
  }
  public boolean isMorning () {
    int hour = getHour();
    return (hour >= 6) && (hour < 12);
  }
  public boolean isAfternoon () {
    int hour = getHour();
    return (hour >= 12) && (hour < 18);
  }
  public boolean isDaytime () {
    return isMorning() || isAfternoon();
  }
}
```

Using this Bean, then, we can construct a JSP page that uses this Bean in combination with our ifProperty tag. Here is the source code for such a page:

```
<%@ taglib uri="/mutlib" prefix="mut" %>
<jsp:useBean id="tod"
            class="com.taglib.wdjsp.advtags.TimeOfDayBean"/>
<html>
<head>
<title>Conditional Tag</title>
</head>
<body>
<h1>Conditional Tag</h1>

<p>The hour is now
```

```
<jsp:getProperty name="tod" property="hour"/>.</p>

<mut:ifProperty name="tod" property="morning">
<p>Good Morning!</p>
</mut:ifProperty>

<mut:ifProperty name="tod" property="afternoon">
<p>Good Afternoon!</p>
</mut:ifProperty>

<mut:ifProperty name="tod"
                property="daytime" action="exclude">
<p>Good Night!</p>
</mut:ifProperty>

</body>
</html>
```

This page first creates an instance of the `TimeOfDayBean` named `tod`, and then displays the value of its hour property via the `<jsp:getProperty>` tag. The remainder of the page contains three uses of the `ifProperty` tag, conditionalizing the content to be displayed based on the Bean's three boolean properties. The first two `ifProperty` tags rely on the default setting of the `action` attribute to include their body content whenever the corresponding property is `true`, while the third explicitly sets its action tag to `"exclude"`. As a result, the body content of the third `ifProperty` tag is only displayed when the value of the corresponding Bean property is `false`.

The results of requesting this page at different times of the day are displayed in figures 14.2 and 14.3.

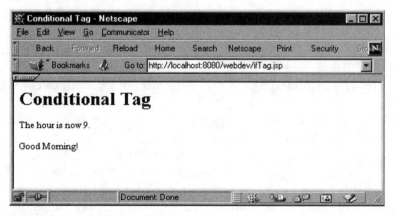

Figure 14.2   Output of the conditional tag

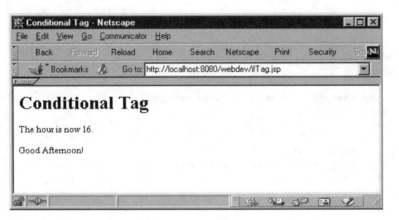

Figure 14.3   Later that same day

14.2.2 *Iteration*

The `forProperty` tag performs iteration over the elements of a JavaBeans indexed property. In retrieving the values of that indexed property, our implementation of this custom action will again utilize the introspection and reflection APIs. In addition, because this tag makes the current element available as a scripting variable, it will require a helper class for use during page compilation.

Here is the syntax for the `forProperty` tag:

```
<mut:forProperty name="bean" property="property"
                 id="id" class="class">
   bodyContent
</mut:forProperty>
```

As was the case for the `ifProperty` tag, the `name` and `property` attributes of the `forProperty` tag have the same meaning as their counterparts in the built-in `<jsp:getProperty>` and `<jsp:setProperty>` tags. These two attributes identify the Bean being accessed, and the specific property over whose elements the tag will iterate. The property identified by the `property` attribute should, of course, be an indexed one.

The body content of this tag will be processed once for each element of that indexed property. The `id` attribute is used to specify the variable name by which the element may be referenced within the body content. Finally, because the custom tag API does not provide enough information for inferring the class of an indexed property's elements during page compilation, the `class` attribute is provided for specifying it explicitly. All four attributes of the `forProperty` tag are required.

Flow of control | 459

Tag Handler

As you recall from the discussion of the tag handler life cycle diagrams in
chapter 11, only the `BodyTag` interface is capable of processing body content iteratively. The tag handler for the `forProperty` custom action is therefore implemented
as a subclass of `BodyTagSupport`. Four instance variables are provided for storing
the tag's attribute values, with corresponding getters and setter:

```
public class ForPropertyTag extends BodyTagSupport {
  private String name, property, id;
  private Class elementClass;

  public void setName (String name) {
    this.name = name;
  }
  public String getName () {
    return name;
  }
  public void setProperty (String property) {
    this.property = property;
  }
  public String getProperty () {
    return property;
  }
  public void setId (String id) {
    this.id = id;
  }
  public String getId () {
    return id;
  }
  public void setClass (String className)
    throws ClassNotFoundException {
    setElementClass(Class.forName(className));
  }
  public void setElementClass (Class elementClass) {
    this.elementClass = elementClass;
  }
  public Class getElementClass () {
    return elementClass;
  }
  ...
}
```

In a slight departure from previous tag handler implementations, note that the setter for the tag's `class` attribute, `setClass()`, automatically performs the translation of the `String` value specified for the attribute into an actual Java class object.
This is accomplished via the `Class.forName()` static method, the result of which is
then stored in the handler's `elementClass` instance variable. Getter and setters

methods are provided for this instance variable, but no getClass() method has been provided for accessing the original String value of the tag attribute.

This is because the handler already has a getClass() method, inherited from java.lang.Object. As with all Java object classes, tag handlers are subclasses of Java's root Object class, which defines getClass() as a method for obtaining an object's class. Furthermore, this method is marked as final, which prohibits subclasses from overriding it. ForPropertyTag therefore cannot define its own get-Class() method, no matter how much we might want it to. The result is that our accessors for the tag's class attribute are somewhat asymmetrical. On the other hand, we are not prohibited from using class as an attribute name, and can thereby support a syntax for the forProperty tag which incorporates familiar elements from the built-in <jsp:useBean> and <jsp:getProperty> tags.

There is additional data that the handler must keep track of, which will also be stored in instance variables. As a result of this tag's iterative nature, run-time performance can be improved by maintaining references to the Bean, the method used for accessing the indexed property's elements, the size of the indexed property, and the current status of the iteration. These references take the form of the following four instance variables:

```
public class ForPropertyTag extends BodyTagSupport {
    ...
    private Object bean;
    private Method elementMethod;
    private int size, index;
    ...
}
```

It is the job of the tag handler's doStartTag() method to initialize these instance variables, and to prepare for the first iteration of the tag's body content. Here is the implementation of that method:

```
public int doStartTag () throws JspException {
  bean = pageContext.getAttribute(name);
  if (bean != null) {
     Class beanClass = bean.getClass();
     initSize(beanClass);
     if (size > 0) {
      initElementMethod(beanClass);
      index = 0;
      assignElement();
      return EVAL_BODY_TAG;
     } else {
      return SKIP_BODY;
     }
```

```
    } else {
        throw new JspTagException("No bean \"" + name
        + "\" available for <forProperty> tag.");
    }
}
```

The first step is to initialize the `bean` instance variable. As was the case for the `eval-PropertyValue()` method of `IfPropertyTag`, this is accomplished by means of the `getAttribute()` method associated with the `pageContext` object for the current page. If the specified Bean is present, the `doStartTag()` method then proceeds to retrieve its `Class` object. If not, an error is signaled.

If Bean initialization succeeds, `doStartTag()` next calls the tag handler's `init-Size()` method to initialize the `size` instance variable. This method is defined as follows:

```
private void initSize (Class beanClass) throws JspException {
    Method method =
        getReader(beanClass, property + "Size", int.class);
    Object sizeWrapper = invokeMethod(method, "size");
    size = ((Integer) sizeWrapper).intValue();
}
```

The first step here is to retrieve the getter method for the indexed property's size. By convention, the size of an indexed property is itself exposed as an integer-valued Bean property with the same name as the indexed property, plus the suffix `Size`. To obtain the size of the indexed property, then, we must first obtain the getter method for this size property. This is accomplished by means of a utility introspection method named `getReader()`, to be presented later in this chapter, which either returns the requested getter or throws a `JspException`.

Once the method is found, it is invoked in order to obtain the property value (i.e., the size property). Another utility method, `invokeMethod()`, is called upon to perform this reflection operation (or throw a `JspException` if for some reason it can't). The `invokeMethod()` method will be described later in the chapter. The final step of the `initSize()` method is to unwrap the `java.lang.Integer` object returned by `invokeMethod()` which contains the actual integer value representing the size of the indexed property.

Returning to the `doStartTag()` method, processing then depends upon whether or not the indexed property actually has any elements. If the indexed property's size is zero, then the tag's body can be skipped altogether. This is accomplished by returning `Tag.SKIP_BODY`.

If one or more elements are present, however, the next step for `doStartTag()` is to call `initElementMethod()` to initialize the tag handler's `elementMethod` instance variable. This method is defined as follows:

```
private void initElementMethod (Class beanClass)
    throws JspException {
    elementMethod =
        getIndexedReader(beanClass, property, elementClass);
}
```

Like the first line of `initSize()`, this method simply relies on a utility introspection method for retrieving the getter method for the indexed property. As before, this utility method will be presented later in the chapter.

The remaining steps in the `doStartTag()` method when elements are present is to initialize the `index` instance variable to zero and then call `assignElement()` to initialize the tag's scripting variable prior to the first iteration. The method then returns `BodyTag.EVAL_BODY_TAG` to indicate that processing of the custom action should continue with its body content.

The `assignElement()` method is also a key element of the tag handler's `doAfterBody()` method, which is defined as:

```
public int doAfterBody () throws JspException {
    BodyContent body = getBodyContent();
    try {
        body.writeOut(getPreviousOut());
    } catch (IOException ex) {
        throw new JspTagException("unexpected IO error");
    }
    body.clearBody();
    if (++index < size) {
        assignElement();
        return EVAL_BODY_TAG;
    } else {
        return SKIP_BODY;
    }
}
```

As was the case in the `doAfterBody()` methods for both `UrlTag` and `HtmlEncodeTag` (chapter 13), the first step is to retrieve the `BodyContent` instance representing the content generated by the tag's body. This instance's `writeOut()` method is then called to actually output that generated content, by sending it to the output stream accessed via `getPreviousOut()`. Its `clearBody()` method is called next to flush the content that was just written. This is particularly important here, since this `Body-Content` instance will be reused in each iteration over the tag's body content.

Once the results of the most recent iteration have been written, the next step is to decide whether or not another iteration is required. The `index` instance variable is incremented, and compared to the stored size of the indexed property. If there are no elements left, then the method returns `Tag.SKIP_BODY` to indicate to the JSP container that no further iterations are required. Otherwise, the `assignElement()` method is called to set the value of the scripting variable for the next iteration, and `BodyTag.EVAL_BODY_TAG` is returned to indicate that the body content should be processed again.

The code for the `assignElement()` method is itself fairly straightforward:

```
private void assignElement () throws JspException {
  Object element =
    invokeMethod(elementMethod, index, "element");
  pageContext.setAttribute(id, element);
}
```

Once again, a utility method, `invokeMethod()`, is called to perform the reflection operations required to retrieve the next element of the indexed property. Its role is to call the getter method for the indexed property, passing it the current value of the `index` instance variable as its sole argument. Then, just as the original Bean was retrieved from the `pageContext` object via its `getAttribute()` method, assignment of the scripting variable for the element is accomplished by calling the `pageContext` object's `setAttribute()` method. This action, in combination with information provided to the JSP container via this handler's helper class, is the only step required for a custom tag to assign a value to a scripting variable. The JSP container handles all of the behind-the-scenes details required to subsequently access this value using the associated page's scripting language.

The final element is the `release()` method, defined as follows:

```
public void release () {
  super.release();
  name = null; property = null; id = null; elementClass = null;
  bean = null; index = 0; size = 0; elementMethod = null;
}
```

Like the `release()` methods presented for previous tag handlers, the primary task of this method is to reset the object's instance variables, so that the tag handler instance may be reused by the JSP container.

The complete source for the `ForPropertyTag` class is presented in abbreviated form in listing 14.8. The definitions of the introspection and reflection utility methods will be presented in the next two sections.

Listing 14.8   Source code for the ForPropertyTag tag handler

```
package com.taglib.wdjsp.mut;

import javax.servlet.jsp.PageContext;
import javax.servlet.jsp.tagext.*;
import javax.servlet.jsp.*;
import java.lang.reflect.*;
import java.beans.*;
import java.io.IOException;

public class ForPropertyTag extends BodyTagSupport {
    private String name, property, id;
    private Class elementClass;

    public void setName (String name) { ... }
    public String getName () { ... }
    public void setProperty (String property) { ... }
    public String getProperty () { ... }
    public void setId (String id) { ... }
    public String getId () { ... }
    public void setClass (String className)
      throws ClassNotFoundException { ... }
    public void setElementClass (Class elementClass) { ... }
    public Class getElementClass () { ... }

    private Object bean;
    private Method elementMethod;
    private int size, index;

    private void assignElement () throws JspException { ... }
    private void initSize (Class beanClass)
      throws JspException { ... }
    private void initElementMethod (Class beanClass)
      throws JspException { ... }

    public int doStartTag () throws JspException { ... }
    public int doAfterBody () throws JspException { ... }
    public void release () { ... }

    private Method getReader (Class beanClass,
                              String property, Class returnType)
      throws JspException { ... }
    private Method getIndexedReader (Class beanClass,
```

```
                                      String property,
                                      Class returnType)
      throws JspException { ... }

   private Object invokeMethod (Method method, String label)
      throws JspException { ... }
   private Object invokeMethod (Method method, int arg,
                                String label)
      throws JspException { ... }
   private Object invokeMethod (Method method, Object[] args,
                                String label)
      throws JspException { ... }
}
```

Introspection methods

The `ForPropertyTag` class defines two utility methods for retrieving Bean property accessors via Java's introspection API: `getReader()` fetches the getter method for a standard Java Bean property; `getIndexedReader()` retrieves the getter method for an indexed Java Bean property.

In the implementation of `ForPropertyTag`, the `getReader()` method is used to obtain the getter method for the property corresponding to the size of the indexed property (i.e., the number of elements over which the iteration is to occur). The `getIndexedReader()` method is used to obtain the getter method for accessing the actual elements of the indexed property.

Given that each of these methods is used only once, it may seem like overkill to provide utility methods for performing these operations. Noting that we have already performed similar introspection operations while implementing the `IfPropertyTag` class, being able to abstract these operations into a set of utility methods that could potentially be reused by multiple tag handler classes is an attractive idea. These utility methods represent a first step in that direction.

Here is the code for implementing the `getReader()` method:

```
private Method getReader (Class beanClass,
                          String property, Class returnType)
  throws JspException {
  try {
    BeanInfo beanInfo = Introspector.getBeanInfo(beanClass);
    PropertyDescriptor[] descriptors =
      beanInfo.getPropertyDescriptors();
    int stop = descriptors.length;
    for (int i = 0; i < stop; ++i) {
      PropertyDescriptor descriptor = descriptors[i];
      if (descriptor.getName().equals(property)
          && (descriptor.getPropertyType() == returnType)) {
```

```
        return descriptor.getReadMethod();
      }
    }
    throw new
      JspTagException("Bean \"" + name +
                      "\" has no property named \"" + property +
                      "\" of type " + returnType.getName() +
                      " for <ifProperty> tag.");
  }
  catch (IntrospectionException e) {
    throw new JspTagException(e.getMessage());
  }
}
```

As might be expected, this method has much in common with the getProperty-Reader() method of IfPropertyTag. The primary difference is that this method has no dependencies on the class's instance variables. Instead, the method's parameters are its primary source of data.

Like the getPropertyReader() method, this method starts out by retrieving the BeanInfo object for the JavaBean class whose properties are being examined (the method's first argument), and then uses this object to retrieve an array of property descriptors. This array is searched for a property whose name and value match those passed in as getReader()'s second and third parameters. Once found, the descriptor's getReadMethod() is called to obtain and return the Method object corresponding to the getter method for the property. If the search fails to turn up an appropriate property descriptor, a JspTagException is thrown. For convenience—given this utility method's intended role in implementing custom tags—if an IntrospectionException is thrown, it is caught and used to initialize a new JspTagException for notifying the caller of any introspection errors.

The implementation of getIndexedReader() is quite similar:

```
private Method getIndexedReader (Class beanClass,
                                 String property,
                                 Class returnType)
  throws JspException {
  try {
    BeanInfo beanInfo = Introspector.getBeanInfo(beanClass);
    PropertyDescriptor[] descriptors =
      beanInfo.getPropertyDescriptors();
    int stop = descriptors.length;
    for (int i = 0; i < stop; ++i) {
      PropertyDescriptor descriptor = descriptors[i];
      if (descriptor instanceof IndexedPropertyDescriptor
          && descriptor.getName().equals(property)) {
        IndexedPropertyDescriptor ipd =
          (IndexedPropertyDescriptor) descriptor;
```

```
      if (ipd.getIndexedPropertyType() == returnType) {
        return ipd.getIndexedReadMethod();
      }
    }
  }
}
throw new
  JspTagException("Bean \"" + name +
                    "\" has no indexed property named \"" +
                    property +
                    "\" of type " + returnType.getName() +
                    " for <ifProperty> tag.");
}
catch (IntrospectionException e) {
  throw new JspTagException(e.getMessage());
}
}
```

The primary difference between getIndexedReader() and getReader() is in the code for checking property descriptors. The introspection API provides a special subclass of PropertyDescriptor, named IndexedPropertyDescriptor, for representing indexed properties. For this reason, the getIndexedReader() method only examines property descriptors that are instances of this subclass. Note also that the IndexedPropertyDescriptor subclass renames the methods for retrieving the property type and getter method. These methods are called getIndexedProperty-Type() and getIndexedReadMethod(), respectively.

Reflection methods

Three utility methods are implemented by the ForPropertyTag class for supporting reflection. All three are variants of the invokeMethod() method, the principal version of which is defined as follows:

```
private Object invokeMethod (Method method, Object[] args,
                              String label)
  throws JspException {
  try {
    return method.invoke(bean, args);
  }
  catch (IllegalAccessException e) {
    throw new JspTagException("Unable to invoke " + label
                              + " method corresponding to property \""
                              + property + "\" of bean \"" + name
                              + "\" for <forProperty> tag.");
  }
  catch (InvocationTargetException e) {
    throw new JspTagException("Unable to invoke " + label
                              + " method corresponding to property \""
                              + property + "\" of bean \"" + name
```

```
                                      + "\" for <forProperty> tag.");
    }
  }
```

Obviously this method is basically a wrapper around the `invoke()` method of class `Method`, which catches any exceptions thrown during method invocation and then throws corresponding instances of the `JspTagException` class. To simplify the argument list, this method uses some of `ForPropertyTag`'s instance variables (specifically, `bean` and `property`), but it would not be too difficult to eliminate this dependency.

To simplify the invocation of methods that take no arguments, the following variant of `invokeMethod()` is provided:

```
private Object invokeMethod (Method method, String label)
  throws JspException {
  return invokeMethod(method, new Object[0], label);
}
```

This form simply provides a default, empty value for the second argument of the original version of `invokeMethod()`. `ForPropertyTag` calls this version of `invokeMethod()` in its `initSize()` method.

A third form of `invokeMethod()` is provided for calling methods which take a single, integer argument:

```
private Object invokeMethod (Method method, int arg, String label)
  throws JspException {
  Integer[] args = { new Integer(arg) };
  return invokeMethod(method, args, label);
}
```

Here, the integer argument is wrapped in an instance of the `java.lang.Integer` class. This `Integer` object is itself packaged in an array, which again serves as the value for the second argument when calling the original version of `invokeMethod()`.

Helper Class

As indicated earlier in this chapter, because the behavior of the `forProperty` tag includes setting a scripting variable, a helper class is required. This class will be instantiated whenever a page using the tag is compiled in order to enable the JSP container to determine the variable's name and type. In this way, references to the scripting variable within the tag's body content can be resolved and statically checked during page compilation. The name of the helper class, as specified by the TLD entry for the `forPropertyTag` provided in listing 14.5, is `ForPropertyTEI`.

> **NOTE** It is standard practice to name the tag helper class after the tag, with an added TEI suffix. As you recall, TEI is an abbreviation for `TagExtraInfo`, the base class that all JSP custom tag helper classes must extend.

The source code for `ForPropertyTEI` is provided in listing 14.9. As required for tag handler helper classes, `ForPropertyTEI` is a subclass of `javax.servlet.jsp.tagext.TagExtraInfo`, and provides implementations for its two primary methods, `getVariableInfo()` and `isValid()`.

Listing 14.9 Source code for the ForPropertyTEI helper class

```
package com.taglib.wdjsp.mut;

import javax.servlet.jsp.tagext.*;

public class ForPropertyTEI extends TagExtraInfo {

  public VariableInfo[] getVariableInfo (TagData data) {
    String varName = data.getId();
    String className = data.getAttributeString("class");
    VariableInfo info =
      new VariableInfo(varName, className,
                       true, VariableInfo.NESTED);
    VariableInfo[] result = { info };
    return result;
  }
  public boolean isValid (TagData data) {
    return true;
  }
}
```

As discussed in chapter 13, `getVariableInfo()` is used to pass information about scripting variables to the JSP container. For the `forProperty` tag, the name of the scripting variable is provided by the `id` attribute, and its type is provided by the `class` attribute. The values for these two attributes are obtained from the `TagData` object passed in as the argument to this method via its `getId()` and `getAttributeString()` methods, respectively.

After retrieving these two attribute values, they are used as the first two constructor arguments in creating an instance of the `VariableInfo` class. The third argument is `true`, indicating that this is a new scripting variable, for which a corresponding declaration may be required (depending upon the page's scripting language). The value for the fourth argument is `VariableInfo.NESTED`, indicating that the scripting variable is only in scope within the body of the `forProperty` tag.

> **NOTE** The `getId()` method of the `TagData` class is shorthand for calling the `getAttributeString()` method with an argument of `"id"`. It is provided in support of the JSP convention that the `id` attribute is used to bind new scripting variables, whereas the `name` attribute is used to reference them. This convention is exemplified by the standard JavaBeans tags: `<jsp:useBean>` has an attribute named `id` for adding a Bean to a page, while `<jsp:getProperty>` and `<jsp:setProperty>` have `name` attributes for accessing an existing Bean's properties. The `getId()` convenience method is only useful in helper classes for custom tags that follow this convention.

Since this tag creates only a single scripting variable, a `VariableInfo` array of length one is then created. The `VariableInfo` instance that was just constructed serves as its sole element. This array is the return value of the `getVariableInfo()` method.

No special checks are performed by the `isValid()` method of `ForPropertyTEI`, so it simply returns `true`, indicating that the tag described by its `TagData` argument is valid. Recall that the JSP container automatically performs certain compile-time checks based on the tag's TLD entry, in addition to calling the `isValid()` method of the tag's helper class (if any).

Unfortunately, the `TagData` object passed in as the argument to both `getVariableInfo()` and `isValid()` provides access only to information about the custom tag currently being compiled by the JSP container. In particular, there is no way for these methods to obtain information about the context in which the custom tag appears.

The methods of `ForPropertyTEI`, for example, could certainly benefit from knowing about the Beans present on the page. During the course of compiling the page, the JSP container will determine the class of the Bean specified by the `forProperty` tag's `name` attribute. If this information were made available to the `isValid()` method, it would be possible for that method to validate the value specified for the tag's `class` attribute, using introspection. Alternatively, if this information were available from the `getVariableInfo()` method, use of the `class` attribute could be avoided altogether. The introspection API could be used to infer the appropriate class of the scripting variable, and supply it to the `VariableInfo` constructor automatically. Perhaps capabilities such as these will be addressed by a future version of the JSP specification.

Example Bean

Before we can demonstrate the use of this tag, we will need a Bean with an indexed property that can be used in an example page. Actually, we will need two Beans, since the elements of the indexed property should themselves be instances of a Bean class. Two such Beans are presented in listings 14.10 and 14.11.

The first class, PlotBean, represents a set of *(x, y)* coordinates by means of two Bean properties, data and dataSize. The first, data, is an indexed property that stores the plot's coordinates as an array of instances of our second example class, DataBean. The dataSize property merely reflects the size of this array. In something of a departure from other indexed properties we have seen, however, the setter for the dataSize property (i.e., setDataSize()) has an important side effect. By calling the Bean class's makeDataPoints() method, the dataSize setter will generate an array of data points, using the zero-argument constructor provided by the DataBean class.

Listing 14.10   Source code for the PlotBean class

```
package com.taglib.wdjsp.advtags;

public class PlotBean {
  private DataBean[] dataPoints;

  public PlotBean () {
    makeDataPoints(0);
  }
  public int getDataSize () {
    return dataPoints.length;
  }
  public void setDataSize (int size) {
    makeDataPoints(size);
  }
  public DataBean getData (int index) {
    return dataPoints[index];
  }
  public void setData (int index, DataBean data) {
    dataPoints[index] = data;
  }

  private void makeDataPoints (int count) {
    dataPoints = new DataBean[count];
    for (int i = 0; i < count; ++i) {
      dataPoints[i] = new DataBean();
    }
  }
}
```

As indicated in listing 14.11, this zero-argument DataBean constructor generates a new Bean that has random values for its x and y properties. This is accomplished by means of randomCoordinate(), a static method defined by the DataBean class which generates random values between 0 and 100. This method in turn relies on a statically stored instance of the java.util.Random class, whose nextDouble() method is used to generate random, double-precision floating-point values between 0 and 1.

The DataBean class also provides a two-argument constructor for specifying its coordinates explicitly, as well as the standard getter and setter methods for the properties corresponding to those coordinates.

Listing 14.11   Source code for the DataBean class

```
package com.taglib.wdjsp.advtags;
import java.util.Random;
public class DataBean {
  private double x, y;

  public DataBean () {
    this(randomCoordinate(), randomCoordinate());
  }
  public DataBean (double x, double y) {
    this.x = x;
    this.y = y;
  }
  public double getX () {
    return x;
  }
  public void setX (double x) {
    this.x = x;
  }
  public double getY () {
    return y;
  }
  public void setY (double y) {
    this.y = y;
  }
  static private Random rnd = new Random();
  static private double randomCoordinate () {
    return 100d * rnd.nextDouble();
  }
}
```

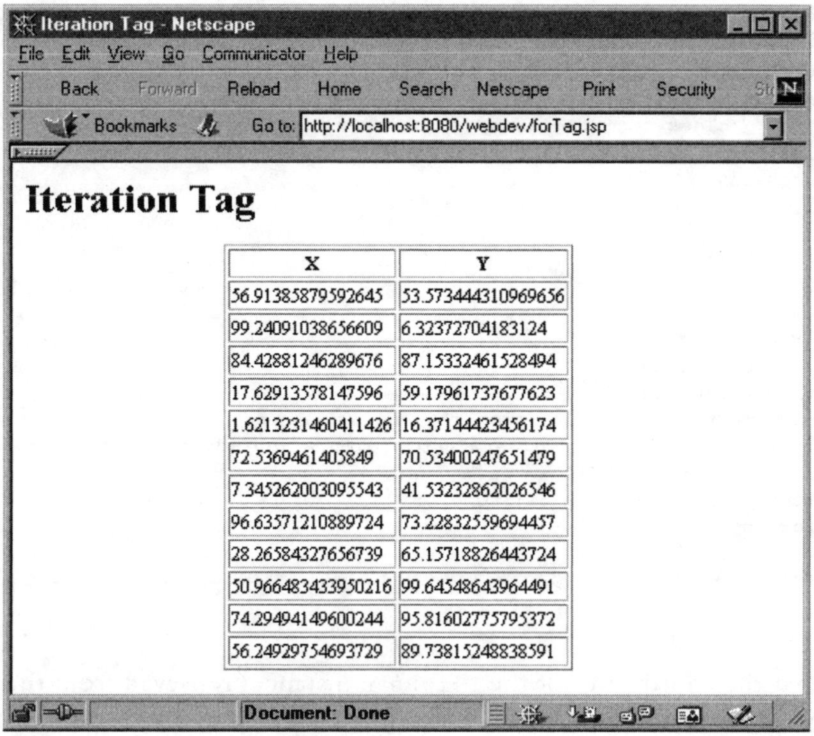

Figure 14.4 Output of the iteration tag

Sample Page

A sample page demonstrating the application of the `forProperty` tag to an instance of the `PlotBean` class is provided in listing 14.12. Note the use of the `<jsp:set-Property>` tag in the body of the `<jsp:useBean>` tag to set the number of data points to 12. Recall that this action has the side effect of replacing the contents of the Bean's `data` indexed property with 12 new, random data points.

The `forProperty` tag appears toward the end of the page, where it is used to iterate through the elements of this `data` property. In the body of the `forProperty` tag, table rows are generated for displaying the coordinates of the data points. The resulting output is depicted in figure 14.4.

Listing 14.12   Source code for the forProperty tag example page

```
<%@ taglib uri="/mutlib" prefix="mut" %>
<jsp:useBean id="plot"
             class="com.taglib.wdjsp.advtags.PlotBean"/>
  <jsp:setProperty name="plot" property="dataSize" value="12"/>
</jsp:useBean>
<html>
<head>
<title>Iteration Tag</title>
</head>
<body>
<h1>Iteration Tag</h1>
<center><table border=1>
<tr><th>X</th><th>Y</th></tr>
<mut:forProperty name="plot" property="data"
                 id="point" class="com.taglib.wdjsp.advtags.DataBean">
  <tr><td><%= point.getX() %></td>
      <td><%= point.getY() %></td></tr>
</mut:forProperty>
</table></center>
</body>
</html>
```

Note that the coordinates of the `DataBean` instances retrieved from the indexed property are displayed by means of JSP expressions. These expressions reference the `point` scripting variable, introduced by the `id` attribute of the `forProperty` tag. Since the value of the `point` variable is actually a Bean (specifically, an instance of `DataBean`), you might prefer to display its value using the `<jsp:getProperty>` tag, instead, as in the following page fragment:

```
<mut:forProperty name="plot" property="data"
                 id="point" class="com.taglib.wdjsp.advtags.DataBean">
  <tr><td><jsp:getProperty name="point" property="x"/></td>
      <td><jsp:getProperty name="point" property="y"/></td></tr>
</mut:forProperty>
```

Unfortunately, the current JSP specification is unclear as to what objects can be accessed using the `<jsp:getProperty>` and `<jsp:setProperty>` tags. Some JSP containers allow all Beans accessible as scripting variables to be manipulated via `<jsp:getProperty>` and `<jsp:setProperty>`, including Beans created using custom tags. Other JSP containers, however, only allow Beans introduced via the `<jsp:useBean>` tag to be referenced by the other two built-in tags. While complete interoperability between custom tags and the standard JSP Bean tags is preferable, if you want to guarantee that your JSP pages are portable, the use of expressions and scriptlets for accessing scripting variables created by custom tags is, at least for now, the recommended approach.

NOTE Another option, that also has the advantage of portability, would be to create your own custom versions of the <jsp:getProperty> and <jsp:setProperty> tags that are compatible with Beans created via custom tags, as well as with those added to a page via <jsp:useBean>. Implementation of their behavior is yet another application of the Java introspection and reflection APIs.

14.3 *Packaging the tag library*

As discussed in chapter 13, tag libraries are deployed in the form of JAR files containing both the tag handler classes and the TLD. The TLD appears in the META-INF directory of the JAR file, under the name taglib.tld. (See listing 13.1 for the basic outline of the TLD for the mut custom tag library.) The tag handler classes are organized into directories according to their package structure.

Any auxiliary classes upon which the tag handlers rely must also be present in the JAR file. This includes all tag handler base classes (such as our OutlineBase class) and inner classes, as well as any helper classes specified in the TLD's <teiclass> entries. The full table of contents listing for the mut library's JAR file is presented in listing 14.13.

Listing 14.13   Contents of the JAR file for the mut tag library

```
META-INF/MANIFEST.MF
META-INF/taglib.tld
com/taglib/wdjsp/mut/DebugBufferTag.class
com/taglib/wdjsp/mut/DebugCookiesTag.class
com/taglib/wdjsp/mut/IfPropertyTag.class
com/taglib/wdjsp/mut/ForPropertyTag.class
com/taglib/wdjsp/mut/ForPropertyTEI.class
com/taglib/wdjsp/mut/EncodeHtmlTag.class
com/taglib/wdjsp/mut/OutlineBase.class
com/taglib/wdjsp/mut/OutlineTag.class
com/taglib/wdjsp/mut/OutlineItemTag.class
com/taglib/wdjsp/mut/UrlTag.class
```

As discussed in chapter 10, deploying the tag library to a JSP container happens at the application level. The library's JAR file is added to the WEB-INF/lib directory associated with the application, and a copy of its TLD is added to the WEB-INF/tlds directory and assigned a library-specific name. A URI for accessing this TLD from the application's JSP pages is then created in the application's deployment descriptor, using a `<taglib>` entry such as the following:

```
<taglib>
   <taglib-uri>/mutlib</taglib-uri>
   <taglib-location>/WEB-INF/tlds/mut_1_0.tld</taglib-location>
</taglib>
```

As a result of including this entry in the application's web.xml file, JSP pages employing the `taglib` directive can reference this TLD via the specified URI. In this example, the URI /mutlib is assigned to the TLD for version 1.0 of the `mut` custom tag library. This URI then serves as the value for the `uri` attribute in the `taglib` directive, as demonstrated in the sample pages presented in this chapter and the previous chapter.

14.4   *For further information*

As stated at the beginning of chapter 13, custom tags are a rather recent addition to JSP, with great promise for expanding the scope and power of the base JSP technology. The range of potential applications for custom JSP tags is vast, and we have only been able to scratch the surface in these two final chapters. For this reason, we invite you to join us at http://www.taglib.com, a web site created by the authors to promote the use of JSP tag libraries and foster a community of developers with expertise in their design and construction. The site will have the usual assortment of news, FAQs and tutorials, but is also intended to serve as a clearinghouse for what we hope will be a large collection of Open Source tag libraries, such as the `mut` library presented here. We hope to see you there.

Running the reference implementation

In June 1999, Sun Microsystems announced it would be turning over to the Apache Software Foundation its internal source code for the reference implementations of the servlet and JSP APIs, for use in the development of an Open Source version of these technologies. This effort, dubbed the Jakarta Project, is aimed at producing world-class implementations of the latest servlet and JSP specifications, by leveraging contributions from major corporations such as Sun and IBM, as well as the developer community at large. The Jakarta software will continue to serve as the reference implementation for these specifications. At the same time, because it is an open platform that can be improved and extended by anyone willing to participate in its development, it should also have performance characteristics that keep it competitive with commercial servlet and JSP containers.

The first public release of software from the Jakarta Project came in December 1999 with Tomcat 3.0. Tomcat is a servlet and JSP container that implements version 2.2 of the servlet specification and version 1.1 of the JSP specification. It is the official reference implementation for these specifications, and may be freely downloaded from the Jakarta website at http://jakarta.apache.org. Tomcat includes a Java-based HTTP server and may be run as stand-alone software. It also includes a connector module supporting integration of Tomcat with the Apache web server.

In its role as the standard reference implementation, Tomcat provides a good platform for developing and testing JSPs, since it enforces compliance with the published specifications. Its suitability for deployment on your production web site, however, depends upon a variety of factors. Other JSP containers—for example, those included with an application server or a J2EE container—may provide additional features required for your site, such as EJB integration, URL rewriting, or automatic servlet reloading, that are not (currently) available with Tomcat. Alternatively, you may already be running an HTTP server to which you wish to add JSP support. Many of the commercial JSP containers support integration with HTTP servers from multiple vendors. Tomcat 3.0 only provides interoperability with the Apache HTTP server, although future versions will include a published interface to enable integration with other HTTP servers.

A.1   Prerequisites

The Tomcat software is written in Java, so the first requirement for running the reference implementation is a working Java Development Kit (JDK), which is a combination of a Java Runtime Environment and a Java compiler. Tomcat 3.0 requires JDK 1.1 or higher. At the time of this writing, this means a JDK that supports Java 1.1 or Java 2. JDKs are freely available from Sun (for the Solaris, Linux, and Microsoft Windows platforms) via the World Wide Web. JDKs for other operating systems are generally available from the corresponding vendor. If you do not already have access to an appropriate JDK on your development server, you will need to download one and install it. (See appendix C for the relevant URLs.) Most JDKs come with installer programs that automate much of the setup process; see the documentation accompanying the JDK download for complete instructions.

A.2   Installation

Once the JDK has been installed and added to your path, the next step is to download and install Tomcat. From the Jakarta home page at http://jakarta.apache.org, select the Binaries link under the Download heading. On the Binary Downloads page, the link for Tomcat 3.0 is listed under Release Builds. Binary versions of Tomcat 3.0 are available in three formats: a compressed Zip archive, a Solaris PKG package, and a Linux RPM package.

> **NOTE** Experienced Java developers may prefer to download Tomcat 3.0 in source code form and compile it themselves. In that case, select the Source Code link under the Download heading on the home page. Tomcat 3.0 and the associated tools for building it yourself are listed under the heading Release Source Drops on the Source Downloads page. Source code is available here as a set of compressed Zip archives. You will need both the Tomcat archive and the accompanying tools archive to compile Tomcat. A third archive contains the Watchdog software, which is used for testing compliance with the published specifications.

For the purposes of this discussion, we will assume that you wish to run Tomcat in stand-alone mode and do not require integration with an existing HTTP server. For those readers interested in running Tomcat with the Apache server, consult the accompanying documentation, which outlines the steps required to set up the JServ module (also available from the Jakarta web site). This module enables an Apache web server to forward requests for URLs corresponding to servlets and JSP pages to Tomcat for processing.

A.2.1 Linux

To simplify installation of Tomcat on the Linux platform, a Redhat Package Manager (RPM) package is provided. Officially, this package is considered to be an experimental version of the 3.0 release. Barring a few minor installation problems, however, our experience indicates that the RPM package can be used to successfully install Tomcat 3.0.

The Tomcat 3.0 RPM package is contained in the tomcat-3.0-0.noarch.rpm file. After downloading this file, it is installed by issuing the following command using the `root` account:

```
# rpm -i tomcat-3.0-0.noarch.rpm
```

At this point, a number of warning messages will be printed, indicating a particular user name (corresponding to a member of the Tomcat development team) is not recognized. These errors are presumably a result of the Tomcat RPM's experimental status, and may be safely ignored.

> **TIP** If you do not have access to the `root` account, you can still install Tomcat on a Linux system using the Zip archive, as described later in this chapter.

After executing the `rpm` command, the Tomcat software will be installed in the `/opt/tomcat` directory, and all files will be owned by `root`. Unfortunately, one file is missing from the RPM package that is required in order to run the server. The simplest way to obtain this missing file is to also download the tomcat.zip file from the same downloads directory as the RPM package, and use the following command to extract the missing file, named xml.jar, from this Zip archive:

```
# unzip tomcat.zip tomcat/lib/xml.jar
```

The extracted file should then be copied or moved into the `/opt/tomcat/lib` directory, as follows:

```
# mv tomcat/lib/xml.jar /opt/tomcat/lib/xml.jar
```

Next, you need to make certain that execute permissions are set on the three Tomcat shell scripts, using the following sequence of commands:

```
# cd /opt/tomcat
# chmod +x startup.sh shutdown.sh tomcat.sh
```

In addition, we recommend that you edit the tomcat.sh script to add a setting for the `JAVA_HOME` environment variable. This will enable Tomcat to readily locate the JRE on your server, without requiring you to add it to `root`'s default path. This environment variable should be set prior to any of the other UNIX commands in the tomcat.sh file. Somewhere near the top of the file (e.g., after the header comments but before the first `if` statement), insert a line such as the following:

```
JAVA_HOME = /usr/java1.2
```

The value of this environment variable is installation-dependent, and should correspond to the top-level directory of the JDK installation you wish to use for running Tomcat. The specified directory should contain a subdirectory named `bin` that contains the `java` executable used for running Java code.

Once these modifications have been made, the Tomcat software can be started and stopped by `root` using the startup.sh and shutdown.sh shell scripts. For additional installation details, consult the "Installation notes" section later in this chapter.

A.2.2 *Solaris*

A PKG package is provided for installing Tomcat on the Solaris operating system, contained in the file ASFtomcat.pkg.tar.Z. After downloading this file from the Tomcat web site, it must first be uncompressed and untarred, using the following command:

```
% uncompress -c ASFtomcat.pkg.tar.Z | tar xvf -
```

This command will result in the creation of a subdirectory named `ASFtomcat` that contains the PKG files needed to install Tomcat.

Installation of the Tomcat PKG requires superuser privileges, so if you have not done so already, log in as `root`, or use the `su` command to switch to that account. Then, from the directory in which you expanded the original, downloaded file, issue the following command to install the package:

```
# pkgadd -d . ASFtomcat
```

At this point, a number of warning messages will be printed, indicating that a particular user name (corresponding to a member of the Tomcat development team) is not in the local password table. The Solaris PKG, like the Linux RPM, is considered experimental for this release of Tomcat. These warnings are a manifestation of that experimental status, but testing by the authors suggests that they may be safely ignored. Even though the `pkgadd` command reports that installation was partially unsuccessful, our experience indicates that the software nevertheless operates as expected.

TIP   If you do not have access to the superuser account, you can still install Tomcat under Solaris using the Zip archive, as described later in this appendix.

After executing this command, the Tomcat software will be installed in the `/opt/tomcat` directory, and all files will be owned by the `root` account. Before running the software, you will need to make the Tomcat shell scripts executable, using the following sequence of commands:

```
# cd /opt/tomcat
# chmod +x startup.sh shutdown.sh tomcat.sh
```

You should also edit the tomcat.sh script to add a setting for the `JAVA_HOME` environment variable. This will enable Tomcat to locate the JRE on your server, without having to add it to the superuser's default path. Note that `JAVA_HOME` should be set prior to any of the other UNIX commands in the tomcat.sh file. Somewhere near the top of the file (e.g., after the header comments but before the first `if` statement), insert a line such as the following:

```
JAVA_HOME = /usr/java1.2
```

The value of this environment variable should be the top-level directory of the JDK installation you wish to use for running Tomcat. This directory should contain a subdirectory named `bin` that contains the `java` executable used for running Java code.

Once these changes have been made, the Tomcat software can be started and stopped by the superuser via the startup.sh and shutdown.sh shell scripts. For additional installation details, consult the "Installation notes" section later in this chapter.

A.2.3 Windows

The Zip archive is used to install Tomcat 3.0 on the Microsoft Windows platform. First create a directory in which you wish to install the software (e.g., C:\tomcat\), and then use your preferred Zip tool to extract the contents of the tomcat.zip archive into that directory. In this directory, you should next edit the tomcat.bat batch file to add the appropriate setting for the JAVA_HOME environment variable. Near the top of the file (e.g., after the comments at the top of the file, but before the other variable settings), add a line such as the following:

```
set JAVA_HOME=C:\jdk1.2.2\
```

The directory to which JAVA_HOME is set should be the top-level directory of your Java installation. This directory should include a subdirectory named bin that contains the java.exe application for running Java programs. Adding this environment variable to tomcat.bat precludes your having to add it to your global startup file.

The top-level Tomcat subdirectory includes two batch files that may be run from the DOS prompt to either start or stop the server. These scripts are named startup.bat and shutdown.bat, respectively.

A.2.4 Other platforms

If you wish to use Tomcat 3.0 on an alternative operating system, or do not have sufficient privileges to install either the RPM or PKG versions on their respective platforms, you may still be able to use the Zip version to install and run it on your platform of choice. Tomcat is a pure Java application, so the only requirement for running it is a JDK that supports Java 1.1 or higher. Installation requires only the ability to extract files from a Zip archive. Given that JAR files use the same format as Zip archives, the jar tool included with the JDK can be used for this purpose in the absence of other Zip-compatible tools, using a command such as the following:

```
jar xvf tomcat.zip
```

Although the details will differ from platform to platform, the basic approach is to create a directory for the Tomcat files and then extract them from the Zip archive into that directory. Using the included scripts (i.e., the files in the top-level directory with the .sh and .bat extensions) as a basis, create platform-specific scripts for starting and stopping the Tomcat software. The basic operation that these scripts must perform is to make sure that the locations of the JRE and the Java compiler are known, and the class path is set properly. The class path should include the following JAR files: webserver.jar from the top-level Tomcat directory, and servlet.jar, jasper.jar, and xml.jar from the top-level Tomcat directory's `lib` subdirectory. If you are using Java 2 (i.e., JDK 1.2 or higher), then the tools.jar archive included with the JDK should also be in the class path for Tomcat. This JAR file contains the Java compiler, which Tomcat uses to compile the servlets generated by JSP pages. Typically, a Java 2 installation will place this file in a subdirectory of its top-level directory named `lib`.

Assuming the JRE is accessible and the class path is properly set, Tomcat 3.0 is started by calling the `main()` method of the `org.apache.tomcat.shell.Startup` class. The server is shut down by calling the corresponding method of the `org.apache.tomcat.shell.Shutdown` class.

A.2.5 *Installation notes*

Several example servlets and JavaServer Pages are included with the reference implementation. The easiest way to test your Tomcat installation is to run the appropriate startup script, and then try to access these examples. If you are running Tomcat as a stand-alone server on its default port (8080), simply point your web browser to a URL of the form http://server:8080/, replacing "server" with the actual host name of your development server. This should bring up the default home page for your Tomcat installation, which includes links to index pages for the documentation, as well as various servlet and JSP examples. Follow these links to test your installation by trying to run the examples.

As you may be aware, the standard network port number for HTTP servers is 80. As suggested above, to access documents on an HTTP server using a non-standard port number, the port number must be explicitly specified in the URL (e.g., http://server:8080/webdev/helloBean.jsp). If you wish to have Tomcat respond to requests on port 80, it is necessary to edit the server.xml configuration file in the top-level directory of your Tomcat installation. In this file, you should find a `<ContextManager>` element that looks as follows:

```
<ContextManager port="8080" hostName="" inet="">
```

The port number used by Tomcat to listen for HTTP requests is changed by editing the value of the `port` attribute of this element and restarting the program. Changing this value from `"8080"` to `"80"` will cause Tomcat to use the standard HTTP port number.

WARNING   On the UNIX platform, only processes owned by the `root` account can use port numbers less than 1024. Tomcat must be run with superuser privileges under this operating system in order to use the standard HTTP port number (80).

If you are running Tomcat 3.0 under Java 2, you may find while testing the examples provided with the installation that the "Simple custom tag example" (corresponding to the jsp/simpletag/foo.jsp file in the `examples` application) does not work. This is a known bug with the binary distributions of Tomcat 3.0, and is due to the fact that the Tomcat class files were compiled using Java 1.1. Under most circumstances, class files produced by Java 1.1 compilers are fully compatible with Java 2. Unfortunately, the compiled class file for the `org.apache.jasper.compiler.TagLibraryInfoImpl` class is one of the rare exceptions to this rule.

As its name suggests, this class is part of Tomcat's implementation of JSP custom tag libraries. The class file for this class included in the Zip, PKG, and RPM binary distributions of Tomcat 3.0 cannot be loaded under Java 2, and causes all requests for JSP pages which use custom tags to fail when running Tomcat with a Java 2 JRE. The only workaround for this problem is to compile the associated Java source yourself. If you wish to run Tomcat 3.0 with Java 2, you will need to download the source distribution for Tomcat 3.0, and compile it using a Java 2 compiler. You can then either run Tomcat using this newly compiled code, or simply replace the incompatible class file for the `TagLibraryInfoImpl` class in an installed copy of the binary distribution. Note that after installing the binary distribution, the `TagLibraryInfoImpl.class` is stored in the jasper.jar file, located in the `lib` subdirectory of the installation's top-level directory.

A second platform-specific issue with Tomcat 3.0 is related to serving static files when running Tomcat under the Windows operating system. In this case, there is a bug in Java 1.1 that causes requests for static files (e.g., HTML documents and image files) to fail when running Tomcat 3.0 on the Microsoft Windows platform. The workaround for this bug is to use Java 2 instead of Java 1.1.

Finally, there also appears to be a problem with the loading of JAR files located in an application's `WEB-INF/lib` subdirectory. Although class files in the `WEB-INF/classes` subdirectory are properly recognized and loaded by Tomcat, class files stored in JAR files in the `WEB-INF/lib` subdirectory are not, at least on some platforms. One way to overcome this problem is to expand the contents of your application's JAR files into the application's `WEB-INF/classes` subdirectory.

Alternatively, you can manually add these JAR files to the class path setting for Tomcat by editing the appropriate control script (i.e., tomcat.sh or tomcat.bat).

A.3 *Constructing an application*

Once you have verified that the reference implementation is operating correctly, the next step is to configure Tomcat to run your own JSP pages, as well. This is done by creating a web application and adding it to the Tomcat configuration file, server.xml, which is located in the top-level directory of your Tomcat installation (i.e., the same directory as the startup and shutdown scripts). For the present discussion, we will simply outline the steps required to get you up and running; for further details on constructing and configuring web applications, see chapter 10.

A.3.1 *Application directory*

The first step is to create a directory structure for the web application that will hold your JSP pages. Create a directory named webdev (i.e., web development) in a convenient location (your home directory, for example), and then add a subdirectory to it named WEB-INF. Underneath this WEB-INF subdirectory, add two more subdirectories, classes and lib. The JSP pages you create will be added to the top-level webdev directory; if desired, you can create additional subdirectories under webdev and place JSP pages in them, as well. Note that any directory that can hold JSP pages can also be used for other web content, such as static HTML documents and image files. The WEB-INF directory holds the configuration files for your web application, which we'll get to momentarily. The subdirectories under WEB-INF are for storing the Java code—i.e.,

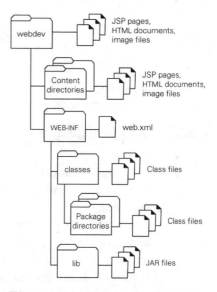

Figure A.1   Application file hierarchy for using the Tomcat reference implementation

servlets, Java Beans, and supporting classes—used by your web application. Code stored as individual class files, organized into directories representing the Java package hierarchy, go in the classes subdirectory. JAR files containing archived Java class files go in the lib subdirectory. This directory structure is depicted graphically

in figure A.1, and should be familiar to those who have already read chapter 10: the
webdev directory structure described here is simply an expanded WAR file.

A.3.2 *Configuration file*

Once the directory structure is in place, the next step is to create the configuration
file. This file is named web.xml and resides in the WEB-INF directory, as indicated in
figure A.1. For simple JSP development, the contents of this file are fixed, as shown
in listing A.1. Customization of this file is required if you need to add servlets and/
or initialization parameters. For further details on the configuration settings supported by the web.xml file, see chapter 10.

Listing A.1 Sample web.xml for JSP development

```
<?xml version="1.0" encoding="ISO-8859-1"?>

<!DOCTYPE web-app
    PUBLIC "-//Sun Microsystems, Inc.//DTD Web Application 2.2//EN"
    "http://java.sun.com/j2ee/dtds/web-app_2.2.dtd">

<web-app>
</web-app>
```

A.3.3 *Server configuration*

The next step is to configure the reference implementation server to recognize this
new web application. You will need to return to the top-level directory of the Tomcat installation, and edit the server configuration file located there, which is named
server.xml.

   This file, as its extension suggests, is in XML format. Various settings that control the operation of the server may optionally be specified, such as the network
port on which the server listens for requests. The configuration file also identifies
the web applications that are known to the server. To add your development web
application, first locate the specification for the Tomcat examples application,
which should look something like the following:

```
<Context path="/examples" docBase="examples"
        defaultSessionTimeOut="30" isWARExpanded="true"
        isWARValidated="false" isInvokerEnabled="true"
        isWorkDirPersistent="false"/>
```

You will need to add a similar entry for your web application. The first attribute,
path, specifies the directory prefix for URLs which should be handled by the web

application. For the `examples` application, then, its `path` attribute indicates that the server should forward to this application all URLs for which the top-level directory is /examples (i.e., URLs of the form http://server:8080/examples/directory/page.jsp). The second attribute, `docBase`, indicates where the files for the application actually reside. For the `examples` application, this is specified as a relative pathname, since `examples` is installed as a subdirectory of the top-level Tomcat installation directory.

Unless you created your `webdev` application directory as a subdirectory of the Tomcat installation directory, you will need to specify an absolute pathname for the `docBase` attribute. For example, if your application directory was created as /home/lora/webdev on the UNIX platform, the entry for your web application would take the following form:

```
<Context path="/webdev" docBase="/home/lora/webdev"
         defaultSessionTimeOut="30" isWARExpanded="true"
         isWARValidated="false" isInvokerEnabled="true"
         isWorkDirPersistent="false"/>
```

Alternatively, if your application directory is C:\lora\webdev on the Windows platform, the entry would instead take this form:

```
<Context path="/webdev" docBase="C:\lora\webdev"
         defaultSessionTimeOut="30" isWARExpanded="true"
         isWARValidated="false" isInvokerEnabled="true"
         isWorkDirPersistent="false"/>
```

In either case, the entry for your web application can be added to the server.xml configuration file right after the entry for the `examples` web application.

A.3.4   *Verifying the application*

Once all of these modifications have been made, you will need to stop and restart the Tomcat server in order for these changes to take effect, by running the appropriate shutdown and startup scripts. Once the server has been restarted, you should be able to access JSPs associated with your new web application using the mapping prefix specified in the server configuration file. To verify this, place a copy of the helloScript.jsp file, presented in chapter 2, into the top-level directory of your web application (i.e., the `webdev` directory). Assuming you configured the web.xml file as described here, you should now be able to run this JSP page using a URL of the form http://server:8080/webdev/helloScript.jsp.

If this test is successful, you can also try to install and run the helloBean.jsp file, which was also presented in chapter 2. In this case, keep in mind that you will also need to install and compile the corresponding Java Beans code.

First, place a copy of helloBean.jsp into the `webdev` directory. Next, create a file named HelloBean.java, inserting the appropriate Java code for that class from chapter 2. Noting that the package for this Bean is `com.taglib.wdjsp.fundamentals`, the Unix path for this source code file should be as follows:

```
webdev/WEB-INF/classes/com/taglib/wdjsp/fundamentals/HelloBean.java
```

If you are running Tomcat on a Microsoft Windows platform, the path should instead be as follows:

```
webdev\WEB-INF\classes\com\taglib\wdjsp\fundamentals\HelloBean.java
```

In both cases, the `classes` subdirectory of the application's `WEB-INF` directory is the appropriate top-level directory for Java Beans that will be referenced from JSP pages. The remaining subdirectories in the path are derived from the Bean's package, each element in the package representing a new subdirectory.

Once the source code is in place, it must be compiled. This is accomplished via the `javac` command, which invokes the Java compiler. Assuming that the `classes` subdirectory is the current working directory, the following command may be executed on the Unix platform to compile the Bean source code:

```
javac -d . com/taglib/wdjsp/fundamentals/HelloBean.java
```

For the Windows platform, this command instead takes the following form:

```
javac -d . com\taglib\wdjsp\fundamentals\HelloBean.java
```

After running this command, there should be a file named HelloBean.class in the same directory as the HelloBean.java file, which contains the compiled bytecode for the Bean.

After the Bean has compiled, all the elements should be in place for successfully accessing the corresponding JSP page. Based on the Tomcat configuration described above, you should now be able to run this second JSP page using a URL of the form http://server:8080/webdev/helloBean.jsp.

Incorporating Java applets B

Java applets are small applications that run within the context of a web browser. Because they can take advantage of the powerful graphical user interface (GUI) class provided by the standard Java AWT and Swing class libraries, applets can be used to implement much richer user interfaces than is typically possible using HTML alone.

Using the latest versions of Java for applet development, however, requires browser-specific code. To simplify the deployment of applets based on Java 2, JSP provides the `<jsp:plugin>` action for cross-platform specification of Java 2 applets.

B.1 *Browser support for Java 2*

Java 2 adds an improved security model, as well as the Swing package of user interface classes. Both of these enhancements are of interest to applet developers, but neither of the two major web browsers—Netscape Communicator and Microsoft Internet Explorer—currently provides built-in support for Java 2. Instead, the latest versions of both browsers provide direct support only for Java 1.1.

Netscape provides versions of Communicator for a wide range of hardware platforms and operating systems. Its current lack of support for Java 2 is therefore a result of what has been a general lack of platform support for Java 2. (Until very recently, release versions of Java 2 were widely available only for the Sun Solaris and Microsoft Windows operating systems.) With the next major release of Communicator, version 5, Netscape will no longer be bundling Java with the browser itself, but will instead provide hooks for applets to use whatever JVM is already present on the local computer. As platform support for Java 2 continues to improve, then, this new version of Communicator will automatically be able to take advantage of those implementations.

At the time of this writing, Sun Microsystems and Microsoft are engaged in a legal battle over Microsoft's implementation of Java for the Windows platform. As a result, changes to the Java-related features of Microsoft Internet Explorer—such as built-in support for Java 2 applets—are unlikely to appear until the legal dispute is resolved.

As a result of this slow adoption of Java 2 by the browser vendors, Sun Microsystems has developed its own browser plug-in for running Java 2 applets. Instead of relying on HTML's standard `<applet>` tag, support for which is provided by the browser itself, Sun has taken advantage of the browser-extension APIs built into these products to implement an alternative mechanism for running Java applets. The Java plug-in relies on its own JVM. By taking advantage of the plug-in mechanism, applet support becomes browser-independent.

Furthermore, even if the browser vendors do add support for Java 2 in the near future, it will likely be some time before use of those new browsers becomes widespread. In many corporate settings, the web browser has become a mission-critical application, leading many business organizations to standardize on specific browser implementations. Upgrades to new versions happen in a phased manner, driven more by company policy than product release cycles.

The majority of home users still relies on analog modems for Internet connectivity. The limited bandwidth of this technology is a major impediment to downloading large files, as is typically required in order to upgrade a web browser. There is therefore little incentive for home users to upgrade their web browser beyond what was originally installed with their operating system.

Fortunately, the plug-in APIs have been present in browser implementations for quite some time. As a result, the Java plug-in is compatible with fairly old versions of the popular browsers. This means that users often need not upgrade their web browsers in order to take advantage of the new features made available through the Java plug-in. In particular, the Java plug-in is compatible with versions 3 and later of both Netscape Communicator and Microsoft Internet Explorer. At the time of this writing, implementations of the plug-in are available for three different operating systems: Solaris from Sun Microsystems, Microsoft Windows, and Hewlett-Packard's HPUX.

B.2   *The plug-in action*

Unfortunately, the HTML for adding an applet to a page using the Java plug-in is browser-specific. In addition, the plug-in code is itself platform-specific, based on the hardware and operating system it will be running on. As a result, configuring a page to run an applet via the plug-in is not very straightforward using HTML alone.

> **NOTE**   Plug-ins for Microsoft Internet Explorer are specified via the HTML `<OBJECT>` tag. Plug-ins for Netscape Communicator are specified via the HTML `<EMBED>` tag.

To simplify this task, then, Java Server Pages provides the `<jsp:plugin>` action, which provides developers with a cross-platform mechanism for specifying the use of the Java plug-in. The syntax for this action is as follows:

```
<jsp:plugin type="type" code="objectCode" codebase="objectCodeBase"
      attribute1="value1" attribute2="value2" … >
   <jsp:params>
    <jsp:param name="parameterName1" value="parameterValue1"/>
    …
    <jsp:param name="parameterNameN" value="parameterValueN"/>
   </jsp:params>
   <jsp:fallback>fallback text</jsp:fallback>
</jsp:plugin>
```

There are four basic elements to this JSP action. First, there are three required attributes for the `<jsp:plugin>` tag itself. There are also several optional attributes, many of which are carried over from `<applet>` tag in HTML. The third element of a `<jsp:plugin>` specification is a set of parameter values, which are indicated via multiple `<jsp:param>` tags within the body of a `<jsp:params>` element, which is itself part of the body of the `<jsp:plugin>` action. Finally, the body of the action can also specify text to be displayed if for some reason the Java plug-in cannot be used. This is accomplished via the `<jsp:fallback>` tag.

B.2.1 *Required attributes*

There are five required attributes for the `<jsp:plugin>` tag, as summarized in table B.1. All have the same meaning as the corresponding attributes of the HTML `<applet>` tag, with the exception of the `type` attribute, for which the `<applet>` tag has no equivalent.

The `type` attribute is used to specify the type of Java component which is to be loaded and run by the plug-in. In addition to applets, which are indicated by providing the keyword `applet` as the value for this attribute, the Java plug-in can also be used to run JavaBeans components within the browser. This latter behavior is specified by supplying the keyword `bean` as the value of the `type` attribute. The two valid values for this attribute, then, are as follows:

```
<jsp:plugin type="applet" … >
<jsp:plugin type="bean" … >
```

The `code` attribute is used to specify the file containing the compiled Java code for the applet or Bean to be run. For applets, its value takes the form of a class file, qualified with the package name—if any—and including the .class extension. Alternatively, for both applets and Beans, a file containing a serialized object may be specified.

The `codebase` attribute indicates the directory on the web server in which the applet or Bean code may be found. Its value takes the form of a URL directory specification. Either an absolute or a relative URL may be provided; if the URL is not absolute, it is assumed to be relative to the URL of the JSP page containing the `<jsp:plugin>` tag. In either case, the filename specified for the `code` attribute is required to be relative to the directory specified for the `codebase` attribute.

The `height` and `width` attributes are used to designate the dimensions of the applet or the Bean. They effectively specify a rectangular region of the browser page which is to be set aside for the display of the applet or Bean.

In the following `<jsp:plugin>` tag, for example, an applet is to be loaded from a class file:

```
<jsp:plugin type="applet" codebase="plugins"
            code="com.taglib.wdjsp.applet.CountDown.class" … >
```

In this case, the applet code may be found in the file plugins/com/taglib/wdjsp/applet/CountDown.class, where the subdirectories are derived by combining the value of the `codebase` attribute with the package names appearing in the value of the `code` attribute. Here, the `plugins` directory should be a subdirectory of the directory which contains the JSP page.

This second example loads a Bean from a serialized object file:

```
<jsp:plugin type="bean" codebase="/resources/objects"
            code="MagicPizzaBean.ser" … >
```

In this case, the serialized object is stored in the file /resources/objects/MagicPizzaBean.ser. In this case, an absolute URL has been specified for the `codebase` attribute, so the `resources` directory should be one of the web server's top-level document directories.

Table B.1   Required attributes of the `<jsp:plugin>` tag

Attribute	Value	Description
type	`applet` or `bean`	Type of Java component to be loaded into browser.
code	Filename	File containing Java component, either a serialized object or a class file qualified with package name, relative to `codebase` value.
codebase	Directory URL	Directory on server containing file specified by `code` attribute.
height	Integer	Vertical dimension (in pixels) of the Java component within the browser window.
width	Integer	Horizontal dimension (in pixels) of the Java component within the browser window.

B.2.2   *Optional attributes*

Several optional attributes are also supported by the `<jsp:plugin>` action, as summarized in table B.2. Those which share the same name as attributes of the original HTML `<applet>` tag have corresponding behavior. Three of these attributes, however, are unique to the `<jsp:plugin>` tag: `jreversion`, `nspluginurl`, and `iepluginurl`.

The `jreversion` attribute is used to indicate which version of the JRE is required to run the applet or Bean. The value of this attribute is used to determine whether or not the JRE being used by the plug-in is compatible with the component that is to be loaded and run. The default value of this attribute is `1.1`, indicating the component is compatible with JRE version 1.1 or higher. The JRE for Java 2 is JRE version 1.2, so for Java 2 applets and Java Beans this attribute should be set to `1.2`.

The `nspluginurl` and `iepluginurl` attributes are used to indicate the URLs from which the plug-in code for the various browsers can be downloaded. The `nspluginurl` attribute specifies the location of the plug-in for Netscape Communicator, while `iepluginurl` provides the location of the plug-in for Microsoft Internet Explorer. Default values for these two URLs are implementation-specific. Because the code for the plug-in can be quite large (i.e., multiple megabytes), you may wish to install copies of the plug-in software on a local server, to improve download performance. In this case, these two attributes are used to point to the local copies so that, if the plug-in has not been installed when the browser encounters the HTML generated by the `<jsp:plugin>` action, it will look for the required software on that local server instead of attempting to load it from some default location on the Internet.

Table B.2   Optional attributes of the `<jsp:plugin>` tag

Attribute	Value	Default	Description
`align`	Text string	`baseline`	Alignment of the Java component relative to other page elements. Allowed values are `left`, `right`, `top`, `texttop`, `middle`, `absmiddle`, `baseline`, `bottom`, and `absbottom`.
`name`	Text string	None	Name by which other components on the same page can reference the Java component.
`archive`	Filenames	None	Comma-separated list of JAR files containing resources (classes, images, data files, etc.) to be preloaded.
`vspace`	Integer	0	Margin (in pixels) that should appear on the left and right sides of the Java component in the browser window.
`hspace`	Integer	0	Margin (in pixels) that should appear above and below the Java component in the browser window.
`jrever-sion`	Version	`1.1`	Version of the JRE required to run the Java component.
`nsplugin`	URL	Implementation-specific	Location from which the Java Plug-in for Netscape Communicator can be downloaded.
`ieplugin`	URL	Implementation-specific	Location from which the Java Plug-in for Microsoft Internet Explorer can be downloaded.

B.2.3   *Parameters*

Applets may be configured on a page-by-page basis by means of parameters passed in from the browser. When using the HTML `<applet>` tag, this is accomplished via the `<param>` tag. When the `<jsp:plugin>` tag is used to specify an applet or Bean, parameter values are set by means of the `<jsp:param>` tag, which takes the following form:

```
<jsp:param name="parameterName" value="parameterValue"/>
```

The `name` attribute designates the name of the parameter to be set, and the `value` attribute specifies its value. An applet accesses these parameters via the `getParameter()` method of the `java.applet.Applet` class, and all applet parameter values are interpreted as character strings. The applet itself is responsible for parsing parameter values that represent other data types, such as numeric values.

Multiple applet parameters can be set via multiple `<jsp:param>` tags. All `<jsp:param>` tags, however, must occur within the body of `<jsp:params>` tag, which itself occurs within the body of the `<jsp:plugin>` action. The overall syntax for specifying applet parameters, then, is as follows:

```
<jsp:plugin ... >
    ...
    <jsp:params>
      <jsp:param name="parameterName1" value="parameterValue1"/>
      ...
      <jsp:param name="parameterNameN" value="parameterValueN"/>
    </jsp:params>
    ...
</jsp:plugin>
```

Note that only one set of parameter values, as bounded by the `<jsp:params>` and `</jsp:params>` delimiter tags, should occur within the body of the `<jsp:plugin>` action.

In addition to applet parameter values, the `<jsp:param>` tag can also be used to configure Beans loaded via the `<jsp:plugin>` action. In this case, the `name` attribute of each `<jsp:param>` tag is interpreted as the name of a Bean property, and the `value` attribute indicates the value to which the property should be set.

B.2.4 *Fallback text*

Successful use of the `<jsp:plugin>` action is dependent upon the end user being able to run the Java plug-in from their browser. As a result of this reliance on the installation and configuration of end-user software, it is convenient to be able to gracefully handle situations in which, for whatever reason, the Java plug-in cannot be run. This is the role of the `<jsp:fallback>` tag.

The `<jsp:fallback>` tag is used to specify content to be displayed in the output of the JSP page in the event the Java plug-in fails to be started by the browser. This content is delimited by matching `<jsp:fallback>` and `</jsp:fallback>` tags, as in the following example:

```
<jsp:plugin ... >
    ...
    <jsp:fallback>
    Sorry, unable to start <b>Java Plug-in</b> to run Java 2 applet.
    </jsp:fallback>
    ...
</jsp:plugin>
```

Note that since the `<jsp:plugin>` action is used to load Java components into a web browser, its utility is generally limited to JSP pages used to construct HTML documents. As a result, however, it is perfectly acceptable for the fallback text in the body of the `<jsp:fallback>` tag to include HTML markup, as in this example.

The fallback text is only displayed when there are problems with the plug-in itself. If, instead, there is a problem with the applet or Java Bean to be loaded via the plug-in, the plug-in will display an error message to that effect. The exact contents and presentation of this error message are implementation-specific.

B.3   *Example: applet configuration*

One particular advantage of combining JSP with applets is that the applet can be configured at run time. This is made possible by the use of request-time attribute values when specifying the `value` attributes of one or more `<jsp:param>` tags. In this way, the values of the corresponding applet parameters are computed by the JSP page at the time the request for the page is processed.

Consider, for example, the Java class presented in listing B.3. This class, `com.taglib.wdjsp.applets.CountDown`, defines an applet that implements a timer, counting down to a date and time specified via applet parameters. Since this is a book on JavaServer Pages rather than applet design, we will not consider the details of this code. In brief, then, the various components specifying the state of the timer are stored as an array of `String` elements, which are updated via a thread represented by the `countdown` instance variable. This thread updates the timer's state every tenth of a second, until the countdown expires. Two parameters, named `endTime` and `endDate`, are used to configure the applet.

To allow the user to set these configuration parameters, a form could be provided for selecting the desired date and time. One such form is presented in figure B.1, with the corresponding (abbreviated) HTML code presented in listing B.1. Note that the value of the `action` attribute for this document's `<form>` tag is set to a JSP page, specifically /webdev/countdown.jsp.

When this form is submitted, then, the values of its form fields are sent via a POST request to the specified page. This page, whose source code appears in listing B.2,

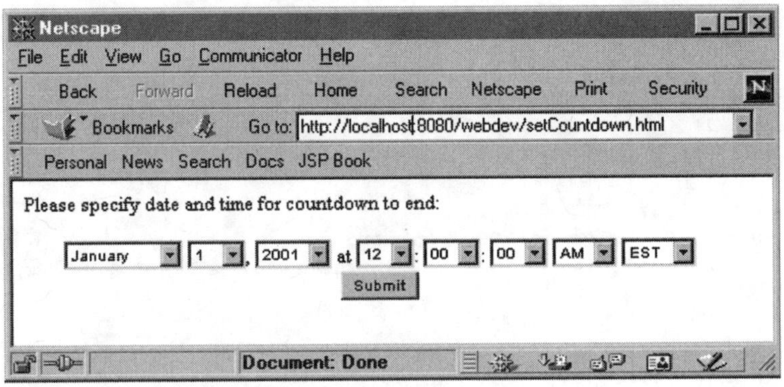

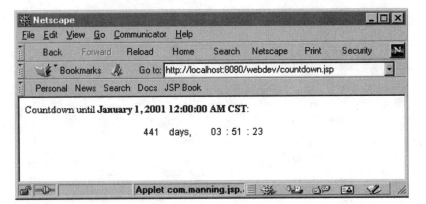

Figure B.1   Form for configuring countdown applet

Figure B.2   Countdown applet running via `<jsp:plugin>` tag

uses those form values to construct a date string and a time string, using a scriptlet to retrieve those parameters from the `request` implicit object. These two strings are then supplied as parameters to the Java applet, via request-time attribute values. The result is presented in figure B.2.

Listing B.1   Abbreviated HTML source code for applet configuration form

```
<html>
<body> Please specify date and time for countdown to end:<br>
<center><form action="/webdev/countdown.jsp" method="POST">
<select name="month" size="1">
  <option value="January" selected>January</option>
  <option value="February">February</option>
```

```
  ...
  <option value="December">December</option>
</select>
<select name="day" size="1">
  <option value="1" selected>1</option>
  <option value="2">2</option> ... <option value="31">31</option>
</select>,
<select name="year" size="1">
  <option value="2000" selected>2000</option>
  <option value="2001">2001</option> ... <option value="2005">2005</option>
</select>
at
<select name="hour" size="1">
  <option value="1">1</option> ... <option value="11">11</option>
  <option value="12" selected>12</option>
</select>:
<select name="minutes" size="1">
  <option value="00" selected>00</option>
  <option value="01">01</option> ... <option value="59">59</option>
</select>:
<select name="seconds" size="1">
  <option value="00" selected>00</option>
  <option value="01">01</option> ... <option value="59">59</option>
</select>
<select name="ampm" size="1">
  <option value="AM">AM</option><option value="PM">PM</option>
</select>
<select name="zone" size="1">
  <option value="EST">EST</option><option value="EDT">EDT</option>
  <option value="CST">CST</option><option value="CDT">CDT</option>
  <option value="MST">MST</option><option value="MDT">MDT</option>
  <option value="PST">PST</option><option value="PDT">PDT</option>
</select><br>
<input type="submit" value="Submit">
</form></center>
</body>
</html>
```

Listing B.2   JSP page for displaying applet via <jsp:plugin> tag

```
<html>
<body>
<% String month = request.getParameter("month");
   if (month == null) month = "January";
   String day = request.getParameter("day");
   if (day == null) day = "1";
   String year = request.getParameter("year");
   if (year == null) year = "2001";
   String hour = request.getParameter("hour");
```

```
    if (hour == null) hour = "12";
    String minutes = request.getParameter("minutes");
    if (minutes == null) minutes = "00";
    String seconds = request.getParameter("seconds");
    if (seconds == null) seconds = "00";
    String ampm = request.getParameter("ampm");
    if (ampm == null) ampm = "AM";
    String zone = request.getParameter("zone");
    if (zone == null) zone = "CST";
    String date = month + " " + day + ", " + year;
    String time =
      hour + ":" + minutes + ":" + seconds + " " + ampm + " " + zone;
 %>
Countdown until <b><%= date %> <%= time %></b>:<br>
<center>
<jsp:plugin type="applet" codebase="plugins"
            code="com.taglib.wdjsp.applets.CountDown"
            width="300" height="50"
            jreversion="1.2">
  <jsp:params>
    <jsp:param name="endDate" value="<%= date %>" />
    <jsp:param name="endTime" value="<%= time %>" />
  </jsp:params>
  <jsp:fallback>Unable to start Java Plug-in for applet.</jsp:fallback>
</jsp:plugin>
</center>
</body>
</html>
```

Listing B.3 Source code for com.taglib.wdjsp.applets.CountDown class

```
package com.taglib.wdjsp.applets;

import java.applet.*;
import java.awt.*;
import java.util.*;
import java.text.*;

public class CountDown extends Applet implements Runnable {
    private Thread countdown;
    private long ends;
    private int height, width;
    Image offscreen;
    private String[] text = new String[FIELDS];
    private int[] textWidth = new int[FIELDS];
    Font font;
    FontMetrics fontMetrics;
    private int fontHeight, ascent;
```

```java
static final int FIELDS = 7;
static final int DAYS = 0;
static final int HOURS = 2;
static final int MINUTES = 4;
static final int SECONDS = 6;

// Constructor
public CountDown () {
 ends = 0l;
 long now = new Date().getTime()/1000l;
 ends = now + 7l * 24l * 60l * 60l; // One week
 ends = now + 24l * 60l * 60l + 30; // One day
 text[HOURS+1] = ":";
 text[MINUTES+1] = ":";
 updateElements();
 width = 0;
 height = 0;
 font = new Font("Helvetica", Font.BOLD, 18);
 fontMetrics = this.getFontMetrics(font);
 fontHeight = fontMetrics.getHeight();
 ascent = fontMetrics.getAscent();
}

// Display code
public void paint (Graphics g) {
 g.setColor(Color.white);
 g.fillRect(0, 0, width, height);
 g.setColor(Color.black);
 int strWidth = 0;
 for (int i = 0; i < FIELDS; ++i) {
     textWidth[i] = fontMetrics.stringWidth(text[i]);
     strWidth += textWidth[i];
 }
 int x = (width - strWidth)/2;
 int y = (height + fontHeight - ascent)/2;
 for (int i = 0; i < FIELDS; ++i) {
     g.drawString(text[i], x, y);
     x += textWidth[i];
 }
}

// Thread code
public void run () {
 boolean updating = false;
 boolean counting = true;
 while (counting) {
     if (! updating) {
       updating = true;
       try {
           counting = updateElements();
```

```
                updateDisplay();
            }
            finally { updating = false; }
        }
        try { Thread.sleep(100); } catch (InterruptedException e) {};
    }
}

// Updating
final static long minuteSeconds = 60l;
final static long hourSeconds = 60l * minuteSeconds;
final static long daySeconds = 24l * hourSeconds;

private boolean updateElements () {
 long now = new Date().getTime()/1000l;
 if (now >= ends) {
     setDays(0);
     setElement(HOURS, 0);
     setElement(MINUTES, 0);
     setElement(SECONDS, 0);
     return false;
 } else {
     long remaining = ends - now;
     long days = remaining/daySeconds;
     setDays(days);
     remaining -= days*daySeconds;
     long hours = remaining/hourSeconds;
     setElement(HOURS, hours);
     remaining -= hours*hourSeconds;
     long minutes = remaining/minuteSeconds;
     setElement(MINUTES, minutes);
     remaining -= minutes*minuteSeconds;
     setElement(SECONDS, remaining);
     return true;
 }
}
private void setElement (int index, long t) {
 if (t < 10) {
     text[index] = "0" + Long.toString(t);
 } else {
     text[index] = Long.toString(t);
 }
}
private void setDays (long d) {
 text[DAYS] = Long.toString(d);
 text[DAYS + 1] = (d == 1l) ? " day, " : " days, ";
}

private void updateDisplay () {
 Dimension size = this.getSize();
```

```java
    if ((offscreen == null)
        || (width != size.width)
        || (height != size.height)) {
        width = size.width;
        height = size.height;
        offscreen = this.createImage(width, height);
    }
    Graphics g = offscreen.getGraphics();
    paint(g);
    g = this.getGraphics();
    g.drawImage(offscreen, 0, 0, this);
}

// Applet Lifecycle
public void init () {
  String endTime = getParameter("endTime");
  if (endTime == null) endTime = "12:00am";
  String endDate = getParameter("endDate");
  if (endDate == null) endDate = "January 1, 2001";
  DateFormat fmt = DateFormat.getDateTimeInstance(DateFormat.LONG,
              DateFormat.LONG,
              Locale.US);
  Date d;
  try {
      d = fmt.parse(endDate + " " + endTime);
  }
  catch (ParseException e) {
      System.err.println("Error while parsing date: " + e.getClass());
      System.err.println(e.getMessage());
      d = new Date();
  }
  ends = d.getTime()/10001;
}
public void start () {
  countdown = new Thread(this);
  countdown.start();
}
public void stop () {
  if (countdown != null) countdown.stop();
  countdown = null;
  }
}
```

JSP resources

C.1 *Java implementations*

http://java.sun.com/jdk
  Sun Microsystem's implementations of the Java platform for the Solaris, Linux, and Microsoft Windows operating systems.

http://www.blackdown.org/java-linux.html
  An Open Source implementation of the Java platform for the Linux operating system.

http://www.developer.ibm.com/java/member/technical/jdk.html
  IBM's implementations of the Java platform for the Microsoft Windows, Linux, AIX, OS/2, AS/400, OS/390, and VM/ESA operating systems. Registration required.

http://www.microsoft.com/java
  Microsoft's implementation of the Java platform for the Windows operating systems.

http://www.sgi.com/developers/devtools/languages/java.html
SGI's implementation of the Java platform for the IRIX operating system.

http://www.unixsolutions.hp.com/products/java
Hewlett Packard's implementation of the Java platform for the HPUX operating system.

C.2   *JSP-related web sites*

http://java.sun.com/products/jsp
Sun Microsystem's official home page for JavaServer Pages technology.

http://www.taglib.com/
Home page for this book, featuring source code and a collection of JSP custom tag libraries.

http://www.burridge.net/jsp/
Resources for developers working with JSP and related technologies.

http://www.gefionsoftware.com/
JSP tag libraries and utilities.

http://www.interpasnet.com/JSS/textes/jsp.htm
More online resources for JSP developers.

http://us.imdb.com/Title?0084827
Critical resources for JSP book authors.

C.3   *JSP FAQs and tutorials*

http://java.sun.com/products/jsp/docs.html
A series of JSP tutorials and reference information from Sun Microsystems.

http://java.sun.com/products/jsp/faq.html
Sun's official online FAQ.

http://www.burningdoor.com/web99/jsp/index.htm
Conference presentation describing JSP.

http://www.esperanto.org.nz/jsp/jspfaq.html
The unofficial online FAQ.

http://www.jguru.com/jguru/faq/faqpage.jsp?name=JSP
An interactive FAQ from jGuru, with visitor-submitted questions.

http://www2.software.ibm.com/developer/education.nsf/java-onlinecourse-bytitle
Online Java tutorials from IBM, including "Introduction to JavaServer Pages."

http://java.sun.com/products/jsp/docs.html
A series of JSP tutorials and reference information from Sun Microsystems.

C.4 JSP containers

http://jakarta.apache.org/
Home page for Tomcat, the official reference implementation of the servlet and JSP specifications. Tomcat is available both as source code and in compiled form.

http://www.allaire.com/Products/Jrun
Home page for JRun, from Allaire.

http://www.caucho.com/
Web site for Resin, a servlet and JSP container supporting both Java and server-side JavaScript as its scripting languages.

http://www.klomp.org/gnujsp/
Home page for GNUJSP, an Open Source implementation of the JSP specification.

http://www.newatlanta.com/
Web site for New Atlanta, makers of ServletExec.

http://www.plenix.org/polyjsp/
An Open Source JSP container that supports multiple scripting languages.

C.5 Java application servers with JSP support

http://java.sun.com/j2ee
Sun Microsystem's home page for Java 2, Enterprise Edition (J2EE). The reference implementation of J2EE, available here, includes a JSP container.

http://orion.evermind.net/
Home page for the Orion application server.

http://www.bea.com/java
Web site for BEA Systems, makers of the WebLogic application server.

http://www.bluestone.com/
Web site for the Bluestone/Sapphire web application server.

http://www.exoffice.com/
An Open Source application server.

http://www.gemstone.com/
Web site for the GemStone application server.

http://www.ibm.com/software/webservers/
Home page for IBM's WebSphere application server.

http://www.inprise.com/appserver/
Web site for the Inprise application server.

http://www.iplanet.com/
Web site for the Sun-Netscape Alliance, makers of the iPlanet web server.

http://www.oracle.com/java/
Web site for Oracle's 8i Jserver.

http://www.silverstream.com/
Web site for the SilverStream application server.

C.6   *JSP development tools*

http://www.allaire.com/Products/HomeSite
Home page for HomeSite, a web page authoring tool from Allaire with built-in support for JSP tags.

http://www.forte.com/
Forte is an integrated JSP development environment.

http://www-4.ibm.com/software/webservers/studio/index.html
Product information about IBM's Websphere Studio, which includes a tool for visually creating and editing JSP pages.

http://www.macromedia.com/software/drumbeat/
Web site for Drumbeat 2000, a visual editor for authoring JSP pages.

http://www.oracle.com/tools/jdeveloper/index.html
Home page for JDeveloper, Oracle's server-side Java development suite.

C.7   *Tools for performance testing*

http://java.apache.com/
Home page for the Java Apache Project, which hosts several Open Source, web-related development projects associated with the Apache Software Foundation. The JMeter tool for measuring servlet and JSP performance is available here.

http://www.allaire.com/products/jrun/ServletAddOn.cfm
Download page for Allaire's free ServletKiller program, used for stress-testing servlets and JSP pages.

http://www.binevolve.com/velometer/velometer.vet
VeloMeter is a web server load tester from Binary Evolution, distributed as Open Source. A commercial version, VeloMeter Pro, is also available.

http://www.eqase.com/
eQase is a suite of tools from AST Engineering Services for measuring the performance of web-based applications and identifying performance bottlenecks.

http://www.klgroup.com/
KL Group's JProbe ServerSide Suite bundles multiple tools for tuning the performance of server-side Java applications.

http://www.optimizeit.com/
Optimize It!, from Intuitive Systems Inc. is a profiling tool for Java applications that can be integrated directly with a large number of JSP containers and Java Application Servers.

C.8 Mailing lists and newsgroups

JSP-INTEREST@java.sun.com
A mailing list for technical discussions among developers who are deploying JSP technology. To subscribe, use the archive site described below, or send an email message to `listserv@java.sun.com` with the text `subscribe JSP-INTEREST` as the body of the message.

http://archives.java.sun.com/archives/jsp-interest.html
These are the online archives for the `JSP-INTEREST` mailing list. Forms are available for searching past messages, as well as for subscribing or unsubscribing to the mailing list.

comp.lang.java.*
This is the Usenet News hierarchy dedicated to discussion of the Java programming language. There are, as yet, no groups dedicated to either servlet or JSP development, but occasional discussions of these topics do appear on some of the existing Java newsgroups, such as comp.lang.java.programmer and comp.lang.java.misc. If you are relatively new to Java programming, you may find the discussions in the comp.lang.java.help and comp.lang.java.setup groups particularly helpful.

JSP syntax reference

In this appendix we'll summarize the usage of all of the JSP tags discussed in this book. This listing is intended primarily as a quick reference to JSP, and repeats information presented elsewhere. If you're in a hurry, reading this appendix will get you started, but is no substitute for studying the thorough discussion and examples of each tag, especially the coverage provided in chapters 1 through 5.

D.1   Content comments

Content comments will be sent back to the browser as part of the response. Since they are comments, they do not produce any visible output, but they may be viewed by the end user via the browser's View Source menu item.

Syntax

XML: `<!-- comment -->`

Shorthand: `<!-- comment -->`

Description

Those familiar with HTML and XML will recognize that this is the standard comment syntax for those two markup languages. Thus, a JSP page that is generating either HTML or XML simply uses the native comment syntax for whichever form of content it is constructing. Content comments are part of the output from the page. You can, if you wish, include dynamic content in them. HTML and XML comments can, for example, include JSP expressions, and the output generated by these expressions will appear as part of the comment in the page's response.

Examples

```
<!-- begin dynamically generated content -->
<%= new java.util.Date() %>
<!-- end dynamically generated content -->

<!-- longs are 64 bits, so 20! = <%= fact(20) %> is the upper limit. -->
```

D.2   JSP comments

JSP comments are independent of the type of content being produced by the page. They are also independent of the scripting language used by the page. These comments can only be viewed by examining the original JSP file

Syntax

XML: none

Shorthand: `<%-- comment --%>`

Description

The body of a JSP comment is ignored by the JSP container. When the page is compiled into a servlet, anything appearing between these two delimiters is skipped while translating the page into servlet source code. For this reason, comments such as this are very useful for commenting out portions of a JSP page, as when debugging.

Examples

```
int y = 0;
int z = 3;
<%-- y = 2; --%>
z = 4;

<table width="150">
<%-- Really should make the width dynamic --%>
<tr><td>Hello There</td></tr>
</table>
```

D.3 *<jsp:declaration>*

Declarations define a variable or method for use on the current page, using the current page's designated scripting language.

Syntax

XML: `<jsp:declaration> declaration(s) </jsp:declaration>`

Shorthand: `<%! declaration(s) %>`

Description

Declarations are used to define variables and methods for use by other scripting elements on a specific JSP page. Multiple declarations may appear within a single tag, but each declaration must be a complete declarative statement in the designated scripting language. White space after the opening delimiter and before the closing delimiter is optional, but recommended to improve readability. Variables defined as declarations become instance variables of the servlet class into which the JSP page is translated and compiled. Since variables specified via JSP declarations are directly translated into variables of the corresponding servlet class, they may also be used to declare class variables, whose values are shared among all instances of a class rather than being specific to an individual instance. Methods defined via declarations become methods of the servlet class into which the JSP page is compiled. Class methods, also known as static methods, are associated with the class itself, rather than individual instances, and may be called without requiring access to an instance of the class. In fact, class methods are typically called simply by prepending the name of the class to the name of the method. Class methods may reference only class variables, not instance variables.

Examples

```
<%! private int x = 0, y = 0; %>

<jsp:declaration> String units = "ft"; </jsp:declaration>

<%!
  public long fact (long x) {
    if (x == 0)
      return 1;
    else
      return x * fact(x-1);
  }
%>
```

D.4   *<jsp:directive.include>*

The include directive enables page authors to include the contents of one file in another. The file to be included is identified via a local URL, and the directive has the effect of replacing itself with the contents of the indicated file.

Syntax

XML: `<jsp:directive.include file="localURL" />`

Shorthand: `<%@ include file="localURL" %>`

Description

There are no restrictions on the number of include directives that may appear in a single JSP page. There are also no restrictions on nesting; it is completely valid for a JSP page to include another JSP page, which itself includes one or more others. All included pages must use the same scripting language as the original page. The value of the include directive's file attribute can be specified as an absolute path on the local server, or relative to the current page, depending upon whether or not it starts with a forward slash character.

Examples

```
<%@ include file="includes/navigation.jsp" %>

<%@ include file="/shared/epilogue/copyright.html" %>
```

D.5   *<jsp:directive.page>*

The `page` directive is used to convey special processing information about the page to the JSP container. The `page` directive supports a wide range of attributes and associated functionality, as summarized in table D.1.

Syntax

XML: `<jsp:directive.page attribute1="value1" attribute2="value2" attribute3=… />`

Shorthand: `<%@ page attribute1="value1" attribute2="value2" attribute3=… %>`

Description

The `page` directive does not directly produce any output that is visible to end users when the page is requested; instead, it generates side effects that change the way the JSP container processes the page. The `page` directive supports a number of attributes. With the exception of the `import` attribute, however, no individual `page` directive attribute may be specified multiple times on the same page.

Table D.1   Attributes supported by the `page` directive

Attribute	Value	Default	Examples
`info`	Text string	None	`info="Registration form."`
`language`	Scripting language name	`"java"`	`language="java"`
`contentType`	MIME type, character set	See first example	`contentType="text/html;charset=ISO-8859-1"` `contentType="text/xml"`
`extends`	Class name	None	`extends="com.taglib.wdjsp.MyJspPage"`
`import`	Class and/or package names	None	`import="java.net.URL"` `import="java.util.*, java.text.*"`
`session`	Boolean flag	`"true"`	`session="true"`
`buffer`	Buffer size, or false	`"8kb"`	`buffer="12kb"` `buffer="false"`
`autoFlush`	Boolean flag	`"true"`	`autoFlush="false"`
`isThreadSafe`	Boolean flag	`"true"`	`isThreadSafe="true"`
`errorPage`	Local URL	None	`errorPage="results/failed.jsp"`
`isErrorPage`	Boolean flag	`"false"`	`isErrorPage="false"`

Examples

```
<%@ page contentType="text/xml" %>

<%@ page import="java.util.*" %>

<%@ page info="This is a valid set of page directives." %>
<%@ page language="java" import="java.net.*" %>
<%@ page import="java.util.List, java.util.ArrayList" %>
```

D.6 *<jsp:directive.taglib>*

The taglib directive is used to notify the JSP container that a page relies on one or more custom tag libraries. A tag library is a collection of custom tags that can be used to extend the functionality of JSP on a page-by-page basis.

Syntax

XML: `<jsp:directive.taglib uri="tagLibraryURI" prefix="tagPrefix" />`

Shorthand: `<%@ taglib uri="tagLibraryURI" prefix="tagPrefix" %>`

Description

In both cases, the value of the uri attribute indicates the location of the Tag Library Descriptor (TLD), and the prefix attribute specifies the XML namespace identifier that will be prepended to all occurrences of the library's tags on the page. Once this directive has been used to indicate the reliance of a page on a specific tag library, all of the custom tags defined in that library become available for use on that page. Because the tag prefix is specified external to the library itself, and on a page-specific basis, multiple libraries can be loaded by a single page without the risk of conflicts between tag names. If two libraries define tags with the same name, a JSP page would still be able to load and use both libraries since it can distinguish between those tags via their prefixes. As such, there are no restrictions on how many taglib directives may appear on a page, as long as each is assigned a unique prefix. If, however, the JSP container cannot find the TLD at the indicated location, or the page references a tag that is not actually defined in the library, an error will result when the JSP container tries to compile the page.

Examples

```
<jsp:directive.taglib uri="/localTags" prefix="my"/>

<%@ taglib uri="/EncomTags" prefix="mcp" %>
<mcp:showUser user="flynn">
  firstname, lastname, idnumber
</mcp:showUser>
```

D.7   \<jsp:expression>

Expressions are code fragments evaluated at run time. The JSP expression element is explicitly intended for content generation, displaying the output of the code fragment's execution into the page content.

Syntax

XML: `<jsp:expression>` *expression* `</jsp:expression>`

Shorthand: `<%=` *expression* `%>`

Description

In both syntax cases, the `expression` should be a valid and complete scripting language expression, in whatever scripting language has been specified for the page. Note that no end of line marker (in Java, the ;) is present. The effect of this element is to evaluate the specified expression and substitute the resulting value into the output of the page, in place of the element itself. JSP expressions can be used to print out individual variables, or the result of some calculation or other operation. Any valid scripting language expression is allowed, so calls to methods are likewise permitted. Expressions can return Java primitive values, such as numbers, characters, and booleans, or full-fledged Java objects, such as `String` objects and Java-Beans. All expression results are converted to character strings before they are added to the page's output.

Examples

```
The value of PI is about <%= Math.PI %>

The time is <%= hours %> <%= (hours < 12) ? "AM" : "PM" %>

Hello <%= request.getRemoteUser() %>
```

D.8 *<jsp:forward>*

The `<jsp:forward>` action is used to permanently transfer control from a JSP page to another location on the local server.

Syntax

XML: `<jsp:forward page="localURL" />`

   or

```
<jsp:forward page="localURL">
  <jsp:param name="parameterName1" value="parameterValue1"/>
  ...
  <jsp:param name="parameterNameN" value="parameterValueN"/>
</jsp:forward>
```

Shorthand: none

Description

The `page` attribute of the `<jsp:forward>` action is used to specify this alternate location to which control should be transferred, which may be a static document, a CGI, a servlet, or another JSP page. Since the `request` object is common to both the original page and the forwarded page, any request parameters that were available on the original page will also be accessible from the forwarded page. If additional parameters are supplied, they are passed to the receiving page.

The browser from which the request was submitted is not notified when the request is transferred to this alternate URL. In particular, the location field at the top of the browser window will continue to display the URL that was originally requested. Any content generated by the current page is discarded, and processing of the request begins anew at the alternate location. For added flexibility, the `<jsp:forward>` action supports the use of request-time attribute values. In addition, the `<jsp:param>` tag may be used to specify additional request parameters.

For the specific case when control is transferred to another JSP page, the JSP container will automatically assign a new `pageContext` object to the forwarded page. The `request` object and the `session` object, though, will be the same for both the original page and the forwarded page. Sharing of the `application` object depends upon whether or not the two pages are both part of the same application. Thus, some but not all of the attribute values accessible from the original page will be accessible on the forwarded page, depending upon their scope: page attributes are not shared, request and session attributes are, and application attributes may or may not be.

Examples

```
<jsp:forward page="showresults.jsp">
  <jsp:param name="header" value="Results of Query"/>
  <jsp:param name="color" value="blue"/>
</jsp:forward>

<% if (! database.isAvailable()) { %>
  // Notify the user about routine maintenance.
  <jsp:forward page="db-maintenance.html"/>
<% } %>
<%-- Database is up, proceeed as usual... --%>
```

D.9   <jsp:getProperty>

The `<jsp:getProperty>` action is the primary way to access a Bean's properties in JSP.

Syntax

XML: `<jsp:getProperty name="bean name" property="property name"/>`

Shorthand: none

Description

Unlike the `<jsp:useBean>` action which performs some work behind the scenes but doesn't produce any output, the `<jsp:getProperty>` action actually produces content that we can see in the HTML generated by the page. The `name` attribute specifies the Bean we are accessing, and should correspond to the identifier we selected for the Bean in the `<jsp:useBean>` tag's `id` attribute. In the resulting HTML that is displayed at run time, this tag is replaced with the value of the property of the Bean being requested. Of course, since we are creating an HTML document, the property is first converted into text by the JSP container. You can use as many `<jsp:getProperty>` tags in your page as you need. You can intersperse them with HTML to not only dynamically generate individual values and blocks of text, but to control attributes of the HTML as well. It is perfectly legal to nest JSP tags inside HTML attribute values. For example, a Bean property could be used to control the page's background color, the width of a table, or the source of an image.

Examples

```
<jsp:getProperty name="user" property="department"/>

<jsp:useBean id="myclock" class="ClockBean"/>
<html>
<body>
The Bean says that the time is now:
<jsp:getProperty name="myclock" property="time"/>
</body>
</html>
```

D.10 <jsp:include>

The `<jsp:include>` action enables page authors to incorporate the content generated by another local document into the output of the current page.

Syntax

XML: `<jsp:include page="localURL" flush="true" />`

or

```
<jsp:include page="localURL" flush="true">
  <jsp:param name="parameterName1" value="parameterValue1"/>
  ...
  <jsp:param name="parameterNameN" value="parameterValueN"/>
</jsp:include>
```

Shorthand: none

Description

The output from the included document is inserted into the original page's output in place of the `<jsp:include>` tag, after which processing of the original page resumes. In contrast to the `<jsp:forward>` tag, then, this action is used to *temporarily* transfer control from a JSP page to another location on the local server. The page attribute of the `<jsp:include>` action is used to identify the document whose output is to be inserted into the current page, and is specified as a URL on the local server. The included page can be a static document, a CGI, a servlet, or another JSP page. As with the `<jsp:forward>` action, the page attribute of the `<jsp:include>` action supports request-time attribute values. The `<jsp:param>` tag may be used to specify additional request parameters.

The flush attribute of the `<jsp:include>` action controls whether or not the output buffer for the current page is flushed prior to including the content from the included page. As of version 1.1 of the JSP specification, it is required that the flush attribute be set to true, indicating that the buffer is flushed before processing of the included page begins. This is a result of current limitations in the underlying servlet API; as such, this requirement may be relaxed in subsequent versions of the specification. Because the output buffer is flushed as the first step in performing the <jsp:include> action, forwarding to another page—including an error page—is not possible. Likewise, setting cookies or other HTTP headers will not succeed if attempted after processing a <jsp:include> tag.

If the included page changes, its changes will be reflected immediately. In contrast, the JSP include directive does not automatically update the including page when the included file is modified. This is because the include directive takes effect when the including page is translated into a servlet, effectively merging the base contents of the included page into those of the original. The <jsp:include> action takes effect when processing requests, and merges the output from the included page, rather than its original text.

Examples

```
<jsp:include page="/headers/support_header.jsp" flush="true"/>

<jsp:include page="topten.jsp" flush="true">
  <jsp:param name="category" value="books"/>
</jsp:include>
```

D.11   <jsp:plugin>

The <jsp:plugin> action provides a cross-platform mechanism for incorporating applets based on the Java 2 platform into JSP pages.

Syntax

XML:

```
<jsp:plugin type="type" code="objectCode" codebase="objectCodeBase"
            attribute1="value1" attribute2="value2" … />
```

or

```
<jsp:plugin type="type" code="objectCode" codebase="objectCodeBase"
            attribute1="value1" attribute2="value2" … >
  <jsp:params>
    <jsp:param name="parameterName1" value="parameterValue1"/>
    …
    <jsp:param name="parameterNameN" value="parameterValueN"/>
  </jsp:params>
  <jsp:fallback>fallback text</jsp:fallback>
</jsp:plugin>
```

Shorthand: none

Description

The `<jsp:plugin>` action uses Sun Microsystem's Java plug-in to run an applet or JavaBean in the end user's browser. Browser-specific code is inserted into the output of the JSP page for loading the Java plug-in, which is based on the Java 2 JVM, and running the specified code. The `code` attribute indicates the Java class to be run, while the `codebase` attribute indicates where this class is located on the server. If value of the `type` attribute is `"applet"`, the specified class is presumed to be an applet. If this attribute's value is `"bean"`, a JavaBean is assumed. The `<jsp:plugin>` action also supports all of the attributes supported by HTML's `<applet>` tag, of which the `height` and `width` attributes are required.

Applet parameters are specified via the `<jsp:param>` tag, and must be delimited as a group in the body of a `<jsp:params>` tag. The `<jsp:fallback>` tag is used to specify the content that should be displayed if the Java plug-in is not available in the end user's browser.

Examples

```
<jsp:plugin type="bean" code="timer.ser" width="100" height="50"/>

<jsp:plugin type="applet" codebase="plugins"
            code="com.taglib.wdjsp.applets.CountDown"
            width="300" height="50"
            jreversion="1.2">
  <jsp:params>
    <jsp:param name="endDate" value="<%= date %>" />
    <jsp:param name="endTime" value="<%= time %>" />
  </jsp:params>
  <jsp:fallback>Unable to start Java Plug-in for applet.</jsp:fallback>
</jsp:plugin>
```

D.12 *<jsp:scriptlet>*

Scriptlets are the primary way to include fragments of code, typically Java, into a JSP page. Scriptlets can contain arbitrary scripting language statements, which—like declarations—are evaluated for side effect only. Scriptlets do not automatically add content to a JSP page's output.

Syntax

XML: `<jsp:scriptlet> scriptlet </jsp:scriptlet>`

Shorthand: `<% scriptlet %>`

Description

For either tag style, the scriptlet should be one or more valid and complete statements in the JSP page's scripting language. Alternatively, a scriptlet can leave open one or more statement blocks, which must be closed by subsequent scriptlets in the same page. In the (default) case where the JSP scripting language is Java, statement blocks are opened using the right brace character (i.e., {) and closed using the left brace character (i.e., }). If a scriptlet opens a new block without also closing it, then the Java statements corresponding to any subsequent static content or JSP elements simply become part of this new block. The block must ultimately be closed by another scriptlet, or else compilation will fail due to a Java syntax error. A page's scriptlets will be run for each request received by the page—any variables introduced in a scriptlet are available for use in subsequent scriptlets and expressions on the same page (subject to variable scoping rules).

Examples

```
<jsp:sriptlet>
Date now = new java.util.Date();
out.println("The time is: " + now);
</jsp:scriptlet>

<table>
<% for (int j=0; j < 11; ++j) { %>
<tr><td><%= j %></td></tr>
<% } %>
</table>
```

D.13 *<jsp:setProperty>*

The `<jsp:setProperty>` action is used to modify the properties of Beans used in the page.

Syntax

XML:

```
<jsp:setProperty name="bean name" property="property name" value="value"/>
```

> or

```
<jsp:setProperty name="bean name" property="property name" param="param"/>
```

> or

```
<jsp:setProperty name="bean name" property="*"/>
```

Shorthand: none

Description

The `<jsp:setProperty>` action can be used anywhere within the page to modify a Bean's properties, as long as it appears after the `<jsp:useBean>` action used to define that Bean. The Bean is identified via the action's `name` attribute, which should correspond to the identifier originally assigned to a Bean via the `id` attribute of its `<jsp:useBean>` tag. Only properties that have public setter methods can be modified via the `<jsp:setProperty>` action. The property to be set is specified via the tag's `property` attribute.

The `value` attribute is used to specify the value to be assigned to the indicated property, and may be a JSP expression representing a request-time attribute value. Alternatively, the `param` attribute can be used to specify the name of a request parameter whose value is to be copied to the Bean property. As a special case, if the value of the `property` attribute is `"*"`, the JSP container will identify all of the request parameters whose names match those of Bean properties, and make the corresponding assignments from the request parameter values to those matching properties. In all cases, the JSP container will attempt to coerce values specified by the `value` attribute or obtained from request parameters into the appropriate type for the specified property.

At run time the JSP container evaluates the tags in a page in the order they appear, from top to bottom. Any property values that you set will only be reflected in JSP elements that follow the `<jsp:setProperty>` tag within the page.

Examples

```
<jsp:setProperty name="user" property="daysLeft" value="30"/>

<jsp:setProperty name="user" property="daysLeft" value="<%= 15 * 2 %>"/>

<jsp:useBean id="clock" class="com.taglib.wdjsp.ClockBean">
  <jsp:setProperty name="clock" property="timezone" value="CST"/>
</jsp:useBean>
```

D.14 <jsp:useBean>

The `<jsp:useBean>` action tells the page that we want to make a Bean available to the page. The tag is used to create a Bean or fetch an existing one from the server.

Syntax

XML: `<jsp:useBean id="`*bean name*`" class="`*class name*`"/>`

or

```
<jsp:useBean id="bean name" class="class name">
    initialization code
</jsp:useBean>
```

Shorthand: none

Description

The attributes of this tag specify the type of Bean you wish to use and assign it a name that can later be used to refer to it. The `<jsp:useBean>` action comes in two forms, a single empty tag and a matching pair of start and end tags that contain the body of the tag, which can be used to specify initialization code. In its simplest and most straightforward form, the `<jsp:useBean>` tag requires only two attributes, `id` and `class`. The attributes of this tag are summarized in table D.2.

Table D.2 Attributes of the `<jsp:useBean>` tag

Attribute	Value	Default	Example Value
id	Java identifier	none	myBean
scope	page, request, session, application	page	session
class	Java class name	none	java.util.Date
type	Java class name	class value	com.taglib.wdjsp.AbstractPerson
beanName	Java class or serialized Bean	none	com.taglib.wdjsp.USCurrency.ser

The `<jsp:useBean>` action creates or retrieves an instance of the Bean and associates it with the identifier specified by the `id` attribute. This identifier can be used to access the Bean from scripting elements, or in subsequent `<jsp:setProperty>` or `<jsp:getProperty>` tags. If an existing Bean is not located in the scope specified by the `scope` attribute, a new Bean instance is created using the Bean class's default constructor, and any content specified in the body of the `<jsp:useBean>` tag is processed. Otherwise, the Bean is simply retrieved from the corresponding scope and the tag's body content is ignored.

Examples

```
<jsp:useBean id="now" class="java.util.Date"/>

<% @page import="com.taglib.wdjsp.*" %>
<jsp:useBean id="user" class="RegisteredUserBean"/>

<jsp:useBean id="user" class="RegisteredUser" scope="session"/>

<jsp:useBean id="news" class="NewsReports" scope="request">
  <jsp:setProperty name="news" property="category" value="financial"/>
  <jsp:setProperty name="news" property="maxItems" value="5"/>
</jsp:useBean>
```

JSP API reference

This appendix provides summary information on the Java classes and interfaces defined by the Servlet 2.2 and JSP 1.1 specifications. It is intended as a quick reference for JSP application developers. Information about inheritance, variables, and methods is provided for each class and interface, where applicable. Note that deprecated methods have been omitted. For certain classes that are managed by the JSP container and do not provide public constructors (e.g., `javax.servlet.Request-Dispatcher`), any alternative methods for obtaining instances of these classes, referred to as *factory methods*, are listed. For convenience, table 4.1, summarizing the JSP implicit objects and their types, is repeated here as well (see table E.1).

DEFINITION In the parlance of design patterns, the use of one type of object to abstract the instantiation of other types of objects is known as the *factory pattern*. Hence, methods for obtaining instances of a class without calling a constructor are described as *factory methods*.

E.1 JSP Implicit Objects

Table E.1 Implicit objects and their corresponding types

Object	Class or *Interface*	Attributes?
page[1]	*javax.servlet.jsp.HttpJspPage*	No
config	*javax.servlet.ServletConfig*	No
request	*javax.servlet.http.HttpServletRequest*	Yes
response	*javax.servlet.http.HttpServletResponse*	No
out	javax.servlet.jsp.JspWriter	No
session[2]	*javax.servlet.http.HttpSession*	Yes
application	*javax.servlet.ServletContext*	Yes
pageContext	javax.servlet.jsp.PageContext	Yes
exception[3]	java.lang.Throwable	No

1. The default type for accessing the page implicit object is java.lang.Object.
2. The session implicit object is only available on JSP pages that participate in session tracking. The default behavior is for all pages to partake in session tracking, but this can be overridden by specifying a value of false for the session attribute of the page directive.
3. The exception implicit object is only available on JSP pages that are designated as error pages by setting the isErrorPage attribute of the page directive to true.

E.2 Package javax.servlet

E.2.1 Class GenericServlet

Inheritance
This is an abstract class.
Implements Servlet, ServletConfig, and java.io.Serializable.

Constructors
```
public GenericServlet ()
```

Methods
```
public void destroy ()
public String getInitParameter (String name)
public java.util.Enumeration getInitParameterNames ()
public ServletConfig getServletConfig ()
```

```
public ServletContext getServletContext ()
public String getServletInfo ()
public void init ()throws ServletException
public void init (ServletConfig config) throws ServletException
public void log (String message)
public void log (String message, Throwable t)
public void service (ServletRequest request, ServletResponse response)
    throws ServletException, java.io.IOException
```

E.2.2   Interface RequestDispatcher

Factory methods

```
ServletContext.getRequestDispatcher(String URL)
ServletContext.getNamedDispatcher(String URL)
ServletRequest.getRequestDispatcher(String URL)
```

Methods

```
public void forward (ServletRequest request, ServletResponse response)
    throws ServletException,
          java.io.IOException, java.lang.IllegalStateException
public void include (ServletRequest request, ServletResponse response)
throws ServletException, java.io.IOException
```

E.2.3   Interface Servlet

Constructors

No public constructors or factory methods.

Methods

```
public void destroy ()
public ServletConfig getServletConfig ()
public String getServletInfo ()
public void init (ServletConfig config) throws ServletException
public void service (ServletRequest request, ServletResponse response)
throws ServletException, java.io.IOException
```

E.2.4   Interface ServletConfig

Factory methods

```
Servlet.getServletConfig()
```

Methods

```
public String getInitParameter (String name)
public Java.util.Enumeration getInitParameterNames ()
public ServletContext getServletContext ()
public String getServletName ()
```

E.2.5   Interface ServletContext

Factory methods
```
ServletConfig.getServletContext()
```

Methods
```
public String getAttribute (String name)
public Java.util.Enumeration getAttributeNames ()
public ServletContext getContext (String uripath)
public String getInitParameter (String name)
public Java.util.Enumeration getInitParameterNames ()
public int getMajorVersion ()
public String getMimeType (String file)
public int getMinorVersion ()
public RequestDispatcher getNamedDispatcher (String URL)
public String getRealPath (String URL)
public RequestDispatcher getRequestDispatcher (String URL)
public java.net.URL getResource (String path)
    throws java.net.MalformedURLException
public java.io.InputStream getResourceAsStream (String path)
public String getServerInfo ()
public void log (String message)
public void log (String message, Throwable throwable)
public void removeAttribute (String name)
public void setAttribute (String name, Object value)
```

E.2.6   Class ServletException

Inheritance
Extends Exception.

Constructors
```
public ServletException ()
public ServletException (String message)
public ServletException (String message, Throwable rootCause)
public ServletException (Throwable rootCause)
```

Methods
```
public Throwable getRootCause ()
```

E.2.7   Class ServletInputStream

Inheritance
This is an abstract class.
Extends java.io.InputStream.

Factory methods

```
ServletRequest.getInputStream()
    throws IllegalStateException, java.io.IOException
```

Methods

```
public int readLine (byte[] b, int offset, int length)
    throws java.io.IOException
```

E.2.8 Class ServletOutputStream

Inheritance

This is an abstract class.
Extends java.io.OutputStream.

Factory methods

```
ServletResponse.getOutputStream()
    throws IllegalStateException, java.io.IOException
```

Methods

```
public void print (boolean b) throws java.io.IOException
public void print (char c) throws java.io.IOException
public void print (double d) throws java.io.IOException
public void print (float f) throws java.io.IOException
public void print (int i) throws java.io.IOException
public void print (long l) throws java.io.IOException
public void print (String s) throws java.io.IOException
public void println () throws java.io.IOException
public void println (boolean b) throws java.io.IOException
public void println (char c) throws java.io.IOException
public void println (double d) throws java.io.IOException
public void println (float f) throws java.io.IOException
public void println (int i) throws java.io.IOException
public void println (long l) throws java.io.IOException
public void println (String s) throws java.io.IOException
```

E.2.9 Interface ServletRequest

Constructors

No public constructors or factory methods.

Methods

```
public String getAttribute (String name)
public java.util.Enumeration getAttributeNames ()
public String getCharacterEncoding ()
public int getContentLength ()
```

```
public String getContentType ()
public ServletInputStream getInputStream ()
    throws IllegalStateException, java.io.IOException
public java.util.Locale getLocale ()
public java.util.Enumeration getLocales ()
public String getParameter (String name)
public java.util.Enumeration getParameterNames ()
public String[] getParameterValues (String name)
public String getProtocol ()
public java.io.BufferedReader getReader ()
    throws IllegalStateException,
            java.io.IOException, java.io.UnsupportedEncodingException
public String getRemoteAddr ()
public String getRemoteHost ()
public RequestDispatcher getRequestDispatcher (String URL)
public String getScheme ()
public String getServerName ()
public int getServerPort ()
public boolean isSecure ()
public void removeAttribute (String name)
public void setAttribute (String name, Object value)
```

E.2.10 *Interface ServletResponse*

Constructors
No public constructors or factory methods.

Methods
```
public void flushBuffer ()throws java.io.IOException
public int getBufferSize ()
public String getCharacterEncoding ()
public java.util.Locale getLocale ()
public ServletOutputStream getOutputStream ()
    throws IllegalStateException, java.io.IOException
public java.io.PrintWriter getWriter ()
    throws IllegalStateException,
            java.io.IOException, java.io.UnsupportedEncodingException
public boolean isCommitted ()
public void reset () throws IllegalStateException
public void setBufferSize (int size) throws IllegalStateException
public void setContentLength (int length)
public void setContentType (String type)
public void setLocale (java.util.Locale locale)
```

E.2.11 *Interface SingleThreadModel*

This interface defines no variables or methods.

E.2.12 Class UnavailableException

Inheritance
Extends `ServletException`.

Constructors
```
public ServletException (String message)
public ServletException (String message, int seconds)
```

Methods
```
public int getUnavailableSeconds ()
public boolean isPermanent ()
```

E.3   Package javax.servlet.http

E.3.1   Class Cookie

Inheritance
Implements `Cloneable`.

Constructors
```
public Cookie (String name, String value)
```

Methods
```
public Object clone ()
public String getComment ()
public String getDomain ()
public int getMaxAge ()
public String getName ()
public String getPath ()
public boolean getSecure ()
public String getValue ()
public int getVersion ()
public void setComment (String comment)
public void setDomain (String domain)
public void setMaxAge (int seconds)
public void setPath (String url)
public void setSecure (boolean flag)
public void setValue (String value)
public void setVersion (int version)
```

E.3.2 Class HttpServlet

Inheritance
This is an abstract class.
Extends `javax.servlet.GenericServlet`.
Implements `java.io.Serializable`.

Constructors
```
public HttpServlet ()
```

Methods
```
protected void doDelete (HttpServletRequest request,
                         HttpServletResponse response)
   throws javax.servlet.ServletException, java.io.IOException
protected void doGet (HttpServletRequest request,
                      HttpServletResponse response)
   throws javax.servlet.ServletException, java.io.IOException
protected void doOptions (HttpServletRequest request,
                          HttpServletResponse response)
   throws javax.servlet.ServletException, java.io.IOException
protected void doPost (HttpServletRequest request,
                       HttpServletResponse response)
   throws javax.servlet.ServletException, java.io.IOException
protected void doPut (HttpServletRequest request,
                      HttpServletResponse response)
   throws javax.servlet.ServletException, java.io.IOException
protected void doTrace (HttpServletRequest request,
                        HttpServletResponse response)
   throws javax.servlet.ServletException, java.io.IOException
protected long getLastModified (HttpServletRequest request)
protected void service (HttpServletRequest request,
                        HttpServletResponse response)
   throws javax.servlet.ServletException, java.io.IOException
public void service (HttpServletRequest request,
                     HttpServletResponse response)
   throws javax.servlet.ServletException, java.io.IOException
```

E.3.3 Interface HttpServletRequest

Inheritance
Extends `javax.servlet.ServletRequest`.

Constructors
No public constructors or factory methods.

Methods

```
public String getAuthType ()
public String getContextPath ()
public Cookie[] getCookies ()
public long getDateHeader (String name)
public String getHeader (String name) throws IllegalArgumentException
public java.util.Enumeration getHeaderNames ()
public java.util.Enumeration getHeaders (String name)
public int getIntHeader (String name) throws NumberFormatException
public String getMethod ()
public String getPathInfo ()
public String getPathTranslated()
public String getQueryString ()
public String getRemoteUser ()
public String getRequestedSessionId ()
public String getRequestURI ()
public String getServletPath ()
public HttpSession getSession ()
public HttpSession getSession (boolean create)
public java.security.Principal getUserPrincipal ()
public boolean isRequestedSessionIdFromCookie ()
public boolean isRequestedSessionIdFromURL ()
public boolean isRequestedSessionIdValid ()
public boolean isUserInRole (String role)
```

E.3.4   Interface HttpServletResponse

Inheritance
Extends `javax.servlet.ServletRequest`.

Constructors
No public constructors or factory methods.

Class Variables

```
public static final int SC_ACCEPTED = 202;
public static final int SC_BAD_GATEWAY = 502;
public static final int SC_BAD_REQUEST = 400;
public static final int SC_CONFLICT = 409;
public static final int SC_CONTINUE = 100;
public static final int SC_CREATED = 201;
public static final int SC_EXPECTATION_FAILED = 417;
public static final int SC_FORBIDDEN = 403;
public static final int SC_GATEWAY_TIMEOUT = 504;
public static final int SC_GONE = 410;
public static final int SC_HTTP_VERSION_NOT_SUPPORTED = 505;
public static final int SC_INTERNAL_SERVER_ERROR = 500;
public static final int SC_LENGTH_REQUIRED = 411;
```

```
public static final int SC_METHOD_NOT_ALLOWED = 405;
public static final int SC_MOVED_PERMANENTLY = 301;
public static final int SC_MOVED_TEMPORARILY = 302;
public static final int SC_MULTIPLE_CHOICES = 300;
public static final int SC_NO_CONTENT = 204;
public static final int SC_NON_AUTHORITATIVE_INFORMATION = 203;
public static final int SC_NOT_ACCEPTABLE = 406;
public static final int SC_NOT_FOUND = 404;
public static final int SC_NOT_IMPLEMENTED = 501;
public static final int SC_NOT_MODIFIED = 304;
public static final int SC_OK = 200;
public static final int SC_PARTIAL_CONTENT = 206;
public static final int SC_PAYMENT_REQUIRED = 402;
public static final int SC_PRECONDITION_FAILED = 412;
public static final int SC_PROXY_AUTHENTICATION_REQUIRED = 407;
public static final int SC_REQUEST_ENTITY_TOO_LARGE = 413;
public static final int SC_REQUEST_TIMEOUT = 408;
public static final int SC_REQUEST_URI_TOO_LONG = 414;
public static final int SC_REQUEST_RANGE_NOT_SATISFIABLE = 416;
public static final int SC_RESET_CONTENT = 205;
public static final int SC_SEE_OTHER = 303;
public static final int SC_SERVICE_UNAVAILABLE = 503;
public static final int SC_SWITCHING_PROTOCOLS = 101;
public static final int SC_UNAUTHORIZED = 401;
public static final int SC_UNSUPPORTED_MEDIA_TYPE = 415;
public static final int SC_USE_PROXY = 305;
```

Methods

```
public void addCookie (Cookie)
public void addDateHeader (String name, long date)
public void addHeader (String name, String value)
public void addIntHeader (String name, int value)
public boolean containsHeader (String name)
public String encodeRedirectURL (String url)
public String encodeURL (String url)
public void sendError (int statusCode)
   throws java.io.IOException, IllegalStateException
public void sendError (int statusCode, String message)
   throws java.io.IOException, IllegalStateException
public void sendRedirect (String location)
   throws java.io.IOException, IllegalStateException
public void setDateHeader (String name, long date)
public void setHeader (String name, String value)
public void setIntHeader (String name, int value)
public void setStatus (int statusCode)
```

E.3.5   *Interface HttpSession*

Constructors
No public constructors or factory methods.

Methods
```
public Object getAttribute (String name) throws IllegalStateException
public java.util.Enumeration getAttributeNames ()
   throws IllegalStateException
public long getCreationTime () throws IllegalStateException
public String getId ()
public long getLastAccessedTime ()
public int getMaxInactiveInterval ()
public void invalidate () throws IllegalStateException
public boolean isNew () throws IllegalStateException
public void removeAttribute (String name) throws IllegalStateException
public void setAttribute (String name, Object value)
   throws IllegalStateException
public void setMaxInactiveInterval (int seconds)
```

E.3.6   *Class HttpSessionBindingEvent*

Inheritance
Extends `java.util.EventObject`.

Constructors
```
public HttpSessionBindingEvent (HttpSession session, String name)
```

Methods
```
public String getName ()
public HttpSession getSession ()
```

E.3.7   *Interface HttpSessionBindingListener*

Inheritance
Implements `java.util.EventListener`.

Constructors
No public constructors or factory methods.

Methods
```
public void valueBound (HttpSessionBindingEvent event)
public void valueUnbound (HttpSessionBindingEvent event)
```

E.3.8   Class HttpUtils

Constructors
```
public HttpUtils ()
```

Class methods
```
public static StringBuffer getRequestURL (HttpServletRequest request)
public static java.util.Hashtable parsePostData (int length,
                                            ServletInputStream in)
   throws IllegalArgumentException
public static java.util.Hashtable parseQueryString (String queryString)
   throws IllegalArgumentException
```

E.4   Package javax.servlet.jsp

E.4.1   Interface HttpJspPage

Inheritance
Extends JspPage.

Constructors
No public constructors or factory methods.

Methods
```
public void _jspService (HttpServletRequest request,
                         HttpServletResponse response)
   throws ServletException java.io.IOException
```

E.4.2   Class JspEngineInfo

Inheritance
This is an abstract class.

Factory methods
```
JspFactory.getEngineInfo()
```

Methods
```
public String getSpecificationVersion ()
```

E.4.3 Class JspException

Inheritance
Extends `Exception`.

Constructors
```
public JspException ()
public JspException (String message)
```

E.4.4 Class JspFactory

Inheritance
This is an abstract class.

Factory methods
```
JspFactory.getDefaultFactory()
```

Class methods
```
public static JspFactory getDefaultFactory()
public static void setDefaultFactory (JspFactory defaultFactory)
```

Methods
```
public JspEngineInfo getEngineInfo ()
public PageContext getPageContext (javax.servlet.Servlet servlet,
                                   javax.servlet.ServletRequest request,
                                   javax.servlet.ServletResponse response,
                                   String errorPageURL,
                                   boolean needsSession, int bufferSize,
                                   boolean autoFlush)
public void releasePageContext (PageContext context)
```

E.4.5 Interface JspPage

Inheritance
Extends `javax.servlet.Servlet`.

Constructors
No public constructors or factory methods.

Methods
```
public void jspDestroy ()
public void jspInit ()
```

E.4.6 Class JspTagException

Inheritance
Extends `JspException`.

Constructors
```
public JspTagException ()
public JspTagException (String message)
```

E.4.7 Class JspWriter

Inheritance
This is an abstract class.
Extends `java.io.Writer`.

Constructors
```
protected JspWriter (int bufferSize, boolean autoFlush)
```

Class variables
```
public static final int DEFAULT_BUFFER;
public static final int NO_BUFFER;
public static final int UNBOUNDED_BUFFER;
```

Instance variables
```
protected boolean autoFlush;
protected int bufferSize;
```

Methods
```
public void clear ()
public void clearBuffer ()
public void close ()
public void flush ()
public int getBufferSize ()
public int getRemaining ()
public boolean isAutoFlush ()
public void newLine ()
public void print (boolean b)
public void print (char c)
public void print (char[] s)
public void print (double d)
public void print (float f)
public void print (int i)
public void print (long l)
public void print (Object o)
public void print (String s)
```

```
public void println ()
public void println (boolean b)
public void println (char c)
public void println (char[] s)
public void println (double d)
public void println (float f)
public void println (int i)
public void println (long l)
public void println (Object o)
public void println (String s)
```

E.4.8   Class PageContext

Inheritance
This is an abstract class.

Factory methods
```
JspFactory.getPageContext(...)
```

Class variables
```
public static final String APPLICATION;
public static final int APPLICATION_SCOPE;
public static final String CONFIG;
public static final String EXCEPTION;
public static final String OUT;
public static final String PAGE;
public static final int PAGE_SCOPE;
public static final String PAGE_CONTEXT;
public static final String REQUEST;
public static final int REQUEST_SCOPE;
public static final String RESPONSE;
public static final String SESSION;
public static final int SESSION_SCOPE;
```

Methods
```
public Object findAttribute (String name)
public void forward (String localURL)
   throws javax.servlet.ServletException,
          java.io.IOException, IllegalArgumentException,
          IllegalStateException, SecurityException
public Object getAttribute (String name)
   throws NullPointerException, IllegalArgumentException
public Object getAttribute (String name, int scope)
   throws NullPointerException, IllegalArgumentException
public java.util.Enumeration getAttributeNamesInScope (int scope)
public int getAttributesScope (String name)
public Exception getException ()
```

```
public JspWriter getOut ()
public Object getPage ()
public javax.servlet.ServletRequest getRequest ()
public javax.servlet.ServletResponse getResponse ()
public javax.servlet.ServletConfig getServletConfig ()
public javax.servlet.ServletContext getServletContext ()
public javax.servlet.http.HttpSession getSession ()
public void handlePageException (Exception e)
   throws javax.servlet.ServletException, java.io.IOException,
         NullPointerException, SecurityException
public void include (String localURL)
   throws javax.servlet.ServletException, java.io.IOException,
         IllegalArgumentException, SecurityException
public void initialize (javax.servlet.Servlet servlet,
                        javax.servlet.ServletRequest request,
                        javax.servlet.ServletResponse response,
                        String errorPageURL, boolean needsSession,
                        int bufferSize, boolean autoFlush)
   throws java.io.IOException,
         IllegalStateException, IllegalArgumentException
public JspWriter popBody ()
public BodyContent pushBody ()
public void release ()
public void removeAttribute (String name)
public void removeAttribute (String name, int scope)
public void setAttribute (String name, Object value)
   throws NullPointerException
public void setAttribute (String name, Object value, int scope)
   throws NullPointerException, IllegalArgumentException
```

E.5   Package javax.servlet.jsp.tagext

E.5.1   Class BodyContent

Inheritance
This is an abstract class.
Extends `javax.servlet.jsp.JspWriter`.

Constructors
```
protected BodyContent (javax.servlet.jsp.JspWriter writer)
```

Methods
```
public void clearBody ()
public void flush () throws java.io.IOException
public javax.servlet.jsp.JspWriter getEnclosingWriter ()
public java.io.Reader getReader ()
```

```
public String getString ()
public void writeOut (java.io.Writer writer) throws java.io.IOException
```

E.5.2   Interface BodyTag

Inheritance
Extends `Tag`.

Constructors
No public constructors or factory methods.

Class variables
```
public static final int EVAL_BODY_TAG;
```

Methods
```
public int doAfterBody ()throws javax.servlet.jsp.JspException
public void doInitBody () throws javax.servlet.jsp.JspException
public void setBodyContent (BodyContent content)
```

E.5.3   Class BodyTagSupport

Inheritance
Extends `TagSupport`, implements `BodyTag`.

Constructors
```
public BodyTagSupport ()
```

Methods
```
public int doAfterBody ()throws javax.servlet.jsp.JspException
public void doEndTag () throws javax.servlet.jsp.JspException
public void doInitBody ()
public BodyContent getBodyContent ()
public javax.servlet.jsp.JspWriter getPreviousOut ()
public void release ()
public void setBodyContent (BodyContent content)
```

E.5.4   Interface Tag

Constructors
No public constructors or factory methods.

Class variables
```
public static final int EVAL_BODY_INCLUDE;
public static final int EVAL_PAGE;
```

```
public static final int SKIP_BODY;
public static final int SKIP_PAGE;
```

Methods
```
public int doEndTag ()throws javax.servlet.jsp.JspException
public int doStartTag () throws javax.servlet.jsp.JspException
public Tag getParent ()
public void release ()
public void setPageContext (javax.servlet.jsp.PageContext context)
public void setParent (Tag parent)
```

E.5.5 Class TagAttributeInfo

Constructors
No public constructors or factory methods.

Class Methods
```
public static TagAttributeInfo getIdAttribute (TagAttributeInfo[] array)
```

Methods
```
public boolean canBeRequestTime ()
public String getName ()
public String getTypeName ()
public boolean isRequired ()
```

E.5.6 Class TagData

Inheritance
Implements `Cloneable`.

Constructors
```
public TagData (Object[][] attributes)
public TagData (java.util.Hashtable attributes)
```

Methods
```
public Object clone ()
public Object getAttribute (String name)
public String getAttributeString (String name)
public String getId ()
public void setAttribute (String name, Object value)
```

E.5.7 Class TagExtraInfo

Constructors
```
public TagExtraInfo ()
```

Methods

```
public TagInfo getTagInfo ()
public VariableInfo[] getVariableInfo (TagData data)
public boolean isValid (TagData data)
public void setTagInfo (TagInfo info)
```

E.5.8 Class TagInfo

Constructors

No public constructors or factory methods.

Class variables

```
public static String BODY_CONTENT_EMPTY;
public static String BODY_CONTENT_JSP;
public static String BODY_CONTENT_TAG_DEPENDENT;
```

Methods

```
public TagAttributeInfo[] getAttributes ()
public String getBodyContent ()
public String getInfoString ()
public String getTagClassName ()
public TagExtraInfo getTagExtraInfo ()
public TagLibraryInfo getTagLibrary ()
public String getTagName ()
public VariableInfo getVariableInfo (TagData data)
public boolean isValid (TagData data)
```

E.5.9 Class TagLibraryInfo

Inheritance

This is an abstract class.

Constructors

No public constructors or factory methods.

Methods

```
public String getInfoString ()
public String getPrefixString ()
public String getReliableURN ()
public String getRequiredVersion ()
public String getShortname ()
public TagInfo getTag (String shortname)
public TagInfo[] getTags ()
public String getURI ()
```

E.5.10 *Class TagSupport*

Inheritance

Implements `Tag`, `java.io.Serializable`.

Constructors

```
public TagSupport ()
```

Class methods

```
public static Tag findAncestorWithClass (Tag from, Class klass)
```

Methods

```
public void doEndTag () throws javax.servlet.jsp.JspException
public void doStartTag () throws javax.servlet.jsp.JspException
public Tag getParent ()
public String getTagId ()
public Object getValue (String name)
public java.util.Enumeration getValues ()
public void release ()
public void removeValue (String name)
public void setPageContext (javax.servlet.jsp.PageContext context)
public void setParent (Tag parent)
public void setTagId (String id)
public void setValue (String name, Object value)
```

E.5.11 *Class VariableInfo*

Constructors

```
public VariableInfo (String variableName, String className,
                     boolean declare, int scope)
```

Class variables

```
public static int AT_BEGIN;
public static int AT_END;
public static int NESTED;
```

Methods

```
public String getClassName ()
public boolean getDeclare ()
public int getScope ()
public String getVarName ()
```

index